COUNTRY MUSIC, U.S.A.

A Fifty-year History

PUBLICATIONS OF THE AMERICAN FOLKLORE SOCIETY

MEMOIR SERIES

General Editor, John Greenway

Volume 54   1968

COUNTRY MUSIC U. S. A.

a fifty-year history by Bill C. Malone

PUBLISHED FOR THE AMERICAN FOLKLORE SOCIETY BY
THE UNIVERSITY OF TEXAS PRESS, AUSTIN AND LONDON

International Standard Book Number 0-292-78377-9
Library of Congress Catalog Card No. 68–66367
Copyright © 1968 by the American Folklore Society
All rights reserved

FOURTH PRINTING, 1973

Manufactured in the United States of America

PREFACE

One of the great American success stories is that of country music and its development. Once confined to small towns and rural areas—largely in the South and Middle West—and rejected or scorned by those who considered themselves musically sophisticated, country music is now deeply rooted in American life and is, in fact, international in scope. Moreover, it is a multi-million dollar industry and one of the most durable forms of American entertainment.

Despite its durability and commercial success, however, country music has yet to be accorded a full-scale, scholarly treatment. This neglect is all the more apparent when one considers the plethora of material, both scholarly and otherwise, that has been written on other musical forms, including "popular" music, blues, and jazz. The neglect of country music is due primarily to two factors: the scarcity of basic source materials and the belief held by many authorities that the music is unworthy of serious attention. But through the years collectors and enthusiasts have been patiently accumulating early phonograph records, songbooks, transcriptions, and handbills and interviewing early commercial performers. However slow and tedious, their work will someday provide the basis for a definitive history of American country music. The John Edwards Memorial Foundation in Los Angeles and the Country Music Hall of Fame and Museum in Nashville are only now beginning to provide the kind of research facilities that country-music historians have always needed.

Although country music still is not fully accepted by many musical sophisticates, and probably never will be, it has experienced a marked rise in status because of its strong involvement in the mid-century urban folk-music boom, and because of the commercial success symbolized by Nashville, Tennessee, with all its recording companies and related industries.

This history is intended as a partial remedy for the previous neglect of country music. The purpose of this study is to give a general, chronological account of the development of American country music from its commercial founding in the 1920's to its present big-business status. It is hoped that the general reader will not only gain some understanding of the complexities of this seemingly simple music form, but that he will perhaps be encouraged to undertake an even deeper study of it. An attempt has been made, therefore, to mention much of the scholarly and semischolarly work on country music that has been done in recent years and to suggest other areas that merit investigation.

Because country music has always reflected the social and economic milieu in which it was found, this study emphasizes the relation of country music to the changing South and to the United States as a whole. This musical culture, although highly complex and semisophisticated, nonetheless emerged from a folk background and must therefore be studied, at least partially, in terms of its origins.

It would perhaps be useful at this point to define the term "commercial country," and explain also what this study does *not* include. Commercial country music developed out of the folk culture of the rural South. Although it has absorbed styles, songs, instruments, and influences from a multitude of nonwhite and noncountry sources, the music has been created and disseminated largely by rural dwellers within the mainstream of the white Protestant Anglo-Celtic tradition. At first uncommercialized and "pure folk" in that its adherents had few monetary outlets open to them and were relatively unaffected by forces outside their native culture, the music became "commercial" when entertainment entrepreneurs learned in the 1920's that a cash market existed for it. Whereas some country boys moved away to the city and became salesmen, truck drivers, or industrial laborers, others, drawn by the lures of radio, television, and recording, became professional country musicians. And in each case, regardless of the occupation chosen, the rural-bred influences remained. After country music became a commercial enterprise, it could not escape radical change and invasion from people and forces outside the rural culture. Apparent external changes, however, will not transform overnight a deeply rooted culture. Rural music did not die when it moved into the cities; it merely adapted itself to changed conditions.

Despite its many modifications, country music is still a distinctive form, and the term "country" is still an apt designation. The music developed lineally out of the rural styles of the past, and the bulk of its performers today, in point of origin, are southerners who came from farms or small towns or who are only a generation away from a farm background. The old attitudes, mores, and social responses which originally produced the rural musical styles still endure in the southern United States. Country music is still as "country" as rapid urbanization and commercial pressures will allow it to be. This study, therefore, accepts the designation of "country music" as the term is used in the music and entertainment trade journals.

Although this study is concerned with "country" music, it does not encompass other forms, such as Negro country blues, which have strong rural roots. Negro country blues and its modern descendants, such as rhythm-and-blues, have deeply influenced white country music, but they are representative of a decidedly different folk culture and therefore deserve a completely separate study. Although country music bears a strong relationship to folk music, this study touches only briefly upon the "pure" folk music styles. Numerous studies, such as those by Bertrand H. Bronson, MacEdward Leach, and Stith Thompson, have analyzed America's folk-music traditions. This study, on the other hand, is concerned only with those individuals who have made or have tried to make money through their presentation of the music. Gospel music, with a history as old as that of country music and with adherents today numbering into the millions, is another southern, rural-based genre which is only peripherally treated in this work. Folk and rural humor, which continues to be such a vital part of the country music tradition, is still another area which is only briefly discussed. The scholar who ventures into these neglected fields will be performing a valuable service for students of folk and popular culture.

Only brief mention is given to the urban folk performers (city-bred and city-based entertainers who perform folk-style music), such as Pete Seeger and the Kingston Trio, even though they bear strong relation to country-music forms. These performers are not rural in origin; they do not direct their performances toward rural audiences; and their style of delivery and approach to the material are different from those of country performers. Because of their consistent use of the word "folk," it is evident that they do not consider themselves part of the country-music world. Conversely, the country-music

practitioners—the Roy Acuffs, the Hank Williamses, and the Bill
Monroes with whom this study is concerned—seldom have called
themselves "folk" musicians, although the term would be correct.
The folk do not think of themselves as "folk"; the term is almost always used by someone outside the culture. The musical line that
began generations ago with unschooled and uncultured mountain
and back-country musicians runs directly through such early commercial performers as Buell Kazee and Uncle Dave Macon to modern
country stars such as Ernest Tubb, Merle Haggard, and George
Jones. It does not run directly to such urban folk performers as Pete
Seeger, Joan Baez, Bob Dylan, the New Christy Minstrels, or Peter,
Paul and Mary. For no matter what their talents might be, and regardless of the skills they might possess in imitating folk styles, they
can never be considered as authentic folk performers. One cannot
join the "folk"; one must be born into the culture. This study, therefore, is an account of a musical form, folk in origin, which has
changed drastically through the years because of the impact of mass
media, but which, throughout its development, has been consistently
reflective and representative of the society which nourished it and of
the changes in that society.

In preparing this work I have been indebted to many people both
in and outside the field of country music. The Graduate Research
Committee of Murray State University helped to lighten my financial
burdens through a generous grant used to allay typing, indexing, and
photographic duplication costs. To Dr. Joe B. Frantz I owe a strong
debt of gratitude, for it was he who recommended the topic as a
relevant area of sociological and economic research and who supervised it in its original form as a doctoral dissertation at The University
of Texas. I am also indebted to Professor Barnes F. Lathrop of the
History Department, and Roger Abrahams of the English Department, who served on my doctoral committee. Dr. Abrahams, in particular, made helpful and perceptive comments about the early
chapters concerning the folk background. Dr. Donald Whisenhunt,
of the Murray State University History Department, also read the
manuscript and contributed helpful criticism of a stylistic nature.

Of the many individuals who contributed to the preparation of this
study, none was more important nor more helpful than Mrs. Jo
Walker, the Executive Director of the Country Music Association in

Nashville, Tennessee. Had it not been for her gracious aid in August, 1961, I could not have arranged necessary interviews and conferences.

At various stages of this study's writing and research, several people contributed new information or criticism. The following list is not definitive but, hopefully, it does include some of the more generous contributors. Guthrie Meade of Fairfax, Virginia, contributed significant information on early radio barn dances; Joe Boyd of Willow Grove, Pennsylvania, placed at my disposal some of his material on Bob Miller; Ronald Foreman, Jr., of Urbana, Illinois, made helpful suggestions about early blues music; Norman Cohen of the John Edwards Memorial Foundation contributed data on early recorded string bands; and Dave Wylie of Wilmette, Illinois, very kindly made available to me the results of his voluminous research on the National Barn Dance. It was also through Wylie's efforts that George C. Biggar, who was connected for many years with WLS and the National Barn Dance, provided me with data of both a musicological and economic nature.

Largely through the intercession of Archie Green, several scholars permitted me to see copies of unpublished manuscripts on various phases of country-music history. Neil Rosenberg's paper on bluegrass music, Richard Reuss's work on Woody Guthrie, and Judy McCulloh's manuscript on hillbilly tune transcription (all of which have been published) proved to be invaluable research aids.

Robert Shelton sent me an advance copy of his *The Country Music Story*, a combination history and photographic study which deserves to be in the library of every country-music enthusiast. Shelton also read my manuscript in its dissertation form and contributed helpful suggestions and critiques.

While this study was in the very early research stage, Ralph Rinzler placed at my disposal much of his research on Bill Monroe and bluegrass music, and, as the study will readily show, I have placed an equally heavy dependence on Rinzler's published studies.

Three individuals who, like Rinzler, have served as directors of the John Edwards Memorial Foundation read portions of the manuscript and contributed information which, it is hoped, has made the study more accurate and perceptive than it was in its original form. Of all the people who have generously given scholarly aid and encouragement, the writer is most deeply indebted to these three: Ed Kahn,

Executive Secretary of the John Edwards Memorial Foundation; Archie Green, of the University of Illinois; and Bob Pinson, country-music collector from Santa Clara, California. Virtually every chapter of this work bears evidence of my debt to these men.

Of course, I can never adequately thank nor repay the countless country musicians of the past, both commercial and otherwise, who captivated my interest from the time I was old enough to recognize a melody. They have contributed to the making of this book, not only through their spoken commentaries, but more especially through the songs and styles which they have implanted in the nation's musical consciousness. These individuals and their songs are, after all, the real sources for this work.

BILL C. MALONE

CONTENTS

ILLUSTRATIONS

COUNTRY MUSIC, U.S.A.

A Fifty-year History

CHAPTER 1

The Folk Background—Before the Coming of Commercialism

MODERN AMERICAN country music emerged out of the varied social and musical currents of the South. It is a vigorous hybrid form of music, constantly changing and growing in complexity but, at the same time, originating from a basically simple form of musical expression. It is a music which is as old as the South—or older—and the commercial paraphernalia it has adopted are both representative and derivative of that larger technological and communications revolution which has so radically transformed American popular tastes and steadily worked to pull the rural, socially static South into the homogenizing mainstream of American life.

Hillbilly music (a once universally accepted designation for country music) developed out of the reservoir of folksongs and ballads brought to North America by the Anglo-Celtic immigrants and gradually absorbed influences from other musical sources until it emerged as a force strong enough to survive, and even thrive, in an urban-industrial-oriented society. Yet, to explain country music solely in terms of its British background is to take a limited and incomplete approach for, after all, the settlers of prerevolutionary America, from Maine to Georgia, came out of essentially the same ethnic and social backgrounds. The British culture was implanted throughout the length and breadth of the American frontier. Why, then, did the music of the South develop in a radically different fashion from that

of the North? And why did the southern culture produce such a con-
geries of regional styles—both Negro and white—that have coalesced
into viable commercial forms in the modern period? The answer lies
in southern history.

Because of a complex variety of influences, involving geographical
and climatological determinism and cultural preconditioning, southerners became committed very early to an agricultural economy and
the rural way of life. In order to preserve that existence, which southerners professed to believe had a value transcending the mere acquisition of material wealth, they adopted a philosophically and socially
conservative position designed to ward off potentially disruptive internal and external influences. Always hovering in the background of
any southern attitude was the fact of Negro slavery, and the racial
hierarchy which derived from it. Recognizing that their socio-
economic system rested on a base of human slavery, the "peculiar institution" that increasingly drew the censure of the civilized world in
the first half of the nineteenth century, southerners grew progressively more defensive as they erected a wall of isolation against their
hostile critics. In their zeal to defend white supremacy and preserve
the supposed blessings of a rural society, southerners—through both
necessity and choice—committed their region to a course of arrested
development in a nation that was rapidly surrendering to the blandishment of urbanism and industrialization. Traditions which had
once been the common property of Americans therefore endured in
the South long after they had ceased to be important elsewhere.[1]
Although British ballads and folksongs were perpetuated in all areas
of early America, only in the South did they contribute to the creation of a lasting regional music.[2]

After a century and a half of concentration in the tidewater areas
of the South, settlements began to appear with substantial frequency
in the Appalachians and back-country areas at about the time of the
Revolution.[3] Confronted with a frontier existence, the people dis-
pelled the loneliness, in part, with the songs that were part of their

[1] An excellent account of the forces that have made the South conservative is
Wilbur J. Cash, *The Mind of the South*.

[2] Other such pockets of traditional British culture have existed, such as rural
New England and Canada's Maritime Provinces; it is significant that southern
country music has caught on in those areas as well.

[3] Clement Eaton, *A History of the Old South*, pp. 9–10.

inheritance and those that were occasionally added to their repertory. Despite the traditional emphasis placed on the mountaineer's commitment to song, it is equally true that the rural southerner, whether he lived in flatland or hill-country region, was passionately fond of singing. The mountaineers and their rural flatland cousins shared the same cultural tradition, and they preserved the same songs and styles.[4] Conditions leading to the creation and preservation of folk traditions were prevalent throughout the southern region.

Although the problem of folk definition is a complex and controversial one, it is reasonably clear that one powerful factor that has worked toward the perpetuation of folk communities is cultural isolation. According to B. A. Botkin, "the folk . . . group is one that has been cut off from progress and has retained beliefs, customs, and expressions with limited acceptance and acquired new ones in kind." Southern mountain people, it is true, preserved folk traditions because of their isolation, deficiencies in education, and lack of communication, but rural lowland southerners, in a society where illiteracy was widespread and where social contact with outsiders was limited, were also characterized by cultural isolation.[5] The socially ingrown rural South, from the tidewater of Virginia to the pine barrens of East Texas, produced a population that, in its commitment to and preservation of traditional cultural values, should be considered as a distinct family unit. The music of these people, lying outside the mainstream of American cultural development, provided the origin and nucleus of what we now call country music.

Although an occasional traveler noticed the pervasiveness of music in the lives of rural southerners, it was not until the turn of the present century that any kind of serious scholarly attention was devoted to the folk music of the rural South. Its seclusion in the back-country areas served to isolate the music from the efforts of music scholars

[4] Alan Lomax, *The Folk Songs of North America.* Lomax said that "the lowland poor whites shared the song preferences of their mountaineer cousins" (p. 153). Arthur Palmer Hudson, in attacking the overemphasis that scholars have placed on the mountains, said that "not only was the singing habit a widely and perhaps equally diffused one in the South as a whole; the songs sung over the South are much the same, irrespective of locality" (A. P. Hudson, "Folk Songs of the Southern Whites," *Culture in the South,* edited by W. T. Couch, p. 520).

[5] B. A. Botkin, "Folk and Folklore," *Culture in the South,* edited by W. T. Couch, pp. 570–572.

throughout the nineteenth century, and those who did come in contact with it were repelled by what they considered its rawness and
crudity. Colleges and universities for many decades were reluctant
to recognize the folksong as a legitimate document for the study of
American culture, and the ballad, if studied at all, was considered as
an example of literature and not as a socially significant musical expression. The publication in 1908 of Nathan Howard Thorp's *Songs
of the Cowboy*, and the 1910 publication of John A. Lomax's influential *Cowboy Songs and Other Frontier Ballads*,[6] signaled the
dawning of an awareness of the importance of folksong scholarship.
In the following ten years small collections containing songs of individual states or distinct regions began to appear.[7] In 1919 Cecil Sharp
introduced to the world, through his significant *English Folk Songs
From the Southern Appalachians*, the richness of the southern mountains as a folksong depository. Sharp's collection, containing both
music and lyrics, became a model for later folklorists, and the Appalachian chain unfortunately became riveted in the popular imagination as perhaps the sole source of traditional music in the United
States. The newly developed interest in mountain songs was only
one facet of a general, romantic obsession with the southern mountains current in the early part of the twentieth century. As a source
of romance and enchantment, the mountains stimulated much regional literature, as exemplified by the novels of John Fox, Jr.[8] The
Appalachians were pictured as a remote sanctuary inhabited by a
pure strain of Anglo-Americans who, untouched by communication
with the outside world, preserved the speech and customs of Elizabethan England. An individualistic, taciturn people with a stern code
of honor, the mountaineers were portrayed as America's purest racial
element and the epitome of Americans as they had lived in the
seventeenth century. In part, therefore, because of the romantic
image that became affixed to the southern mountains, folk scholar-

---

[6] *Cowboy Songs and Other Frontier Ballads* appeared in a revised and enlarged edition in 1938 and has since been reprinted many times. A new printing
was issued by the Macmillan Company in 1965.

[7] These include Josephine McGill, *Folk Songs of the Kentucky Mountains*;
Howard Brockway and Loraine Wyman, *Twenty Kentucky Mountain Songs*;
and Robert Hughes and Edith B. Sturges, *Songs from the Hills of Vermont*.

[8] John Fox, Jr. (1862–1919) was the author of such popular works as *The
Little Shepherd of Kingdom Come* and *The Trail of the Lonesome Pine*.

ship tended to concentrate upon that region, and ultimately the term "mountain music" came to be applied to the commercial country music that emanated from the South.

The emphasis upon mountain folksongs has tended to obscure the importance of other rural sectors in creating a southern regional music. This overemphasis, in regard to the realm of folksong scholarship, is largely a legacy of Cecil Sharp, who was a recognized authority on the folksongs of both America and his native England. Through the encouragement of Mrs. Olive Dame Campbell, whose husband, John Campbell, was head of Pine Mountain Settlement School in Kentucky, Sharp traveled to the United States in 1916 to collect those British ballads supposedly still extant in the Appalachians. From 1916 to 1918 Sharp spent forty-six weeks in the mountain regions of North Carolina, Kentucky, Virginia, Tennessee, and West Virginia. He was amazed not only by the existence of traditional ballads but also by the prevalence of singing among both young and old. The British folklorist found that singing was "almost as universal a practice as speaking," and that mountain singers depended upon their traditional store of songs for a convenient repertory. Sharp noted that "when, by chance, the text of a modern street-song succeeds in penetrating into the mountains it is at once mated to a traditional tune and sometimes still further purified by being moulded into the form of a traditional ballad."[9] Sharp, of course, was concerned primarily with the British songs that he discovered in the mountains, and, as a result, he neglected some of the musical influences that were just as strong, if not stronger, than those of British origin. He noted the strong Calvinistic-tinged religious faith of the people but neglected to collect and analyze their religious songs, feeling that they were not a legitimate source of folk material.[10] Despite its omissions, however, Sharp's research was of major importance in that he illustrated the wealth of the mountains and attempted to denote the melodies of the secular songs. Many of the songs had

[9] Cecil J. Sharp, *English Folk Songs from the Southern Appalachians*, I, xxv–xxvi.

[10] George Pullen Jackson, in commenting on Sharp's neglect of religious folk songs, said that it probably came about because Sharp believed that the songs were "organic with 'psalmody' or 'hymnody' and hence not a part of folk-lore at all, not important or even interesting" (*White Spirituals in the Southern Uplands*, p. vii).

been collected previously in narrative form, but, until Sharp heard the songs from native singers and noted them down, the melodies were virtually unknown. The day was approaching, therefore, when not only would southern folksongs be made public, but the southern folksingers and folk style would also become known to the outside world. The diverse vocal and instrumental approaches used by rural southerners to perform their native songs developed into definite "folk styles" which provided the basis for modern country music.

The door that Sharp opened provided the outlet for later folklorists who uncovered other deposits of folk music in the United States. Some explored more deeply into the mountain resources, while others conducted their investigation in lowland back-woods areas. It was ultimately revealed that traditional British ballads could be discovered in every part of the United States. In fact, folk researchers have found as many Child ballads in New England as in the South.[11] And in the South the traditional ballads have been discovered in many areas outside the mountain regions. Arthur Palmer Hudson has shown, for example, that Mississippi is a fertile field for the collection of traditional ballads, while William A. Owens has discovered the existence of British ballads in his native East Texas.[12] As scholars have demonstrated, the early settlers and their descendants carried the traditional songs with them wherever they went. As the southern frontier moved steadily westward, the southern musical culture moved with it. Southern migration in the early nineteenth century moved down from Pennsylvania into the Appalachian chain and either remained there or pushed on into other regions of the South. Southern frontier expansion generally demonstrated the tendency of pioneer farmers to move into areas that contained soil and climatological conditions similar to those left behind. As a result, southern migrations flowed in a southwesterly direction toward the potential cotton-producing regions of Arkansas, Louisiana, and Texas.[13] Rural

[11] Bruno Nettl, *An Introduction to Folk Music in the United States*, p. 39. The Child ballads are those included in Francis James Child's, *The English and Scottish Popular Ballads*.

[12] Arthur Palmer Hudson, *Folksongs of Mississippi and their Background*; and William A. Owens, *Texas Folk Songs*.

[13] The general flow of migration in the South has been described by Clement Eaton in *A History of the Old South* (pp. 9–25). See also Frank L. Owsley, "The Pattern of Migration and Settlement of the Southern Frontier," *Journal of Southern History*, XIX (1945), 147–176.

isolation, religious conservatism, and ethnic homogeneity produced a people who made up a relatively distinct social unit and performed a common type of music.

The rural southerners did not depend solely upon their inherited store of songs. They created songs based upon their own experiences, and acquired songs from other sources. With the passage of time the country people built up a body of songs of native-American origin which sang, not of knights and fair English damsels, but of scenes and events in their own American experience. And, in the mountains and rural areas of the South, the ancient British ballads underwent, in terms of subject matter, a degree of Americanization. American names and places often replaced those of British origin, and American expressions superseded the quaint language common in the sixteenth and seventeenth centuries.[14] The British tradition continued to be strong, however, as long as communication with outside cultures remained limited. Many of the songs discovered by Sharp and other collectors in the early twentieth century were in the modal scale of an older musical culture.[15]

Rural singers continued to sing their songs in melodies of ancient origin or of an ancient pattern until they became familiar with modern melodic patterns. Abandonment of the modal scale was largely the product of the modern inclination to adopt the practice of harmony and the use of instruments.[16] The necessity for harmony led to abandonment of the modal scale, whereas such instruments as the guitar produced a modification of the existing melodic patterns so that they would more easily fit the instrument's chords. The traditional patterns slowly gave way to modern techniques, though they lingered to a longer degree in the more isolated regions of the country.

[14] The best study of British traditional songs found in North America is Tristram P. Coffin, *The British Traditional Ballad in North America* (Vol. II of the Bibliographical and Special Series of the American Folklore Society).

[15] The music of the older British ballads found in the South was in a style that dated back to the Middle Ages. Bruno Nettl has said that "most of the tunes do not make use of the seven-tone scale, as do those of eighteenth and nineteenth century origin, but are restricted to five or six tones. Many of the tunes are modal; that is, they do not fit into the major and minor scales to which we are accustomed, and hence sometimes sound incomplete to our ears. In many of the tunes the melody rises to a peak about the middle and then descends slowly to its original level" (*An Introduction to Folk Music in the United States*, p. 42).

[16] Jean Thomas and Joseph A. Leeder, *The Singin' Gatherin'*, pp. vii–ix.

As a whole, the South held on to the traditional melodic structure longer than the remainder of the country, expressing in this respect an over-all tendency of the section to perpetuate customs and manners that had been characteristic of an earlier America.

The continued existence of old-world ballads and the steady addition of native products provided an immense repertory for the native singers, who performed in styles that were also products of folk tradition. The matter of song performance leads to the consideration of a fact long neglected by folklorists: in considering the problem of folk music, folk "style" must be stressed as well as folk "song." Not only are certain songs transmitted from generation to generation, but the manner of performing them, both vocally and instrumentally, is also passed on through the years. A folk style, created by the interchange of musical ideas and techniques among folk musicians and singers, proves to be a very tenacious factor. A folk "style" will persist long after the folk "songs" are forgotten.[17] With the coming of urbanization the old "rustic"-based songs are discarded and the new ones become largely devoid of "rural" settings; however, in the style of its performance and in its basic construction the song is, in point of origin, rural in nature. A rural inhabitant or an urban dweller who has formerly lived in the country will likely render a song in a "country" manner even though the words of the song describe an urban scene or event. This is significant in view of the fact that migration from southern rural areas to southern and northern urban centers has been a steady factor in southern life.[18] Southern cities have been populated largely by individuals of rural origin who carry with them their musical appreciation and tastes. These cities, then, to a great extent continue to be affected by rural attitudes and values. This in great measure explains why country music has endured in an urbanizing South, and why its lyric content has changed to fit the needs of a rural people who no longer live in rural surroundings. That music which thrives in a honky-tonk atmosphere or depicts the problems inherent in an urban existence can accurately be termed "country" music since it sprang from a rural origin.

[17] The most significant study of American musical styles is Alan Lomax, "Folk Song Style," *American Anthropologist*, LXI, No. 6 (December, 1959), 927–955. Much of the same discussion can be found in Alan Lomax, *The Folk Songs of North America*.

[18] Howard Odum, *Southern Regions of the United States*, p. 463.

It is, of course, not entirely accurate to speak of a single southern country style, since the southern region is divided into several subsections: the mountains, the lowlands, the piedmont, the pine barrens, the delta, the Texas plains, etc. In several of the subsections, too, the white singers were subjected in varying degrees to the influence of other musical cultures: that of the Negroes in most of the lowland areas, the Cajuns in Louisiana, the Mexicans in the Southwest, and commercial influences that might have emanated from the cities, or vaudeville-type shows that came in from the North. Despite the multitude of influences that have worked upon country music, it is reasonably clear that the process involved essentially the gradual transformation of a major style by the acquisition of minor traits and styles.[19] When southern people moved into new areas, their music acquired new characteristics from the cultures with which they came in contact. Still, a distinct southern backwoods style predominated and provided the basis for other styles that ultimately arose. It is for this reason that such urban-oriented styles as "western swing" and "honky-tonk" music developed when rural people adapted their older music to new environments. Western swing, specifically, is the product of the change that took place when southerners moved to Texas and Oklahoma and adapted the rural- or mountain-based music to new developments and surroundings.

Although the study of folk style is still in the embryonic stage, one of the best introductions to the study is a 1959 article by Alan Lomax which appeared in *American Anthropologist*.[20] Lomax has described the southern white rural style as the product of the "security patterns" of the white community. In reference to its social function, "the primary effect of music is to give the listener a feeling of

[19] W. J. Cash has made some acute observations about those factors that serve to unify the South socially and intellectually. They help to explain the existence of an over-all musical style. "Nevertheless, if it can be said there are many Souths, the fact remains that there is also one South. That is to say, it is easy to trace throughout the region . . . a fairly definite social pattern—a complex of established relationships and habits of thought, sentiments, prejudices, standards and values, and associations of ideas, which, if it is not common strictly to every group of white people in the South, is still common in one appreciable measure or another, and in some part or another, to all but relatively negligible ones" (*The Mind of the South*, p. viii).

[20] Alan Lomax, "Folk Song Style," *American Anthropologist*, LXI, No. 6 (December, 1959), 927–955.

security, for it symbolizes the place where he was born, his earliest childhood satisfactions, his religious experience, his pleasure in community doings, his courtship and his work—any or all of these personality-shaping experiences." A musical style, then, is "one of the most conservative of culture traits," because it is so deeply interwoven in the security framework of the community. "An entirely new set of tunes or rhythms or harmonic patterns may be introduced; but, in its overall character, a musical style will remain intact."[21]

In the American South there have been basically two important musical traditions or styles: the Afro-American and the rural white. Both styles have had dynamic effects in American society, and both have borrowed from and influenced each other for many decades. The white style has borrowed many of its rhythms, songs, and instrumental styles from the Negro. And the debt of the Negro to the white has been equally as heavy. Still, regardless of the debt and despite the generations of mutual collaboration, "the white folk pattern in America," according to Lomax, "still resembles the familiar folk-song style of Western Europe more than it does that of its Afro-American neighbors."[22]

In its purest state, this white folk pattern was marked by a number of definite characteristics. Usually solo voiced and instrumentally unaccompanied, it was performed with a rigidly pitched voice, high, rubato, and nasal. Lyrics, considered to be the most important part of a song, were set to simple melodies and rhythms and rendered in a highly impersonal manner by a singer who sang either for his own enjoyment or for close friends or relatives. Public performances were rare and, when held, were usually for a limited group and the source of considerable embarrassment. The more accomplished singer gradually gained a reputation in the neighborhood and was invited to perform at various social functions.[23] With the acquisition of instruments an individual performer would occasionally join with some of his neighbors in the formation of a rudimentary string band. Thus, in the environs of their own native neighborhood, country singers developed styles and techniques and transmitted them to other people.

[21] *Ibid.*, pp. 929–930.
[22] *Ibid.*, pp. 931–932.
[23] *Ibid.*, p. 931; Alan Lomax, *The Folk Songs of North America*, p. 153.

When the commercial music forces decided to exploit the South, they found a music culture already there, vigorous and thriving.

Southern country music, working from a definite solo style, changed as instruments made their way into the back-country recesses. The early settlers, with rare exceptions, had few instruments, and those possessed were usually of a homemade variety. In some remote areas of the southern mountains—particularly Kentucky—the dulcimer, an ancient instrument of Germanic origin, gained a considerable degree of popularity. A delicate instrument of weak volume, the dulcimer lost favor as other instruments were circulated in the mountain areas. The fiddle, universally popular on the frontier, was brought into the South as early as the seventeenth century and, though one can only speculate, it probably entered the back country along with the first permanent settlers. Brought to this country by white settlers, the fiddle was taken up by Negro musicians who played for white social gatherings, then finally made its way into the hands of lower-class whites in the hinterlands.[24]

The banjo, an instrument of Negro origin which gained tremendous popularity among country entertainers, is sometimes called America's only native instrument. This appellation is correct, however, only in terms of its final state of development, because the instrument can be traced back ultimately to an African instrument, the *bania*.[25] Originally a four-stringed instrument, the banjo was "revolutionized" in the early nineteenth century by the addition of a fifth, or drone, string which made it more adaptable and flexible. Although the banjo was popular throughout the United States in the mid-nineteenth century, and was the favorite instrument among the "Forty-Niners," it did not gain wide currency in the southern mountains until the late nineteenth century.[26] The five-string banjo became

[24] A general discussion of the entry of musical instruments into the Southern backwoods can be found in the notes for *Blue Ridge Mountain Music*, Southern Folk Heritage Series (Atlantic LP 1347, recorded in the field and edited by Alan Lomax).

[25] Nettl, *An Introduction to Folk Music in the United States*, p. 56.

[26] There is no definitive history of the five-string banjo, but the student can learn much of both its history and of various instrumental styles by consulting *Banjo Songs of the Southern Mountains* (Riverside RLP 12–610, notes by John Greenway). Also very helpful are Alan Lomax's notes for *Blue Ridge Mountain Music* (Atlantic LP 1347).

the mountain or hillbilly banjo, while the four-stringed instrument
became the province of Dixieland or jazz musicians. The five-string
banjo, with its melancholy phrasing, became the perfect accompaniment for the lonely laments and doleful dirges of the early country
singers and was one of the most popular instruments among the early
commercial performers. With the acquisition of the banjo, along with
the other instruments that were added periodically, country singing
styles changed—indeed, they had to change in order to meet the requirements of the instruments. The old songs, with their minor keys
and modal structure, were flattened out in order to allow easier accompaniment. The acquisition of the guitar in the late nineteenth
century, and of such instruments as the mandolin in the early twentieth century, led to even more changes, particularly in reference to
rhythm and timing structure.[27]

As performers acquired instruments, they first learned basic
chords, then made various embellishments either invented or learned
from others, and possibly derived techniques from Negro country
musicians. The instrumental styles, transmitted from one musical
performer to another and circulated in a relatively isolated environment, became the basis for the later commercial hillbilly styles. Instrumental style, therefore, worked as a folk process in much the
same way as did the country singing style.

Musical stringed instruments were one of two major forces working for the modification of the old country solo singing style. The
other was the growing predilection for harmony singing throughout
the nineteenth century. The acceptance of harmony throughout the
Western world led to the abandonment of the modal scale.[28] In the
back-country areas of the South the use of harmony—like most new
ideas and fashions—gained slower acceptance, although the process
was initiated at a rather early date. Because of the rawness and un-

[27] Information about other hillbilly instruments such as the guitar and mandolin, which ventured into rural areas later than the fiddle and banjo, is extremely
scarce. Lomax thinks, however, that these instruments entered the rural South,
along with instruction manuals, through the mail-order route. He quotes mountain folk singer Hobart Smith as saying that he saw his first guitar about the
time of World War I when a Negro construction gang laid rails into Saltville,
Virginia. (Notes, *Blue Ridge Mountain Music*, Atlantic LP 1347). The guitar
evidently was a flatland phenomenon long before it ventured into the mountains.
[28] Thomas and Leeder, *The Singin' Gatherin'* pp. viii–ix.

trained nature of the southern country singing voice, harmonizing took on a quainter and more primitive form than it did in more refined centers. The high, wailing style, so characteristic of solo singing, was transferred to harmony singing, in which the tenor sang in a high, nasal fashion considerably above the lead singer. Country tenors strove to achieve a clear "bell-like tone" in order that ornamentation could be made upon the melody. The high, nasal harmony became an easily recognizable characteristic of white country music, and can still be heard on many commercial country records, especially the "bluegrass" recordings of such performers as Bill Monroe and the Stanley Brothers.[29]

The introduction and refinement of harmony singing was primarily the product of the church singing schools. In the shaping of southern musical style and in the introduction of various songs, the itinerant singing-school master played a profound role. This individual, and the practice of group singing, seem to have originated in New England, because it was there that the English manner of solmization entered North America.[30] Group singing first developed there in the late eighteenth century and then spread in the early part of the next century to the rural areas of the South. The Yankee singing-school master traveled alone into the frontier areas of the United States, carrying with him a technique of musical education simple enough for the relatively unlettered backwoodsmen to understand. This technique, eventually to gain wide vogue throughout the southern states, was referred to as the "shape-note" method. It was a highly simplified plan, designed to appeal to the musically illiterate, in which the pitch of musical notes was indicated by their shapes, independently of the lines and spaces of the staff. Originating in New England, the shape-note singing school entered the South from Philadelphia and eastern Pennsylvania. From northwestern Virginia,

[29] The above statements should be qualified. In the absence of sound reproduction of nineteenth-century country singing, no conclusive evidence exists as to the true nature of the singing styles of that period. As far as the writer can ascertain, no exhaustive studies have been made of old-time country harmony singing with the exception of congregational vocalizing. Future investigations among the older people in remote country areas may reveal styles of harmony radically different from what are considered old-fashioned styles today. Bluegrass music (discussed in Chapter 10), and other old-timey styles, may be products of twentieth-century commercial factors.

[30] Jackson, *White Spirituals in the Southern Uplands*, p. 5.

the scene of the earliest southern shape-note activity, the music eventually penetrated as far west as Texas and Arkansas. This style of musical instruction, embodied in such books as William Walker's *Southern Harmony*, became a deeply imbedded facet of southern musical culture and was largely responsible for the prominence of harmony singing among generations of rural southerners.[31]

In the North shape-note singing had almost disappeared by the late nineteenth century. Here, as had been the case with the traditional British folksongs, factors came into play which served to destroy the simpler traditional music of the past. The growth of cities, economic prosperity, urban-continental-Nordic immigration, and European musical influences alienated the northerners from the more primitive rural music style. These factors, on the other hand, did not exist in the southern region. Thus, in the words of George Pullen Jackson, "when the singing schools came into the South, they stuck."[32] The South illustrates again, in this respect, a tendency to hold on to those customs and values which were characteristic of an older America.

Harmony singing preceded the introduction of musical instruments. For a long period instruments were difficult to obtain, and in many instances church tenets forbade their acquisition. According to George Pullen Jackson, southern country music in the early nineteenth century grew up "as an exclusively vocal development. The charm of harmony, since it could not be delegated to an instrument, had to be produced vocally."[33] From a solo style of performance, therefore, southern rural music developed a style of harmony that affected both the secular and religious songs of the region.

There has been no greater influence on country music than southern religious life, both as to the nature of the songs and to the manner in which they were performed. The fundamentalist and revivalist sects —the Methodists, Baptists, and Presbyterians—began moving into the southern back country shortly after the American Revolution.[34] These groups, moving down the Appalachian chains into the frontier

[31] *Ibid.*, pp. 15–16, 22–26, 81.

[32] *Ibid.*, p. 22.

[33] *Ibid.*, p. 427.

[34] Information on the evangelical religious denominations has been gathered principally from the following books: Charles A. Johnson, *The Frontier Camp Meeting*; and Bernard Weisberger, *They Gathered at the River: The Story of the Great Revivalists and their Impact upon Religion in America.*

areas of the South, brought a popular brand of religion to the socially isolated and religion-starved pioneers of the back country. This religion, striking out against formalism and the maintenance of a church hierarchy, appealed to the democratic instincts of the people. Rather than the cold reserve and formality of the established churches, the frontier sects stressed democratic individualism and the necessity for emotionalism. The popularity of frontier evangelical groups was due as much to their congregational singing as to any other factor. The Methodist church, in particular, was often called the "singing church."[35] American backwoodsmen, who had neither the time nor the means to acquire an education, could respond joyfully to the command of song, whereas theology or sermons might leave them cold. The frontier camp meetings gave birth to spirited songs which, set to familiar or simple melodies, described the heavenly joys awaiting men of good faith. Although printed manuals containing the more popular tunes began to appear in the early nineteenth century, there were never enough books to go around. The song books were passed from person to person until the better songs were committed to memory. Another memorization technique was the practice of "lining the hymn,"[36] a process especially beneficial to those who could not read. In this procedure the preacher read the verses, usually two lines at a time, to his congregation, which then proceeded to sing them. The camp meetings, as important for their social significance as for their religious impact, inspired songs and song styles that have endured in rural America.

The frontier church doctrines were just as profound in their influence as were the camp-meeting songs. The frontier religious groups combined in their doctrines a liberal mixture of both Calvinistic predeterminism and Arminian free will. God was, in truth, an omniscient Being who consigned souls to everlasting damnation because of their misdeeds, but He was also an all-merciful, benevolent ruler who would spare an individual if he asked for forgiveness. The Creator was pictured as a very personal Being who interceded in the daily affairs of mankind. A feeling developed among the southern country people, then, that God was ever present, was keeping close watch upon humanity, and would punish any transgression. A feeling

[35] Johnson, *The Frontier Camp Meeting*, p. 192.
[36] *Ibid.*, p. 195.

of guilt and a conviction that, despite the frivolity and waywardness of the moment, God would ultimately punish, pervaded the rural mind. This religious conviction, born of Calvinism and the rigorousness of rural living, cast a somber and melancholy mood over much of the religious and secular music of the southern rural dweller. The southerner, despite his occasional lapses into wickedness, and despite his concern with day-to-day living, developed an otherworldly attitude. Rather than developing a music of protest and striking out against the evils in society, the rural southerner more often looked toward life beyond the grave as the ultimate solace or consolation.[37] Scores of religious songs, such as "This World Is Not My Home," and "Farther Along, We'll Know All About It," became great favorites in the back-country South. The songs of unrequited love, as "The Little Rosewood Casket" and hundreds of similar examples will indicate, often expressed the idea that only the grave could bring peace and solace to a heart broken by an unfortunate love affair.

By the 1920's southern country music had had well over a century of American existence in which to develop. A body of songs had become the common property of rural southerners, and an over-all style—marked by many sub-stylings—had been formulated in which to perform the songs. Although the southern rural musical culture had been marked by a largely indigenous development, that development had never been unaffected by external urban or commercial forces. The modern researcher must rid his mind of the idea that country music had no commercial history prior to the 1920's. He must also rid himself of the romantic but tenaciously lingering idea of complete folk isolation. No southern area (or any other American area, for that matter) has ever been totally isolated from the world at large. The currents of change that have swept over the United States, making it the most advanced, industrially oriented nation in the world, have also moved across the South. The South has changed slowly, and often with dogged resistance, but it has changed.

The southern pockets of rural folk culture—whether mountain, hill country, or flatland—have never been completely immune to the

[37] As Bernard Weisberger has said, "for plain men and women, in fact, the hopes of mansions bright and blessed and crowns of glory were the stellar consolations of hard-driven lives of work" (*They Gathered at the River*, pp. 106–107).

forces of technological or social change. Scarcely a rural community in the decades before 1920 was not visited at one time or another by some kind of peripatetic agent of the world outside who brought news, business, religion, education, or amusement.[38] It might be the Methodist circuit rider braving the flooded streams and frozen wilderness to bring not only the gospel but gossip from the towns and cities. It might be the singing-school teacher boarding with farm families until his shape-note method had been learned by the entire community. Or it might be any number of salesmen or agents of mercantile houses, the "rider" sent out by the general store to see if the farmer's crops would enable him to meet his credit obligations, or the Yankee or Jewish peddler in his horse-drawn wagon carrying a valuable cargo of needed items—which might even include a musical instrument.[39]

Neither have our rural areas—prior to the coming of radio, television, and rural electrification—been totally immune to the musical trends emanating from the cities. The popular music originating in Tin Pan Alley or on the vaudeville stages of northern cities entered the rural districts in a variety of ways. The city could most effectively transport its musical ideas to the country through the medium of the traveling show. Perhaps the most common of these shows, but one as yet inadequately documented, was the medicine show. The "physick" wagon, with its glib-talking "doctor" and cargo of patent medicines, was a familiar phenomenon to rural Americans as late as the 1930's. Nearly all of the medicine shows employed an entertainer—often blackface—to warm up the crowd by singing, cracking jokes, or playing an instrument. Not only were songs introduced to rural America in this manner, the medicine shows also provided an early commercial outlet for country musicians, who were often employed by the traveling shows. On the physick wagons, country entertainers gained invaluable show business experience which would later serve them well when they set out on their professional careers. And the list of country performers who learned in this manner is long indeed. It in-

[38] A general account of early American peripatetic occupations is found in Richardson Wright, *Hawkers and Walkers in Early America.*

[39] An excellent account of post-Civil War merchandising and peddling in the South is Thomas D. Clark, *Pills, Petticoats and Plows: The Southern Country Store.*

cludes Uncle Dave Macon, Jimmie Rodgers, Roy Acuff, Lew Childre, Clarence Ashley, and Hank Williams.[40]

On a larger scale, and almost as common as the medicine show until the 1930's, was the traveling tent operation—often called the "tent repertoire" show. The tent show brought to the rural regions a touch of vaudeville, including everything from magicians, acrobats, and trained bears to Irish tenors, Swiss yodelers, and dancing girls. These organizations, transported by horse-drawn wagons, would move into a rural community, stake out their tents, hold nightly shows that might run as long as a week, and then move on to another excited community. The communities visited, it is clear, often included the very smallest villages imaginable. My father remembered a tent show which, just before World War I, lingered for a week in his rural home community of Galena, an East Texas village near Tyler so small that it could not be located on the map. Practically every man, woman, and child attended the shows—night after night —spending money if they had it, but just as often bartering eggs, vegetables, or canned goods for the price of admission.[41]

Although the traveling shows were important vehicles for transmitting urban culture to the rural regions, a more common, and obvious, means was the movement of country people to and from the town. As long as the city has existed, it has beckoned the rural dweller. Often pictured in American myth and story as the center of vice, corruption, and lost innocence, the city has more often exerted a contrary pull on the rural mind. Country youth have traditionally seen the city in many different lights: as a place of employment, a means of escape, and a source of amusement. It would therefore be more accurate to say that the city has exerted an ambivalent influence on country people. They often have sought the city's advantages while at the same time attacking its values and longing for the rural life which they readily extol but to which they would not return. The catalogue of country music is filled with songs extolling the farmer[42]

---

[40] For a full and interesting picture of medicine-show life at the beginning of the twentieth century see Ralph and Richard Rinzler's notes to *Old-Time Music at Clarence Ashley's*, Folkways FA 2355.

[41] Cleburne Malone to the writer, Dallas, Texas, December 28, 1966.

[42] Joe D. Boyd of Willow Grove, Pennsylvania, has been compiling the data which will eventually give the large field of farming and agricultural songs the scholarly treatment it has long deserved.

and the whole scheme of rural values, and with scores of others describing the innocent ruralite lost in the big city and at the mercy of the city slicker. But, attacked and ridiculed as the city may have been, the statistics of the past hundred years reveal the irresistible appeal the city has had for rural Americans.

Southern country boys burdened by the rigors of farm work and by the social isolation of country living have traditionally longed for the bright lights of the city that lay somewhere down the road or beyond the mountains. By the thousands they have ventured into such cities as Louisville, Memphis, Nashville, Atlanta, New Orleans, and Houston. Many of them went only for temporary employment, later going back to the farm, but the great majority remained as part of the swelling ranks of the urban lower-middle class. In the decades before 1920 the city was never too far away for the country boy whose dreams and longings were intense enough. By foot, by wagon, by horseback, by flatboat or steamboat, the trek to the city was made. And increasingly after the Civil War another transportation device— the railroad—played its powerful role in uniting city and farm. No other industrial phenomenon has held such a magnetic and romantic fascination for Americans, and it is doubtful that any ever again will, even though the automobile has had a greater impact on the breaking down of regional barriers. No one can document the number of farmboys who have lain awake in quiet and darkened farmhouses listening to the lonesome wail of a distant freight train or have seen it belching smoke as it thundered down the mountain side and longed for the exciting world that the iron monster seemed to symbolize.[43]

So off they went to the textile mills of the Carolina piedmont, the coal mines of eastern Kentucky, the dockyards of New Orleans and Galveston, the railroad shops of Atlanta and Richmond, and, in this century, to service installations, defense plants, and industrial jobs all over the United States. Many of those who roamed had no particular destination in mind but were part of that nameless throng of drifters that has always been such a visible part of American life. Whether they came to visit or stay, they were exposed to a multitude of musical influences that in time would be taken back to their rural homes. In the mid-nineteenth century one of the more popular urban

[43] For a sampling of the best-known railroad ballads of the past see Sterling Sherwin and Harry K. McClintock, *Railroad Songs of Yesterday*.

musical sources was the minstrel show, which contributed a brand of humor and stage patter, banjo styles, and very popular songs—such as "Old Zip Coon," "Blue Tailed Fly," and "Old Dan Tucker"—that have endured in the rural tradition. Rivaling the minstrel performance was the vaudeville show, a variety extravaganza which introduced "pop" tunes and styles from the North and also occasionally used country talent. Long before the coming of radio, several country entertainers—one of them Uncle Dave Macon—toured the southern theater circuits: Loew's, RKO-Pathe, Keith-Orpheum. During the 1920's Al Hopkins, Jimmie Rodgers, Otto Gray, the Weaver Brothers and Elviry, and a host of other country performers continued to travel the vaudeville circuits.[44]

The city held a thousand attractions, and not all of them were of the formalized, respectable, vaudeville variety. Nearly every southern city had its "sin street"—Beale Street in Memphis and Basin Street in New Orleans, for example—where blues, ragtime, and jazz techniques were learned. These techniques would eventually find their way into the repertories of almost all country musicians from Jimmie Rodgers and Milton Brown to the Delmore Brothers and Hank Williams. Or it might be a street like "deep Elm (Ellem)," Dallas' notorious red-light district, which lured East Texas farm boys until the 1930's. Here one could find amusement in the white taverns or Negro juke joints, or listen to street singers—both white and Negro— who could be heard with frequency in any southern city in those days before ordinances drove them from the streets. In the twenties the great Negro country-blues artist, Blind Lemon Jefferson, made Dallas his main base of operations.[45] Many of the white country boys who heard Blind Lemon and other blues performers in clubs or on street corners were permanently influenced by what they heard.

Whatever they heard, or wherever they heard it, if the song or style attracted their fancy, the country people would take it back home. It might be a song learned from a Swiss yodeler, the latest tune from the pen of a Tin Pan Alley songwriter, a sentimental melody intro-

[44] See *Billboard* of the 1920's and 1930's for confirmation.

[45] Old-time Texas musician William Ernest Porter has attested to the fact that he and other young white musicians learned the finger style of guitar playing from Blind Lemon Jefferson and other Negro musicians whom they heard on the streets of Dallas in the late twenties (interview with William Ernest Porter, Dallas, Texas, September 13, 1966).

duced by a touring Hawaiian string band, or a ragtime, blues, or jazz melody learned from Negro performers. Regardless of the origin or style, once an urban melody was introduced into a rural region the folk esthetic began to assert its process of natural selection and the song (or style) was either accepted or rejected. More importantly, through some kind of musical chemistry the urban songs and styles were radically transformed into country songs. As the years passed, the social conservatism of the rural South not only influenced the modification of urban song structure, it also preserved these songs and styles long after they were forgotten elsewhere. Songs once known in the cities and then discarded would emerge decades later as part of the recorded repertory of country music. And as far as the casual observer could tell, the songs were not only "country" but always had been.

If the rural South received musical ideas from various internal and external sources, then what kind of songs did it make its own? In considering this question, it should be made clear that the origin of a song is no criterion as to whether it is in the "folk" or "country" category. Whether the song comes from urban or nonsouthern areas makes no difference: if the rural people accept it as one of their own and perform it in their native manner, then it becomes a "country" song. And if the song enters oral tradition it becomes a "folk" song regardless of its origin or quality.[46]

On the verge of commercial exploitation in the 1920's, southern country music had developed a large repertory consisting of both southern and nonsouthern songs, of both folk and nonfolk origin. At the core of the country depository of songs was the store of traditional songs, both British and American. Many of them were ballads; that is, narrative songs that told a story.[47] The beloved British ballads,

[46] The term "folksong" is used here in the pure sense, as meaning a traditional song of unknown origin existing in the form of scattered variants. But the point to be made is that the song could have come from the pen of a professional composer writing for contemporary tastes and could be of the poorest musical quality and still be a folksong. If the folk accept a song, then it is a folksong regardless of its origin or quality.

[47] In modern usage the ballad has come to be any kind of lyrical love song as opposed to other kinds of musical forms such as novelty or blues numbers. For a discussion of the nature of the traditional ballad, and the difficulty of an adequate definition, consult Gordon Hall Gerould, *The Ballad of Tradition* (pp. 1–14).

brought to America by the early immigrants, continued to exert a powerful attraction on later generations, who found in the old songs a means of dispelling the monotony and loneliness of rural existence. In time, the traditional store was enlarged by the addition of American songs and ballads. These songs recounted the experiences with which southerners were acquainted, or they told the story of significant events, such as "The Death of Little Mary Phagan."[48] The old ballad style, then, was perpetuated by southern singers and used as a communicative device in a semiliterate society that of necessity emphasized the oral-aural means of communication and expression.

The southern taste in ballad and song ran the gamut from the ridiculous to the tragic—from "Froggie Went a Courtin'" to "The Fatal Flower Garden." Although the songs depicted every aspect of rural life and temper, the rural taste ran heavily toward the mournful and lonesome tunes. In part, this inclination was a legacy from the British tradition, because many of the British songs dealt with somber themes and were cast in minor-sounding keys which evoked melancholy responses in the minds of the singer and listener.[49] The sad songs continued to be loved by later generations of southerners long after instrumentation and modern harmonic devices had diminished the influence of the ancient modal patterns.

The preference for the mournful derived its existence from several sources. One source was the religious life, which stressed an otherworldly attitude and the depiction of this world as a vale of sorrow. Southern backwoodsmen, imbued with the doctrines of Calvinism, labored under a conviction of sin. It is not surprising that their choice of songs and style of singing would reflect this tragic outlook. The average rural dweller in the pre-1920 period needed few reminders to know that life was indeed tragic—a brief period filled with sad-

[48] "Little Mary Phagan" (sometimes spelled Fagan) related the story of the little fourteen-year-old factory worker who was allegedly assaulted and murdered by her factory superintendent, Leo Frank, in Atlanta, Georgia, April 27, 1913 (F. W. Bradley, "Little Mary Fagan," *Southern Folklore Quarterly*, XXIV, No. 2 [June, 1960], 144–146).

[49] In fact, when the Americans extracted songs from the British tradition, they seem to have selected the sad ones and rejected the gay and bawdy ones, of which there were many. The old-time love songs, as Alan Lomax has said, "gather together the sorrowful themes from England, Scotland, and Ireland, with little of their gaiety and sensuality" (*The Folk Songs of North America*, p. 196).

ness and disappointment and ultimately ending in death. Bernard Weisberger has described well the preoccupation with death held by many Americans of the late nineteenth century: "parting and death were real terrors to that generation. The sentimentality which overflowed in the short stories of both the popular and religious presses, however mawkish it might be, had a foundation in real anguish."[50] His statements would just as easily apply to the popular music of the late nineteenth century. Many of the sentimental tunes from Tin Pan Alley—such as "I'll Be All Smiles Tonight," "Just Tell Them that You Saw Me," and "The Fatal Wedding"[51]—filtered into the rural areas and, finding a natural habitat, remained there. Such songs experienced their births in urban areas and gained extensive popularity in a nineteenth-century America that, despite its rapid industrialization, still contained a population that yearned nostalgically for the departed farm and village. Long after these songs had faded into obscurity in urban areas and had ceased to be known by "popular"-music fans, they continued to be known and loved by rural southerners who held on to the simple and sentimental values of a bygone era. The home, the family, and the church continued to be emotional and security-laden facets of southern culture long after industrialization made its long-delayed impact.

Although the sad, lonesome tunes were probably preferred, the more joyful, boisterous tunes also became an important part of the rural singers' repertory. From the singers' Celtic forebears came a legacy of jigs, reels, and novelty songs, and from the English came country dances and melodies. The fiddle, despite its being frowned upon by many Christians as the devil's instrument, provided the chief source of instrumentation at country dances[52]—the large, and often boisterous affairs at which country people obtained relief from a

[50] Weisberger, *They Gathered at the River*, p. 217.

[51] The reader can find examples of popular sentimental favorites from the nineteenth century in *Read 'Em and Weep* and *Weep Some More My Lady*, both edited by Sigmund Spaeth.

[52] The popularity of the mountain dances, and the corresponding disapprobation of the churchgoing elements, has been vividly described in John C. Campbell, *The Southern Highlander and His Homeland* (pp. 130–131). Country dances, however, were not confined to the mountains. They could be found all over the South, as is exemplified by the "fais dodos" (the all-night dances of Cajun Louisiana), and by the "house parties" in Texas where fiddlers like Bob Wills laid the basis for modern western swing.

period of toil or solitude. The rural southerner, in his moral outlook, could be a man of extreme contradiction. On one occasion he could be an individual of stern piety and devout reverence toward his God, and on another he could be a hard-swearing, hard-drinking, militant hellion. The passive, taciturn southerner could suddenly erupt into a man of violence, especially when in the company of his fellows and when plied with liberal amounts of liquor. Country dances, therefore, quite often provided an outlet for the more raucous or libertine aspects of the southerner's nature. But as W. J. Cash has pointed out, through it all, while the fiddles whined their melodies of merriment, the southerner knew amidst his moment of exultation that ultimately the revelry must end and he must pay the fiddler.[53]

The fiddle dance tunes are among the most genuine folk melodies produced or preserved in the United States. These melodies, of unknown authorship, have been transmitted from generation to generation, often from father to son. Many of the country fiddlers came to know hundreds of tunes simply by learning them aurally from others. Some of the tunes, such as "Soldier's Joy," were of English origin, while others were of native vintage. Illustrative tunes are "The Eighth of January," composed in commemoration of the battle of New Orleans, and "The Orange Blossom Special," composed by fiddler Ervin Rouse and perhaps the most popular and exciting fiddle tune of the modern period.[54] The fiddle was the backbone of the early hillbilly string bands, and the village dances at which the fiddle held sway were the forerunners of the radio barn-dance shows.

White country music received many of its songs and rhythms from the various ethnic groups that composed the South. In the Southwest country music acquired both guitar techniques and songs from Mexican sources. "El Rancho Grande," for example, came to be included

[53] Cash, *The Mind of the South*, p. 56.

[54] "The Eighth of January" had the unusual distinction in 1959 of attaining the number one position on the nation's music popularity charts. Refurbished with words by Jimmie Driftwood, and entitled "The Battle of New Orleans," the song achieved "hit" status when recorded by Johnny Horton on Columbia 41339. "The Orange Blossom Special," first recorded in 1939 by the Rouse Brothers, is now in the repertories of most country musicians. The original Rouse Brothers' recording can be heard on *The Railroad in Folksong*, RCA Victor Vintage album, LPV 532 (notes by Archie Green).

in the repertory of nearly all the western-swing bands.[55] In Louisiana country music was affected by the music of the Cajuns, the French-American inhabitants in the southern part of the state who contributed a distinctive type of rhythm, produced chiefly by the concertina, which came to be applied to the hillbilly fiddle. In addition, such songs as "Jole Blon" emerged out of Cajun folk music and became a standard part of country music.[56]

Of all the southern ethnic groups, none has played a more important role in providing songs and styles for the white country musician than that forced migrant from Africa, the Negro. Nowhere is the peculiar love-hate relationship that has prevailed among the southern races more evidenced than in country music. Country music—seemingly the most "pure white" of all American musical forms—has borrowed heavily from the Negro. White southerners who would be horrified at the idea of mixing socially with Negroes have enthusiastically accepted their musical offerings: the spirituals, the blues, ragtime, jazz, and a variety of instrumental techniques. In our own era the Negro rhythms of rhythm-and-blues, rock-and-roll, and folk rock have captivated southern youth whose parents in some cases may be Ku Klux Klan and Citizens' Council members. It has never been possible in this country to segregate musical forms.[57]

Although Negro songs and styles have moved freely into white country music, Negroes have not. One of the striking characteristics of country music has been the almost total absence of Negro performers. (In fact, a Negro spectator at a country concert has been

[55] "El Rancho Grande" has become a standard song in American country music. Some of the more significant recordings have been by Milton Brown and his Musical Brownies on Decca 5071 and 46000, and by the Light Crust Doughboys on Vocalion 03017.

[56] For a representative selection of the old-time French songs found in Louisiana, see Irene Therese Whitfield, *Louisiana French Folk Songs*. For a more modern sampling of the various musical strains in Cajun Louisiana, and a discussion of the hybridization of the music, see *Folksongs of the Louisiana Acadians*, Folk-Lyric IFS-A-4 (collected and edited by Harry Oster from 1956 to 1959, under the auspices of the Louisiana Folklore Society).

[57] Negro influence on white country music is a subject worthy of a separate and definitive study. An extremely useful beginning has been made by John Cohen in "The Folk Music Interchange: Negro and White," *Sing Out: The Folk Song Magazine*, XIV, No. 6 (January, 1964), 42–49.

and is a rare phenomenon.) An important exception to the exclusive rule was DeFord Bailey, a harmonica player, who long performed on the Grand Ole Opry and who may have been the first person recorded in Nashville. In the modern period Charley Pride holds the distinction of being the only member of his race to be a featured country and western vocalist and the only Negro country singer ever to be recorded by a major company (RCA Victor).[58] The rigid segregation that has kept country music lily white has been only a facet of that larger scheme of values that has kept the southern races apart, but the apartness derives additionally from the fact that Negro rural music has developed in its own independent fashion and has spawned a profusion of sub-styles. But, regardless of the segregation of personnel, Negro musical styles and songs have always freely made their way into the world of white country music.

Prior to the commercial period Negro influence was extended in a variety of ways. Anywhere that Negroes and whites mingled on construction or work projects, as in railroad section gangs or in coal mines, there was bound to be a mutual cultural transmission. Not even the mountains were too remote for this kind of musical intermingling. Both the guitar and the blues form may have ventured into the mountains with Negro laborers who followed the railroads as they gradually inched their way up the Appalachian ridges. But everywhere in the South—in flatland rural areas, in the delta country, as well as in the mountains—Negro musicians contributed a variety of songs from "John Henry" to "Trouble in Mind." The blues form, which has been such a durable facet of country music, is largely derived from the Negro experience.[59] Although the white country dweller had many musical outlets, both religious and secular, through which to express his loneliness and soul-misery, the blues pattern became a favorite manner of expression for many white singers.

Of perhaps greater significance than the introduction of Negro

[58] For information on DeFord Bailey's 1928 recordings see Robert Shelton, *The Country Music Story*. The best introduction to the style and songs of Charley Pride is his long-play album *Pride of Country Music*, RCA Victor LPM 3775.

[59] The most comprehensive account of early Negro country-blues performers and their instrumental styles is Samuel Charters, *The Country Blues*. Another incisive interpretation of the origin of the blues is Paul Oliver, *Blues Fell This Morning*.

songs and vocal styles was the contributing of rhythms, such as eight-to-the-bar and the rag styles, and certain instrumental techniques. Primarily through the influence of the Negro, the guitar came to be more than a simple accompanying instrument; it came to be a device for punctuating the moods and sentiments expressed in the songs. The Negro country guitarist commonly interspersed runs and instrumental patterns at the end of verses or lines in order to emphasize the lyrics being expressed. Guitar and voice were equally important, with the guitar, in effect, serving as a second voice.[60] The early white guitarists, on the other hand, played in a relatively simple style, using a back-up style marked by no more than three or four basic open chords with perhaps an occasional run thrown in. But partially under the influence of Negro guitarists white stylings gradually became more complex. White musicians began to play the guitar as it was probably designed to be played—with the fingers picking the melody on the treble strings while the thumb maintained a steady rhythm on the bass strings. The enduring influence of Negro instrumentation is attested by the fact that among white country performers the most complex guitar styles are known as "nigger picking."[61] The list of white country guitarists who were influenced by Negro instrumental styles is very long, and it includes some of the most respected names in country music: Sam McGee, the Delmore Brothers, Dorsey Dixon, Ike Everly, Chet Atkins, and Merle Travis.

Despite the richness of its vocal, instrumental, and stylistic repertory, and despite the antiquity and diversity of its heritage, southern country music remained unnoticed by the outside world until the 1920's. Radio had not yet ventured into the southern region; indeed, it was only in the experimental stage in the remainder of the country. The phonograph industry, though in existence since the 1890's and in a relatively thriving condition, had neglected to tap the southern folk-music reservoir, either Negro or white. The neglect had resulted either from ignorance of the music's existence or from prejudice

---

[60] There have been several important reissues of the Negro country-blues recordings of the 1920's. Among these are two Folkways items, *The Country Blues*, Vol. I, RF 1, and Vol. II, RF 9 (both edited by Samuel Charters). The most significant albums, however, are those produced by the Origin Jazz Library, an assemblage of collectors who have done extensive field research on the early blues performers.

[61] Alan Lomax, *The Folk Songs of North America*, p. 276.

against its quality and content. The dignitaries of the northern recording companies were repelled by the harshness and rawness of the untrained country voices and were unable to realize that an audience could be attracted by the music. Statements about the commercial world's neglect of southern folk music must of course be qualified. The musical products of the Negro had certainly been recognized for several decades, as is evidenced by the national popularity of such pseudo or imitative Negro entertainments as the minstrel show, ragtime music, and the "coon" songs employing Negro dialect which were so popular at the turn of the century. Few Negroes, however, participated in these musical forms. And by the 1920's jazz, which was largely a creation of the folk, had virtually lost its folk basis and had become the province of sophisticated urbanites. Still, folk music had not been totally ignored by the commercial recording companies. Folk and folk-style songs of the Stephen Foster variety had long been recorded, but almost always by nonfolk performers. The one major exception to the neglect of southern folk artists was the international recognition given to those famous Negro gospel singers from Nashville, the Fisk Jubilee Singers.[62] White country performers, on the other hand, were seldom recorded prior to 1923; however, researchers are periodically finding examples of country peformances on the old cylinder recordings. Country people bought the cylinder records in rather large quantities, but they had to be content with the same musical offerings that were being disseminated among city people. When they ventured into town, rural dwellers heard the new recordings, and when they took the cylinders back home (paying as little as 35 cents for them), they listened to Harry Lauder, Gene Austin, Henry Burr, the Peerless Quartet, Al Jolson, Vernon Dalhart, and other "popular" singers of the early twentieth century. Only rarely could one hear a performance by an authentic country act, such as Fiddlin' Bob Haines and His Four Aces, who were probably the first country string band to record on Edison cylinders.[63] Recording executives had not yet realized that an untapped musical goldmine existed in the rural regions of the United States.

In addition to commercial neglect, country music gained little acceptance either from the realm of academic scholarship or from

[62] Foreword (p. 2), *Anthology of American Folk Music*, Folkways FA 2951–53, (edited by Harry Smith).
[63] Shelton, *The Country Music Story*, p. 27.

the world of musical culture, although there had been a start as far as scholarship was concerned. The devotees of musical appreciation could see no merit in American backwoods folk music. In fact, the "better music" people historically had tended to see only in European music, or music similar to it, those qualities that were worthy of appreciation. For centuries the musicologists and professional musicians and their patrons tended to look upon music as something apart from life. Within the past hundred years this attitude became intensified when large-scale musical organization required the support of wealth and fashion. As a result, the rare and difficult came to be emphasized rather than the common and simple. Fine-art music, therefore, became "good" music, and any other kind of musical expression was "bad" or outside the pale of serious consideration.[64] If folk material was considered, it was changed or reshaped in such a manner as to be accepted in polite society. Charles Seeger has stated that basically two forces have been at work in the United States in the furtherance of American music: the "Make-America-Musical" and "Sell-America-Music" groups. Throughout the eighteenth, nineteenth, and early twentieth centuries, the "Make-America-Musical" group, composed of the well-to-do classes (and their imitators), endeavored to educate the people to the values of "good" music through the media of concerts, recitals, and musical education courses. To this group, "good" music was European fine-art music or its imitation. It was something that all Americans should enjoy. But folk or popular music was anathema to these people.[65]

The "Sell-America-Music" fraternity, of course, was the commercial-minded people—those who strove to make a profit from the sale of music, both good and bad, to the public. Until the twentieth century, the music industry was not overly interested in the rural population, because the bulk of that population lived in areas not easily susceptible to commercial interests. The recording industry and the purveyors of sheet music made no effort to find out the musical tastes of the people living in the hinterlands. And they cared not at all for the musical products of these people.[66] The entrepreneurs

[64] Charles Seeger, "Folk Music as a Source of Social History," *The Cultural Approach to History*, edited by Caroline F. Ware, pp. 318–319.

[65] Charles Seeger, "Music and Class Structure in the United States," *American Quarterly*, IX, No. 3 (Fall, 1957), 287–288.

[66] *Ibid.*

first had to be convinced that a market for rural music existed and that a profit could be made from it. Southern folk music, therefore, was not extensively subjected prior to the 1920's to the manipulation of either the fine-art or the commercial groups.

At the dawn of the 1920's, southern folk music remained virtually unknown outside the southern region. Largely ignored and unobserved by outsiders, it was left to develop on its own. The songs of the southern region, however, were gradually being presented to Americans at large through the publication of such folksong compilations as those by Lomax and Sharp. Sharp's publication constituted the first attempt to include the musical notation as well as the lyrics for the South's traditional store of songs. But nothing had been done as yet to publicize the singers of the songs themselves, and little was known of the musical culture they had developed. Those forces that would ultimately serve to break down the isolation and cultural barriers of the South would also present its rural music to the rest of the nation. In the words of Alan Lomax, the country music business "had a late and fortuitous beginning."[67]

[67] Alan Lomax, *The Folk Songs of North America*, p. 280.

CHAPTER 2

The Early Period of Commercial Hillbilly Music

AT THE OPENING of the twentieth century American music was urban-oriented. Both the fine-art and commercially directed groups neglected the rural population and catered to the interests of people in the cities. But in the following decades these two "pressure groups," as Charles Seeger has shown,[1] were transformed into organizations that served the musical interests of the people as a whole. The "Make-America-Musical" group became a "more nearly realistic, accultura-tive segment of the population," while the "Sell-America-Music" fra-ternity cast off much of its commercial opportunism and acquired a broader concept of public service.[2]

In the satisfying of the musical and entertainment needs of Amer-ica's rural population, the commercial fraternity was the first to re-spond. The music industry—employing chiefly the media of radio, phonograph, sheet music, and live entertainment—at first directed its approach to urban areas because it was there that the greatest profits were made. Few people recognized the possible existence of a rural buying population. Rural performers were rejected because they sounded strange and primitive to urban music executives, who

[1] Discussed in Chapter 1.

[2] Charles Seeger, 'Music and Class Structure in the United States," *American Quarterly*, IX, No. 3 (Fall, 1957), 288.

believed that the urban buyer would be repelled by the quaint country sound. The commercial people, of course, were not displeased when country people bought their products, but the product was usually urban produced and urban performed. The employment of a country performer was almost unthinkable.

The music industry's antirural attitude might have persisted had it not been for the emergence of one medium of communication and the temporary submergence of another. In general, the discovery of southern backwoods music was only one result of a general communications revolution which has gradually broken down southern rural isolation. Along with the automobile, which has progressively narrowed the distance between city and farm, the phenomenon that has exerted perhaps the most profound urbanizing influence upon rural areas is the radio, a device that in the 1920's temporarily stifled the growth of the phonograph industry and brought a welcome measure of entertainment and information to the rural populace.

In the research stage during World War I and chiefly a diversion for amateur operators, radio became a craze in the twenties and experienced a phenomenal growth in sales and popularity. In only a few years radio was transformed from an expensive plaything to a widely popular and inexpensive diversion for millions of Americans. Social observers recognized immediately that radio would revolutionize rural existence.[3] Not only did it do that, but it revolutionized American popular tastes as a whole.

The financial figures on radio sales during the twenties are little short of astounding. From a relatively modest figure of $60,000,000 in 1922, sales rose to a total of $842,548,000 in 1929, and some observers estimated that radio had penetrated every third home in the country.[4] According to the federal census of 1930, 12,078,345 families owned radio sets. Of this number, the smallest percentage of ownership was in the South. This low figure was due in part, however, to the existence of a low-income Negro population which possessed few radio sets. One report maintained that "the ownership ratios among the white populations of Southern states would doubtless be much higher

---

[3] "Removing the Last Objection to Living in the Country," *Country Life*, XLI, No. 4 (February, 1922), 63.

[4] Frederick Lewis Allen, *Only Yesterday*, pp. 147–148.

than general state ratios indicate."[5] Broadcasting stations, the majority of them small and low-powered, made early appearances in the South. Of 510 active broadcasting stations operating on 360 meters at the end of 1922, 89 of them were in the South. The numbers ranged from Texas' 25 to Mississippi's one.[6]

The development of southern radio broadcasting was important in the discovery, refinement, modification, and eventual standardization of southern country music. With the coming of radio, southern folksingers had an additional outlet for their entertainment energies. No longer would they be confined to their limited native environments, but would be enabled to exhibit their skills before a wider audience. This process, in addition to other commercial factors, first presented the folk musician to the American public, but it also served gradually to transform that same folk musician into a self-conscious commercial performer. The folksinger-turned-commercial performer now had a chance to perfect his skill, and he would tend to stress those techniques which most pleased his listeners.

Many southern broadcasting stations, therefore, featured live country entertainment almost from the day they opened their doors. In the years following 1920, radio remained the most important means of country-music dissemination, eventually in the form of disc-jockey programs. The first high-powered radio station in the South, and possibly the first to feature country music, was WSB in Atlanta, Georgia. This station, owned by the Atlanta *Journal*, first went on the air on March 16, 1922, with a 100-watt transmitter, which was subsequently increased to 500 watts on June 13. Within a few months several folk performers—including Rev. Andrew Jenkins, a blind gospel singer, and Fiddlin' John Carson, well known because of his musical performances during Georgia political campaigns—had appeared on station broadcasts catering to the wide popularity of folk music in the central Georgia region. For approximately one year before the first recording expedition went to Atlanta searching for folk talent, singers and string bands had been appearing on WSB,

[5] President's Research Committee on Social Trends, *Recent Social Trends in the United States*, pp. 211–212.

[6] "All States Broadcast Except Wyoming," *The Literary Digest*, LXXV, No. 6 (November 11, 1922), 29.

providing a reservoir of talent for any recording scout who might venture into the city.[7]

With WSB probably leading the way, radio stations all over the South and Midwest began featuring country talent in the early twenties. Although exhaustive research on the relationship between broadcasting and early country music has not yet been completed, collector and folklorist Guthrie T. Meade, who is the most knowledgeable authority on this particular subject, has pointed to the very significant role played by WBAP in Fort Worth.[8] WBAP can justly lay claim to having produced one of the first, if not the first, radio barn dances in the United States—about a year and a half before the WLS National Barn Dance, and about three years before the WSM Grand Ole Opry.

In the first several months of its existence WBAP—as was true of almost all early radio stations—programmed nothing but popular, jazz, sacred, and semiclassical music. But on the night of January 4, 1923, WBAP featured an hour-and-a-half program of square-dance music directed by an old-time fiddler and Confederate veteran, Captain M. J. Bonner. The music was performed by a string band which normally played only Hawaiian music (Fred Wagner's Hilo Five Hawaiian Orchestra), and Captain Bonner's was the only fiddle music provided. The program provoked the largest audience response—in the form of telegrams and telephone calls—that the station had experienced in its short history.[9] Touching an unexploited but eager audience, WBAP inaugurated the hillbilly radio barn dance in the Southwest and may have influenced the formation of such shows elsewhere. In those early unregulated days of American broadcasting, WBAP programs were picked up by listeners as far away as New York, Canada, Hawaii, and Haiti, and the square-dance shows which followed periodically—featuring such groups as the Peacock

[7] Archie Green, "Hillbilly Music: Source and Symbol," *Journal of American Folklore*," LXXVIII, No. 309 (July–September, 1965), 209. See also Fred G. Hoeptner, "Folk and Hillbilly Music: the Background of their Relation, Part II," *Caravan: The Magazine of Folk Music* (June–July, 1959), 20.

[8] Letter to the author from Guthrie T. Meade, College Park, Maryland, February 21, 1967.

[9] On a tip from Guthrie Meade, I checked the Fort Worth *Star-Telegram* for the period from late 1922 to May, 1923, and found a goldmine of information about the early WBAP barn-dance shows.

Fiddle Band from Cleburne, Texas—may have triggered the entire wave of hillbilly barn dances that began appearing on radio stations throughout the United States. After the striking success of the first program on January 4, 1923, WBAP presented the country-music shows on a rather unplanned, periodic basis, usually two or three times a month, but by 1927 a regularly scheduled Friday night program was broadcast.[10] Broadcasting executives at stations like WBAP, WSB, WLS, and WSM, were the first members of the commercial fraternity to devote any consideration to the musical interests of America's folk-music population.

In the commercial exploitation of southern folk music the phonograph industry was only a step behind the broadcasting business. This exploitation came at the precise moment when the record business as a whole was experiencing a sharp downturn in volume of sales, due largely to the competition of radio, which lured listeners away and gave them a greater variety of entertainment. Business dropped off tremendously in 1923 and 1924 as radio became an established facet of American entertainment.[11] People preferred to sit in comfort and listen to an entire program of music without having to change records every few minutes. The public discovered, too, that the better-grade radio sets were superior in tone and quality to the then-existent phonographs.[12] The peak in record sales had been reached in 1922, when the figure neared one hundred million, but the market diminished during the next ten years under the combined assaults of radio and the national depression.[13] In the period between 1927 and 1932 record sales declined to one-fortieth of what they previously had been.[14]

Although radio competition forced the phonograph industry to search for new marketing outlets, it had moved in this direction before radio made such terrific inroads. At least a few of the recording executives earlier had recognized that a market might exist among

---

[10] Letter to the author from Guthrie Meade, February 21, 1967.

[11] Leroy Hughbanks, *Talking Wax; or the Story of the Phonograph*, p. 113.

[12] *Ibid.*, p. 79.

[13] Radio Corporation of America, *The 50-Year Story of RCA Victor Records*, p. 26.

[14] American Society of Composers, Authors and Publishers, *Nothing Can Replace Music*, p. 1.

America's rural population. This recognition came first as a result of the new-found buying habits of American Negroes in the post-World War I period. Because of the war thousands of Negroes migrated to northern urban centers in pursuit of employment in shipyards and mills.

In the spring of 1920, Ralph Peer, recording director for Okeh Records, recorded a Negro blues singer, Mamie Smith. This recording generated a boom for blues music and launched Okeh into a ranking position as a record company. A market for Negro music was found to exist among the Negroes themselves.[15] This was music produced in the cities and by city people, however. As yet, the record companies had not signed the "country blues" performers, and when the recording executives learned that southern rural Negroes desired to purchase recordings by members of their own race, such enterprising recording men as Ralph Peer determined to venture into the South to find native singers in their own habitats. Through this kind of scouting activity the white hillbilly recording industry came into being.

Before the actual signing of white country performers, the commercial success of a popular Victor recording of "It Ain't Gonna Rain No Mo," by Wendell Hall, "The Redheaded Music Maker," presaged the wide market that hillbilly music might attain. Hall, in no sense a hillbilly entertainer, took an old country-dance melody, gave it funny lyrics, and catapulted it to the top of Victor best-seller lists. Okeh, acting under this stimulation, set up recording studios in several southern localities, including Asheville, North Carolina; Atlanta; Bristol and Johnson City, Tennessee; St. Louis; and Dallas, Texas. Of these locations, however, Atlanta, with its wealth of folk talent was given top priority.[16] Ralph Peer then was sent into the South to ferret out folk performers wherever they might be found. In doing so, Peer was performing, perhaps unwittingly, a valuable function as a folklorist. He and other field-recording men, such as Frank Walker, Eli

[15] Kyle Crichton, "Thar's Gold in Them Hillbillies," *Colliers*, CI (April 30, 1938), 24; Samuel B. Charters, *The Country Blues*, pp. 47–48.

[16] Green, "Hillbilly Music: Source and Symbol," *Journal of American Folklore*," LXXVIII, No. 309 (July–September, 1965), 208. See also Jim Walsh, "Favorite Pioneer Recording Artists: Vernon Dalhart," *Hobbies: The Magazine for Collectors*, LXV, No. 5 (July, 1960), 36.

Oberstein, and Arthur Satherly,[17] were the first individuals to present southern folksingers to the American public.

Despite the forays made by field-recording men into the commercially unexploited southern territory, it is doubtful that the first commercially recorded hillbilly was discovered in this manner. Discographical researchers are constantly disclosing the existence of early fiddle recordings, even on cylinders which have not as yet been thoroughly investigated and documented. Although historians and folk scholars may yearn for this kind of information, the knowledge of country music's "earliest" recording performer may never be conclusively known. Nevertheless, recent research indicates that Eck Robertson, champion old-time fiddler from Amarillo, Texas, and Henry Gilliland, old-time fiddler from Virginia, were among the very first individuals to make disc recordings during the phonograph industry's first hesitant and "casual encounter"[18] with country music. In June, 1922, Robertson—who is still making occasional appearances at Old Fiddler's Contests—traveled to Virginia to play for a Civil War veterans' reunion. On the spur of the moment, he and Gilliland decided to go to New York to make some records. The Victor recording people must have been taken aback when Gilliland and Robertson, dressed in Confederate uniform and cowboy suit respectively, marched into the Victor offices and asked for auditions. Largely to get rid of them, Victor allowed them to perform, and their selections were subsequently released. Although Victor released a publicity blurb describing the recordings, and although sales were reasonably good, the company did not immediately follow through in its exploitation of the untapped folk reservoir. In fact, Robertson himself was not again recorded until 1930, when Ralph Peer, by then a Victor talent scout, arranged another session for the Texas fiddler and his family.[19] On March 29, 1923, about a year after his unsolicited New

[17] Mike Seeger has discussed Ralph Peer and Frank Walker (whom he interviewed) in *The New Lost City Ramblers Song Book* (pp. 25–29).

[18] The phrase was used by Archie Green in a letter to the author, February 6, 1967.

[19] John Cohen, "Fiddlin' Eck Robertson," *Sing Out: The Folk Song Magazine*, XIV, No. 2 (April–May, 1964), 55–59. Additional information on the Robertson-Gilliland recordings was supplied by Ed Kahn in a letter to the author, February 1, 1967.

York recording venture, Robertson performed on WBAP the two numbers that he had earlier recorded, "Sally Goodin" and "Arkansas Traveler." These radio performances may have been the first by a folk musician who had earlier recorded for commercial records. In doing these numbers, in fact, Robertson—termed a "Victor Artist" by the Fort Worth *Star Telegram*—may have been the first country performer to "plug" his recordings on a radio broadcast.[20] This important Texas folk musician thus played significant roles in two important commercial media whose dual exploitation of folk talent coincidentally converged in the early twenties to produce that brand of music which we now call country music.

Almost a year after Robertson's first trip to New York, a similar incident occurred: Henry Whitter, a Virginia textile worker and hillbilly singer, traveled uninvited to New York in March, 1923, and recorded one of the most famous of the early hillbilly songs, "The Wreck on the Southern Old 97." Whitter's recording was not released, however, until December, 1923.[21] By that time, Ralph Peer's field trips were reaping a rich harvest of old-time performers.

Although Ralph Peer was the agent who first presented country music to the American public and thereby inaugurated its development as a commercial force, Polk Brockman was the catalyst. As director of the phonograph department of his grandfather's furniture store, James K. Polk, Inc., in Atlanta, Brockman had by 1921 built up a flourishing business selling race records and had made his firm the largest regional distributor of Okeh records in the country. A business trip to New York in June, 1923, kindled in Brockman an idea which led directly to Ralph Peer's historic 1923 trip to Atlanta and the subsequent birth of the hillbilly industry. During Brockman's stay in New York he visited the Palace Theatre on Times Square, where he saw a newreel of a Virginia fiddlers' contest. The astute Brockman, who was well acquainted with the country talent of his own Georgia area and particularly with those who had been performing on WSB for the preceding year, immediately recognized the commercial possibilities of recorded hillbilly music. He instantly thought of one person—an old-time fiddler, house painter, well-

[20] *Fort Worth Star-Telegram*, March 30, 1923.

[21] Green, "Hillbilly Music: Source and Symbol," *Journal of American Folklore*, LXXVIII, No. 309 (July–September, 1965), 210.

known musical performer in political campaigns, and acknowledged Georgia moonshiner—Fiddlin' John Carson, who had built up a wide popularity performing over Station WSB. As he thought of Carson, Brockman picked up a memorandum pad and wrote the following words: "Let's record."[22]

Out of Brockman's brainstorm came Ralph Peer's Atlanta recording session of mid-June, 1923. Preceded into the city by the Okeh engineers, Charles Hibbard and Peter Decker, who brought the acoustical recording equipment, Brockman rented an empty loft on Nassau Street, where Peer began listening to and recording the assembled performers. Several performers—mostly in the blues and popular categories—were auditioned and recorded: Warner's Seven Aces, a collegiate dance band; Eddy Heywood, a Negro pianist; Bob White's syncopating band, and others. But with the recording of Fiddlin' John Carson on June 14, 1923, Ralph Peer made his initial venture into the unexploited field of country music. When Peer listened to the two songs which Carson chose to record—"The Little Old Log Cabin in the Lane" and "The Old Hen Cackled and the Rooster's Going to Crow"—he responded as one might expect of a northern urbanite upon first being initiated into the exotic world of southern folk music. He thought the singing was awful and insisted that only Carson's fiddle tunes be recorded. Brockman, however, understood the Georgia entertainment market and realized that the small farmers and mill workers enjoyed Fiddlin' John's vocalizing as much as his instrumental virtuosity. Brockman offered to buy five hundred copies of Carson's first recorded and unpressed numbers immediately. Unable to conceive of a regional or national market for such items, Peer issued the record uncatalogued, unadvertised, unlabeled, and for circulation solely in the Atlanta area. By late July, 1923, when the first shipment of five hundred records had been sold and after Brockman had ordered another shipment, Peer acknowledged his early mistake and gave the recording the label number 4890, a move which placed the songs in Okeh's popular catalogue and gave them national publicity. In November, as sales continued to mount, Carson was asked to come to New York, where he recorded twelve more songs and signed an exclusive Okeh contract.[23]

[22] *Ibid.*, p. 208.
[23] *Ibid.*, p. 210.

Fiddlin' John Carson, therefore, became the first hillbilly performer to have his selections recorded and marketed on a commercial basis. This was the real beginning of the hillbilly music industry. Peer now remembered the recorded but unreleased tunes of Henry Whitter, who had earlier persuaded New York Okeh executives to test record some of his numbers. Two songs, "Lonesome Road Blues" and "The Wreck on the Southern Old 97," were released in late November with the number 40015.[24] The popularity of these songs, plus that attained by Fiddlin' John Carson and Eck Robertson, encouraged other record companies to cash in on the popularity of native white performers as a means of bolstering lagging sales capacity. In the next several years other recording companies—Columbia (through its famous 15000 series), Vocalion, Brunswick, Gennett, Victor (hesitantly), and several minor organizations—rushed into the South and Southwest with their field units, recording almost indiscriminately any country musicians they could find. In those early days it was the general practice for recording companies to send their technical equipment into an area and record country performers on the spot. The recording engineer, carrying suitcases of wax discs and equipment, accompanied the artists and repertory man in his country talent hunts. Almost any building with ample space could be converted into a recording studio in a manner of moments.[25] Country musicians, upon learning of the phonograph companies' interest (subsequently through newspaper advertisements), would often flock to the makeshift studios in hopes of becoming recording stars. In their indiscriminate haste to capitalize on the fast-developing field, recording men accepted much that was both good and bad and, unfortunately, devoted little care toward achieving the best possible sound reproduction. Hillbilly performers did not receive the same scrupulous attention given to popular and classical entertainers, and their recorded efforts were treated indifferently as necessary devices that, though not quite respectable, had to be considered because of their profit-making possibilities. Hillbillies were often recorded without adequate preparation, and after only one hasty recording.[26]

[24] *Ibid.*

[25] Thurston Moore, ed., *The Country Music Who's Who*, First Annual edition, p. 52.

[26] Bill Bolick, of the Blue Sky Boys, claims that the lackadaisical attitude shown by the recording men toward country performers lasted well into the

The belated recognition given to southern folk music by the phonograph industry produced in the 1920's two types of commercial music. Both folk in origin and orientation, they were white country, popularly called "hillbilly," and Negro country, most often designated as "race." The coining of these terms is usually attributed to Ralph Peer. The word "hillbilly," as Archie Green has noted in a discerning *Journal of American Folklore* article,[27] has been used in print since at least 1900 as a catch-all designation for the southern backwoods inhabitants. Not until 1925, however, was the term used in association with the music of the rural South. Employment of "hillbilly" as a generic term for the commercial country music of the South may be traced to a January 15, 1925, recording session in the Okeh studios in New York City. A string band composed of members from the mountain counties of Watauga, North Carolina, and Grayson and Carroll, Virginia, had journeyed to the Okeh studios after an earlier unsuccessful attempt with Victor. The group—composed of Al and Joe Hopkins, Tony Alderman, and John Rector—had no official name, and, after they had recorded six numbers for Ralph Peer, their leader and vocalist, Al Hopkins, suggested that Peer find a suitable name for them. Hopkins said, "call the band anything you want. We are nothing but a bunch of hillbillies from North Carolina and Virginia anyway." Peer then instructed his secretary to list the six selections on company ledger sheets as performed by the "Hillbillies" (later changed to the "Original Hillbillies" after other organizations began appropriating the term).[28]

Despite considerable misgivings on the part of some of the band members about the seemingly disreputable name, the group was advertised in the Okeh catalogues and on personal appearances as the Hillbillies. Hopkins and his associates became more confident about the use of the title after an old friend and highly respected Vir-

thirties (interview with Bill Bolick, Greensboro, North Carolina, August 24, 1965). Mike Seeger has found, on the other hand, that Frank Walker of Columbia attempted to put his performers at ease by creating a "homey atmosphere" (Seeger, *The New Lost City Ramblers Song Book*, p. 27).

[27] The Green article, "Hillbilly Music: Source and Symbol," is probably the most significant work ever written on early country music. I am, obviously, heavily indebted to it.

[28] *Ibid.*, p. 213. See also "Meet Charlie Bowman," *Disc Collector*, No. 16 (n.d.), 3.

ginia musician, Ernest "Pop" Stoneman, told them he approved of the term.[29] They lived to see "hillbilly" applied widely to the entire field of country music.

"Hillbilly" became a common if not always admired term among country musicians and enthusiasts alike. But the record companies remained rather hesitant about labeling the songs with such an appelation. In the 1920's the record companies' release sheets and catalogues camouflaged the songs under a variety of titles, most of them evoking a romanticized conception of southern rural music: for example, "hill country tunes," "songs of the hills and plains." Columbia, after the inauguration of the 15000-D series devoted to country music, referred to the songs as "old familiar tunes." Okeh Records quite often labeled the tunes as "old-time music." (The recording companies evidently had a slight inkling of the folk nature of the music even if scholars did not.) After the decade of the twenties, as further evidence of the companies' self-consciousness about the country songs steadily building up in their catalogues, the hillbilly songs were shunted on to subordinate labels, such as Victor's Bluebird label.[30]

The early hillbilly entertainers were in the unique position of being transitional figures. They were folk performers who had acquired their style and repertories from traditional sources, but who now found themselves in a milieu where the necessity of pleasing both the recording executives and their audiences would cause them to alter their styles. In this period the entertainers possessed an audience, the southern rural population, which was also deeply steeped in the folk tradition and which did not place excessive demands upon its native singers to perform in a "slicked up" or sophisticated manner. The period of the 1920's and 1930's has been described as the "Golden Age of Hillbilly Music," a phrase first used by John Edwards of Cremorne, Australia, who until his death in 1960 was the world's foremost hillbilly record collector.[31] Although the phrase is controversial

[29] Green, "Hillbilly Music: Source and Symbol," *Journal of American Folklore*, LXXVIII, No. 309 (July–September, 1965), 214.

[30] See any record catalogue of the twenties for examples. For comments on the "covert" listings of hillbilly records during the early period see Fred G. Hoeptner, "Folk and Hillbilly Music: The Background of their Relation" (*Caravan: The Magazine of Folk Music* [April–May, 1959], 42).

[31] Quoted in "Noted Country Collectors," *Country Directory*, No. 1 (November, 1960), 5.

and unfortunately denigrates the country music which came later, to Edwards and others who believe as he did, the decades before World War II were golden, because the music remained a relatively regional phenomenon and was largely free from big-city commercial control. The performers were rural southerners (and midwesterners) who drew upon their inherited folk traditions. Radio and the phonograph industry did not create country music; these commercial media merely exploited and popularized a pre-existent tradition of singing and string-band playing. Although subjected to new commercial influences in the 1920's the hillbilly performer remained a folk musician who was molded and shaped by the complex religious, social, cultural, and economic patterns of his traditional environment. The folk musician did not (and does not) cease to be folk merely because he stepped in front of a microphone. The commercial hillbilly recordings of the twenties provide one of the most fertile fields of investigation for folklorists, since the early hillbillies were the first white folk musicians to be commercially recorded in the United States. Their selections, which were performed in the styles that had been characteristic of rural southerners for decades, were the first oral renditions of many of the traditional songs ever heard by the American public.

Generally, the performers of the early commercial period were the more accomplished local entertainers, although many entertainers, such as Uncle Dave Macon and Charlie Poole, had been entertaining regularly in vaudeville and medicine shows for several years. The early hillbillies recorded with their own accompaniment, or with no more than two or three accompanying instruments. The guitar, five-string banjo, and fiddle were the most commonly used instruments, although the mandolin, autoharp, and Hawaiian steel guitar were often employed.[32] In fact, everything from the piano (on Al Hopkins' records) to accordions (on Cajun records) and kazoos,

[32] The best introduction to the hillbilly music of the twenties is, of course, the old 78 rpm recordings themselves. But for the listener who does not have access to the original recordings, there are a few companies which have produced important reissues. Of most historic importance is the *Anthology of American Folk Music* (Folkways FA2951–53), which includes selections by such people as Dock Boggs, Clarence Ashley, Uncle Dave Macon, and the Carter Family. The two labels which have done most to reintroduce the early commercial performers to modern America are County, a New York company, and Old-Timey, a Berkeley, California concern.

whistles, jew's-harps, and comb-and-paper could be heard frequently on the rich assortment of recordings produced in the twenties. The singers' vocal deliveries and types of voice were just as diverse as their instrumental styles, depending in part on the geographical regions from which the entertainers came. No generalization about vocal styles, therefore, could be valid, although the listener could generally be certain that the singer was southern and rural. Some singers sang in the vital, energetic style of Uncle Dave Macon; some sang in the soft, largely emotionless style of Bradley Kincaid; some sang with a noticeable nasal twang, as in the case of Dock Boggs or Charlie Poole; and a few sang, as did Vernon Dalhart, with the studied affectation of a trained concert singer.

Regardless of the myriad styles they possessed, the early hillbilly singers performed the songs that had endured in the United States for generations. Rather than creating their own songs, in most cases, the singers depended upon the songs that had been common in their native heritage. A perusal of the hillbilly section of any record catalogue, or of the Sears-Roebuck or Montgomery Ward mail-order catalogues, will reveal the overwhelming preference among hillbilly musicians for traditional songs. The songs ran the gamut of the events and emotions that were common among rural southerners, although the preference for the sad, tragic, and sentimental seemed to be decisive. Traditional songs in the hillbilly repertory included such numbers as Ernest Thompson's "Little Rosewood Casket," Riley Puckett's "Boston Burglar," Al Craver's (Vernon Dalhart) "Barbara Allen," Gid Tanner's "Cumberland Gap," and Samantha Bumgarner's "Fly Around My Pretty Little Miss."[33] No certainty exists as to the number of traditional songs to be found on commercial recordings, but D. K. Wilgus, who has done extensive research on the problem, estimates that about one-third of the songs from any large general collection from the South have been recorded on hillbilly records.[34]

[33] The examples cited were taken from *Columbia Record Catalogues,* 1925 through 1928. A perusal of any other record catalogue of the period would produce the same result. The best printed collection of early hillbilly songs, and some of the best discussions of performers and styles, is *The New Lost City Ramblers Song Book.*

[34] From an address delivered by D. K. Wilgus before the seventy-third annual meeting of the American Folklore Society, Austin, Texas, December 28, 1961. The address was subsequently reprinted in *A Good Tale and a Bonnie*

The value of this still largely untapped depository should be obvious to students of folk culture, and, as Judith McCulloh has asserted, "to ignore this potentially rich source of text, tune, style, social commentary . . . is nonsensical."[35]

Instrumental styles on the early records, although always influenced by the dominant pop, swing, and jazz techniques of the day, were also products of traditional influences. The hillbilly string bands of radio and phonograph were the direct descendants of (and in many cases were the same as) the folk entertainers who played for house parties, barn dances, church socials, tent shows, and political gatherings in the decades before 1920. The identity of the first recorded string band is about as shadowy as the name of the first recorded hillbilly. If a string band can be considered as consisting of as little as two members, then, as Norman Cohen has suggested, Gid Tanner and Riley Puckett (who recorded with fiddle and banjo on March 7–8, 1924), and Samantha Bumgarner and Eva Davis (who recorded with fiddle and banjo on April 22–23, 1924) may hold the distinction of being the first recorded string bands.[36] Of the more conventional-sized groups, several organizations vie for the position of the earliest to be placed on commercial records. In April, 1924, Fiddlin' John Carson recorded with a group called the Virginia Reelers, and Henry Whitter made a few records in late July, 1924, with a group named the Virginia Breakdowners. In late August of the same year Fiddling Powers and his family recorded a few breakdown instrumentals for Victor. In November, 1924, Chenoweth's Cornfield Symphony Orchestra became perhaps the first Texas string band to record. Ernest "Pop" Stoneman, performing with a group called the Dixie Mountaineers, made his first recording for Okeh on September 1, 1924.[37] In the course of a long and distinguished

---

Tune, edited by Mody C. Boatright, et. al., (*Publications of the Texas Folklore Society,* XXXII), pp. 227–237.

[35] Judith McCulloh, "Hillbilly Records and Tune Transcriptions," a paper read at the April 10, 1965, meeting of the California Folklore Society at UCLA (unpublished copy made available to the author).

[36] Letter to the author from Norman Cohen, Los Angeles, California, February 25, 1967.

[37] *Ibid.;* Archie Green, "Hillbilly Music: Source and Symbol," 211. *Journal of American Folklore,* LXXVIII, No. 309 (July–September, 1965). Information on the Fiddling Powers recordings was obtained from a letter written by Brad

entertainment career, Stoneman introduced some of the most durable and legendary country songs—such as "The Titanic" (his first recording) and "We Parted By the Riverside"—and thrilled listeners with his ability to pick out melodies note-for-note on the autoharp, a talent which only a few folk musicians have possessed. Until his death in June, 1968, Stoneman continued to appear in concerts with his children in one of the most sensational bluegrass bands of the modern period.[38]

Also of historic importance, but minus the longevity experienced by Stoneman, was a five-string banjoist, Charlie Poole, and his North Carolina Ramblers. Although Poole died in 1931 at the height of his career, his name is still remembered with reverence among country musicians and fans in the mountain region of the South. Poole was both a vocalist and an accomplished five-string banjoist whose repertory included everything from mountain instrumentals to vaudeville and ragtime tunes. The history of the North Carolina Ramblers provides additional refutation of the idea that country music was spawned by the radio and phonograph. Poole and the two other original Ramblers—fiddler Posey Rorer and guitarist Norman Woodlieff—had been entertaining at dances and fiddlers' conventions in the area around Spray and Leaksville, North Carolina, since at least 1918. It was not until 1925, however, when they made their first records for Columbia in New York, that they gained enough financial security to free them from the textile employment at which they had periodically worked during their earlier musical career. In their first recording session on July 27, 1925, they recorded the song which would always be their most popular number, "Don't Let Your Deal Go Down." After the success of their first recording, the Ramblers became much sought after for personal appearances, mostly in the upper South and in Ohio. In the years before Poole died, the Ramblers personnel changed, first in 1926 with the addition of an outstanding guitarist named Roy Harvey (who later made some important duet recordings with Leonard Copeland and Jess Johnson), and then in

---

McCuen, of RCA Victor, to Norman Cohen, March 2, 1967 (copy made available to the author by Norman Cohen).

[38] The modern Stoneman Family bluegrass band (including Pop Stoneman) can be heard on any one of several long play albums. Of particular importance is MGM 4363, *Those Singin', Swingin', Stompin', Sensational Stonemans.*

1928 when fiddler Lonnie Austin replaced Posey Rorer. Poole and the North Carolina Ramblers were not only popular in their own time and milieu, they have also exerted a profound influence upon modern country performers, particularly those in the bluegrass category. Charlie Poole's banjo technique (performed with thumb and three fingers) is generally recognized as one of the progenitors of the modern bluegrass style, a sensational three-finger style popularized by Earl Scruggs.[39]

Another valuable string band of the early commercial period was the previously mentioned Al Hopkins group, who recorded as the Original Hillbillies for Okeh and Vocalion, and as the Buckle Busters for Brunswick. An extremely popular organization, the group performed on Station WRC in Washington, D.C., and through the recognition gained on these broadcasts received invitations to appear at schools, political rallies, and social functions from South Carolina to New York. This commercial pattern—the acquisition and promotion of personal appearances through radio broadcasts—became standard procedure for most of the country groups that followed. The Hopkins organization was typical of the early southeastern string bands in its use of the fiddle, five-string banjo, and guitar, but was unique in its employment of the piano (a portable one played by Hopkins himself), an instrument which until recent times was rarely heard in country music.[40]

One of the most highly respected string bands of the early period traces its commercial origin to a Columbia recording session in New York on March 7, 1924, where a chicken farmer and old-time fiddler from Dacula, Georgia, James Gideon (Gid) Tanner, met with a blind guitarist from Alpharetta, Georgia, George Riley Puckett, to become that label's first hillbilly talent. This duo, who had long been popular attractions on Station WSB in Atlanta, were joined in Columbia recording sessions in 1926 by two other popular WSB performers and Georgians, fiddler Clayton McMichen and five-string banjoist Fate Norris. McMichen and Norris had been the nucleus of a group called the Lick the Skillet Band, and this humorous title became the

[39] David Freeman has produced two albums of reissued Charlie Poole selections, both entitled *Charlie Poole and the North Carolina Ramblers*, on County 505 and 509. County 505 includes a written discussion of both Poole and the North Carolina Ramblers.

[40] "Meet Charlie Bowman," *Disc Collector*, No. 16 (n.d.), 3.

source of the new group's name: Gid Tanner and his Skillet Lickers, a usage that was a continued irritation to McMichen, since the original band had been his creation.[41] In their Columbia recording period from 1926 to 1931, the Skillet Lickers recorded, in a highly infectious and often raucous style, everything from traditional ballads, breakdowns, and rural "dramas" (humorous skits) to the latest popular hits from Tin Pan Alley. The real backbone of the band was the virtuoso fiddling of Tanner and McMichen, with a driving rhythm provided by the bass strings of blind guitarist and singer Riley Puckett. Puckett, along with Maybelle Carter, Sam McGee, and Charlie Monroe, was among the most influential hillbilly guitarists before the coming of Merle Travis.

Beginning with a large nucleus of traditional material, the Skillet Lickers had by 1931 moved toward a much heavier inclusion of jazz and pop-style numbers, largely through the collective influence of McMichen and Puckett, who had more eclectic repertories and less dedication to tradition than Tanner. In fact, McMichen's later organizations—such as the Georgia Wildcats—played as many pop as country tunes. After 1931 McMichen left the Skillet Lickers to found several other organizations, and Tanner retired after a 1934 session with a reorganized Skillet Lickers band. Riley Puckett continued to perform as a soloist, and sometimes with an instrumental group, until his death in 1946.[42]

As the previous material would indicate, the fiddle was usually the featured instrument of the early hillbilly bands, with the five-string banjo—played in a variety of styles—coming in a close second as the most popular instrument. Although the hillbilly bands quite often featured vocal music, many of their recordings were purely instrumental. In fact, the early radio barn dances were built around instrumental and dance music. The Grand Ole Opry, now a haven for country crooners, had no featured big-time singer until the 1930's.

Among the early hillbilly vocalists, perhaps none preceded or had

[41] Most of the material on the Skillet Lickers was taken from Norm Cohen's notes to *The Skillet Lickers* (County 506). Of additional aid were the notes to *Gid Tanner and His Skillet Lickers*, a now out-of-print album produced by The Folksong Society of Minnesota. See also John Edwards, "A Tribute to Riley Puckett," *Disc Collector*, No. 12 (n.d.), 8.

[42] Norm Cohen, notes to *The Skillet Lickers*, County 506.

more success on commercial records than Riley Puckett. Born in about 1890 in Alpharetta, Georgia, Puckett was accidentally blinded at the age of three months when a lead acetate solution was used to treat a minor eye irritation. He attended the School for the Blind at Macon, Georgia, and later, with the normal avenues of employment closed to him, he turned to music for a profession—as did many other southern blind people such as Blind Lemon Jefferson, Ernest Thompson, Pete Cassell, and Leon Payne. Puckett was one of many folksingers who gained their initial reputations in the environs of Station WSB in Atlanta. His recording career began in 1924 with "Little Log Cabin in the Lane" and "Rock All Our Babies to Sleep" (Columbia 107-D). On the second song he yodeled, becoming probably the first hillbilly singer to do so and preceding Jimmie Rodgers, of "blue yodel" fame, by about three years. He remained with Columbia until the 1930's, when he changed over to Decca and Bluebird. Although most of Puckett's songs were of a rural or traditional nature, he ranged far and wide for his repertory and showed no reluctance to record any song that caught his fancy. Some of his songs, like "Let Me Call You Sweetheart," came from the sentimental period at the turn of the century; others, such as "How Come You Do Me Like You Do," came from the pop repertory of the Golden Twenties.[43]

Another early vocalist, and one who never wavered in his determination to perform only the native songs of his people, was Bradley Kincaid, "The Kentucky Mountain Boy." Although born in the foothills of the Kentucky Mountains and thoroughly knowledgeable about the folksongs of the region, Kincaid made no deliberate efforts to become a professional folksinger; he became one largely by accident. While attending George Williams College in Chicago, preparing for a career as a YMCA secretary, Kincaid began singing occasionally with the college quartet. A fellow classmate and member of the quartet informed Don Malin, the WLS Music Director, that Kincaid was a folksinger. Malin contacted Kincaid about doing a fifteen minute show on WLS, and Kincaid, who had not sung folksongs for years, borrowed a guitar and began brushing up on the old songs from back home. His initial show evoked a tremendous audience response, and

[43] John Edwards, "A Tribute to Riley Puckett," *Disc Collector*, No. 12 (n.d.), 8–9. Cohen, notes to *The Skillet Lickers*, County 506.

by the fall of 1926 he had become a regular on the National Barn Dance, where he remained for about four years.[44]

With a repertory composed chiefly of traditional mountain ballads and sentimental songs, Kincaid gained a loyal radio following in the Midwest and upper South. After leaving WLS in 1930, he moved to WLW in Cincinnati and then to other stations in the Northeast and mid-South, performing finally during the 1940's over the Grand Ole Opry in Nashville. From the very beginning of his long career Kincaid bitterly resented being called a "hillbilly." He preferred to be called a "singer of mountain songs."[45] Most of his renditions were characterized by a simple guitar accompaniment, and he sang them in a high, sweet, nasal tenor. His tastes ran toward sad, beautiful ballads such as "Barbara Allen" and "Fatal Derby Day," or religious ballads such as "The Legend of the Robin Red Breast." Kincaid made his first recordings for Gennett, one of the more important companies recording hillbilly talent in the twenties. These early recordings were made in an old warehouse; he was not recorded in a fully-equipped sound studio until 1929, when Brunswick issued some of his songs. In those early days country singers seldom signed exclusive contracts with record firms, and their songs could be found on many different labels, quite often under assumed names. Kincaid's songs were placed on several labels, including minor labels in England, Ireland, and Australia.[46]

It would be almost impossible to name all of the early hillbilly performers, but among those who relied heavily upon the traditional songs were Buell Kazee, Clarence Ashley, Dock Boggs, and Kelly Harrell. The first three individuals were five-string banjoists, but Kelly Harrell played no instrument. Each of them possessed a repertory of old-time American and British songs. Buell Kazee was much

[44] The essential biographical information on Bradley Kincaid was supplied by George C. Biggar, who was connected for many years with both WLS and the National Barn Dance. Mr. Biggar, in turn, obtained the information from Bradley Kincaid in the form of a single-spaced typewritten sheet, a copy of which was passed on to me. Additional information on Kincaid can be found in D. K. Wilgus' liner notes to *Bradley Kincaid*, Bluebonnet, Vol. 4, BL 112.

[45] Cited by James McConnell, former head of Acuff-Rose Artists Service, in an interview with the author, Nashville, Tennessee, August 28, 1961.

[46] John Edwards, "Bradley Kincaid, The Story of the Kentucky Mountain Boy," *Disc Collector*, No. 11 (n.d.), 4–5.

like his fellow Kentuckian, Bradley Kincaid, in that he had both a college education and a musical education. And like Kincaid, he was a genuine mountain boy from Magoffin County, Kentucky, and he grew up in a family of traditional singers. He began picking around on the banjo when he was five years old and, at an early age, became a popular performer at neighborhood festivities. At the age of seventeen he became a Missionary Baptist minister. He then attended college at Georgetown, Kentucky, where he studied voice and music and majored in English. His study of Elizabethan literature revealed to him the importance of the ballads he had known all his life. As a result, his concerts in the college area were marked by an erudition rare among country performers. From 1926 to 1930 he recorded fifty-two selections for Brunswick. When the Brunswick Company collapsed in 1930 at the onset of the depression, Kazee terminated his recording career. He was never a full-fledged commercial performer, however, because he had committed himself fully to the Baptist ministry.[47] Recording for Brunswick, Kazee sang in a resonant, mournful fashion such songs as "The Lady Gay," "The Butcher's Boy," and "The Waggoner Lad." Charles Seeger referred to Kazee's "Lady Gay" as "about the finest variant of 'The Wife of Usher's Well' " that he knew.[48] "The Waggoner Lad" is one of the more beautiful songs found in the hillbilly collection, and Kazee performed it and the others over a galloping banjo background.

Clarence Ashley, recently rediscovered and re-presented to the American public via the concert stage, performed as both an individual act and as part of various musical units. Born in Bristol, Tennessee, in 1895, as Clarence Earl McCurry, he legally adopted the name of his grandfather Enoch Ashley, who reared him. He had become an accomplished banjoist and guitarist by the time he reached his early teens and had absorbed an extensive repertory of traditional material from friends and relatives in the Mountain City area of northeastern Tennessee, where his family had moved in 1899. As yet another example of country music's long commercial history prior to the coming of radio and recording, Ashley had been a commercial

[47] Notes to *Buell Kazee Sings and Plays*, Folkways FS 3810. See also John Edwards, "Buell Kazee: A Biographical Note," *Caravan* (June–July, 1959), 42–43.

[48] Charles Seeger, "Reviews," *Journal of American Folklore*, LXI (April–June, 1948), 217.

performer for several years before he made records. At the age of sixteen he joined a medicine show in Mountain City as a featured singer
and remained on the medicine-show circuit, with some exceptions,
until World War II. As a medicine-show entertainer he gained invaluable experience and met other performers—including Roy Acuff,
who would eventually be the great country singing star of the 1940's.

Ashley was also involved periodically in what he termed "busting."
This was the practice of singing in streets, carnivals, or anywhere that
a few dollars might be obtained. In this activity he was sometimes
joined by George Banman Grayson, a blind fiddler who later made
recordings with Henry Whitter on Victor. Ashley's own recording
career came in the mid-twenties when he joined with fiddler Clarence Greene, harmonica player Gwen Foster, autoharpist Will Aber-
nathy, and lead guitarist Walter Davis to form the Blue Ridge
Mountain Entertainers. In this and other organizations, such as the
Carolina Tar Heels and Byrd Moore and His Hotshots, Ashley played
the guitar. To many modern country-music enthusiasts, however,
Ashley's chief claim to fame is his banjo renditions of such songs as
"The Coo Coo Bird" and "The House Carpenter," first recorded when
he was a member of Byrd Moore and His Hotshots. These were his
"lassy-makin'" tunes, so called because they were learned at
molasses-making time back home, and were among the oldest songs
he knew.[49]

Moran Lee "Dock" Boggs also occupies an honored niche in
country-music history, not only because of his use of traditional material but because of his unique banjo style. He was born on February 7, 1898, in West Norton, Virginia, a mountainous area in the
southwestern portion of the state, rich in both coal deposits and
traditional music. Although he began playing the banjo when he was
about twelve years old, his musical activity was never more than a
sideline. Boggs was a coal miner who worked in the mines from the
age of twelve until he retired forty-one years later, in 1952. His recording career began in 1927 with the Brunswick Company. His
recorded repertory is distinctive in its inclusion of blues material,
such as "Down South Blues" and "Mistreated Mama Blues," which he

[49] Ralph and Richard Rinzler, notes to *Old-Time Music at Clarence Ashley's,*
Folkways FA 2355.

learned from Negro performers. Also unique is his banjo technique on both ballads and blues numbers, which is unlike that of any other performer. Boggs picked out the melodies note for note while singing the lyrics. His renditions of such tunes as "Country Blues" and "Pretty Polly" have been continuing favorites among folk music devotees. Many fans had long assumed him dead, but, as is true with Clarence Ashley, Boggs has been rediscovered and once again is making concert appearances.[50]

Kelly Harrell, who recorded for Victor and Okeh, was a Ralph Peer discovery. Harrell was born in Drapers Valley, Wythe County, Virginia, in 1889. After wandering around the country for a number of years, Harrell returned to Fries, Virginia, and was working in a cotton mill when Peer found him in 1924. On his first records Harrell, who played no instrument, was accompanied by a guitarist and a fiddler. In later years he made a number of recordings in which a five-string banjo was added to the guitar and fiddle. Harrell recorded chiefly traditional songs such as "Cuckoo, She's a Pretty Bird" and "Charles Guiteau," but he also composed some of his own numbers. Most famous of these were "Away Out on the Mountain," recorded by Jimmie Rodgers, and "The Story of the Mighty Mississippi," recorded by Ernest Stoneman. Harrell made little profit from his recordings, and at the end of his career was employed at a towel factory in Fieldale, Virginia.[51]

The growing awareness of rustic entertainment in the mid-twenties spurred people, not necessarily of a southern rural persuasion, to attempt to capitalize on hillbilly popularity. Such an individual, and perhaps the most important, was Vernon Dalhart (Marion Try Slaughter). Dalhart was not unfamiliar with Southern rural life and singing; he was born in Jefferson, Texas, of a family of moderate circumstances. His career began in New York, where he gained employment as a popular and light-opera singer, spent several years with the Century Opera Company, and later appeared at the New

[50] The information on Dock Boggs has been obtained from two sources: Michael Seeger, notes to *Dock Boggs,* Folkways Album FA 2351; and Dock Boggs, "I Always Loved the Lonesome Songs," *Sing Out,* XIV, No. 3 (July, 1964), 32–37.

[51] Wilbur Leverett, "The Kelly Harrell Story," *Disc Collector,* No. 11 (n.d.), 5–6.

York-Hippodrome in a Gilbert and Sullivan production in 1913–1914.[52]

Dalhart began recording for Edison in 1916 and later free-lanced for practically every recording company in the United States.[53] When searching for a stage name, he took the names of two Texas towns, "Vernon" and "Dalhart," but he recorded under countless pseudonyms. Prior to 1924, he was listed in the record catalogues as a "tenor,"[54] and few of his songs were even remotely close to the hillbilly category. As a popular singer, Dalhart was only moderately successful. In fact, by 1924 his popularity on Victor was waning, and he desperately needed some means of increasing his depleted financial resources. Dalhart recognized the growing popularity of hillbilly songs, and asked the directors of the Victor record company to allow him to record a hillbilly number. Although Dalhart's financial woes were shared by the Victor record company in 1924, they were hesitant to allow one of their popular singers to record a hillbilly song.[55] Their final affirmative decision, however, gave hillbilly music a national boost, bolstered the sagging Victor sales capacity, and made Vernon Dalhart one of the best-known recording stars of the 1920's.

Two songs served to convert Dalhart to the status of "hillbilly singer" and catapulted him to national attention. These were "The Wreck of the Old 97" and "The Prisoner's Song." "The Wreck of the Old 97" is characteristic of the multitude of native ballads which Americans composed about the events—disasters, wrecks, murders—which caught their fancy. One of many train songs, the ballad tells of the fatal crash of the Fast Mail of the Southern Railway on its run between Monroe and Spencer, Virginia, on September 27, 1903. Engineer Joseph A. (Steve) Broady and twelve others died in the tragedy. Several ballads, including one by Fred Lewey and another by Charlie Noell, were composed about the wreck. In 1927 a Virginia farmer named David Graves George, seeing the great commercial success that the song enjoyed, filed a claim for compensation assert-

[52] Jim Walsh, "Favorite Pioneer Recording Artists: Vernon Dalhart," Part I, *Hobbies*, LXV, No. 3 (May, 1960), 33–34.

[53] Walsh, "Death of Three Recording Artists," *Hobbies*, LIII, No. 10 (December, 1948), 32.

[54] Quoted from *Columbia Record Catalogue* (1923), p. 64.

[55] Walsh, "Favorite Pioneer Recording Artists: Vernon Dalhart," Part III, *Hobbies*, LXV, No. 6 (August, 1960), 33.

ing that he was the real author of the song that Dalhart and others had recorded. Although the Circuit Court of Appeals concluded in 1934 that Graves was not the composer and had, in fact, copied his version from the Dalhart recording, the song's legitimate authorship has never been conclusively ascertained.[56]

"The Wreck on the Southern Old 97" had been subjected to the molding influence of oral tradition for over twenty years before it was recorded in 1923; the "finished" product, therefore, was probably the work of several people. One individual who contributed to the song's structure and popularity was a well-known Virginia hillbilly singer named Henry Whitter, who had kept the ballad alive through local performances in the Fries, Virginia, area. Using the melody of "The Ship that Never Returned," he recorded the great railroad ballad in 1923 on Okeh 40015. His recording was not only one of the very earliest in the commercial hillbilly field, its popularity also directly inspired the entrance of Vernon Dalhart (and others) into hillbilly music. Although Whitter later made some important recordings with the blind fiddler G. B. Grayson, including the well-known "Little Maggie," "Handsome Molly," and "I've Always Been a Rambler," his individual performances often had an unintended result. Many people were inspired to become performers because they were convinced they could do a better job than Whitter![57]

Regardless of Dalhart's motives, he persuaded the Victor Company to allow him to record the number which he had already recorded on Edison Diamond disc No. 51361, and he used the lyrics from the Whitter recording and sang them in a nasal fashion similar to that of Whitter's.[58] The Victor directors asked Dalhart to find something to go on the other side of the record, and he produced the manuscript of a song supposedly written by a cousin, Guy Massey. Nathaniel Shilkret, the Victor Company's staff accompanist, added a few words to the song and thought up a melody. This song, added to the record almost as an afterthought, was "The Prisoner's Song": "If I had the wings of an angel, over these prison walls I would fly." The biggest

---

[56] The complex story of the "Old 97" and the litigation concerning it is best told in Henry M. Belden and Arthur Palmer Hudson, eds., *The Frank C. Brown Collection of North Carolina Folklore*, II, 512–516.

[57] *The New Lost City Ramblers Song Book*, p. 51.

[58] Walsh, "Favorite Pioneer Recording Artists: Vernon Dalhart," Part II, *Hobbies*, LXV, No. 5 (July, 1960), 37.

selling record in Victor's pre-electric recording history,[59] it approached the six-million mark. After the recording of these two numbers, Dalhart remained firmly in the hillbilly category, recording only rural and folk-flavored melodies.

Dalhart, therefore, helped to make hillbilly music more nationally prominent, and, at a time when popular record sales were declining, hillbilly records sold well. Although coming out of a light-opera background, Dalhart knew how to perform the rural songs in a sincere, plaintive style that rural people loved. In his first Edison hillbilly recording, he was accompanied by his own mouth harp and the Hawaiian guitar of Frank Ferara. Ferara was a Hawaiian native of Portuguese descent who had come to the United States in 1900; he claimed to have introduced the Hawaiian guitar to Americans.[60]

From 1925 to 1931 Dalhart became one of the highest-ranked hillbilly singers and recorded songs under many different pseudonyms. "The Prisoner's Song," which he recorded for a dozen or more companies, is said to have brought him well over a million dollars in royalty.[61] "The Death of Floyd Collins" was also a big-selling record for Dalhart. Dalhart's repertory, recorded by practically every recording company of even the slightest importance in the United States, was found on literally thousands of records and included both traditional numbers and newly written ones. The Dalhart collection includes nearly every type of song with which the rural southerner was familiar. There were comical tunes like "The Little Black Mustache," tragic songs like "The Fatal Wedding," bad man ballads like "Sydney Allen," train songs like "The Wreck of the Old 97," sentimental-religious tunes like "The Dying Girl's Message," and, of course, unrequited love ballads like "I'll Be All Smiles Tonight."[62] In many of Dalhart's recordings he was accompanied by Adelyne Hood and a professional whistler and guitarist, Carson Robison.[63]

[59] Released on many labels and under many different numbers, the song's Victor number is 19427. For information on its selling power, see Radio Corporation of America, *The 50-Year Story of RCA Victor Records*, p. 49.

[60] Walsh, "Favorite Pioneer Recording Artists: Vernon Dalhart," Part II, *Hobbies*, LXV, No. 5 (July, 1960), 37.

[61] Walsh, "Death of Three Recording Artists," *Hobbies*, LIII, No. 10 (December, 1948), 32.

[62] Taken from *Columbia Record Catalog* (1928), pp. 248–249.

[63] Walsh, "Death of Three Recording Artists," *Hobbies*, LIII, No. 10 (December, 1948), 32.

Born in Chetapa, Kansas, in 1890, Robison had a career similar to Dalhart's, in that he began his career as a popular entertainer. He became a professional musician in the Midwest at the age of fifteen, and in the early 1920's he worked for a short while in Chicago with Wendell Hall, "The Red-Headed Music Maker." In 1924 he went to New York and made records with Victor, chiefly as a whistler. In the same year he became associated with Vernon Dalhart, and that arrangement lasted for three years. His association with hillbilly music, however, lasted until his death in 1957 and made him one of the most colorful and influential hillbilly performers.

Carson Robison was one of a number of individuals who were able to write songs that would appeal to the hillbilly public. After his first successful hillbilly composition, "Way Out West in Kansas," Robison wrote many of the top songs of the twenties, and many of them were recorded by Vernon Dalhart.[64] Robison, along with people like Bob Miller, composed a type of song—the "event" song—that was a throwback to the British broadside and was perhaps most characteristic of the hillbilly music of the twenties. The leading news topics of the day, especially the violent or sensational events, were chronicled in the event songs. It had long been a habit among southern folksingers to make up songs about striking events, but Robison developed the practice almost to a science. Robison supposedly read all the newspaper accounts of an event; then, in writing the song, he began by establishing a happy mood, which degenerated into tragedy. The last stanza pointed out the moral to be learned.[65]

Robison knew exactly how to gauge the temper of his naive, sentimental listeners, and he strove to present the songs in the manner that a native hillbilly bard would present them. Many of his lyrics, therefore, were presented rather tongue-in-cheek, as is exemplified by the concluding moralistic stanza of "The John T. Scopes Trial," in which Mr. Scopes is warned of the dangers of doubting the "old religion."[66] Robison, therefore, was analogous in certain respects to the eighteenth-century ballad vendors who composed their "event"

[64] Walsh, "Favorite Pioneer Recording Artists: Vernon Dalhart," Part IV, *Hobbies*, LXV, No. 8 (October, 1960), 34.

[65] Mrs. Henry Parkman, "Now Come All You Good People," *Collier's*, LXXXIV (November 2, 1929), 21.

[66] Edison 51609-R. For the words of the song, see *Caravan* (April–May, 1959), 23.

songs on broadside sheets and peddled them on English and colonial street corners. These men, too, were "popular" composers in every sense of the word, adept at producing the kind of songs that the people desired, and more of these songs have endured in the folk tradition than the Child or Popular ballads.[67] In the same manner, the hillbilly songwriters produced songs that were loved by the American rural populace, and some of the songs have gone into "oral tradition." Anything was grist for the mill of the hillbilly composers, and very little has escaped their attention in the years since 1920.

One of the most continuingly popular songwriters in the country genre, from the 1920's until his death in 1955, was the "event" composer par excellence, Bob Miller. Miller was not of country origin; he was born in 1895, in Memphis, Tennessee. Memphis, however, provided him with a social milieu in which he could obtain a close acquaintance with southern melodies. In the early twenties Miller played the piano for a dance band called the Idlewild Orchestra, which performed on the steamer Idlewild on the Mississippi River. In 1928 he moved to New York where he worked as an arranger for the Irving Berlin Company before establishing his own music concern, the Bob Miller Publishing Company. Although he composed numerous blues and popular tunes, the most important items in his repertory of over seven thousand songs were the hillbilly items. In the decades following the 1920's Miller produced scores of lucrative and lastingly popular compositions, including the well-known "Eleven Cent Cotton and Forty Cent Meat"; the prison song which has inspired countless others, "Twenty One Years"; the sentimental favorites "When the White Azaleas Start Blooming" and "Rocking Alone In An Old Rocking Chair"; and the World War II hit "There's a Star Spangled Banner Waving Somewhere."[68] As an event-song writer Miller was always alive to the possibility of exploiting any incident that struck the fancy of the people. In fact, he was sometimes ahead of a story. He supposedly prepared an obituary song for Huey

[67] Gordon H. Gerould, *The Ballad of Tradition*, pp. 261–262.

[68] The information on Bob Miller was supplied by Joe D. Boyd of Willow Grove, Pennsylvania, who is preparing a full-scale study of Miller. The relevant biographical material is the Memphis *Press-Scimitar*, May 5, 1939; and the Memphis *Commercial Appeal*, February 7, 1953.

Long two years before his assassination, and even went so far as to predict accurately that the killing would occur in the state Capitol.[69]

A real folk bard of the 1920's, and one who produced some of the most popular hillbilly songs, was Rev. Andrew Jenkins. Born in Jenkinsburg, Georgia, in 1885, Jenkins, who became totally blind in middle-age, developed a proficiency for several instruments, including the French harp, banjo, guitar, and mandolin. In 1910 he became a Holiness preacher, and except for occasional odd jobs—such as selling newspapers on the streets of Atlanta—he remained a revivalist until his death in 1956.

His second marriage, in 1919, brought him into a musical family. When station WSB opened its doors in 1922, the Jenkins family (probably the first country music family to be recorded) was well prepared to move into studio entertainment. Although Jenkins was an accomplished musician and entertainer, he achieved his greatest fame as a songwriter. He composed well over eight hundred songs, the majority of them sacred. His repertory of compositions includes "Little Marian Parker," "God Put a Rainbow in the Clouds," "Ben Dewberry's Final Run," "Kinnie Wagner," "Billy the Kid," and one of the most popular songs of the 1920's, "The Death of Floyd Collins."

"The Death of Floyd Collins," recorded by Vernon Dalhart and others, chronicled the sad story of a young spelunker who became trapped in a sandstone cave near the Mammoth Cave in Kentucky in 1925. The incident gained national attention because of radio coverage,[70] and Polk Brockman (the talent scout and record distributor who had been instrumental in Fiddlin' John Carson's discovery), who at that time was in Jacksonville, Florida, communicated with Andrew Jenkins and asked him to write a ballad. Jenkins' composition, arranged by his stepdaughter, Mrs. Irene Spain, was then mailed to Brockman, who paid twenty-five dollars for it.[71] Brockman in turn

[69] Doron K. Antrim, "Whoop-and-Holler Opera," *Collier's*, CXVII (January 26, 1946), 85.

[70] Described in Frederick Lewis Allen, *Only Yesterday*, p. 174.

[71] The information on Andrew Jenkins was obtained from an address made by D. K. Wilgus at the seventy-third annual meeting of the American Folklore Society at Austin, Texas, December 28, 1961 (reprinted in *A Good Tale and a Bonnie Tune*, edited by Mody C. Boatright, et. al. [Publications of the Texas Folklore Society, XXXII], pp. 227–237).

sold it to Frank Walker of Columbia Records, who gave it to Dalhart for recording purposes.[72] The song was typical of the event songs of the period in that it was highly moralistic in tone and informed the listener of the dire fate that awaited the young man who disregarded his father's warnings.

This song and similar ones produced by commercial hillbillies were accepted by the folksingers in southern rural communities, people who would never attempt to make a living through professional singing. Therefore, when later generations of folklorists traveled through the South in search of material, they collected such songs as "The Death of Floyd Collins" as authentic specimens of the folk-produced songs of the region. In the words of D. K. Wilgus, "a commercialized tradition was being established."[73]

Most of the folksingers recorded during the twenties were from the southeastern states, and the styles and songs they contributed continued to set the pattern for the hillbilly music produced in future decades. Essentially, two forms of music developed within hillbilly music during the early period, two forms that dominated it until the emergence of "western" music in the 1930's. These, for lack of better labels, can be called "country" and "mountain." Both were country, or rural, in origin, but mountain music came to be identified in the minds of many people as the type that originated in the Appalachians. Country music was that type which stressed more individual solo singing, utilized more nontraditional instruments, and was influenced by popular music and Negro blues music. Its chief exponent and most influential performer was Jimmie Rodgers. Mountain music tended to be more conservative and to rely more on the traditional songs and instruments, and it was performed in the traditional, high-nasal harmony. This type, today represented by bluegrass music, owes many of its essential characteristics to the style produced by the famous Carter Family.

The recording of both Rodgers and the Carter Family was the work of the indefatigable commercialist-folklorist, Ralph Peer. Peer journeyed to Bristol, on the Tennessee-Virginia border, for a ten-day visit in late July and early August, 1927, laden with his recording

---

[72] Dalhart's performance appeared on at least nineteen different labels. The Columbia number, however, was 15064-D.

[73] Wilgus, *Anglo-American Folksong Scholarship Since 1898*, pp. 283–284.

apparatus in quest of hillbilly talent. Many hillbilly performers, lured by advertisements in the local newspapers, appeared before Peer, and perhaps as many as twenty were recorded. Among these were Alfred Karnes, a powerful-voiced gospel singer, and the Tenneva Ramblers, who earlier had performed in and around Asheville, North Carolina, as the Jimmie Rodgers' Entertainers. Of the several groups recorded, however, only two, Rodgers and the Carters, were to experience any kind of long-range success. The two acts, recorded within two days of each other (the Carter Family on August 1 and 2, and Rodgers on August 4),[74] became the two most influential groups within the hillbilly-music field during the early period, and provided it with two of its basic styles. Rodgers, in his six-year recording career, became the country's biggest-selling hillbilly star, and set the music on a course that would make it more commercial and more oriented toward the individual star.

The Carter Family continued to be important country-music performers until the early 1940's. Although they ceased to make commercial records in 1941, they did not actually retire from radio work until 1943. Their retirement date is significant in that it coincided with the coming of World War II, which, to some people, was the ending of country music's golden age. The Carter Family, which in many respects dominated the so-called golden age, was composed of A. P. Carter, his wife Sara, and A. P.'s sister-in-law, Maybelle Addington Carter. The Carter Family perpetuated many traditional songs that might otherwise have been lost, and contributed styles that influenced later generations of hillbilly performers.

Alvin Pleasant Carter was born at Maces Spring, Scott County, Virginia, in 1891. Reared in a strict Christian environment, A. P. learned to love religious songs but was attracted also by lively fiddle music. Because the fiddle was looked upon as the devil's instrument by his religious parents, he had to wait until he had earned enough money as a fruit-tree salesman to acquire such an instrument. While visiting relatives on Copper Creek in Scott County, he met Sara Dougherty (born in 1898 in Wise County, Virginia), who was an accomplished young singer and instrumentalist. After their marriage on June 18, 1915, they settled at Maces Spring, where their home became a neighborhood attraction because of A. P.'s and Sara's singing.

[74] Letter to the author from Ed Kahn, February 1, 1967.

Maybelle Addington, born in 1909 at Nickelsville, Virginia, married E. J. Carter in 1926. She brought to the Carter Family an exceptional talent for the autoharp, banjo, and guitar. When Ralph Peer arrived in Bristol, the Carter Family was well prepared to record.[75]

The Carters, according to statements made by Sara Carter, recorded over three hundred sides for various companies.[76] Victor and Columbia, in the early period, and Decca, in the late 1930's, were the most important. Their Victor recordings of 1927, inaugurated with "Wandering Boy" and "Poor Orphan Child" (Victor 20877), were among the very first recordings made by the electrical process that led to vastly improved sound reproduction. In most of the Carter Family's recordings Sara led the singing, Maybelle provided the alto and A. P. sang bass. The accompaniment was provided by autoharp chords, played by Sara, and a guitar melodic line produced by Maybelle. The Carter Family's rhythmic style influenced most of the folk musicians who came afterward. Their unique style, immediately recognizable to country music enthusiasts, was largely the product of Maybelle Carter's guitar-playing style, which she learned from her brothers.[77] In the decades following 1927 it became the height of accomplishment for southern country guitarists to learn the Maybelle Carter guitar style, especially her rendition of "Wildwood Flower," which has become a classic instrumental piece.[78] Her style has been detected also in the guitar techniques of such urban-oriented folk

[75] Basic biographical information on the Carter Family has been obtained from Archie Green, "The Carter Family's 'Coal Miner's Blues,'" *Southern Folklore Quarterly*, XXV, No. 4 (December, 1961), 227–229. A definitive analytical study of the Carter Family is now being done by Ed Kahn, of the University of California at Los Angeles, and I am deeply indebted to him. Another very interesting study of the Carter Family has been written by one of Maybelle's daughters, June Carter ("I Remember the Carter Family," *Country Song Roundup*, XVII, No. 90 [October, 1965], 16–17, 30–32; and *ibid.*, No. 91 [December, 1965], 16–20).

[76] Harry Smith, ed., notes (p. 11) *Anthology of American Folk Music*, Folkways FA 2951–2953.

[77] Interview with Mrs. Maybelle Carter, Nashville, Tennessee, August 26, 1961. For an explanation of the "Carter Family Lick" see Alan Lomax, *The Folk Songs of North America*, p. 603.

[78] D. K. Wilgus has said that "almost every young guitarist plays (even if he cannot sing) a 'Wildwood Flower' ultimately traceable to the Carter version" (quoted in "Record Reviews," *Journal of American Folklore*, LXXV, No. 295 [January–March, 1962], 87).

singers as Huddie (Leadbelly) Ledbetter and Woody Guthrie. When Woody Guthrie made his first coast-to-coast radio appearance, he supposedly received a postcard from Virginia signed "the Carters" and saying "you're doing fine, boy." Upon receipt of the postcard, Guthrie acknowledged his debt.[79]

The Carter Family never made extensive tours; most of their activities were confined to the upper South, although they did occasionally go up into Pennsylvania. Their popularity was gained through phonograph recordings and through radio broadcasts made over the powerful Mexican border stations after 1938.[80] The Family sang both traditional songs and their own compositions. Most of their own songs were written by A. P., who was one of the first individuals to protect his repertory by securing copyrights on the music—even on that very large percentage which was in the public domain. Carter readily admitted that he took many of his songs from traditional sources, but as Archie Green has said "every time A. P. Carter recorded a song or published it in a folio, he 'collected' a variant as does any folklorist in the field with his notebook, acetate disc, or tape."[81] It is not surprising, therefore, to find A. P. Carter listed as author of songs that he could not possibly have written—"I'll Be All Smiles Tonight," "Wabash Cannon Ball," and others.[82] In fact, from the lyrics of some of his numbers, it is evident that the words must have come to him in a somewhat garbled fashion. "Wildwood Flower," traceable to a nineteenth-century parlor tune called "The Pale Amaranthus," has such quaint lines as "I'll twine with my mingles and waving black hair," and "the pale and the leader, and eyes look like blue."[83]

In recording these songs the Carter Family presented versions of many traditional songs that had never been heard by the American public, and by presenting them in a simple and easily singable style they made it possible for these songs to be perpetuated. One writer claimed that one of the Carter Family's "greatest contributions to

[79] John Greenway, *American Folksongs of Protest*, p. 285.

[80] Interview with Mrs. Maybelle Carter, August 26, 1961.

[81] Green, "The Carter Family's 'Coal Miner's Blues,'" *Southern Folklore Quarterly*, XXV, No. 4 (December, 1961), 231.

[82] Ed Badeaux, "The Carters of Rye Cove," *Sing Out*, II, No. 2 (April–May, 1961), 14.

[83] The Carters' version can be heard on *The Famous Carter Family*, Harmony HL 7280.

American folk music was the way in which they perpetuated the
traditional Anglo-Saxon ballad, making it live anew in the hearts of
succeeding generations of Americans."[84] The process by which they
did this was a product of their religious training and their employment of musical instruments. The Carters' use of harmony, learned in
the church singing schools, and their use of the guitar and autoharp
necessitated a change in the basic structures of many of the traditional songs. Many of the old ballads were in modes that did not lend
themselves to instrumental accompaniment or harmony. The Carters,
instead of tuning their instruments modally, changed the melodies so
they would fit instrumental accompaniment. Their version of "Sink-
ing in the Lonesome Sea" has few similarities to the original ballad
("The Golden Vanity"), but it lends itself more readily to modern
singing styles.[85]

The Carter Family's strong preference for religious songs was evident in their repertory.[86] Their recording of "Little Moses" remains a
great favorite among traditional-minded hillbilly fans and folklorists, and modern concert singer Joan Baez has made it a standard part
of her routine and has recorded the song on a long-play album.[87]
Most of the Carters' religious songs, originating in the fundamentalist tradition, stressed the importance of holiness, emphasized the sadness and wickedness of this life, and related the joys of the heavenly
home beyond the grave. The song which they used as their radio
theme, "Keep on the Sunny Side," has continued to be a favorite
among country entertainers.

Religious attitudes also influenced the secular songs of the Carter
Family (as they have those of most other hillbilly performers). The
travail of earthly existence and the despair brought by lost or unrequited love have been pictured as being assuaged by death (or by
cathartic songs about death). For example, the mournful love ballad
"Little Darlin', Pal of Mine" expresses a prevailing death wish, or a
desire to find solace in the "coffin, shroud, and grave."[88] These were

[84] Badeaux, "The Carters of Rye Cove," *Sing Out*, II, No. 2 (April–May,
1961), 14.

[85] *Ibid.*

[86] One of the better Carter Family discographies is by Bill Legere in *Country
and Western Spotlight*, No. 34 (June, 1961), 6–14.

[87] On *Joan Baez*, Vanguard VRS-9078.

[88] On *The Famous Carter Family*, Harmony HL 7280.

the utterances of an unsophisticated people who expressed their feelings in a simple, straightforward manner. Many of the lyrics found in Carter Family songs appear maudlin to those who are not country-music enthusiasts. For example, the well-known "Can the Circle Be Unbroken" tells of a heart-broken person who follows the hearse as it carries his mother to the burial ground.[89] Although the words may be maudlin, they are not unrealistic. They sprang from and were representative of a Victorian culture which was acutely conscious of death and the sorrow it could bring to tightly-knit family groups. Country music received much of its repertory from a sentimental nineteenth-century America which valued songs about dying orphans, poor blind children, and departed mothers. The social conservatism of the rural South preserved these songs in a nation that was rapidly becoming too sophisticated to appreciate down-to-earth lyrics about death and sorrow, regardless of how real these emotions might be. The Carter Family, in its choice of songs and style of presentation, was strongly representative of musical attitudes as they had developed among southern whites for many generations. But in their instrumentation, and in their arrangements, the Carter Family presaged new developments in southern rural musical taste and performance.

It is difficult to measure fully the Carters' influence. Their records sold well into the millions. The influence of their radio broadcasts on country people who decided to take up the guitar or become professional singers must have been amazingly wide. There are still groups, exemplified by the A. L. Phipps Family of Kentucky,[90] who closely copy the songs and techniques of the Carter Family.

Record sales are no real criterion of the popularity of hillbilly music during the twenties and thirties, because the music was directed toward an audience that could not afford periodic record purchases. The real source of entertainment for the country-music fan during the early period, and one that can be only inadequately measured, was the radio. Hillbillies, both amateur and professional,

---

[89] "Can the Circle Be Unbroken," which has been recorded many times, can be heard on *The Famous Carter Family*, Harmony HL 7280.

[90] A good introduction to the Phipps Family style is *Just Another Broken Heart*, Folkways FA 2375. One of the best tributes to the Carter Family is the Lester Flatt and Earl Scruggs album, *Songs of the Carter Family*, Columbia CL 1664.

had short segments of radio time in areas all over the South and Midwest. These programs led to the development of the hillbilly radio barn dances, which today have become meccas for top-ranking country artists.

Although earlier stations such as WSB and WBAP had featured barn-dance shows as early as 1922, the first show to experience any kind of longevity or national recognition was the one produced by WLS in Chicago. WLS inaugurated a hillbilly show about a week after the station went on the air on April 12, 1924. WLS (World's Largest Store) was a Sears-Roebuck station from its beginning until September, 1928, when it was purchased by the *Prairie Farmer* newspaper. From the very first it aimed many of its broadcasting features at rural and small-town listeners in the Midwest.[91] The first WLS barn-dance show got off to a rather inauspicious beginning on the small mezzanine of the Sherman Hotel in Chicago on the night of April 19, 1924. On this first program, a group of country-style fiddlers were booked to alternate with the popular Isham Jones dance band from the College Inn. The music was so well received that hundreds of requests for various fiddle numbers poured into the station in the next few days.[92] The humble beginning on April 19 ultimately led to the development of the popular National Barn Dance.

Throughout its long history (it is now carried on WGN in Chicago) the National Barn Dance has had a broader musical perspective than most country-music shows. From the time of its inception in 1924 the WLS Barn Dance (as it was then called) featured a high proportion of sentimental pop tunes and "heart songs" along with its basic repertory of country and folk music. Although criticized by some observers, the inclusion of old-fashioned pop music was perhaps natural in that, to most midwesterners, such songs as "Down By the Old Mill Stream" were the closest approximations of folk music that they knew. These songs were the songs of their youth, and they remained important ingredients of the Barn Dance shows long after performers from the South and West brought their mountain and

[91] Boris Emmet and John E. Jeuck, *Catalogues and Counters: A History of Sears, Roebuck and Company*, p. 624.

[92] Clarence B. Newman, "Homespun Harmony," *The Wall Street Journal*, XXXVII, No. 141 (May 3, 1957), 6.

cowboy tunes to the Chicago radio show.[93] Fiddle bands and ballad-eers appeared from the very beginning, but often in conjunction with performers of old-time pop and standard melodies. Organist Ralph Waldo Emerson played such songs as "Silver Threads among the Gold" while Ford and Glenn (Ford Rush and Glenn Rowell), the Maple City Four Quartet, and Bill O'Connor (The Irish Tenor) sang sentimental melodies and novelty tunes from earlier years. The two most important singers of "heart songs" ever to appear on the Barn Dance—and two of the more important "popular singers" of the early twentieth century—were Henry Burr and Grace Wilson. Burr did not join the Barn Dance until 1934, but he came with a well-established reputation as a tenor who had performed extensively on the theater and concert circuits since World War I. Although he had often sung with such groups as the Peerless Quartet, his greatest success came as a soloist, and his World War I recording of "Just a Baby's Prayer at Twilight" sold a million copies.[94]

Grace Wilson, a popular contralto, was one of the most valuable members, both historically and musically, to appear on Barn Dance programs, and her career is illustrative of both midwestern musical tastes and of the Barn Dance's wide-ranging repertory. Born in Owesso, Michigan, on April 10, 1890, Miss Wilson became a professional singer in 1906 in musical comedy and vaudeville. Between this time and her radio debut in 1922 on WTAS in Elgin, Illinois, she introduced such songs as "In the Shade of the Old Apple Tree" and "I'd Love to Live in Loveland with You." She already had a wide following, therefore, when she joined both WLS and the Barn Dance in 1924. From 1924 until her retirement in 1960 Grace Wilson remained one of the best loved Barn Dance stars, and her most popular rendition was "Bringing Home the Bacon." During her thirty-six-

[93] I am deeply indebted to Dave Wylie of Wilmette, Illinois, for the bulk of the material on the National Barn Dance. Mr. Wylie, whose exhaustive knowledge of WLS and the National Barn Dance will someday lead to a definitive study of those institutions, has kindly made available to me the results of his interviews and research findings. In addition, through the intercession of Wylie, George Biggar, who was connected in a business capacity with WLS for many years, has also graciously contributed information.

[94] Letter to the author from George C. Biggar, Laguna Hills, California, March 18, 1967.

year career on the Barn Dance (the longest of any performer) she received over one million fan letters and was generally billed as "The Girl with a Million Friends." Upon retiring from professional singing Grace Wilson moved to Sun City, Arizona, where she died in 1962.[95]

Despite the continuing appearance of pop-style entertainers, hillbilly entertainers comprised the real nucleus of the Barn Dance shows. In the early years of the show, mountain and old-time influences were exerted by such people as Tommy Dandurand and his Barn Dance Fiddlers, who provided square dance music with calls; Walter Peterson (the Kentucky Wonder Bean), who sang old-time ballads; and five-string banjoist Chubby Parker (the Stern Old Bachelor), who performed such songs as "Little Old Sod Shanty" which he had learned back home in Kentucky. Of special significance among the early old-time performers was Luther Ossenbrink, who, although coming from Missouri, billed himself as Arkie the Woodchopper. Arkie knew a wide variety of mountain, country, and cowboy ballads, and his career on WLS, which ran almost continuously from 1929 to 1960, was second in longevity only to that of Grace Wilson. (He is, in fact, still appearing on the WGN Barn Dance).[96] All of these performers, along with Bradley Kincaid, who performed on WLS from 1926 to 1931, gave the Barn Dance a richly distinctive old-time flavor and made it the nation's leading country-music show in the days before Nashville's Grand Ole Opry became the top country spectacular.

According to George Biggar, former program director for WLS, the Barn Dance experienced its greatest development in the seven or eight years immediately following 1930.[97] In that period the cast of Barn Dance performers gradually expanded and the program's radio listening range increased to take in most of the United States. Some of the entertainers—like Gene Autry—stayed for only a couple of years; but others—like Lulu Belle and Scotty (Myrtle Cooper and Scott Wiseman)—were to remain for twenty years and more. One of the more valuable of the early groups was the Cumberland Ridge Runners, an assemblage of singers and musicians who came to the

[95] Letter to the author from Dave Wylie, March 24, 1967.
[96] Letter to the author from George C. Biggar, March 18, 1967.
[97] *Ibid.*

Barn Dance in 1930 from the areas around Mt. Vernon and Berea, Kentucky. The Cumberland Ridge Runners definitely strengthened the show's old-time orientation. John Lair, the group's leader, was and is a folk music authority, and his library of old-time music, still maintained in Renfro Valley, Kentucky, is of great value to the student of folk culture. Lair wrote some of the best country songs of the early thirties, such as "Freight Train Blues," and after leaving WLS founded the continuingly popular Renfro Valley Show. Several individuals, including Clyde (Red) Foley and Hugh Cross, appeared periodically with the Ridge Runners. Probably the most tradition-oriented members were Slim Miller, an old-time fiddler; Doc Hopkins, who sang traditional ballads; Linda Parker, who sang old favorites like "I'll Be All Smiles Tonight;" and Karl Davis and Harty Taylor, a mandolin and guitar combination, who introduced such well-known favorites as "I'm Just Here to Get My Baby Out of Jail."[98]

Because of the Barn Dance's immediate popularity after its founding in 1924, WLS became the first radio station to construct a studio theater. By 1932, with reservations being made seven months in advance for the show, WLS began looking for larger audience accommodations, and as a result, took over Chicago's Eighth Street Theatre, broadcast the program in two complete shows, and charged admission.[99] The Eighth Street Theatre remained the home of the National Barn Dance for the next twenty-five years. Only one year after moving into the theater, the Barn Dance moved well beyond its midwestern scope when Alka-Seltzer, in 1933, began the sponsorship of a one-hour Saturday night segment on NBC.[100] This coast-to-coast radio coverage, in addition to the road-show units that left WLS in an ever widening arc after 1932, made the National Barn Dance the nation's leading country-music show in those years before the Grand Ole Opry became predominant.

The modern-day giant among country-music radio shows, the

---

[98] Much of the basic biographical information on Karl and Harty came from *Stand By* magazine ([November 2, 1935], p. 9) and was supplied in a letter to the author from Dave Wylie, April 3, 1967. Additional information on John Lair and the Cumberland Ridge Runners is from a letter to the author from George Biggar, March 18, 1967.

[99] *The Billboard*, LXVI, No. 15 (April 10, 1954), 5.

[100] Letter to the author from George Biggar, March 18, 1967.

Grand Ole Opry, had a slightly later beginning than the WLS program and, for a number of years, had a lesser influence and popularity. The Grand Ole Opry was the brainchild of George D. Hay, who had also been instrumental in the creation of the WLS Barn Dance, on which he served as an announcer. Shortly after World War I, Hay, at that time a reporter for the Memphis *Commercial Appeal*, went to the Ozark foothills town of Mammoth Spring, Arkansas, to cover the funeral of a war hero. The night following the funeral he visited a country hoedown held in a log cabin about a mile up a muddy road. While there he received the idea which later grew into the National Barn Dance and the Grand Ole Opry.[101]

In 1925 the National Life and Accident Insurance Company began the operation of Station WSM in Nashville, and the company hired Hay as its first station director.[102] On November 28 of that year he launched a hillbilly radio show, the WSM Barn Dance, with only two entertainers, an eighty-year-old fiddler named Uncle Jimmy Thompson and his niece, Mrs. Eva Thompson Jones, who played the piano. Uncle Jimmy was seated in a comfortable chair in front of an old carbon microphone, while Mrs. Jones played his piano accompaniment. At the end of an hour, Hay asked the old fiddler if he was tired of playing, and Uncle Jimmy replied: "Why, shucks, a man don't get warmed up in an hour. I just won an eight-day fiddling contest down in Dallas, Texas, and here's my blue ribbon to prove it." [103] Uncle Jimmy claimed to know a thousand tunes, and he evidently wanted to be given a chance to play all of them.

The fiddle playing brought an immediately favorable response, and telegrams and letters requesting tunes poured into the station. As a result, Uncle Jimmy, his niece, and announcer Hay carried on for an hour each Saturday night for several weeks. This small group did not long remain the total personnel of the Barn Dance show. Their success inspired other country performers to try their luck at radio entertaining. As George Hay later recalled, "after three or four weeks of this fiddle solo business, we were besieged with other fiddlers, banjo pickers, guitar players, and a lady who played an old zither."[104] Most anyone who could perform was accepted; the enter-

---

101 George D. Hay, *A Story of the Grand Ole Opry*, p. 23.
102 William R. McDaniel and Harold Seligman, *Grand Ole Opry*, p. 17.
103 Hay, *A Story of the Grand Ole Opry*, p. 1.
104 *Ibid.*

tainers (mostly from the middle Tennessee region) performed without pay, and the performances were given without commercials. The entertainers for the most part were amateur musicians who worked as farmers and laborers during the week and then performed at WSM on Saturday night. The programs were very informal affairs conducted by people who had no thought of making far-flung professional tours. The entertainers performed as much for their own enjoyment as they did for that of their listeners.

As was common on nearly all early radio stations, the early WSM shows emphasized instrumental music. The first old-time string band to be featured was Dr. Humphrey Bate and the Possum Hunters. Dr. Bate, a physician and surgeon from Sumner County, Tennessee, played the harmonica. He brought along five or six of his neighbors who played various stringed instruments.

Shortly after the arrival of Bate's group, three similar string bands joined the regular Saturday night broadcast. These were the Crook Brothers, the Gully Jumpers, and the Fruit Jar Drinkers.[105] Following not far behind these groups was a brother team from the rural area around Franklin, Tennessee, Kirk and Sam McGee. Sam was one of the finest finger-style guitarists of the early period. Although the McGee boys were raised in a family that often played string music (their father was an old-time fiddler), Sam did not become interested in the guitar until shortly before World War I when he heard it being played by Negro street musicians in Perry, Tennessee. From that time forward, although he also played the five-string banjo competently, Sam McGee's chief instrument was the guitar, an instrument which he put to proficient use in 1923 when he began touring and playing with Uncle Dave Macon. By 1925 the two McGees were playing on Grand Ole Opry broadcasts and touring along with Dr. Bate and the Possum Hunters on Opry-sponsored shows on the RKO vaudeville circuit in the Midwest and upper South.[106]

Sometime in the early thirties the McGee brothers teamed with the famous old-time fiddler from Humphries County, Tennessee,

[105] *Ibid.*

[106] Jon Pankake, "Sam and Kirk McGee from Sunny Tennessee," *Sing Out*, XIV, No. 5 (November, 1964), 47–49. Other very useful sources on the McGee Brothers are Ralph Rinzler's notes to *Uncle Dave Macon*, Decca DL 4760; and Pankake's notes to *The McGee Brothers and Arthur Smith*, Folkways FA 2379.

Arthur Smith, to form a group called the Dixieliners. Under this name the group performed regularly on WSM broadcasts and also toured extensively in the central Tennessee region, where they played in schoolhouses and theaters. Despite their radio and road-show appearances, the McGee brothers and Arthur Smith did not record together. The McGees recorded as a team and with Uncle Dave Macon, but when Arthur Smith made his Bluebird recordings with the Dixieliners and the Arthur Smith Trio he was accompanied by Alton and Rabon Delmore. Known not only as one of the great fiddlers in country-music history, Arthur Smith is also credited with composing some of the classic songs within the country genre, including "Beautiful Brown Eyes" and "There's More Pretty Girls Than One," both of which were recorded by the Arthur Smith Trio.[107]

All of the original string bands, with the exception of the Dixieliners, still appear on the Grand Ole Opry, although some of the old-timers, including Dr. Bate, have passed away. One of the tragedies of these groups' careers, however, is the fact that, despite their many contributions to the country-music field, they have been all but engulfed by the wave of superstars who have dominated the Grand Ole Opry since the 1940's. The presence of the old-timers is scarcely noticed except by the dwindling band of old-time enthusiasts who attend the show. Although they played pre-eminent roles in the twenties and thirties, the original string bands gradually have been relegated to the position of fill-ins and play only an occasional number, usually of the breakdown variety. Sam McGee, for instance, rarely gets the opportunity to display his virtuoso talents on the guitar, a skill which only an occasional folk-festival audience is fortunate enough to witness. Ironically, it has been the folk festival—such as the one at Newport, Rhode Island—and not the Grand Ole Opry that has afforded many of the old-time country performers the recognition that they have long deserved. Sam and Kirk McGee, Arthur Smith, and the Crook Brothers have recently won new acclaim because of the national folk-music boom; they have made appearances at folk festivals (usually in the North) and have been newly recorded.[108]

[107] Jon Pankake, notes to *The McGee Brothers and Arthur Smith,* Folkways FA 2379.

[108] Mike Seeger has been most instrumental in giving the old-time string bands

Although the early Grand Ole Opry string bands featured vocal numbers as well as instrumental, none of them had a featured vocalist. The chief singing star of the Grand Ole Opry, before the coming of Roy Acuff, was a colorful five-string banjoist named Uncle Dave Macon. David Harrison Macon, one of the greatest five-string banjoists and most gifted entertainers in the history of the United States, was born between McMinnville and Smartt, Warren County, Tennessee, on October 7, 1870.[109] The musical education that would one day make him such an accomplished performer began when his parents moved to Nashville in 1873 and opened a boardinghouse which catered to theatrical people. At an early age he learned songs, stories, and instrumental techniques from the colorful vaudeville personalities who passed through the city. After his marriage to Mathilda Richardson, he moved to a small farm in Kittrell, not far from Readyville, Tennessee, where in 1900 he established the Macon Midway Mule and Wagon Transportation Company, which hauled material from Woodbury to Murfreesboro for the next twenty years. (The company is immortalized in Uncle Dave's recording of "From Earth to Heaven.")[110]

Before 1918 music was no more than an amusing diversion for Uncle Dave. He was known for miles around as a first-rate comic, an extraordinary banjoist, and a thorough professional in his musical skills, but he had never performed for money. His performances at picnics and social functions had been strictly for fun. The commercial world of show business beckoned, however, in 1918 when he demanded fifteen dollars to play at a large party given by a farmer whom he believed to be a bit pompous. To Uncle Dave's great surprise the farmer accepted. A talent scout for Loew's Theatre Circuit, who happened to be present at the party, approached Macon after the performance and booked him for a concert at a leading theater

---

the recognition which they deserve among folk music devotees, and he was the producer of *The McGee Brothers and Arthur Smith*, Folkways FA 2379.

[109] The most important biographical sketch and musical analysis of Uncle Dave Macon is that in Ralph Rinzler's notes to *Uncle Dave Macon*, Decca DL 4760.

[110] Rinzler, notes to *Uncle Dave Macon*, Decca DL 4760. "From Earth to Heaven" can be heard on *Uncle Dave Macon*, RBF album RF 51.

in Birmingham. Thus began a career in commercial country music which was not to terminate until his death in 1953.[111]

When Uncle Dave Macon joined the Grand Ole Opry in 1926, he was fifty-six years old, had been a professional entertainer for eight years and had been a semi-professional for much longer. He brought to the Grand Ole Opry the versatile skills of a seasoned vaudeville and minstrel entertainer and a storehouse of folk material garnered from a host of southern sources. He brought also a wide variety of complex frailing and picking styles which modern banjoists might well envy. In his commitment to traditional styles he certainly deserves the praise given to him by Ralph Rinzler: "with the exception of the Carter Family, Uncle Dave preserved more valuable American folklore through his recordings than any other folk or country music performer."[112] Many of the songs he recorded were learned before 1900 from both white and Negro laborers who had worked at railroad, mining, and river occupations. "Way Down the Old Plank Road" (Vocalion B15321) describes life on a Georgia chain gang, and "Buddy, Won't You Roll Down the Line" (Brunswick 292) discusses the bitter labor upheavals in Tennessee in the 1880's, which were occasioned by the use of convict labor in the coal mines. Uncle Dave's recordings are important sources of social commentary about the industrial revolution that steadily moved across the South in the decades following the Civil War.[113]

Uncle Dave's recording career, which preceded his first Opry appearance by about two years, spanned the period from 1924, when he first recorded for Vocalion, to 1938. He recorded occasionally as a solo act, and often with accompanists who were fellow Tennesseans and Grand Ole Opry performers. In his first two recording sessions in 1924 and 1925 he was accompanied by Sid Harkreader, who was both a fiddler and guitarist. In most of his later sessions—primarily for the Brunswick Company—he was supported by those talented brothers

[111] Rinzler, notes to *Uncle Dave Macon*, Decca DL 4760.
[112] *Ibid.*
[113] "Way Down the Old Plank Road" and "Buddy Won't You Roll Down the Line" can both be heard on the *Anthology of American Folk Music*, Folkways FA 2951–2953. Both songs are also printed in *The New Lost City Ramblers Song Book* (pp. 218, 220). The violence occasioned by the use of convict labor in Tennessee coal mines has been described by C. Vann Woodward (*Origins of the New South, 1877–1913* [Vol. IX of *A History of the South*], pp. 232–235.

from Tennessee, Sam and Kirk McGee, along with old-time fiddler Mazy Todd.[114]

Until his death at the age of 83, Uncle Dave Macon played with a zest and enthusiasm which few, if any, modern country entertainers can equal. Although thoroughly professional in his approach to show business and in his musical skills, Macon was totally unaffected and unpretentious, and he loved to perform for the pure personal enjoyment of it. When the Grand Ole Opry began sending out tours in the late twenties and early thirties, Uncle Dave was a source of considerable consternation to the show's directors. Harry Stone, a former manager of the Grand Ole Opry, said that Macon sometimes had to be restrained from giving the whole show away through his willingness to perform in hotel lobbies, free of charge, before the main program got underway.[115] He cut a striking figure in his double-breasted waistcoat, high wing collar, bright red tie, and broad-brimmed hat of black felt. He looked the part of a gay country gentleman of the 1890's, and with his old-time songs, homey sayings, shouted enthusiasms, and boundless vitality, he captivated his audiences and recaptured the spirit of rural, small-town America that was about to be submerged by the sophistication and glamor of urban twentieth-century America. Modern country-music enthusiasts who are accustomed to seeing performers experience a brief period of success and then fade might well ponder the words of Ralph Rinzler: "no one figure will ever again dominate the field single-handedly for fifteen years as did the extraordinary singer, banjo picker, raconteur and humanitarian known fondly as 'The Dixie Dewdrop' . . . Uncle Dave Macon."[116]

The popularity of the WSM show necessitated its gradual enlargement. The show's cast had grown to about twenty-five when Uncle Dave Macon joined it, so WSM decided to build a much larger studio, Studio B. A large plate-glass window was provided in order to allow spectators to watch the show. Eventually, however, the

[114] Rinzler, notes to *Uncle Dave Macon*, Decca DL 4760. A discography of Uncle Dave's recordings is printed in the notes to *Uncle Dave Macon*, RBF album RF 51.

[115] Interview with Harry Stone, Nashville, Tennessee, August 28, 1961.

[116] Rinzler, notes to *Uncle Dave Macon*, Decca DL 4760. For another good personal description of Uncle Dave see Rufus Jarman, "Country Music Goes to Town," *Nation's Business*, XLI (February, 1953), 48.

WSM executives decided to allow about fifty or sixty people to listen from within the studio. From this small beginning WSM gradually expanded the facilities for the show, first building an auditorium studio with a seating capacity of five hundred, and later renting the Hillsboro Theatre, which proved to be too small for the program's fans. The show moved next to a large tabernacle in East Nashville and then to the War Memorial Auditorium before finding a suitable location.[117] In 1941 the show moved to its present location, a converted tabernacle replete with church pews and a balcony dedicated as a Confederate memorial, the historic Ryman Auditorium.[118]

In 1926 announcer George D. Hay gave the WSM Barn Dance its present title of Grand Ole Opry. The program, then three hours long, followed NBC's Musical Appreciation Hour, conducted by Dr. Walter Damrosch. While introducing a number on one of his evening programs, Dr. Damrosch remarked that "while most artists realize that there is no place in the classics for realism, I am going to break one of my rules and present a composition by a young composer from Iowa. This young man has sent us his latest number, which depicts the onrush of a locomotive . . ." When the WSM country-music show came on the air, Hay announced that while there was no room for realism in the classics, the following three hours would be devoted to nothing but realism. Then in an obvious, good-natured jibe at Dr. Damrosch, Hay introduced Deford Bailey, a Negro harmonica player, who played a country version of a train song, "Pan American Blues." When the performance was over, Hay said that "For the past hour we have been listening to music taken largely from grand opera, but from now on we will present 'The Grand Ole Opry.' "[119] The name proved to be popular with the listeners, and came to be the official title of the show.

The popularity earned by the Grand Ole Opry was only one facet of the general popularity being garnered by country music at the beginning of the 1930's. The music gave every indication of being a potentially lucrative entertainment venture, and its followers numbered into the millions. The popularity of the barn-dance shows presaged country music's coming commercial success.

[117] McDaniel and Seligman, *Grand Ole Opry*, pp. 21–24.
[118] Hay, *A Story of the Grand Ole Opry*, p. 13.
[119] *Ibid.*, pp. 9–10.

CHAPTER 3

The Emergence of the First Country Singing Star: Jimmie Rodgers

THAT COUNTRY MUSIC took on a more commercial, star-oriented development and lost much of its southeastern-based attributes is largely the legacy of Jimmie Rodgers. One of the top Victor record sellers of the 1920's and the "father of modern country music," Rodgers introduced novel techniques and styles to the music and created a legion of followers who strove to emulate the master. By doing this, he provided a spark to the industry, and launched it on a course that emphasized the individual singing star. In his repertory of 111 recorded songs,[1] Jimmie Rodgers exhibited his debt to the diverse strains that made up the South's musical culture. He recorded almost every type of song with which the rural southerner was familiar. Rodgers, however, introduced a new form to commercial hillbilly music, one that was a product of his native environment. This was the "blue yodel."

"Blues" music antedated Jimmie Rodgers by many years[2] and the yodel had existed for generations, but he was the first to merge the two forms into a unique musical expression. Before Rodgers' com-

[1] A complete listing can be found in John Greenway, "Folk Song Discography," *Western Folklore*, XXI, No. 1 (January, 1962), 73–74.

[2] The blues had been commercially recorded, however, only since 1920. Paul Oliver, "Blues to Drive the Blues Away," in *Jazz*, edited by Nat Hentoff and Albert J. McCarthy, p. 86.

mercial career, the Negro blues had come to be a part of American popular music and was well-known all over the United States. When Ralph Peer, in the employment of Okeh Records, recorded a Negro blues singer, Mamie Smith, he generated a boom for blues music. Negro blues records sold widely among both whites and Negroes, and Mamie Smith's success inspired many others to record such numbers. The early blues recordings, however, were songs of urban origin, and some of the most popular were imitations produced by white composers. Eventually, the phonograph companies realized that the bulk of the blues-buying population was made up of America's Negro population, and this new-found audience preferred to hear renditions by its own members. As a result of World War I, thousands of Negroes in search of defense work had migrated to northern cities, where they constituted a new buying public. These people, along with the steadily expanding rural buying public reached by the mail-order companies, yearned to hear the authentic blues creations of their own race. Increasingly, the phonograph companies turned their attention toward the rural blues of the South, for it was here that the folk blues could be found at its source.[3]

In its most well-defined and distinct phase, the blues form developed in the period between 1885 and World War I and in fact paralleled and derived from the hardening of racial segregation in the South. But the emotions and styles that characterized the blues had been part of Negro musical life since the day the first Negro was brought to American soil. Developing out of the old worksongs and spirituals, the blues came to be the expression of the Negro's outlook on life. Arising out of poverty, oppression, and the numerous miseries and injustices which the Negro experienced, the blues had taken on a fairly established form by 1920.[4] Although it originally resembled the spirituals and ballads in its basic bar structure, the folk blues came more and more to take the pattern of twelve-bar stanzas of three lines each. In this form the repetition of the first line gives the singer an opportunity to extemporize the third line in any manner he chooses.[5] Long before any record company decided to exploit coun-

---

[3] Samuel Charters, *The Country Blues*, pp. 46–48.
[4] Jerry Silverman, *Folk Blues: One Hundred and Ten American Folk Blues*, pp. 4–5.
[5] Paul Oliver, *Blues Fell This Morning*, p. 6.

try-blues material, Negro blues singers were performing and perfecting their varied arts all over the South. Street singers, blues
shouters, and string and jug bands could be found anywhere that
Negroes congregated, and the music performed was as diverse as the
southern environment which nourished it.

The secular music produced by rural southern Negroes became
known as the "country blues," and it laid the basis for modern race
or rhythm-and-blues music and underlies, in fact, the whole con-
geries of modern popular music ranging from rock-and-roll and folk
rock to England's Mersey Beat. The country-blues performers, many
of whom have been reintroduced to contemporary America through
the valuable albums produced by the Origin Jazz Library,[6] were a
primitive and uninhibited breed of musicians who produced a music
that was vigorous and refreshingly frank in its lyrical and textural
structure. Equally important as the deeply expressive lyrics of the
country blues was the intricate and unorthodox instrumentation of
its performers. In the country blues the guitar was much more than
a simple accompanying instrument. It was, in effect, a second voice,
a device used to heighten the general effect of a song through its
intricate and often dominant interplay with the singer's voice. The
guitar was often used to imitate the flattenings and shadings that the
singers achieved with their voices. This instrumental effect could be
achieved by sliding the fingers or some hard object such as a bottle
or pocket knife down the strings, or by using diminished chords or
"blue notes."[7]

The gallery of Negro country-blues performers of the 1920's is as
rich and varied as that of white country music. Through the loving
dedication and persistence of blues collectors, such as those associated with the Origin Jazz Library, the story of these important Negro
folk musicians is gradually being revealed to the American public.
Sam Collins, Furry Lewis, James "Rabbit" Brown, "Sleepy John"
Estes, Willie Johnson, "Ragtime Texas" Henry Thomas, and of course,
the almost legendary figures of Huddie "Leadbelly" Ledbetter, Mississippi John Hurt, and Blind Lemon Jefferson are only a few of the

---

[6] The Origin Jazz Library, previously mentioned in Chapter 2, is based in
Berkeley, California.

[7] Paul Oliver, "Blues to Drive the Blues Away," *Jazz*, edited by Hentoff and
McCarthy, pp. 87–88.

talented Negro performers who have enriched American culture and contributed to the broadening of American popular music.[8]

Blind Lemon Jefferson, who performed most extensively in the area ranging from Marlin to Dallas, Texas, was one of many blind country performers, both Negro and white, who entertained in amateur or professional capacities in the South during the twenties and thirties. Recording for Paramount Records, Jefferson performed in a remarkably free manner employing a vocal style suggestive of field shouts and a guitar technique that was among the most intricate of the early commercial period. It is a tribute to his greatness that many of the later blues performers claimed to have learned their techniques from him. In fact, both Huddie Ledbetter and modern blues-guitarist Josh White claimed to have served as "lead men" for the blind singer for short intervals during their youth.[9]

Negro country-blues performers could not have helped but influence white hillbilly musicians in both song content and performance. This influence was exerted by both the commercial performers like Lemon Jefferson and the countless amateurs who made no money from their performances. The influence of the amateurs was strongest, of course, in areas where Negro population was most concentrated: in the black-belt areas of the deep South and in the Mississippi delta region. Anywhere that Negroes and whites mingled, especially on work projects, an excellent opportunity existed for cultural borrowing or transmission.

To assess accurately the influence of Negro blues music on white country music is difficult, because the conditioning attitudes which produced the "blues" form had existed among white country people for many generations. The loneliness and arduousness of rural life combined with the other-worldly vision of southern religion to produce a spirit that was often melancholy and fraught with self-pity. The somber old ballads and "lonesome tunes" of the pioneer period can be pictured as "blues expressions." The Elizabethans, in fact,

[8] The most useful approach to the early country-blues performers is through reissued recordings such as those released by the Origin Jazz Library and the Folkways Company. An interesting profile of one of the most important blues entertainers is Lawrence Cohn, "Mississippi John Hurt," *Sing Out: The Folk Song Magazine*, XIV, No. 5 (November, 1964), 16–21.

[9] Silverman, *Folk Blues*, pp. 5–7. Blind Lemon Jefferson can be heard on *Blind Lemon Jefferson*, Riverside RLP 12–136.

had described melancholy as "the blue devils."[10] The southern whites evidently borrowed the Negro blues pattern to express their deep-seated feelings of loneliness and alienation.

Jerry Silverman has described the white blues as a hybrid type of song: the product of the mingling of the Negro blues, the southern mountain ballad, and the cowboy song.[11] This statement is suggestive of the acculturative process that took place in the rural South, although it is doubtful that the cowboy song had an appreciable effect upon the formation of white blues or any other type of country song. The white blues was often composed of three-line stanzas, as was its Negro counterpart, but the white blues was characterized, according to Silverman, by "the steady, rhythmic accompaniment of the Southern mountain ballad, and the long-held-often yodeled notes of the cowboy song."[12] The preceding statement is correct if one substitutes "rural" for "mountain," and "Swiss-influenced" or "indigenous-country" for "cowboy." Since the rural white blues was probably of ancient origin, it is doubtful that this origin was either mountain or cowboy. More likely it was of a general southern origin, emerging from the flatland regions of the South and strongly influenced by Negro music.

The white country singer most influenced by Negro music, and the one who perfected the white blues pattern, was Jimmie Rodgers. James Charles Rodgers was born in Meridian, Mississippi, on September 8, 1897, the son of Eliza Bozeman Rodgers and Aaron W. Rodgers, an extra gang foreman on the Mobile and Ohio Railroad.[13] His mother, who came from the rural Pine Springs Community just north of Meridian, died when he was only four years old, and his father was left with the sole responsibility of rearing him to manhood. The young Rodgers had only an occasional encounter with formal schooling and learned what he knew in the "school of hard

[10] Alan Lomax, *Folk Songs of North America*, p. 576.

[11] Silverman, *Folk Blues*, p. 24.

[12] *Ibid.*

[13] Biographical information on Jimmie Rodgers was obtained from a series of interviews in Meridian, Mississippi, August 23–25, 1966. These included talks with Jimmie Rodgers' aunt, Mrs. Pearl Rodgers; his step-brother, Jake Smith; and his sister-in-law, Mrs. Elsie McWilliams. An additionally useful interview was held on August 25, 1966, with Rodgers' half sister, Mrs. Lottie Mixon, in York, Alabama. The only full-length study of Rodgers, useful though highly romanticized, is Mrs. Jimmie Rodgers, *My Husband, Jimmie Rodgers*.

knocks," while following his father from place to place as he pursued his railroad duties. Aaron Rodgers' work as an extra gang foreman took him for extended periods to different cities in the South, including New Orleans, because it was the duty of the extra gang to travel by railroad car to those sections of the line that needed repairing. In this manner Jimmie Rodgers perhaps gained a broader knowledge of life's varieties—both the exciting and the sordid—than did the typical small-town southern boy.

Before he decided upon a professional entertainment career, Jimmie Rodgers was subjected to almost every conceivable type of musical influence that the South possessed, with the possible exception of gospel music, since he was never known to be a religious or church-going person. One of the most important sources of his songs and styles was the rich musical repertory of the Negro railroad workers who traveled on the extra gang. Mrs. Pearl Rodgers, the widow of Jimmie's oldest brother Talmadge (a long-time Meridian city policeman) remembers that, at the age of fourteen, Jimmie and a young friend named Mike Murphy began carrying water for the railroad workers in the Meridian railroad yards. It was in this capacity that he learned songs and fragments of songs from the Negro workers, who also taught him to play the banjo and guitar.[14]

Rodgers retired from railroad work after fourteen years, when tuberculosis sapped him of the strength necessary for a rigorous, outdoor existence. During his railroad career he worked on lines all over the Southwest, usually as a flagman or brakeman, but the line he worked most was the New Orleans and Northeastern on the run between Meridian and New Orleans.[15] Rodgers became thoroughly conversant with the vocabulary and music of the railroad workers, a hardy race of men that he was later to commemorate so well in his best-selling Victor records.

Although Rodgers had been fond of music since childhood, he made no serious efforts to build a professional career until tuberculosis forced his railroad retirement at the age of twenty-eight. He had learned to play the guitar and banjo at a very early age and often

14 Interview with Pearl Rodgers, Meridian, Mississippi, August 23, 1966.

15 Railroad influence in the life and career of Jimmie Rodgers has been discussed in Silverman, Folk Blues, pp. 9–10; and in John Greenway, "Jimmie Rodgers—A Folksong Catalyst," Journal of American Folklore, LXX, No. 277 (July–September, 1957), p. 232.

entertained his fellow workers during lunch and rest breaks. In his off hours he occasionally played with Negro musicians down around Tenth Street in Meridian or for his favorite southern belles, who would gather in their well-chaperoned parlors to hear him play.[16] His closest approach to a musical career before he left the railroad in 1925 was his membership in a small combo that played dance music at fairs, picnics, political rallies, and other functions in and around Meridian in the early twenties. Rodgers played rhythm guitar, and occasionally the banjo, in a group that featured the violin, played by a man named Rozell, and a grand piano, played by Rodgers' sister-in-law Elsie McWilliams. Rodgers did not sing at all, and the music performed was exclusively of the waltz and popular dance variety.[17] This brief musical interlude provided him with a touch of the show-business experience that would later prove to be invaluable, and it also introduced him to a repertory of pop music that would one day appear with great frequency in his hillbilly-oriented recordings.

Rodgers decided upon a full-fledged professional career in 1925 when he signed on as a blackface entertainer with a medicine show that toured the mountain and hill-country districts of the upper South. This type of show-business experience—shared by so many other big-time country stars—helped to give him ease and confidence in front of audiences and further kindled his desire for stardom as he heard the people applaud and saw their delighted faces. After spending a brief period on the medicine-show circuit, he and his wife Carrie—whom he married in 1920—moved to the mountain resort city of Asheville, North Carolina, in search of a more healthful climate and of outlets for his entertainment ambitions. In Asheville he organized the Jimmie Rodgers Entertainers, a small group composed of Jack Pierce and the Grant Brothers (Jack and Claude), whom Rodgers called his "hillbilly ork."[18] He performed on Station WWNC in Asheville in early 1927, singing both popular and country music, but, although his performances seemed to be popular with the lis-

[16] Interview with Mrs. Claudia Rigby Vick, Meridian, Mississippi, August 23, 1966.

[17] Interview with Mrs. Elsie McWilliams, Meridian, Mississippi, August 24, 1966.

[18] Letter to the author from Bob Pinson, Santa Clara, California, September 4, 1966.

tening audiences, the station canceled his contract after a few weeks. Despairing now of his chances of ever achieving stardom, Rodgers went to work as a city detective. He worked as a detective and performed locally until Ralph Peer came south on one of his recording ventures in late July, 1927.[19]

By 1927 Peer had left Okeh Records and had gone into business for himself as a music publisher. He arranged a business association with Victor Talking Machine Company in which he selected artists and supervised hillbilly recordings for Victor. In return, Peer's publishing firm owned the copyrights, and he was compensated by the royalties resulting from the compositions which he had selected for recording. Under this new arrangement he made a survey of various southern cities and decided to make initial recordings for Victor in Atlanta, Savannah, Memphis, and Bristol, which sits directly astride the Virginia and Tennessee border. Although the statement is open to question, Peer claims that he ran a column on the front page of the Bristol newspaper advertising his search for talent.[20] Whatever the advertising techniques he used, they proved to be very successful. In the words of Peer, "This worked like dynamite and the very next day I was deluged with long-distance calls from the surrounding mountain region. Groups of singers who had not visited Bristol during their entire lifetime arrived by bus, horse and buggy, trains, or on foot."[21]

One of those singers who made a hopeful long-distance call was Jimmie Rodgers, who came down from Asheville, North Carolina, with his little "hillbilly ork." And in one of the most interesting coincidences of country-music history, the Carter Family journeyed to Bristol from Maces Spring, Virginia, for their initial recording venture. If there had been some doubt about it earlier, Victor—with the chance recording of these important groups—vaulted into the lead in the recording of hillbilly talent. After reaching Bristol, Rodgers was

[19] This period of Rodgers' life is more fully related in *My Husband, Jimmie Rodgers*, pp. 55–95.

[20] Ed Kahn says that, in his extensive research on Ralph Peer and the Carter Family, he has been unable to find corroboration for the stories about Peer's newspaper advertising prior to the Bristol trip (letter from Ed Kahn, Los Angeles, California, February 1, 1967).

[21] Ralph Peer, "Discovery of the First Hillbilly Great," *Billboard*, LXV, No. 20 (May 16, 1953), 20.

disappointed to learn that the Jimmie Rodgers Entertainers had decided to try their luck at recording without him. Inspired probably by Bristol's unique location on the border line of two states, Jack Pierce and the Grant Brothers reconstituted themselves as the Tenneva Ramblers and made a number of important recordings, including an interesting variant of "In the Pines" called "The Longest Train."[22] Rodgers' personal audition was held in an abandoned warehouse that had not been used for years.[23] Since he no longer had a string band to accompany him, Rodgers nervously sang his selections solo fashion for Peer and accompanied himself on the guitar.

In his Asheville performances, Rodgers' song material had usually been the current hits, the compositions of New York publishers. But in his first recording session he chose two deeply sentimental country tunes for his first renditions. Recorded on Victor 20864, these were his reworking of an old ballad, "The Soldier's Sweetheart,"[24] and an old lullaby which he had revised, "Sleep, Baby, Sleep." These song choices reveal Rodgers' deep involvement in the rural southern tradition and should be a corrective to those who picture him exclusively as a blues singer. He yodeled on "Sleep, Baby, Sleep" and inaugurated a trend that was to continue in country music for at least a decade. These initial recordings were among the first of the electrical recordings and proved to be the beginning of the most influential career in the history of country music.[25]

Rodgers' first quarterly royalty check reached the discouraging total of twenty-seven dollars, and his life and his career continued briefly to be unpromising. By the end of 1927, however, his popularity had begun to mount, and the Victor executives realized that they had signed a potential star. Rodgers was soon granted another recording session, this time at the Victor studios in Camden, New Jersey. Armed with some of his own compositions and at least nine songs

[22] Letter to the author from Bob Pinson, September 4, 1966.

[23] Peer, "Discovery of the First Hillbilly Great," *Billboard*, LXV, No. 20 (May 16, 1953), 20.

[24] "The Soldier's Sweetheart" is usually attributed to Rodgers, although Vance Randolph has collected Ozark variants (which he calls "Once I Had a Sweetheart") which mention the Spanish-American War *Ozark Folksongs*, IV, 310.

[25] Both selections can be heard on recently-issued Victor Memorial albums: "Sleep, Baby, Sleep" on *Jimmie the Kid*, Victor LPM-2213; and "Soldier's Sweetheart" on *Country Music Hall of Fame*, Victor LPM-2531.

written by Elsie McWilliams, who accompanied him on his Camden trip, Rodgers journeyed to the historic New Jersey session that would catapult him to recording fame.[26] At the Camden session the first blue yodel, "T for Texas," was recorded.[27] this was the first of twelve such recordings by Rodgers, and it caught the imagination of the American people. In its structure it resembled the typical blues form, but at the conclusion of the third line, Rodgers raised his voice to a higher octave and uttered the blue yodel that made him the most famous hillbilly star in history.[28]

From 1927 until 1933 Jimmie Rodgers became a household name in thousands of rural and small-town American homes, particularly in his native Southland. His recording popularity was augmented by vaudeville and tent-show appearances and by radio performances throughout the southern region. Rodgers' barnstorming potentiality was greatly hindered by his affliction with tuberculosis, the grim disease which curtailed his activities and forced him to seek a permanent home in the drier regions of central Texas. About this affliction he wrote a song of ridicule, "The T. B. Blues" (Victor 23535).[29]

Jimmie Rodgers gained little immediate popularity north of the Mason-Dixon Line. In fact, he made no tours in the northern United States. Ralph Peer planned such a tour for Rodgers on the RKO circuit in which he was to appear as a single act in most of the leading vaudeville theaters at a salary of $1,000 a week, but the tour was canceled after an intensification of Rodgers' disease.[30] Rodgers, therefore, restricted himself to performances in the South, particularly in the Southwest, where he made his home during the last years of his life. He appeared in southern vaudeville theaters during 1928; the most important of these theaters were on the Loew circuit. When he completed his tour of the circuit in December, he joined a tent repertoire show, The Paul English Players, working out of Mobile, Ala-

[26] Interview with Mrs. Elsie McWilliams, August 24, 1966.

[27] My Husband, Jimmie Rodgers, pp. 151–153. "T for Texas" ("Blue Yodel No. 1") was recorded on Victor 21142.

[28] According to Mrs. Rodgers, her husband had been performing the song for quite a long time before he recorded it; it had proved to be popular with his radio fans in Asheville (My Husband, Jimmie Rodgers, p. 109).

[29] Issued on Country Music Hall of Fame, Victor LPM-2531.

[30] Peer, "Discovery of the First Hillbilly Great," Billboard, LXV, No. 20 (May 16, 1953), 21.

bama. The employment of a "name attraction" for limited engagements was said to be something new in the tent repertoire line, and the appearance of Rodgers doubled the company's business.[31] Rodgers remained with the English Players until March, 1929, and traveled with them from Mobile, Alabama, to Texas. Working only as a concert feature, about fifteen to twenty minutes a night, he earned $600 a week. His performances greatly increased the company's receipts and stimulated the sale of Victor records, since the show had tieups with Victor dealers in all of the towns visited.[32]

In the following years Rodgers made occasional solo performances, usually in lodge halls, schoolhouses, auditoriums, and occasionally on radio, and traveled with assorted tent-show groups similar to the Paul English organization. His sporadic appearances with these groups depended on the state of his health or on the necessity for recording trips to such cities as Atlanta, Dallas, or New York. With each show Rodgers usually was considered to be the major attraction. During the spring and summer of 1930 he traveled with the W. I. Swain show, Hollywood Follies, through Louisiana and Texas. The show carried a number of acts, including an Irish comedian, a Hawaiian group, and a blues singer, but according to *Billboard* Jimmie Rodgers was "the outstanding hit of the show." The Swain show drew capacity crowds during its one-night stands in Texas, but when the company moved into Kansas and Oklahoma business declined considerably. The decline was attributed to Rodgers' being unknown in that area. As a result, he was replaced by movie comedian Ben Turpin.[33]

During the last few years of his life Rodgers made most of his appearances in Texas. At Kerrville, in the heart of the Texas hill country, he built in May, 1929, a $50,000 mansion, "Blue Yodeler's Paradise." He lived there with his wife Carrie and daughter Anita until mounting medical costs and luxurious living necessitated the sale of the house. Thereafter, until his death in 1933, he and his family lived in a much more modest cottage in San Antonio.[34]

In the spring of 1931 he and Will Rogers conducted a benefit tour

[31] *Billboard,* XL, No. 52 (December 29, 1928), 30.

[32] *Ibid.,* XLI, No. 7 (February 16, 1929), 3.

[33] *Ibid.,* XLII, No. 14 (April 5, 1930), 30; *ibid.,* No. 19 (May 10, 1930), 30; *ibid.,* No. 29 (July 19, 1930), 30.

[34] Mrs. Jimmie Rodgers, *My Husband, Jimmie Rodgers,* 211–212, 244–245.

in northeast Texas for the victims of a recent Red River flood. The pair also gave a number of charity performances throughout the Southwest for the unemployed.[35] In March of that year he journeyed to Austin, where he was appointed an honorary Texas Ranger;[36] he took great pride in this honor, and eventually composed a song called "The Yodeling Ranger." When the Texas Rotary Club held its statewide meeting in Austin in March, 1931, Rodgers appeared as the featured attraction. Upon receiving an invitation from the chairman of the program committee, Adjutant General W. W. Sterling, Rodgers responded with these words: "I am ready and happy to obey any order from my superior officer." The audience gave his performance an enthusiastic reception, and at the conclusion he presented Ranger chief Sterling with one of his fabulous Weyman guitars, worth an estimated $1,500.[37]

The last year and a half of Rodgers' life was filled with recording dates, radio shows, appearances with tent theaters, costly medical treatments, and never realized plans for nationwide tours. During the winter of 1931–1932 he appeared with Leslie E. Kell's tent theater company in an extended engagement in Houston and a shorter one in San Antonio. The Kell Company was a variety show which featured, in addition to Rodgers, a fan dancer named Holly Desmond.[38]

Rodgers and Kell made elaborate plans for an extensive tour which would carry them through the Northwest, British Columbia, eastward through Canada to New York, and finally back to Texas.[39] The plan was never completed, however, because Rodgers left Kell in March, 1932, with the intention of joining the J. Doug Morgan show for its spring and summer tent tour.[40] The affiliation with Morgan was never consummated, for Rodgers remained in San Antonio because of his health and became a twice-weekly feature over Station KMAC, with studios in the Blue Bonnet Hotel.[41] Here he remained

---

[35] *Billboard*, XLIII, No. 7 (February 14, 1931), 26.

[36] *Ibid.*, No. 11 (March 14, 1931), 24.

[37] William W. Sterling, *Trails and Trials of a Texas Ranger*, pp. 189–191.

[38] Houston *Post-Dispatch*, December 20, 24, 1931, and January 1, 1932. *Billboard*, XLIV, No. 3 (January 16, 1932), 24; *ibid.*, No. 4 (January 23, 1932), 22; *ibid.*, No. 6 (February 6, 1932), 22.

[39] *Ibid.*, No. 3 (January 16, 1932), 24.

[40] *Ibid.*, No. 13 (March 26, 1932), 42.

[41] *Ibid.*, No. 42 (October 15, 1932), 22.

until an intensification of his disease necessitated his entry into the Baptist Hospital in Houston in January, 1933. He remained in the Houston hospital for about a month, charming the nurses and keeping Mickey, his Boston Terrier, beside his bed despite the hospital restrictions banning dogs. He returned to San Antonio in February, 1933, partially recuperated and with orders to remain in the Alamo City for at least a six-month rest.[42] But, despite the doctors' orders and despite a prediction made two years earlier by Dr. I. W. Cooper that he could not live longer than two years,[43] Rodgers decided to make a recording trip to New York in May, 1933, knowing probably that it would be his last.

His last recording session is one of the most heart-rending episodes in show-business history. His condition had become so weakened that the Victor Company provided him a special cot in the studio. At the conclusion of each recorded number, he would lie down until he regained adequate strength for another performance. He recorded almost to the very end; his last session was on May 24, two days before he succumbed in the Taft Hotel.[44] On the day of his death he went to Coney Island on a sight-seeing tour with his private nurse, and while there suffered an attack of spasms. He died that night in his hotel room, far from his native Mississippi and from his beloved family.[45] When his death train pulled into Meridian, Mississippi, late at night, the engineer, Homer Jenkins, blew the whistle in a long moaning wail that grew in intensity as the train rolled toward the terminal station. This was the train crew's tribute to the "Singing Brakeman" who now lay in a coffin in one of the baggage cars.[46]

In assessing Jimmie Rodgers' influence on American folk music and on a later generation of commercial performers, one can safely use the adjective "phenomenal." Indeed, one would be hard pressed to find a performer in the whole broad field of "pop" music—whether it be Al Jolson, Bing Crosby, or Frank Sinatra—who has exerted a more profound and recognizable influence on later generations of

[42] Interview with Mrs. Lottie Mixon, York, Alabama, August 25, 1966.

[43] Interview with Mr. Nate Williamson (Jimmie Rodgers' brother-in-law and personal lawyer), Meridian, Mississippi, August 23, 1966.

[44] *Train Whistle Blues: the Legendary Jimmie Rodgers*, RCA Victor LPM-1640 (notes by Jim Evans).

[45] Interview with Mrs. Lottie Mixon, August 25, 1966.

[46] Mrs. Jimmie Rodgers, *My Husband, Jimmie Rodgers*, p. 261.

entertainers. No one as yet has made a full-scale attempt to determine how many of his songs have been accepted by the folk or gone into oral tradition, and there is no way to measure the number of people, amateur and professional, who have been inspired by him to take up the guitar or try their luck at singing. Rodgers singlehandedly originated a new tradition in country music and stimulated legions of his followers—most of whom heard him only on records—to become country musicians. The center of country-music activity shifted more heavily toward the Southwest, and a new generation of hillbilly entertainers, captivated by Rodgers' blue-yodel techniques, began to dominate the country-music scene. The new group of performers arising in the late twenties and early thirties would have repertories of a less traditional character and would perform them in styles that were often direct imitations of Jimmie Rodgers. Ernest Tubb, a Rodgers-worshiper and present-day country music great, estimated that perhaps 75 per cent of modern country-music performers were directly or indirectly influenced to become entertainers either through hearing Rodgers in person or through his recordings.[47] Rodgers' popularity and influence, moreover, were not confined to this country. His records sold widely in various parts of the British Empire, and John Greenway found that in Australia "all contemporary country singing is clearly attributable to Rodgers' compositions, themes and styles." Greenway found, too, that Rodgers' popularity reached beyond the confines of the English-speaking world—one of his correspondents reported seeing a large collection of the "Blue Yodeler's" records in an Eskimo's hut near Point Barrow.[48]

No other hillbilly star of the twenties rivaled Rodgers in popularity. He was one of the few country performers to receive any notice in the major trade publications, and his records, which sold more widely than those of any other hillbilly star, exceeded the sales of most pop performers in the Victor catalogue. When he died in 1933 an estimated twenty million of his records had been sold and he was earning well over $100,000 a year.[49] His earnings were quickly ex-

[47] Interview with Ernest Tubb, Austin, Texas, March 24, 1962.

[48] John Greenway, "Folk Song Discography," *Western Folklore*, XXI, No. 1 (January, 1962), 71–72.

[49] Any figure on record sales is, of course, an estimate. But Mrs. Rodgers

hausted, however, through his penchant for extravagant living and because of mounting medical costs. His commercial popularity is amazing considering his chronic physical incapacity and the fact that his personal appearances were limited to the southern United States during the depression years. Rodgers occasionally had professional managers, such as Ray McCreath of WTFF in Washington, D.C., and Paul Dempsey of the Herbert Hoey office in New York, but on the whole he did not benefit from modern promotional techniques.[50] In fact, for his personal appearances in Houston, newspaper accounts gave simply his name (always misspelled as Rogers), listing him as a "Victor Recording Artist."[51] Perhaps in a southern territory no other advertisement was needed.

Any discussion of Jimmie Rodgers' remarkable popularity would be incomplete without at least some attempt to analyze his distinctive style and personality. His success came largely through his own personal and individualistic approach to both his songs and audiences. Although he recorded with a diverse assortment of instrumental accompaniment—violins, banjoes, ukeleles, Hawaiian steel guitars, and Dixieland jazz bands—his personal appearances were almost always made in solo fashion, just Jimmie and his guitar. For his stage appearances he generally dressed in a white or tan light-weight suit and sported a jauntily cocked straw sailor hat. (He often posed for publicity pictures in a cowboy uniform or railroad brakeman's attire, but seldom dressed this way during a performance). He looked and acted the part of a young man-about-town out for an evening of pleasure. He would put his foot in a chair, cradle his guitar across his knee, and captivate his audiences with a selection of both rakish and sentimental tunes that generally consumed no more than twenty minutes. In a voice unmistakably southern, he kidded his audiences in a whimsical fashion and beguiled them with songs that seemed to catalogue the varied memories, yearnings, and experiences of small-town and rural Americans: nostalgia for the departed mother or "the old southern town" of childhood; pathos for the homeless hobo dying

---

claimed that the "blue yodeler" received an average of two thousand dollars a month in royalties (*My Husband, Jimmie Rodgers*, p. 178).

[50] *Billboard*, XLIV, No. 36 (September 3, 1932), 9.
[51] Houston *Post-Dispatch*, December 20, 1931; December 24, 1931.

in a boxcar or trying to bum a South-bound freight; unrequited memories of the sweetheart who proved unfaithful; laughter for the rakes and rogues who "loved and left them" in every town; and a variety of other experiences with which most people could identify.

As he sang and recorded he kidded both himself and his accompanying musicians with a running patter of commentary. As an accompanist took an instrumental break, Rodgers would occasionally say something like "play that thing, boy," or he would say to himself or no one in particular, "sing them blues, boy," "hey, hey, it won't be long now," or "hey, sweet mama." The total effect of his performances was an air of effortless informality, marked by a very personal approach which insinuated its way into the hearts of listeners, making them feel that the song was meant just for them. His voice—a nasal tenor distinguished by the lazy drawl of the Mississippi black belt—was capable of adjusting itself to almost every kind of song, a spirited railroad song, a rollicking blues number, or a tender, plaintive lullaby. He sang them all with sincerity and in the particular spirit in which they were written. When his audiences of railroad workers, truck drivers, laborers, farmers, and small-town people heard his songs, they recognized him as one of their own and the deadening, bleak years of the depression were thereby made more endurable.

Rodgers' influence on folk music, or the noncommercial music world, is incalculable. The people who bought his records were those normally considered to be the "folk" or people who were strongly imbued with the folk tradition. They heard his songs, accepted them, and eventually gave them back to folklorists who traveled through the South in search of materials. Rodgers' songs can be found listed in the Library of Congress checklists and in the published compilations of a number of folklorists.[52] Among the folklorists, however, only Vance Randolph mentions Rodgers' name. He misspells it, and refers to the "Blue Yodeler" simply as a "popular radio entertainer in the 1930's."[53] Perhaps the other folklorists believed that anonymity lent authenticity to the songs they were presenting, or perhaps they had never heard of Jimmie Rodgers.

In recent years folklorists have become increasingly aware of

[52] These compilations are listed in Greenway, "Jimmie Rodgers—A Folksong Catalyst," *Journal of American Folklore,* LXX, No. 277 (July–September, 1957), 233.

[53] Randolph, *Ozark Folksongs,* IV, 310.

Jimmie Rodgers' influence on American folk music. Although folk-lorists had been unknowingly collecting Rodgers' material for a number of years, the first scholarly investigation of him did not come until the publication of John Greenway's *Journal of American Folk-lore* article.[54] Greenway was interested primarily in Rodgers' blues material, and referred to Rodgers as a "folk catalyst" who preserved the fragmentary, ephemeral phrases of the Negro folksinger" and molded them into a fixed form. In doing so, "Jimmie Rodgers gave us an opportunity to see how folksong evolved through the ages."[55]

Rodgers' blues songs actually were a minority element in his re-corded repertory, but they attracted more interest than his other renditions. Rodgers worked as a railroadman at the very time when the blues form was originating, and, as a waterboy for Negro con-struction groups, he accumulated maverick blues fragments and work-song stanzas and later incorporated them into his own songs.[56] They might perhaps have vanished had he not done so.

In commercial performances of his blues songs, Rodgers height-ened the effect of the numbers by his individualistic guitar technique, also of Negro origin, and by the employment of his famous blue yodel, uttered usually at the end of each stanza. Yodelers had been commercially recorded before Rodgers. Riley Puckett, in fact, had recorded a song complete with yodel as early as 1924,[57] but nothing corresponding exactly to the blue-yodel song had been collected in American folklore.[58] The blue yodel is Rodgers' unique contribution to American folksong, but the origin of the form is unknown and lends itself to a great deal of speculation. In the nineteenth century, Swiss groups, touring through the Midwest, popularized their brand of yodeling, and their styles were copied later by some American popular singers. Alan Lomax maintains that Rodgers' yodel was di-rectly inspired by the Swiss style, and by that alone.[59] This expla-

---

[54] Greenway, "Jimmie Rodgers—A Folksong Catalyst," *Journal of American Folklore*, LXX, No. 277 (July–September, 1957), 233.

[55] *Ibid.*, p. 232.

[56] For example, see "Blue Yodel No. 8" ("Mule Skinner Blues") Victor 23503, with the lines "Hey little waterboy, bring that water around . . ."

[57] Riley Puckett, "Rock All Our Babies to Sleep," Columbia 107-D.

[58] Greenway, "Jimmie Rodgers—A Folksong Catalyst," *Journal of American Folklore*, LXX, No. 277 (July–September, 1957), 233.

[59] Alan Lomax, *The Folk Songs of North America*, p. 281.

nation seems too simple, however, for Rodgers' yodel was unlike the Swiss model. His was more of a wail or moan which was used to intensify the mood being expressed in his song. Perhaps partially influenced by the Swiss style, Rodgers' yodel was his own unique creation, produced by factors in his native environment. As in the case of the blues form, Negro influence again may have been a contributory factor, particularly through the field hollers and the work shouts.[60] Or perhaps the yodel may have ventured into the South through the influence of Mexican song, characterized by shouts and wails which were similar to the hillbilly yodel. The blue yodel, too, may originally have been carried into the lower South by cowboys returning to their southern homes from brief employment on the ranges of the West.[61]

At any rate, regardless of its origin, Jimmie Rodgers fashioned the blue yodel into a distinct form which captivated his listeners and stimulated a new generation of hillbilly performers. As Alan Lomax has said, "Jimmy's [sic] yodeling songs sounded as if they might have been composed by a lonesome Texas cowboy or a hobo kicked off a freight in Tucson or Albuquerque."[62] Rodgers' yodels expressed a variety of emotions, ranging from the nostalgic moan of "Daddy and Home," to the blue-lament of "Never No Mo' Blues," and the spritely yodel of "My Little Lady."

The popularity of the Rodgers yodel and of his blues renditions should not obscure the fact of his multi-faceted repertory. He recorded almost every conceivable type of song—serious, humorous, maudlin, religious, risque, and rowdy. There were railroad songs such as "The Southern Cannonball" and "Waiting for a Train"; "rounder" tunes such as "Frankie and Johnny" and "My Rough and Rowdy Ways"; risque numbers such as "Pistol Packin' Papa"; lullabies such as "Sleep, Baby, Sleep"; "cowboy" songs such as "When the Cactus Is in Bloom"; hobo melodies such as "Hobo Bill's Last Ride"; and a large number of sentimental songs depicting semireligious,

[60] John Greenway suggested this possibility in his "Folk Song Discography," *Western Folklore*, XXI, No. 1 (January, 1962), 72.

[61] Mrs. Rodgers maintains that the blue yodels were first "flung out over the Texas plains" in the years before Rodgers' commercial career began, when the Rodgers family moved through the Southwest in quest of railroad employment (*My Husband, Jimmie Rodgers*, p. 92).

[62] Alan Lomax, *The Folk Songs of North America*, p. 281.

nostalgic, and romantic themes. Sentimental love tunes were quite popular in the twenties, and in his recording of such songs as "My Carolina Sunshine Girl" and "Old Pal of My Heart" Rodgers performed the same type of melody that his friend Gene Austin was recording for the popular-music audience. In fact, Jimmie Rodgers was the first person to record and publicly perform "The One Rose," a song which has gained its most lasting fame in popular music.[63] Jimmie Rodgers' own tastes ran toward such sentimental and melancholy tunes as "Daddy and Home,"[64] which evoked memories of "an old Southern town" and the only parent he had ever known. As further evidence of his preference for sentimental tunes, it is significant that he chose as his first recordings a tender lullaby, "Sleep, Baby, Sleep," and "Soldier's Sweetheart," which told of an old friend who died in "that awful German war." Rodgers' sentimental songs have had a more lasting effect on country entertainers than his other offerings.[65] Blue yodels, or songs similar to them, were performed for a few years after his death but are a rarity in country music today. His other songs, however, have made an enduring impression. Love songs are now predominant in country music, although the sentimental, nostalgic ballad—of the "Mississippi Moon" and "Carolina Sunshine Girl" variety—is rarely heard. Otis Dewey (Slim) Whitman is perhaps the chief exponent of the sentimental-ballad style still recording.[66]

Like many of the country performers who followed him, Rodgers —usually in conjunction with his sister-in-law, Mrs. Elsie McWilliams—wrote a large number of the songs he recorded. After the first Bristol recording session Rodgers felt a need for fresher song ma-

[63] "The One Rose" was written by Lani McIntyre, popular Hawaiian band leader, who backed Rodgers on some selections. It began, "You're the one rose that's left in my heart dear."

[64] "Daddy and Home" was recorded on Victor 21757, and can be heard on the memorial album *Never No Mo' Blues*, RCA Victor LPM-1232.

[65] John Greenway has made the unusual statement, however, that Rodgers' "miscellaneous and sentimental songs are of little interest to folklorists" (Greenway, "Jimmie Rodgers—A Folksong Catalyst," *Journal of American Folklore*, LXX, No. 277 (July–September, 1957), 232). It would seem, however, that folklorists should be interested in anything that the folk accept.

[66] Otis Dewey (Slim) Whitman is a popular country star of the modern period who has recorded for RCA Victor and Imperial. His most representative album, perhaps, is *Love Song of the Waterfall*, Imperial 9277.

terial, so he contacted Mrs. McWilliams, his wife Carrie's oldest sister, who was then teaching in a Meridian business college. Elsie McWilliams played the piano and had had musical training, and she already had acquired the reputation of local poet and songwriter with her writings for church and club periodicals. She accompanied her brother-in-law on some of his recording trips and wrote some of her most famous numbers in a hurried fashion in hotel rooms and recording studios. She wrote or helped to write thirty-eight songs recorded by Rodgers, some of which do not bear her name on the composer credits. These include the beautiful sentimental ballads "Sailor's Plea," "I'm Lonely and Blue," and "Mississippi Moon," and novelty tunes like "My Little Lady" and "Everybody Does it in Hawaii."[67] Mrs. McWilliams, however, was only one of several individuals who either wrote songs for Rodgers or collaborated on songs with him. The list includes Kelly Harrell ("Away Out on the Mountain"), Clayton McMichen ("Peach Picking Time in Georgia"), Shelly Lee Alley ("Traveling Blues"), Waldo O'Neal ("Hobo Bill's Last Ride"), and Carey D. Harvey ("Down the Old Road to Home"). The most famous of these composers, however, was Rev. Andrew Jenkins, of "Floyd Collins" fame, who wrote such songs as "The Drunkard's Child" and "Ben Dewberry's Final Run."

Jimmie Rodgers' popularity was not limited to his own lifetime; with the release of his reissued recordings, a new generation of Rodgers enthusiasts has arisen.[68] During his lifetime, however, Rodgers' popularity was most intensive in the Southwest, particularly in his adopted state of Texas. His Texas popularity can be attributed in part to his residence in that state and to his tours and radio broadcasts there. He became so closely identified with Texas that many people believed him to be a native, and even Alan Lomax has referred to him as a Texas brakeman.[69] Rodgers took great pride in the Texas heritage, especially its romantic cowboy past. He must be given much of the credit for starting the trend toward the "singing cowboy" and the association of country music with the romantic

[67] Interview with Mrs. Elsie McWilliams, August 24, 1966; a letter to the author from Mrs. McWilliams, April 4, 1962.

[68] Each of the Jimmie Rodgers long-play albums released by RCA Victor has sold in excess of thirty thousand copies within a year after its release (*Billboard Music Week*, LXXIII, No. 42 [October 30, 1961], 18).

[69] Alan Lomax, *The Folk Songs of North America*, p. 281.

"western" image. In the lyrics of his Texas songs Rodgers revealed a conception of the west typical of that held by many Easterners; that is, the depiction of the cowboy as a self-reliant, selfless individual, free from the shackles and restraints of society, who whiled away the lonely hours with song. This attitude was expressed in "The Yodeling Cowboy" by the following line: "My cowboy life is so happy and free, out where the law don't bother me." And again in "The Yodeling Ranger"[70] which described "that old ranger band" singing carefree songs as it rode into dangerous situations. The Rangers were no doubt a courageous group, but it is doubtful that any of them went into a dangerous situation in as lighthearted a manner as that described in the song. Indeed, if Rodgers' philosophy had been the accepted one of the Texas lawmen, "that old ranger band" might well have vanished.

Rodgers' reverential and romantic concept of the West was expressed in a variety of songs that were the progenitors of a spate of similar melodies during the next decade. In the thirties other phenomena, such as the Hollywood movie industry, further implanted the image of "the singing cowboy" in the minds of the American people, and "western" came to be the term used by many to denote country music. "Western," however, is just as erroneous or misleading as "mountain."[71]

Whatever the source of his popularity, Rodgers made a profound impression on many of the young country boys who heard him. Some of them went on to found country-music traditions of their own. Bill Bruner, a seventeen-year-old Western Union messenger boy in Meridian, Mississippi, substituted for Rodgers one night when the Blue Yodeler became too ill to fill an engagement with the Paul English Players. After this engagement in February, 1929, Bruner began touring with tent shows as "The Singing Messenger Boy" and singing Jimmie Rodgers' songs in a yodeling style that was almost a carbon copy of Rodgers'.[72] Until the mid-thirties scores of other country singers, partly through their own inclinations and partly through the encouragement of recording men, began producing records that bore strongly the imprint of the Rodgers style. Frankie Marvin, Bill Cox,

[70] "The Yodeling Cowboy" and "The Yodeling Ranger" were recorded on Victor 22271 and Victor 23830 respectively.

[71] The emergence of the western image will be discussed in Chapter 5.

[72] Interview with Bill Bruner, Meridian, Mississippi, August 24, 1966.

Jimmie Davis, Cliff Carlisle, and Leon Huff were only a few of the future big-name stars who, at the beginnings of their careers in the late twenties, used a style that not only employed the Rodgers repertory and yodel technique but borrowed his "hey hey hey" style of spoken commentary as well.

If the modern enthusiast has access to early country-music recordings and will listen to those recorded in the period running roughly from 1928 to 1935, he can understand just how pervasive the Rodgers influence was. The Carter Family, known for its repertory of old-time mountain and gospel songs, was no more immune to the Rodgers appeal than were the newer western singers who were continually cropping up during the thirties. Sara Carter yodeled on a few songs, and the entire Carter Family joined in at least two recording sessions with Rodgers.[73] Gene Autry, known to most modern fans as a Hollywood cowboy and big-business entrepreneur, got his initial start as a singer of Jimmie Rodgers songs. Equally important as Autry, because of his longevity within the country-music field, was Ernest Tubb of Crisp, Texas, who idolized Jimmie Rodgers and in his early recording years tried to recreate the identical sound of the Blue Yodeler. Although Tubb never met Rodgers personally, he can almost be considered his protege because of the personal encouragement he received from Mrs. Carrie Rodgers.[74]

The Rodgers appeal was felt in far off Canada. Motivated by reports of Rodgers' commercial success, the RCA Victor offices in Montreal decided to branch out into country music. The Canadian country-music industry dates, therefore, from the signing in 1932 of a young yodeler named Wilf Carter,[75] a native of Nova Scotia, who gained his first musical inspiration from a traveling Swiss yodeler. Carter was for many years Canada's most popular country entertainer. He also built up a large and loyal following in the United States, where he was known as "Montana Slim." Although born in

[73] Four of the joint Rodgers-Carter Family recordings can be heard on the Jimmie Rodgers LP, *My Time Ain't Long*, RCA Victor LPM-2865.

[74] Both Tubb and Autry will be discussed in later chapters, particularly in Chapters 5 and 6.

[75] The information on Wilf Carter was obtained from Eleanor M. Burdo, "Montana Slim Story," *Disc Collector*, No. 12 (n.d.), 3–4; and Stella Cameron, "Wilf Carter," *Country and Western Spotlight*, No. 19 (July–September, 1957), 8–10.

Nova Scotia, Carter moved to Calgary, Alberta, as a young man and worked as a trail rider in the Canadian Rockies. He was, therefore, an authentic cowboy, and he recorded many songs employing the cowboy or prairie theme: for example, "My Little Grey Haired Mother in the West," "The Fate of Old Strawberry Roan," and "Midnight, the Unconquered Outlaw."[76] Although his yodeling inspiration did not come directly from Rodgers, in the years following Rodgers' death Carter's repertory reflected the Blue Yodeler's influence, and he persistently maintained the yodel as a basic element of his style.

The Rodgers influence was exerted more directly in the case of a young Nova Scotia farm boy who became so enthralled with Rodgers' recording of "Moonlight and Skies" that he resolved to become a country entertainer. He taught himself the guitar and sat by the phonograph for hours trying to master the Rodgers technique. His recording career began with Victor in 1936 when he recorded two of his own compositions, "Lonesome Blue Yodel" and "Prisoned Cowboy." Calling himself the "Yodeling Ranger," by the end of the 1930's he rivaled Wilf Carter for the title of Canada's most popular country performer. After his voice deepened, his yodeling facility began to vanish. He thereupon changed his performing title to "The Singing Ranger" and went on to become one of the greatest stars in the United States. This was Clarence E. (Hank) Snow, the only country singer who has continued the train-song tradition of Jimmie Rodgers.[77]

Although the continuing careers of people like Hank Snow and Ernest Tubb are lasting memorials to the greatness of Jimmie Rodgers, the more immediate memorials were the songs of tribute that were recorded at the time of his death by such singers as Gene Autry, Bradley Kincaid, and Leon Huff of the W. Lee O'Daniel and Light Crust Doughboys' organization.[78] Even more important, perhaps, as

[76] The modern enthusiast can sample the Wilf Carter style on several albums that RCA Victor has released on the Camden label: *Wilf Sings*, CAL 527; *Reminiscin'*, CAL 668; *By Request*, CAL 701; and *32 Wonderful Years*, CAL 787. As late as 1968 Carter was still making occasional recordings; Starday Records released an album containing several of his more popular old-time numbers on *Living Legend*, SLP 300.

[77] *The Hank Snow Twenty-Fifth Anniversary Album*, p. 28.

[78] For a partial discography of these songs, see John Edwards, "Memories of Jimmie Rodgers," *Disc Collector*, No. 15 (n.d.), 16–18.

testimoniés of his popularity, are his Victor recordings, which have continued to enjoy a wide sale in the thirty-five years since his death. The interest in Rodgers has remained so strong that a major fan club, world-wide in scope, has attracted thousands of devotees who never saw or heard the Blue Yodeler during his lifetime. Founded by Jim Evans of Lubbock, Texas, where its headquarters is located, The Jimmie Rodgers Society strives to collect all relevant material pertaining to Rodgers.

The bulk of Jimmie Rodgers' recording career came during the bleak years of the greatest depression the United States has experienced. Yet his record sales outranked those of most of the performers in the Victor catalogue. And they were marketed and sold, for the most part, in the southern region, where farmers and workers spent their few hard-earned dollars to buy his songs. The notes to one of his memorial albums relates a legend concerning his popularity among hard-pressed depression dwellers: "Legend has it that in his heyday, general-store customers would approach the counter and say: 'Let me have a pound of butter, a dozen eggs, and the latest Jimmie Rodgers record.' "[79] When Rodgers died in 1933, he was unknown to the great majority of the American people, but in the Southland, where hillbilly music has always gained its most devoted following, Rodgers had become a hero to millions of rural people.

[79] Roy Horton, notes to *Country Music Hall of Fame*, RCA Victor LPM-2531.

CHAPTER 4

Country Music during the Depression —
Survival and Expansion

WHEN JIMMIE RODGERS died in 1933, one decade had elapsed since Fiddlin' John Carson made his first Okeh record and inaugurated country music's commercial history.[1] The music had become a secure part of American entertainment and gave every indication of expanding both in popularity and personnel.

Country music, however, had been shorn of many of its traditional characteristics. Although a tremendous number of traditional songs were still being recorded by such country singers as Mainer's Mountaineers, the Monroe Brothers, the Carter Family, and the Blue Sky Boys, the ancient ballads and folksongs were steadily ceasing to comprise the bulk of the country performer's repertory. Newly written compositions or arrangements of older songs were gradually edging the traditional ballads aside. The newer tunes, nevertheless, reflected the performer's folk origins, because they were couched in traditional terms and styles and employed melodic structures of age-old derivations. The country singer still sang tunes that reflected his cultural conditioning, a conditioning that was largely fundamentalist protestant, Anglo-Celtic, and small-town-rural. And whether he moved to a city or performed before an urban audience would make no immediate difference. His newly composed songs would be

---

[1] The problems inherent in this statement are discussed in Chapter 2.

shaped by his prior experiences and by the circumscribed limits of his pre-existent culture.

Of course, the use or nonuse of traditional songs has nothing to do with one's status as a member of the folk. (In fact, most of the folk do not sing at all.) It should be stated, too, that the singing of folksongs has little bearing on whether one is a "folksinger," because although the folk perpetuate and sing traditional songs, they also compose their own. The hillbillies of the 1930's, despite the diminution of traditional material within their repertories, sang melodies that were derived from and representative of their culture and were thereby firmly within the folk tradition.

Nevertheless, the early 1930's witnessed a definite turning point in country-music history. Thereafter, the performers tended to be more polished and self-conscious about their commercial status. Jimmie Rodgers success stimulated hundreds of country performers who, although strongly imbued with the folk tradition, attempted to gain their success through emulation of "The Blue Yodeler." Their own desires for recognition, added to the recording executives' insistence upon innovation, served to modify the hillbilly singers' traditional styles. And, too, younger singers who had less contact with the older styles and more with the newer commercial styles naturally sounded considerably different from the performers of the twenties. The recordings of the new group of singers were bought in the following decades by rural dwellers, who, in many cases, gave the songs back to folklorists traveling through the country in search of material. New traditions, therefore, were being created.

It is significant that in 1933, the year of Rodgers' death, the Library of Congress, employing the use of discs, began its systematic field recording of Southern folk music. Although the Archive of American Folk Song is generally associated with the names of John and Alan Lomax, who directed its field recording after 1933, the depository owes its real existence to the labors of Robert Winslow Gordon, a pioneer in the area of recorded folk music. Gordon was the first folklorist to conduct recording expeditions through extensive areas of the country, from the Southern Appalachians to the Canadian side of the Great Lakes. Sponsored by Harvard University, Gordon began his expedition in 1927, and the one thousand cylinder recordings which he produced became the original nucleus of the Archive of American Folk Song. According to D. K. Wilgus, Gordon was one of the first to take "into account evidence from contemporary singers and their sources."[2]

After 1933, with John Lomax serving as Honorary Consultant and Curator, the Archive began employing the disc recording as a folkloristic tool for collecting the traditional songs of the United States.[3] That many of the southern-collected songs in the Archive had been recorded on commercial records is evidence of the cultural impact made by ten years of recorded hillbilly music. Some of the songs had in fact been written by hillbilly performers, while others had been learned by traditional singers from hillbilly records. Of equal significance is the fact that some of the singers recorded by the Library of Congress in the thirties and forties—such as George Roark, Bascom Lamar Lunsford, Uncle Alec Dunford, and Jilson Setters—had been commercial hillbilly performers in an earlier period.[4]

While the southern folk were perfecting new styles and creating new songs, the Library of Congress and independent folklore expeditions were collecting the songs of a previous era, those of commercial origin and otherwise. Much of the folklore collecting of the thirties was done under the auspices of the W.P.A. Federal Writers' Project,[5] a New Deal agency which sponsored intellectuals and unemployed scholars of one kind or another on their journeys through the South searching for folk material. At about the same time, or roughly between 1929 and 1932, a number of northern labor organizers came into the southern mill and coal-mining districts and participated in the series of bitter strikes that made such names as Gastonia, Marion, and Harlan well known to Americans of the depression period. Archie Green has described well the musical phenomenon that resulted from the mating of radical and intellectual ideas from the North with the conservative and rural tradition of ballad-making in the South: "From this setting came a group of topical songs using old melodies to set off intensely stark and mili-

---

[2] Wilgus, *Anglo-American Folksong Scholarship Since 1898*, pp. 180; see also *ibid.*, p. 110.

[3] Harold Spivacke, "The Archive of American Folk-Song in the Library of Congress," *Southern Folklore Quarterly*, II, No. 1 (March, 1938), 31–32.

[4] For examples see *A Check List of Recorded Songs in the English Language in the Archive of American Folk Song to July, 1940*.

[5] Daniel M. Fox, "The Achievement of the Federal Writers' Project," *American Quarterly*, XIII, No. 1 (Spring, 1961), 18–19.

tant texts. In a sense, Piedmont mill villages and Cumberland mine camps became meeting grounds for the ideologies of Andrew Jackson and Karl Marx, Abraham Lincoln and Mikhail Bakunin."[6]

Through these various song-collecting ventures—folkloristic, sociological, or labor inspired—southern rural songs and melodies were not only introduced to the North, they also acquired radical and intellectual connotations which they have never really lost. The folk, and their music, were glorified during the depression as they had not been since the days of Andrew Jackson. Reformers, radicals, and people generally left-of-center adopted folksongs, folk styles, and folk instruments as weapons to fight the enemies of the working classes: depression, hunger, the capitalistic system, and Fascism. The thirties saw the emergence, therefore, of that musical phenomenon which has flourished so strongly in the sixties: "urban folk music." Drawing primarily on the musical traditions of the rural South, the "city-billies" (the urban performers who employed the songs and instruments of an alien rural culture) created a musical tradition that has always been closely allied with the liberal movements of the northern United States. It was because of this movement, and the concomitant association of the words "folksong" and "protest," that a distinction between "folk" and "hillbilly" music developed among the devotees of popular culture. "Folk" music, which had become largely the province of intellectuals and reformers, became increasingly removed from the folk, while "hillbilly" music, the creation of the folk, developed in its own independent fashion.

The great depression of the thirties, which spawned the urban folk movement, also wrought extensive changes in hillbilly music. By 1933 the phonograph companies had been forced to curtail their operations. The contracts of some of the hillbilly performers, especially those who had exhibited little commercial appeal, were not renewed. In the year 1932 only six million records were sold, a striking contrast to the 104 million records that had been sold in 1927.[7] Field recording was ceasing to be a major aspect of the large companies' recording techniques. Some record companies followed the course of Victor, which established a cheaper subsidiary line,

---

[6] Quoted in the notes to Sarah Ogan Cunning, *Girl of Constant Sorrow*, Folk-Legacy FSA-26.

[7] Roland Gelatt, *The Fabulous Phonograph*, p. 255.

Bluebird, to take care of its race and white country artists. The Okeh label (originally owned by the General Phonograph Corporation but bought by Columbia in 1926) was re-established in 1940 (after a six-year submergence) as Columbia's country and race subsidiary. Brunswick, one of the traditional leaders of the record business, had been taken over by the American Record Company, a producer of cheap discs sold by chain stores (under such labels as Melotone, Perfect, Banner, Oriole, and Romeo). Gennett, another old-time company, went out of business and sold its catalogues and labels to the newly formed Decca Company. Sears-Roebuck and Montgomery Ward continued to issue their low-priced records (dubbed from the big companies' masters) aimed at the rural population.[8]

American Decca was organized in 1934, and, because of its low-priced records, immediately became a front-runner among phonograph companies. The issuance of Decca's thirty-five cent records encouraged the other companies, which had generally charged seventy-five cents, to lower their prices, and a "platter war" began. Decca made a successful "raid" on the major record companies and emerged with some of their leading performers; their most important acquisition was Bing Crosby.[9]

From the very beginning, Decca endeavored to build a hillbilly catalogue. In this enterprise it was led primarily by recording man David Kapp, who traveled over the South laden with portable apparatus. Although Kapp's travels ranged far and wide, his most productive efforts came in the Southwest: Louisiana, Oklahoma, and Texas.[10] The thirties definitely saw a shift in the recording of hillbilly personnel from the Southeast to the Southwest, and a corresponding shift in the character of the music. The newer group of performers were more influenced by "western" styles, and employed fewer traditional songs and instruments. For instance, the five-string banjo never became popular in southwestern bands. Instead, the four-string tenor banjo, of jazz origins, was used quite often.

[8] John Edwards, "The Old Labels—No. 2," *Country and Western Spotlight* (Special John Edwards Memorial Edition, September, 1962), 14–15. Archie Green has compiled a useful chronology of the Okeh-Columbia relationship in Appendix III of "Hillbilly Music: Source and Symbol," *Journal of American Folklore*, LXXVIII (July–September, 1965), 228.

[9] "Platter War," *Business Week* (November 10, 1934), 14.

[10] *Time*, XXXVI, No. 10 (September 2, 1940), 45.

In the exploitation of southwestern performers, Decca was in the forefront. A perusal of Decca's hillbilly catalogues[11] for the thirties will show a decided preponderance of entertainers from the Southwest, particularly the state of Texas. The Shelton Brothers (Bob and Joe) were the first of the Texas groups to gain wide popularity, largely through their recordings of "Just Because" and "Deep Ellem Blues." The Shelton Brothers (born Attlesey but renamed "Shelton" because it sounded more commercial) were born at Rylie Springs in Hopkins County, Texas. The Shelton Brothers included both modern and traditional songs in their repertory and performed them in a flavor more reflective of southeastern hillbilly styles than of the "swing" rhythms of the Southwest. As their career progressed, the Sheltons added more instruments and musicians (including their brother Merle in 1935). They eventually came to resemble the typical country bands of the Southwest.[12]

Another early Texas acquisition made by Decca was Stuart Hamblen of Kellysville, Texas.[13] His recording of "Out on the Texas Plains" became one of the country favorites of 1934. Hamblen, who made his base in California and performed for a time with the "Beverley Hillbillies," has continued to be one of the most successful country songwriters. He composed in the 1930's many songs that were to become country perennials, such as "My Brown Eyed Texas Rose," "Golden River," "Just A Little Old Rag Doll," and the famous "My Mary" (best known because of a Jimmie Davis recording). In the mid-fifties he experienced a major show-business comeback through the writing and recording of the nationally famous sacred songs "It is No Secret" and "This Old House." ("This Old House" also gained recognition as a pop-novelty song when recorded by Rosemary Clooney.) Although he was the son of a Methodist minister, Hamblen had the reputation of a hell-raiser in his younger years. In the 1950's he was converted in a Billy Graham Revival

[11] An almost complete listing of Decca's early hillbilly recordings made from 1934 to 1945 (the 5000 Series) is in *Record Research*, No. 23 (June–July, 1959), 13–16. A shorter listing is in *Country and Western Spotlight*, No. 42 (June, 1963), 4–6.

[12] Interview with Merle Attlesey, Dallas, Texas, September 7, 1963.

[13] Pertinent biographical information on Stuart Hamblen was obtained from "Stuart Hamblen and His Lucky Stars," *Picture-Song Book*, pp. 16–17; and from Linnell Gentry, *A History and Encyclopedia of Country, Western, and Gospel Music*, p. 237.

Crusade, and, thereafter, his repertory became heavily oriented toward gospel music. As an extreme example of just how far his conversion had gone, he was a candidate for President on the Prohibition ticket in 1952.

Another early and important Decca acquisition whose career has not yet terminated is James Houston (Jimmie) Davis of Louisiana. Born on a farm near Shreveport, Davis earned a B.A. from Louisiana College and an M.A. from Louisiana State University. After a short tenure as a professor of history and social science at Dodd College, he became an entertainer and in 1936 was among the first group of hillbilly singers signed by Decca. Showing a strong Jimmie Rodgers influence, Davis had been making records for Victor since 1928 and was already a territorial favorite when Decca signed him. Davis achieved fame as both a singer and songwriter and was, in fact, the writer or co-writer of many of the most popular songs of the decades following 1934, including "Nobody's Darling But Mine," "Sweethearts or Strangers," and the national favorite "You Are My Sunshine."[14] Davis' entertainment success brought him not only wealth and prestige, but also the governorship of Louisiana, where he was able to successfully buck against the powerful Long Machine in 1944 and 1960.

One of the significant aspects of recording in the thirties was the fact that, despite the severity of the depression and despite the general woes of the phonograph industry, the recording of hillbilly talent continued. Throughout the depression new hillbilly singers were continually discovered and placed on records. Since phonograph companies have never released specific data on record sales, any statement regarding country music's profitability during the depression can be only an estimate. Compared with popular music sales, hillbilly sales were low. Paul Cohen, former director of Decca's country-music division, estimated that during the depression a "hillbilly hit" was one which sold a total of ten thousand copies. Hillbilly

[14] Hearings before the Subcommittee on Communications of the Committee on Interstate and Foreign Commerce, United States Senate, Eighty-Fifth Congress, Second session, on S. 2834. (A Bill to provide that a license for a radio or television broadcasting station shall not be granted to, or held by, any person or corporation engaged directly or indirectly in the business of publishing music or of manufacturing or selling musical recordings). March 11 through July 23, 1958, 521.

music was still a profitable venture for the record companies, however, because of the low expense of recording.[15]

Regardless of the low individual record sales, hillbilly records sold on a steady and general basis. Both Goddard Lieberson, one-time president of Columbia Records, and Ralph Peer have remarked that hillbilly record sales remained as high during the depression as they had been during previous years.[16] That many country families who lacked money to buy not only luxuries but necessities periodically spent a portion of their scanty income to buy a hillbilly record illustrates again the strong position that music held in the life of the southern rural dweller. It has long been demonstrated, too, that hillbilly records experience a long commercial life. Some records were advertised in Montgomery Ward and Sears-Roebuck catalogues for many years. As an example of hillbilly durability, Bradley Kincaid's "Fatal Wedding" was listed in the Sears-Roebuck catalogue from 1929 to 1940.[17]

The thirties was also a period of expanding radio coverage for hillbilly music. Radio stations in the South and Midwest increasingly recognized the popularity of hillbilly music, and advertisers began to sponsor hillbilly programs in order to popularize their products. Both small stations and high-powered, 50,000-watt units stressed mail-order-purchase advertising aimed at their rural listeners. In the early thirties the Aladdin Mantle Lamp Company became the first company to sponsor half an hour on the National Barn Dance, a segment which featured the Cumberland Ridge Runners. By 1935 a one-hour segment of the Barn Dance was being sponsored by Alka-Seltzer and broadcast to all forty-eight states via NBC.[18] One of the first companies to employ country music as an advertising medium on a national basis was the Crazy Water Crystals Company of Mineral Wells, Texas, a concern that marketed a patent medicine good for numerous internal ailments. Crazy Water Crystals sponsored hillbilly talent far afield from its southwestern headquarters: in Canada, in

[15] Interview with Paul Cohen, Nashville, Tennessee, August 29, 1961.

[16] Ralph Peer, "Rodgers' Heritage," *Billboard*, LXVI, No. 21 (May 22, 1954), 17; Goddard Lieberson, "Country Sweeps the Country," *The New York Times Magazine* (July 28, 1957), 48.

[17] This sentimental song from the 1890's was actually listed in the 1928 catalogue also, but by Ernest Stoneman.

[18] Letter to the author from George C. Biggar, March 18, 1967.

the Midwest (even in Detroit), and over the powerful Mexican border stations. According to president Carr P. Collins, New York and New England were the only areas in the United States where the hillbilly programs did not have wide appeal.[19]

It became common practice in the thirties for business concerns marketing products popular with country people—such brands as Black Draught, Wine of Cardui, Garrett Snuff, Stevens Work Clothes, Royal Crown Cola, or Light Crust Flour—to sponsor a hillbilly band at a strategic period during the day,[20] early in the morning or at noontime, and then to send the group on tour through the area where the program seemed to be popular. The hillbilly audience was loyal not only to the performers but to the companies that sponsored them as well. The 50,000-watt stations were particularly energetic in pushing country music, presumably because of their large rural audience.[21] Not only were the products of various advertisers given wider coverage by the big stations, but hillbilly performers were thereby presented to a larger and ever increasing audience. High-powered stations which featured country music included KWKH in Shreveport, Louisiana; KVOO in Tulsa, Oklahoma; WOAI in San Antonio, Texas; WLW in Cincinnati, Ohio; and WSM in Nashville, Tennessee.

In the dissemination of country music throughout the United States, nothing was of more importance than the powerful Mexican border stations. The X-stations (so-called because of their call letters), operating just across the American border in Mexico, boomed throughout much of the United States and were sometimes heard quite clearly in Canada. The border stations operated on wattage that was as much as two or three times in excess of the maximum limit in the United States. This practice was condoned by the Mexican authorities presumably because of a prior snubbing of Mex-

[19] Interview with Carr P. Collins, Dallas, Texas, April 20, 1962.

[20] See the statements of George Biggar in *Billboard*, LII, No. 15 (April 13, 1940), 64.

[21] In discussing radio popularity in the 1930's, Edmund de S. Brunner said that "radio programs . . . have greater values for rural people than for others. The radio has become one of the most potent of those agencies such as the telephone, the automobile and the rural free delivery, that are rapidly banishing the physical and cultural isolation to which rural people of a few decades ago were inevitably subjected" (*Radio and the Farmer*, p. 5).

ico by her northern neighbors. The American and Canadian governments had divided between themselves the entire long-wave broadcast band, leaving neither Cuba nor Mexico any clear channels at all. Therefore, for many years Mexico rejected American protests about the border stations.[22]

These stations, normally owned by American businessmen, aimed their transmitters toward the United States, and, operating on 100,-000 to 150,000 watts,[23] cut in on wave lengths used by United States and Canadian stations. With this powerful means of transmission American advertisers were able to exploit their products throughout most of the United States. The type of products advertised ranged from old-time religion to medical cure-alls and were aimed at rural American listeners. The border station era was inaugurated in 1930 when Dr. J. R. Brinkley's XER (changed to XERA in 1935) began operations at Villa Acuna, Mexico. Brinkley had formerly operated a station at Milford, Kansas, where he pushed his goat-gland operation, designed to restore sexual potency to men. At his Kansas radio station Brinkley had employed the services of hillbilly performers such as fiddler Uncle Bob Larkin. Brinkley's use of a hillbilly band in his race for governor of Kansas in 1930 made him the predecessor of such famous hillbilly politicians as Texas' W. Lee O'Daniel and Louisiana's Jimmie Davis.[24]

When his radio license was revoked in Kansas, Brinkley moved to Del Rio, Texas, and became the first of the X-station manipulators. Not only did he advertise his own medical remedies, he also pushed products of businessmen from the United States. In addition to the almost incessant advertising, the radio listener was given a steady diet of religious evangelists, hillbilly singers (mostly by transcription), and, on many occasions, right-wing politicians. Brinkley, on XERA and later acquisitions XEPN and XEAW,[25] set a pattern that was closely followed by later border entrepreneurs. His success inspired numerous other individuals in the following decades—some of them, like Norman Baker, of a not-too-savory reputation. Norman

[22] J. C. Furnas, "Country Doctor Goes to Town," *Saturday Evening Post,* CCXII, No. 43 (April 20, 1943), 50.

[23] It has been estimated that at one time (1932) XER reached as high as 500,000 watts (Gerald Carson, *The Roguish World of Dr. Brinkley,* p. 177).

[24] *Ibid.,* pp. 89, 156.

[25] *Ibid.,* p. 205.

Baker plugged his cancer-cure over XENT, across from Laredo, before he was convicted of using the mails to defraud.[26] Brinkley sold XEAW, his station at Reynosa, to Carr Collins, who made himself a millionaire through the selling of Crazy Water Crystals. XEAW, like most of the other border stations, sold commercial time to a motley assortment of patent-medicine proprietors, evangelists, and small business establishments, such as chick farms. Collins felt that in his programming he was giving listeners the unsophisticated material that the big networks neglected.[27] The X-stations profited, therefore, from the popularity of hillbilly music in southern and midwestern rural areas. These powerful stations squeezed out their American rivals during normal operating hours and pre-empted those hours after midnight which most American stations neglected. Through this type of programming the border stations touched not only the farmer, who listened during the earlier hours, but also the truck driver, the night-shift worker, and the insomniac.

If one could endure the seemingly never ending advertising, he could occasionally hear a hillbilly song of the best quality. The border stations did not on the whole attempt to attract the urban listener. The hillbilly songs featured tended to be of a more traditional nature, and border programmers made less effort to compromise on the selections offered in order to attract a wider audience. On the border stations hillbilly music has continued to the present day to be of a more old-time and religious nature.[28] These stations, viewed with contempt and suspicion by many American listeners and broadcasters, nonetheless circulated southern country music throughout the bulk of the United States. There has been no accurate investigation, and probably can be none, of the effect of border programming upon American listeners. It is clear, however, that the border stations played an important role in spreading country music, traditional and otherwise, to nonsouthern areas. No one can ever know the number of traditional ballads, including the venerable Child ballads, that may have found their way into some remote midwestern area solely through the means of Mexican radio transmission, an oral process

[26] *Ibid.*, p. 4.

[27] Interview with Carr P. Collins, Dallas, Texas, April 20, 1962; Carson, *The Roguish World of Dr. Brinkley*, p. 205.

[28] The Mexican border stations now usually amount to no more than 50,000 watts, and their programs are no longer live but taped.

that perpetuated the lives of these songs and made it possible for them to be collected by some folklorist at a later date. The Mexican border station XERA, for example, carried the Carter Family in the last three years of their professional recording career, from 1938 to 1941.[29] Songs and ballads of a perhaps more authentic southeastern origin became known throughout much of the United States because of the Carter Family broadcasts. Other important country groups and individuals with strong traditional orientation—Mainer's Mountaineers, the Callahan Brothers, the Delmore Brothers, the Pickard Family, and Cowboy Slim Rinehart—broadcast over the border stations during the late thirties and early forties. The Mexican border stations, along with the 50,000-watt American stations, popularized hillbilly music throughout the United States and laid the basis for country music's great popularity in the late forties and early fifties.[30]

Radio coverage inevitably led to an expansion of the hillbilly performers' activity. Popularity gained through a radio program quite often led to a demand upon the part of the listener for an opportunity to see as well as hear the performer. The demand for photographs and illustrated song books was very high, but the personal appearance was an even better method of establishing closer listener-performer contact. Personal appearances became increasingly common in the late thirties. The barnstorming path that eventually would be followed by all country entertainers was blazed by such performers as Otto Gray and His Oklahoma Cowboys and the Weaver Brothers and Elviry. The Weaver group (Frank, Leon, and June Weaver) stressed country comedy and music as they played on the vaudeville circuit during the twenties and thirties. They helped to lay the groundwork for hillbilly popularity in the North and were one of the few country groups to gain notice in such trade publications as *Billboard*. For example, a full-page ad in January, 1931, announced that the group had recently played the RKO Circuit in Madison, Brooklyn, and Chester, New York.[31]

The Weaver Brothers and the WLS barn-dance groups were only

[29] Archie Green, "The Carter Family's 'Coal Miner's Blues,'" *Southern Folklore Quarterly*, XXV, No. 4 (December, 1961), 229.

[30] Interview between Ed Kahn and Don Howard (station representative for XERF), Del Rio, Texas, July 18, 1963 (made available to the author by Kahn).

[31] *Billboard*, XLIII, No. 5 (January 31, 1931), 21.

a few of the scores of hillbilly crooners, yodelers, and string bands that were now swarming around the country. Hillbilly music was becoming a sturdy, if unnoticed and scorned, facet of American show business. Hillbilly performers became acquainted with the intricacies of commercial entertainment—recording contracts and percentage data—and were ceasing to be the naive bumpkins of a previous period. It was increasingly difficult for a music executive or promoter to sign a hillbilly to a contract or take over his song without adequate compensation. Nevertheless, there still existed numerous examples of country songwriters who sold the complete rights to their songs for a mere pittance, usually twenty-five dollars, only to see the songs emerge as national hits.

In the early days of hillbilly commercial tours, the majority of the bookings were scheduled by correspondence between the performer and listeners. Hillbilly entertainers tried to estimate from their fan mail where their greatest popularity lay and the size of the crowd that could be expected for a personal appearance. If the number of letters received indicated that the show had a large following in a particular area, a performance was arranged. Shows were booked at such functions as county fairs, barn dances, school activities, and civic affairs, and dates were usually set on a basis of fifty per cent of the gross to the entertainer, although the figure had been raised to as high as sixty or seventy per cent by the end of the thirties. For many years hillbilly performers remained in rather circumscribed limits. By booking themselves at such functions as county fairs, they learned to regard themselves as territorial favorites. They tended to remain, therefore, within the scope of their radio listening audience.[32]

Although many of the details of personal appearances—such as the posting and distribution of placards—were handled by the performers, the thirties saw the gradual appearance of promoters who would devote their entire careers to the handling of hillbilly talent. Some of these, like Dick Bergen, came to country music through established promotional agencies.[33] Others, and these made up the majority, became acquainted with country music through their connections with the radio barn dances and other radio hillbilly shows. As the radio

[32] *Ibid.*, LVII, No. 10 (March 10, 1945), 29.
[33] *Ibid.*, LV, No. 10 (March 6, 1943), 7.

shows grew in popularity, a corresponding growth occurred in the demand for personal appearances, and individuals and organizations arose to handle the demand.

Although the Grand Ole Opry sent out a touring unit in 1925 which traveled on the RKO circuit in the Midwest,[34] most of the show's tours were confined to the middle Tennessee area until the mid-thirties and were handled largely on an individual basis. By the late thirties the WSM tours were becoming big business and were branching out all over the southern United States. Most of the tours were arranged by Station WSM through its Artists Bureau, although an occasional act was promoted by some outside promoter such as Joe Frank, Oscar Davis, or Colonel Tom Parker (later to gain fame as the manager of Elvis Presley). The WSM Artists Bureau continued to provide most of the Grand Ole Opry's talent handling until well into the fifties, when it began to lose out in the competition with independent organizations.[35]

Well in advance of WSM, and one of the pioneers in launching personal appearances, was the National Barn Dance station, WLS. WLS performers, usually booked by independent agents, began making personal appearances as early as 1925, when Ford and Glenn appeared in midwestern theaters. By 1927 Chubby Parker, Bradley Kincaid, and the Maple City Four were making independent tours, and Kincaid was earning between $150 to $500 for each performance in his theater appearances. It was not until 1932, however, that Earl Kurtze and George Ferguson organized the WLS Artists Bureau and began booking Barn Dance performances on a percentage basis. Such acts as Lulu Belle and Scotty, the Maple City Four, and the Three Little Maids earned grosses of from $1,000 to $2,500 a day.[36] A striking example of just how lucrative the Barn Dance performances could be came in the fall of 1932 when Dick Bergen, an independent booking agent in Chicago, conceived the idea of booking some leading WLS artists in theaters. Against the advice of Great States Theaters' executives, Bergen booked a group, including the

[34] Jon Pankake, "Sam and Kirk McGee from Sunny Tennessee," *Sing Out: The Folk Song Magazine*, XIV, No. 5 (November, 1964), 49.

[35] Interview with James Denny, Nashville, Tennessee, August 25, 1961.

[36] The financial information concerning the National Barn Dance performers was obtained from a letter written by George Ferguson to George Biggar, March 21, 1967 (made available to the author by George Biggar).

Three Little Maids and the Cumberland Ridge Runners, into the Rialto Theatre in Peoria, Illinois. When the show, a relatively inexpensive production, proved to be a financial success, booking agencies became convinced of hillbilly music's popularity and its financial possibilities; from that time forward bookings of hillbilly radio favorites grew rapidly.[37]

During the thirties the National Barn Dance expanded its touring operations into Illinois's neighboring midwestern states. Working usually through WLS's own booking bureau, the Barn Dance sent several road units into midwestern areas, where they played two- and three-day stands at theaters, fairs, benefits, and similar functions.[38] The Barn Dance tours and the radio hillbilly shows combined to make country music a well-known part of midwestern musical life. The Barn Dance itself, at the Eighth Street Theatre in Chicago, played normally to capacity crowds and revealed that country music could attract followers even in the large metropolitan areas. In the ten year period from 1932 to 1942 over one million people paid a total of $662,000 to see the shows.[39]

By the late thirties hillbilly music had become one of the staple fares for midwestern small-town audiences. WLS sent its barn-dance performers all over the Midwest, popularizing country music to such an extent that Lewis Atherton, in a later discussion of the phenomenon, remarked that hillbilly music was "surpassing even the minstrel show in popularity" and "had become the favorite of Main Street."[40]

Although country music assumed new forms in the 1930's and acquired many of the commercial techniques of show business, the decade witnessed the emergence of scores of individuals and groups firmly grounded in the folk tradition. Numerous performers still based the bulk of their repertory on the traditional melodies. Despite the development of complexity within country music, and the ever growing pressure upon the performer to modify his style, many singers arose who, in their selections and styles, were just as "authentic" as the pioneer recording stars of the twenties. In these years before World War II made country music a national phenomenon,

---

[37] *Billboard,* LV, No. 10 (March 16, 1943), 7.
[38] *Ibid.,* XLV, No. 6 (February 11, 1933), 12; *ibid.,* XLV, No. 11 (March 18, 1933), 12.
[39] *Movie-Radio Guide,* XI, No. 28 (April 18–24, 1942), 33.
[40] Lewis Atherton, *Main Street on the Middle Border,* p. 296.

the hillbilly entertainer could generally perform in his own desired and accustomed manner and, providing he had talent or caught the listeners' fancy, could expect to be successful. His audience, by and large, shared his tastes and musical and cultural heritage.

Some of the recording artists of the twenties, such as Bradley Kincaid, Gene Autry, Jimmie Davis, and the Carter Family, survived the rigors of the early depression years, but most of the others were released because of phonograph company cutbacks. Some of the important pioneer hillbilly recording artists, including Ernest Stoneman and Buell Kazee, gave up professional hillbilly music (at least temporarily) when their recording companies folded.[41] In the meantime newer groups were recorded who demonstrated in their performances the increased vocal and instrumental variations that had been stimulated by the radio and phonograph. Developing out of the Gid Tanner-Al Hopkins string-band tradition were scores of hillbilly bands all over the South and Midwest (and in fact throughout the nation); they performed on both large and obscure radio stations, or wherever they could obtain a hearing.

In the transitional bands of the thirties, despite the growing emergence of an orchestral style, the breakdown fiddle remained the dominant instrument. This popular instrument was perhaps the strongest tie that hillbilly music had with its folk heritage, and it became the basic instrument in practically all the musical styles that developed within country music. The guitar also remained a popular instrument and was joined as a rhythm instrument by the string bass, probably borrowed from jazz and popular swing bands. Other instruments were employed from time to time, depending, quite often, upon the particular area in which the band was prominent: the five-string banjo in the Southeast and the tenor banjo in the Southwest. The mandolin gained increased popularity during the thirties, while the steel guitar, at first unelectrified, gained more and more adherents until it came to rival the popularity of the fiddle in the forties.

Scores of vocal and instrumental groups appeared on radio and recordings during the thirties. They ranged from the traditional breakdown-style bands of the Southeast to the Cajun-influenced bands of Louisiana and the "western"-style bands of the Southwest. Each of

---

[41] See Ralph Rinzler's notes to *Stoneman Family*, Folkways FA 2315; and Buell Kazee's notes to *Buell Kazee Sings and Plays*, Folkways FS 3810.

them shared a number of common characteristics: the use of the guitar, and often the string bass, as rhythm instruments, and the usual employment of the fiddle as the lead instrument. For the string band the day of the featured vocalist had not yet arrived,[42] and various members of the band took turns at filling the vocal requirements. Group singing (usually duet, trio, or quartet) was prevalent, and almost universally the traditional high harmony persisted.

One of the lesser-known duos of the period, but one which had a significance and influence far beyond its reputation, was the team made up of Tom Darby and Jimmie Tarlton. Although their most important recordings were made in the late twenties, their instrumental styles anticipated those of a later period. Darby and Tarlton recorded at least seventy-five songs for Columbia, Victor, and the American Record Corporation over a period which ranged from April, 1927, until the 1930's. Their recordings featured duet singing and the steel-guitar playing of Jimmie Tarlton, who was one of the very first individuals to play such an instrument on hillbilly records. Johnny James Rimbert Tarlton, who came out of a South Carolina family of textile workers and folksingers, is one of the most interesting figures in the rich history of country music. He possessed a penetratingly clear tenor voice and an individualistic instrumental and vocal style which places him in the front rank of country singers of that or any other era. Beginning with the banjo but capable of playing almost all the stringed instruments, he eventually settled upon the steel guitar, which he played bottle-neck style until he learned the steel technique from Hawaiians whom he met in California at about the time of World War I. By the time of his first recording session in 1927, he had already hoboed around the country, working in everything from cotton mills to oil fields and singing his way as far north as New York and as far west as California. At their second recording session in Atlanta on November 10, 1927, Darby and Tarlton made recording history. They recorded two songs arranged by Jimmie Tarlton: "Columbus Stockade Blues" and "Birmingham Jail." These two songs, which are known by country-music fans around the world, earned Darby and Tarlton seventy-five dollars—the only remuneration they ever received for the songs. If for no other reason, Jimmie Tarlton— who recorded several songs without the aid of Darby—deserves a

[42] Jimmie Rodgers' success, however, was changing this factor rapidly.

place in the memory of all country-music partisans because of his recomposition of the folk-music perennial, "Birmingham Jail."[43]

Country music has always been characterized by a high incidence of "brother" or "family" groups—from the Jenkins Family and Carter Family to such modern groups as the Louvin Brothers and Stanley Brothers. In the thirties appeared a number of brother groups who influenced the future development of country music. Of the full-fledged string bands of the period few were more versatile and accomplished than a North Carolina group from Buncombe County, Mainer's Mountaineers. This organization, headed by fiddler J. E. and banjoist Wade Mainer, was an important transitional group in that it maintained strong connections with the traditional country heritage—breakdowns, reels, ballads—and at the same time developed various instrumental techniques that anticipated the super-charged bluegrass music of modern times. The group featured the full retinue of instruments now associated with bluegrass music: fiddle, five-string banjo, mandolin, guitar, and string bass.

J. E. Mainer was yet another country entertainer who came out of a textile mill environment and, until he became a professional entertainer in 1932, music for him was never more than an amateur diversion, although he earned a modest reputation in western North Carolina as a consistent winner at fiddlers' conventions. In 1932 J. E., Wade, an old friend and guitarist named Daddy John Love, and Claud (Zeke) Morris began performing over WBT in Charlotte, North Carolina, as J. E. Mainer's Crazy Mountaineers, a name inspired by their first sponsor: the Crazy Water Crystals Company, whose Charlotte representative, J. W. Fincher, was a consistent employer of hillbilly talent. Although the personnel of the Mainer organization changed from time to time (eventually including Homer Sherrill, Steve Ledford, and two of Zeke Morris's brothers, Wiley and George) the four original members remained the nucleus of the group.

The Mainer repertory, first recorded on Bluebird in 1934, included an amazing number of traditional songs, including many zestful

---

[43] Information on Darby and Tarlton is from Norman and Anne Cohen, "The Legendary Jimmie Tarlton," *Sing Out*, XVI, No. 4 (September, 1966), 16–19; and from Graham Wickman, *Darby and Tarlton* (Special Edition of Doug Jydstrup's *Blue Yodeler*, 1967). Wickman includes a complete Darby and Tarlton discography (pp. 20–27).

fiddle breakdowns such as "Run Mountain" and "What'll I Do With the Baby-O?"[44] The Mainer group, performing with great gusto and abandon characterized by whoops and hollers, evoked a tangy backwoods atmosphere while they ranged from raucous novelty tunes to southern gospel songs. Although they featured many vocal offerings—such as "John Henry" (a well-done version of Uncle Dave Macon's earlier rendition) and the influential "Maple on the Hill" (performed by Wade Mainer and Zeke Morris)—Mainer's Mountaineers remained primarily an instrumental organization. For the student of folk music the Mainer organization's extensive traditional repertory and perpetuation of old-time country fiddling marks them as one of the most important groups in country-music history.[45]

Of importance perhaps equal to Mainer's Mountaineers, but for different reasons, were Rabon and Alton Delmore, brothers from Elkmont, Alabama. Their recording career lasted from 1931, when they signed with Columbia, until 1952, when Rabon's death broke up the duo. Their recording ventures included stints with Bluebird from 1934 to 1939, and with Decca and King after that period. The Delmore Brothers, important because of their use of traditional material, which was extensive, were more important because of their adaptation of Negro songs and rhythms. The Delmores were greatly influenced by deep-South Negro styles, which they incorporated in many of their songs. In contrast to most of the string bands of the period, the Delmore Brothers featured guitars (the six-string and tenor) as lead instruments. In many of their novelty and rhythm tunes they used a ragtime guitar technique similar to that of the Negro blues performer Blind Boy Fuller—an eight-to-the-bar progression heard in such songs as "Step It Up and Go" and "Don't Let the Deal Go Down." The Delmore Brothers recorded a multi-assorted variety of country songs—most of them written by Alton Delmore—which included the sentimental favorites "When It's Time for the Whippoorwill to Sing" and "Southern Moon." Their greatest popularity and influence, gained largely through performances on WSM, came from

[44] John Edwards, "Wade Mainer," *Country and Western Spotlight* (September, 1962), 24; see also J. E. Mainer's notes to *J. E. Mainer's Mountaineers*, Vol. I, Old Timey 106.

[45] King Records has released two LP albums of songs by the Mainer group: *J. E. Mainer and His Mountaineers*, King 765; and *Good Ole Mountain Music*, King 666.

their performance of novelty numbers such as "Brown's Ferry Blues," and the greatest tribute to their work is the large number of Delmore Brothers songs still found in the repertories of modern country singers.[46]

Another group that ranged far and wide for its material, yet was firmly based in tradition, was Kentucky's Carlisle Brothers. Cliff and Bill Carlisle performed virtually every type of country song, both gospel and secular. Performing throughout the thirties, the Carlisle Brothers became noted chiefly for their novelty, blues, and risque numbers. Instrumentally, they featured Bill's rhythm-guitar playing and Cliff's steel-guitar stylings on the dobro guitar. Cliff, who was among the very first to play the dobro, was one of the finest steel guitarists of the thirties and had accompanied Jimmie Rodgers on some of his recordings.[47] He directly influenced many fine steel guitarists, including Buck Graves of the Flatt and Scruggs organization, who takes great pride in owning a guitar that contains parts of Carlisle's old dobro.[48]

Cliff Carlisle had been recognized as a top-ranking country entertainer long before the brother act was organized. As a boy he had toured the southern states as a vaudeville entertainer on the B. F. Keith circuit, and had performed everything from hobo songs to Hawaiian numbers. His recording career began in 1930 when, along with guitarist Wilbur Ball, he signed a contract with Gennett records. He and Ball were the first blue-yodeling duet to appear on records.[49] As a yodeler Carlisle ranked very close to Jimmie Rodgers in excellence, and his early recordings, both in choice of songs and in style of performance, reveal a strong debt to the Mississippi Blue Yodeler.

From 1930 until his retirement in 1947 Cliff Carlisle recorded for nearly every major company in the country, sometimes alone and occasionally with his brother Bill or other entertainers such as Wilbur

[46] John Edwards, "The Delmore Brothers," *Country and Western Spotlight* (September, 1962), 16.

[47] For example: "Looking for a New Mama," Victor 23580, and "When the Cactus Is in Bloom," Victor 23636.

[48] Jack Hurst, "Hound Dog Wails of Fires and Corn Whiskey," Nashville *Tennessean*, January 15, 1967.

[49] John Edwards, "The Story of a Great Folk Artist—Cliff Carlisle," *Country and Western Spotlight* (September, 1962), 9. A short biographical sketch of Cliff Carlisle can be found in Gentry, *A History of Country, Western and Gospel Music*, pp. 195–196.

Ball and Fred Kirby. Carlisle's repertory contains some of the finest specimens of prison and hobo songs ever recorded in American music: "The Girl in the Blue Velvet Band," "Hobo's Fate," "Just a Lonely Hobo," and "Ramblin' Jack." His recorded material is interesting also because of its inclusion of risque and "rowdy" numbers, such as "Wild Cat Woman and Tom Cat Man," and "Tom Cat Blues." Carlisle's rowdy tunes were often recorded under the alias of "Bob Clifford." Regardless of the nature of the song, Carlisle's recordings were characterized by his easy, natural style and his expert guitar-playing. His solo recordings, along with those made with his brother, were among the more distinctive of the thirties.[50]

Another important brother act which featured the dobro was the Dixon Brothers. Howard and Dorsey Dixon came from Darlington, South Carolina, from the same type of textile-mill environment that produced such important country performers as Henry Whitter, Kelly Harrell, and Jimmie Tarlton. Although music was always an integral part of their lives, the Dixon Brothers were never permanently away from the mills. Howard died on the job, and Dorsey finally retired in 1951.

Both brothers played instruments—Howard, the guitar, and Dorsey, the fiddle and guitar—from the time they were in their late teens, but, although they played semiprofessionally throughout the late twenties, they made no serious attempt at a professional career until the thirties. In 1931 Jimmie Tarlton, in one of his frequent forays through the country, stopped in East Rockingham, North Carolina, where he gained temporary employment at a mill where the Dixon Brothers were working. Because of this chance encounter Dorsey was inspired to develop a finger-picking style on the guitar and Howard started playing the steel guitar, both in emulation of Tarlton. In 1934 the Dixon brothers inaugurated their professional career with a performance on J. W. Fincher's Crazy Water Crystals Saturday Night Jamboree, carried over WBT in Charlotte, North Carolina. They recorded for only two years—a stint with Victor which began on February 12, 1936 in Charlotte. Although their recorded repertory of over sixty songs never earned them enough money to free them from textile employment, they introduced several songs

[50] Many of Cliff Carlisle's original recordings can be heard on two valuable Old-Timey reissues: *Cliff Carlisle*, Vol. I, OT-103, and Vol. II, OT-104.

(most of them written by Dorsey, a prolific songwriter) which have endured in country music: "Intoxicated Rat," the widely-circulated "Weave Room Blues," and Roy Acuff's great hit, "Wreck on the Highway," which the Dixon Brothers entitled "I Didn't Hear Nobody Pray."[51]

Although many of the influential string bands and vocal groups of the thirties were, like the Dixon Brothers, of southeastern origin, some of them gained popularity far beyond the bounds of their native states. Homer and Walter Callahan (known as Bill and Joe) received their basic musical training in the mountains of western North Carolina. As was typical of most of the country performers of the period, they were reared on a musical diet of traditional ballads and gospel songs, which they learned at home and at mountain social gatherings and church services. In emulation of the contemporary hillbilly string bands they learned to play such stringed instruments as the mandolin and guitar. They both played guitars in their early career, although Bill Callahan switched to the mandolin in the late thirties. After performing at folk festivals in western North Carolina and on small radio stations in the South, they gained a recording contract with the American Record Company in 1934. Their career led them all over the South: WHAS in Louisville, Kentucky; WWVA in Wheeling, West Virginia; WLW in Cincinnati, Ohio (with Red Foley); Springfield, Missouri, where they performed with the Weaver Brothers and Elviry; KVOO in Tulsa, Oklahoma; and finally, in 1941, to Texas, where they had radio shows on KRLD in Dallas and KWFT in Wichita Falls. They became one of the most popular bands of the Southwest.

Performing daily over KRLD, they built up an immense listening audience, as evidenced by the sale of their illustrated song books. Their personal appearances were usually made in listening range of their broadcasts, although they sometimes traveled as far as Mississippi. The Callahan Brothers, with their traditional southeastern orientation, therefore became popular in an area less imbued with the "mountain" tradition and one in which the newer "western swing" music was becoming dominant. Their recorded repertory thus shows evidence of both major influences. They performed many songs with

[51] Archie Green, "Dorsey Dixon: Minstrel of the Mills," *Sing Out*, XVI, No. 3 (July, 1966), 10–13. Green has also edited and written the notes for the important Dorsey Dixon album, *Babies in the Mill*, Testament T-3301.

deep roots in the past, such as the murder ballads "Banks of the Ohio" and "The Silver Dagger" ("Katie Dear"); and in April, 1935, they made one of the earliest recordings of a song now well known in urban folk music circles: "The House of the Rising Sun," which they called "Rounder's Luck." But they also included, and this became pronounced in the forties, many rhythm novelties of the Delmore and Carlisle Brothers variety such as "Rattlesnaking Daddy" (written by Bill Carlisle) and "Step It Up and Go." The Callahan Brothers are an important example of the country musicians'—or folk musicians', for that matter—propensity to accept material from any source so long as it fits in well with their own personal styles. The Callahans built up a diversified country repertory, but their instrumentation was like that of the Mainer Brothers and similar groups. And their style of harmony—the high harmony was performed by Bill Callahan—definitely marked them as a group of southeastern rural origin.[52]

In terms of their tremendous impact upon modern country music, by far the most important recording group of the thirties was a Kentucky organization, the Monroe Brothers. This group, composed of brothers Birch, Bill, and Charlie (later only Bill and Charlie), produced out of their folk heritage a myriad of styles and songs that influenced perhaps thousands of country, and eventually city, musicians. The Monroe Brothers, a smaller ensemble than most of the string combinations of the time, featured Bill's intricate mandolin style and high harmony singing and Charlie's lead singing and dynamic guitar playing. Largely through his own independent work after the forties, Bill Monroe became one of the four or five most influential performers in country-music history. His mandolin style provided the base from which most modern bluegrass music developed.[53] The Monroe Brothers recorded for Victor traditional ballads, love songs, mountain instrumentals and novelties, and sacred melodies. They first popularized many of the songs which became standards in country music—including "What Would You Give in Exchange For Your Soul" and "Nine Pound Hammer"—and many,

[52] Interview with Homer Callahan, Dallas, Texas, August 23, 1963. See also Bob Pinson, "The Callahan Brothers," *Country Directory*, No. 2 (n.d.), 5–13; this article is particularly valuable because it contains a complete discography of Callahan recordings (pp. 7–13).

[53] A fuller discussion of Bill Monroe, bluegrass, and the earlier Monroe Brothers will be found in Chapter 10.

such as "Feast Here Tonight" and "All the Good Times Are Past and Gone," which have been accepted by urban folksingers.[54] Of all the hillbilly groups of the thirties, the Monroe Brothers, because of their repertory and musical styles, are probably the most respected among folklorists. The Monroe Brothers dissolved their organization in 1938 and thereafter Charlie and Bill organized their own independent groups.

The Monroe Brothers were part of a host of guitar-mandolin combinations that gained popularity in the thirties. The mandolin gave indications of supplanting the five-string banjo as the most popular hillbilly instrument. The banjo, in fact, has had a very curious history in country music. It came late to the southern mountains but in the twenties became a widely used accompanying instrument on hillbilly recordings. By the thirties, however, it was rarely heard. If used by hillbilly bands, the five-string banjo was seldom featured as a lead instrument, and when employed as a rhythm instrument it was always unobtrusively in the background. The mandolin, however, became widely popular as both a rhythm and lead instrument. This instrument, of ancient European origin, was ideal for fast rhythmic flourishes and for sad, wistful accompaniment. Southern rural musicians acquired mandolins largely through the mail-order catalogues, and they learned to play the instrument by using the instructional manual which accompanied it. It was in this way, perhaps, that a bit of the musical rhythm of Italy entered American country music.

Two mandolin-guitar ensembles who used the National Barn Dance as their primary base of operations were the well-known Mac and Bob, and Karl and Harty. Lester McFarland and Robert A. Gardner (Mac and Bob) came from Kentucky and Tennessee respectively, but they first joined their musical interests in 1915 at the Kentucky School for the Blind, where both were enrolled as students. They were among the many fine blind performers who have enriched the field of country music. Mac generally sang tenor on their duet performances and picked the instrumental leads on his mandolin. His mandolin playing on their Brunswick recordings after 1926 did much to stimulate the general popularity of the instrument among country musicians. Along with Bob, who played guitar and sang lead,

[54] A complete Monroe Brothers discography, compiled by Brad McCuen, can be found in *Country Directory*, No. 2 (n.d.), 14–16.

Mac began performing in schoolhouses and on the vaudeville circuit in 1922. From 1925 until 1931 Mac and Bob (using their full names) performed over WNOX in Knoxville, Tennessee, and began disseminating melodies that would later find their way into the recorded repertories of other hill-country musicians. During this same period, beginning in 1926, Mac and Bob recorded for Brunswick and the American Record Company and in the process introduced some of the classics of country music: for example, "When the Roses Bloom Again" (their first recording), "Twenty One Years" (the great country prison song written by Bob Miller), and "That Little Boy of Mine." McFarland and Gardner actually had one of the most extensive repertories in country music, including everything from "I'm Forever Blowing Bubbles" to "Midnight on the Stormy Deep" and "The East Bound Train." They first began using the label "Mac and Bob" during their initial years on the National Barn Dance from 1931 to 1934 (they had a second stint on the WLS show from 1939 to 1950). After their retirement from show business in the early fifties, Bob became a director of religious rescue missions, and Mac joined the recreation staff of the Chicago State Hospital. They remain in these capacities today.[55]

Karl Davis and Hartford Connecticut Taylor (Karl and Harty) came to the National Barn Dance in 1931 as part of John Lair's Cumberland Ridge Runners. Both musicians came from the vicinity of Mount Vernon, Kentucky, and received part of their grade-school instruction from John Lair, the man who would eventually accompany them to the WLS country show and back in the late thirties to the Renfro Valley show in Kentucky. Although they often performed as part of a larger group, Karl and Harty made their most distinctive mark on country music through their duet harmonies, mandolin and guitar instrumentation, and influential songs. Karl had learned to play the mandolin at the age of twelve after hearing the instrument played by Doc Hopkins, the well-known mountain balladeer and later member of the Cumberland Ridge Runners. Along with Harty, who had taught himself to play the guitar, Karl began playing for local parties in Mount Vernon. In their later recording and perform-

[55] Letter to the author from Dave Wylie, March 24, 1967; letter to the author from George C. Biggar, March 18, 1967. See also John Edwards, "McFarland and Gardner," *Country and Western Spotlight* (September, 1962), 15.

ing career the duet introduced a number of songs which have endured in the country-music tradition. "I'm Just Here to Get My Baby Out of Jail," recorded by entertainers as diverse as the Blue Sky Boys and the Everly Brothers, is only one of many popular hillbilly songs first introduced by Karl and Harty.[56]

Of the many mandolin-guitar groups of the thirties, none was of greater importance, in terms of tradition, than Bill and Earl Bolick, popularly known as "The Blue Sky Boys." In the long list of stars who have been connected with country music since the thirties, none has more deserved to be called authentic than the Blue Sky Boys. In their style of singing and instrumentation, and in their selection of old-time songs, they uncompromisingly adhered to traditional patterns. In a sense, the Blue Sky Boys emerged from and sang for a rural society that was suspended in time, a society that still clung to the values of the past while hovering on the edge of the industrial system that would destroy the traditional values and submerge the old-time music under a wave of commercialism. Their personal popularity, gained largely through radio and personal appearances, was exceeded by no other duet—not even the Monroe Brothers—in the southeastern states during the late thirties. However, the World War which was to come would bring to an end the society that produced and sustained the Blue Sky Boys' style. As William A. Farr said in a *Sing Out* article, "the Blue Sky Boys' music could not survive the culture which had sustained it."[57] After the Bolick Brothers returned from service in World War II they found that their plaintive old-time songs were unwanted by the new generation of country-music enthusiasts, who were being lured away by the upbeat sounds of electric instruments. Resolutely refusing to compromise on either material or style of performance, the Blue Sky Boys, still young men, retired from professional music. Bill Bolick went to work for the post office in Greensboro, North Carolina, and Earl, in a gesture symbolic of the industrial transformation that was doing so much to subvert the old music, went to work for Lockheed Aircraft in Tucker, Georgia.[58]

[56] Basic information on Karl and Harty is from *Stand By* magazine, (November 2, 1935), 9 (made available to the writer by Dave Wylie).

[57] William A. Bolick, "Bill Bolick's Own Story of the Blue Sky Boys," (Introduction and commentary by William A. Farr), *Sing Out*, XVII, No. 2 (April–May, 1967), 20.

[58] Interview with Bill Bolick, Greensboro, North Carolina, August 24, 1965.

The student of American folksong would do well to study the Blue Sky Boys' repertory, for here one can find a myriad of examples of the song types that found their way into the hearts and homes of southern country people. The Bolick family, too, serves as an archetypical example of the hill-country people whose values were shaped by both the conservative force of tradition and by the changing realities of modern America. Bill and Earl Bolick were descended from German immigrants who moved, as did countless other hill-country people, down from Pennsylvania into the North Carolina piedmont. Their father, Garland Bolick, grew tobacco and worked in textile mills. When Bill and Earl were growing up on a farm near Hickory, near the edge of the mountain district known as the "Land of the Blue Sky," they were exposed to a variety of song sources that would one day provide the nucleus of their professional repertory. They learned from friends and relatives in the mountains, from Church of God services that they attended, and from the country-music recordings that they loved so well. Both young men had a passionate commitment to traditional songs and styles, and Bill Bolick, in particular, viewed his song-making role as a folkloristic one of collecting and preserving the ballads and gospel songs of earlier years. The Bolick Brothers, in fact, were one of the few country groups who referred to their music as "folksongs," and, like Bradley Kincaid, they resented the term "hillbilly" music.[59]

Bill Bolick sang briefly in 1935 for a group called the East Hickory String Band (renamed the Crazy Hickory Nuts after they moved to Asheville and gained sponsorship by the Crazy Water Crystals Company), and, in that same year, he and Earl began their duet singing career on WWNC in Asheville. Their duet harmony, probably the closest in country-music history, was produced by the skillful blending of Earl's nasally resonant baritone voice with Bill's smooth tenor. They were immediately popular on WWNC and gained a loyal regional following through radio broadcasts and personal appearances. They augmented their popularity through the acquisition of a Victor recording contract in June, 1936. From the date of their first Bluebird

[59] Basic biographical information on the Bolick Brothers is from an interview with Bill Bolick, August 24, 1965. The best printed source for both the style and career of the Blue Sky Boys is Archie Green's notes to *The Blue Sky Boys,* Camden CAL797; another excellent source is Ed Kahn's notes to *The Blue Sky Boys,* Capitol T2483.

recording of "The Sunny Side of Life," a gospel tune written by Bill Bolick, The Blue Sky Boys never compromised on either material or style of performance.[60] When they retired they were still an old-time singing group with a style almost identical to that with which they had begun in 1935.

The Blue Sky Boys' repertory occasionally included a novelty song such as "Cindy," "Hang Out the Front Door Key," or their radio theme song, "Are You From Dixie?" Despite the occasional exception, however, the dominant theme of their music was the "tragic side of life." In mournful, close harmony they sang tales of death, sorrow, and unrequited love, and they approached each number with a compassion and tenderness that has seldom been equalled in country music. Their instrumentation, characterized by the expert mandolin stylings of Bill Bolick produced against a background of deep, rhythmic guitar tones supplied by Earl Bolick, created a mood similar to that evoked by their vocalizing.

In choosing their selections for recording, the Blue Sky Boys sometimes chose numbers that had already demonstrated popularity when recorded by earlier performers such as the Carter Family, Ernest Stoneman, or Karl and Harty. In other cases, they merely recorded those songs that were often requested on their radio shows.[61] The Blue Sky Boy's inclination toward somber and sentimental melodies was evidently shared by their listeners. The bulk of their recorded numbers were traditional songs like the American murder ballad "Banks of the Ohio" and the British broadside "The Butcher's Boy"; sentimental melodies like "There'll Come a Time," "I Believe it for My Mother Told Me So," and "Sing a Song for the Blind"; unrequited-love songs like "The House Where We Were Wed" and "Who Wouldn't Be Lonely"; and religious songs like "Only One Step More" and "When the Stars Begin to Fall."[62]

After their return from service in World War II, the Blue Sky Boys added a fiddle to their recordings. This instrument, however, was the only change or addition ever made in their instrumentation, and

---

[60] Archie Green, notes to *The Blue Sky Boys*, Camden CAL797.

[61] Letter to the author from Bill Bolick, August 25, 1966.

[62] The best selection of Blue Sky Boys recordings now available is the re-issued numbers on *The Blue Sky Boys*, Camden CAL797; a complete Blue Sky Boys discography, compiled by Brad McCuen, is in *Country Directory*, No. 1 (November, 1960), 20–25.

they successfully resisted pressure from RCA Victor to add an electric guitar to their records.[63] Refusing to surrender to commercialism, the Blue Sky Boys retired, and, except for a few rare appearances before college groups and folk-festival audiences, they have not returned to the field of professional music.

The technological revolution that did so much to drive singers like the Blue Sky Boys from the entertainment business affected country music from its very beginnings and was, in fact, responsible for its dissemination throughout the United States. The very commercial process that introduced rural music to a receptive national audience has also incessantly absorbed that music. Country music, therefore, cannot be studied as a purely rural phenomenon. It must always be considered in relation to the dominant society that lies around it, the industrial-technological-urban society that has modified and transformed all American values.

To this point in this study most country music considered has been of the traditional, blues, or gospel variety, and has been that which evokes images of quaint pastoral life: the rural church, the placid mountain brook, the family fireside, and the hillside farm. Country music, however, has encompassed much more than this, and the South itself has possessed more than just a rural tradition. As pervasive as the rural ethos has been, the South has agonizingly and slowly succumbed to the inroads made by the industrial revolution. A steady and never ending procession of forces—the railroads, the iron and coal interests, timber companies, textile mills, and oil operators—have gradually transformed the South, its inhabitants and the music which they have made.

Southern rural music, both before and after commercialization, has persistently chronicled the developing stages of industrialization,[64] sometimes with disgust, often with amusement, and nearly always with fascination. Literally hundreds of songs have described the rural folk's open-eyed wonder and curiosity about the new gadgets and inventions that have revolutionized southern and American society. The first great economic phenomenon to break through the

[63] Letter to the author from Bill Bolick, Greensboro, North Carolina, July 31, 1963.

[64] Although much more needs to be done, Mike Seeger has made a valuable beginning toward the recording of industrial country songs in *Tipple, Loom, and Rail*, Folkways 5273.

South's wall of isolation—the railroad—inspired a body of songs that comprise one of the single largest categories in country and folk music. Such songs as "Wreck on the Southern Old 97," "Casey Jones," "Waiting for a Train," and "Wabash Cannon Ball" have thrilled generations of American listeners.[65] In more recent times the train songs have given way to songs about more modern means of communication, as is witnessed by the spate of truck-driving songs, such as "Six Days on the Road."[66] In accepting and chronicling the story of innovations, however, the southern country folk have not lost their age-old tendency to moralize and to use the objects of this life to symbolize eternal truths. "Life's Railway to Heaven," "The Automobile of Life," "Life's Elevator," and scores of songs similar to them have all emphasized the ancient theme of the transience of temporal life. The only difference between these and older songs is the depiction of modern transportation devices to symbolize the brief passage of man's life through earth's vale of tears.

This literary-musical device was effectively used by Dorsey Dixon in a song in which the automobile collision supplants the classic motif of the train tragedy: "Wreck on the Highway," recorded and made famous by Roy Acuff.[67] Universally known by country- and folk-music fans, "Wreck on the Highway" reminds the listener that despite the accelerating changes of modern life, some things never change. The Grim Reaper still exacts his deadly toll, and even when life seems its gayest, the very vehicle that has contributed most to one's pleasure may also be the means through which this pleasure turns into tragedy.

Southerners have not viewed the industrial revolution as an unmixed blessing, and, though it is often overlooked by historians, a strain of radicalism—as evidenced by the Populist movement—has run through the fabric of southern history.[68] Southern country music, therefore, has occasionally lent itself to a form of expression which has been of continuing interest to folklorists and social historians:

[65] Sherwin and McClintock, *Railroad Songs of Yesterday*.

[66] For a sampling of songs in the truck driving genre see Dave Dudley, *Truck Drivin' Son-of-a-Gun*, Mercury 21028.

[67] Dorsey Dixon's version can be heard on *Babies in the Mill*, Testament, T-3301. Roy Acuff's original recording was released on Okeh 6685.

[68] The best account of southern populism is in C. Vann Woodward, *Origins of the New South*.

protest music.[69] The civil rights revolution of the sixties, with its use of stirring songs to dramatize and inspire the movement,[70] serves as a modern reminder that the protest song has played a vital role in the unceasing efforts to reform and humanize American society. Through the study of folk music, the folklorist and social historian can gain a greater understanding of the attitudes and ideals of those stratums in American society which leave few if any written documents. The scholar may obtain his source of information directly from the lips of the informant, or perhaps more easily through the medium of a phonograph recording. Both folksongs and folk attitudes of the depression years of the thirties have evoked continuing response from scholars who have demonstrated an intellectual and social concern for the plight of suffering farmers and unemployed laborers. Few eras have elicited more responses of a protest nature, and no groups in American society had greater traditions of expressing their basic attitudes in song than did rural white and Negro southerners.

The question of protest music presents some interesting problems. It is obvious that the southern people were confronted by conditions that needed to be protested, but did they protest, and if so, how was their protest directed? Southern poor whites—tenant farmers, coal miners, textile workers—were beset with the problems of low prices, low wages, poor housing, and job insecurity. Despite the multitude of problems, and despite the persistence of the ballad tradition of expressing stories in song, the number of protest songs in country music, commercial and otherwise, is extremely low. Although individual items can be detailed, as a class of songs they comprise a small percentage of the total folk repertory. Of course, the number of social "comments" in recorded hillbilly music make up a tremendous percentage of the over-all total, but they certainly cannot all be construed as protest songs. Admittedly, however, since the

[69] Archie Green is the most knowledgeable authority on the subject of industrial and protest music in the United States. A major work in the area of protest music is John Greenway, *American Folksongs of Protest*.

[70] Probably the best source to the contemporary "freedom songs" is *Broadside*, a monthly topical song magazine edited by Sis Cunningham in New York. Also excellent as a source for modern protest material is *Sing Out* magazine. A short general study of the topical songs of the sixties is Josh Dunson, *Freedom in the Air*.

recording companies are profit-minded business organizations, it would be generous indeed for them to allow a large quantity of protest songs to be placed on the market.

It should be made clear at the outset that in this discussion "protest" means "overt" protest—an utterance or outcry against social and economic grievances, or a call for action against them. The outcries of a poor farmer against the landlord or the credit system, or of a laborer against the lords of capital, have been few indeed. Instead, the southern rural white has more often directed his protests against other factors in society, usually individual personal misfortunes. The sorrows of this world, fatalistically explained as the fruits of individual error or as divine payments for past sins, are expressed through songs of self-pity or of yearning for solace through heavenly reward. But the system that produced these sorrows is seldom attacked.[71]

Regardless of their relatively minor position in the field of folk music, protest and semi-protest songs became a fairly important part of southern rural music during the thirties. This type of song could be heard in both commercial and noncommercial country music. The most explosive areas in the South, and those where class hostility was most extreme, were the drought-ridden Southwest, the textile-mill region of the Carolinas, and the coal fields around Harlan, Kentucky. All three areas have been important ballad-producing regions, and each has contributed greatly to the formation of country music.

The unhappy region of Harlan County, Kentucky, particularly produced some of the most bitter class feeling and labor violence that the country has known. It has also produced some of the truest expressions of protest music and labor songs that are available in the American experience. In this region of eastern Kentucky singing and the tradition of ballad-making were deeply ingrained. The Kentucky mountain people, who provided the bulk of the work force, carried

[71] The above statements are, of course, open to argument. I realize that, despite the paucity of protest material in the standard folksong compilations, this may not be a valid criterion for judging their total number. As John Greenway has indicated, most protest songs are ephemeral by nature and do not survive long enough to be collected. (*American Folksongs of Protest*, pp. 4–5). It is possible, too, that many of these songs may have been omitted from collections because the folklorist did not consider them folksongs.

their stubbornly individualistic attitudes into the Kentucky coal fields. The stark misery and oppressive conditions of the coal mines made the mountaineers loyal union people, and their individualism made them among the most militant of American union members. In their organizational drives and on the picket lines, they sang melodies that expressed their discontent or the necessity for unity. Generally, their protest songs were set to traditional or sacred melodies.[72]

The most productive and talented spokesman of the Kentucky coal miners was Aunt Molly Jackson, the wife of a union member.[73] Along with her sister Sarah Ogan Gunning, she did much to popularize labor and protest music in New York and other areas outside Kentucky. Aunt Molly made only one commercial recording (Sarah Gunning has been recently recorded),[74] but she was a favorite informant of the folklorists who gathered material for the Library of Congress. Her store of ballads and folksongs was almost limitless, and she generally set her labor lyrics to some older melody with which she was familiar. Aunt Molly took her songs from wherever she could get them—from traditional or commercial sources. An example of the traditional influence was her "Dreadful Memories"— the story of coal miners' children who had died because of malnutrition—which was modeled upon the popular southern gospel song, "Precious Memories."[75] Aunt Molly Jackson, Sarah Ogan Gunning, and similar individuals, such as Woody Guthrie, are interesting examples of people who sprang from the folk and sang melodies that were partly influenced by commercial sources. They were border-line cases who borrowed their songs from a variety of sources and in their appeal went far beyond the limits of their native folk audiences.[76] In

[72] Greenway, *American Folksongs of Protest*, pp. 147–149.

[73] A biographical account of Aunt Molly Jackson can be found in Greenway, *American Folksongs of Protest*, pp. 252–275. The *Kentucky Folklore Record* has devoted a special edition to the life and career of Aunt Molly (VII, No. 4 [October–November, 1961]).

[74] Aunt Molly's single commercial recording was "Kentucky Miner's Wife" ("Hungry Ragged Blues"), Columbia 15731D (both sides); see Archie Green, "An Aunt Molly Jackson Discography," *Kentucky Folklore Record*, VII, No. 4 (October–December, 1961), 159–169. Sarah Ogan Gunning was recorded on a long play album in 1965: *Girl of Constant Sorrow*, Folk-Legacy FSA-26 (notes by Archie Green).

[75] D. K. Wilgus, "Aunt Molly's 'Big Record,'" *Kentucky Folklore Record*, VII, No. 4 (October–December, 1961), 174.

[76] Aunt Molly moved to New York in 1936 after being black-listed in Ken-

fact, they were enthusiastically accepted by northern urban groups, and at least in the case of Guthrie they became more identified with the urban "folk" than with the rural.

Woodrow Wilson (Woody) Guthrie occupies an unusual position in American country and folk music. He began as a hillbilly singer with strong traditional roots and advanced to the position of America's most revered urban folksinger and writer. Born in Okemah, Oklahoma, in 1914, Woody learned a wide variety of traditional melodies from his parents. In 1929, his parents being in an impoverished condition, he went out on his own and traveled over much of the Southwest doing odd jobs. In Pampa, Texas, where he experienced the dust storms for the first time, he learned a few basic guitar chords from his uncle Jeff, one of the local deputy sheriffs. The two of them formed a hillbilly band and began entertaining at local functions in the Pampa area.[77]

Woody Guthrie gained his earliest experience in the small towns of Oklahoma and Texas when those areas were experiencing the social flux of the twenties and thirties. The late twenties and early thirties saw the eruption of the southwestern oil boom, and, with its passage, the coming of the dust storms and the Great Depression. In this atmosphere of social upheaval Woody Guthrie developed the style and politics that made him the "darling" of urban folksong enthusiasts. Building upon a traditional repertory, Guthrie perfected his technique in the southwestern oil-town honky-tonks.

Guthrie was imbued with a strong sense of social consciousness, and the unfortunate decade of the thirties inflamed this feeling, as it did with many people, to outright rebelliousness. Guthrie moved to California and, in typical hillbilly fashion, obtained a job on Station KFVD in Los Angeles.[78] California at that time was being deluged with victims of the depression and the southwestern dust bowl. Guthrie felt a strong emotional kinship with the homeless migratory workers, especially his fellow Okies, and he began to compose songs

tucky for her union activities. She became well known in union circles there (Greenway, *American Folksongs of Protest*, pp. 259–260).

[77] Woody Guthrie, *Bound for Glory*, pp. 36–39, 231; see also Greenway, *American Folksongs of Protest*, pp. 275–302.

[78] Guthrie described the manner in which the depression and dust bowl aroused his awareness of social injustice in *Bound for Glory*, (pp. 231–232).

which expressed his sympathies with these people and his anger at the system which caused their misfortunes. Thus, Guthrie began to change from a simple singer of hillbilly songs to a full-fledged performer of protest music. By the end of the thirties he had accumulated an extensive aggregation of original compositions dealing with the dust storms. These ballads, usually set to traditional Oklahoma and Texas melodies, included "Dust Bowl Refugee," "Talking Dust Bowl Blues," and "I Ain't Got No Home in This World Anymore."[79] The songs were performed with Guthrie's distinctive southwestern twang and his rhythmic, Carter Family-inspired guitar playing.

In 1938 Guthrie moved to New York where he gained the attention of folk-music enthusiasts in that area. He recorded for the National Archives, performed on New York radio stations, and recorded his "Dust Bowl Ballads" for Victor.[80] With his sojourn in New York Guthrie all but severed his ties with the southern rural folk, and became instead the chief apostle of the urban folk movement. Guthrie immediately became associated with assorted intellectuals and folk-music devotees who wished to use the music as a propaganda vehicle for liberal programs. Guthrie, along with Aunt Molly Jackson and Negro folksinger Huddie Ledbetter, were readily accepted by New York intellectual groups. Guthrie seemed to be a living example of exactly the sort of person the liberals were fighting for, a flesh-and-blood proletarian from the poverty-stricken dust bowl who lent his support to liberal causes. And better yet, he sang protest songs. Here was a proletarian, of almost storybook proportions, who acted as a proletarian should act. Woody Guthrie became a popular and sought after performer before college groups, union organization meetings, and intellectual gatherings of one kind or another. Along with Pete Seeger, Lee Hays, and Millard Lampell, he organized in 1940 a folksinging group called the Almanac Singers,[81] who sang labor and patriotic songs, such as "The Good Reuben James," during World War II. Before his tragic death from Huntington's chorea in 1967, Woody Guthrie had been most responsible for the course that the

[79] Guthrie's dust-bowl ballads were recorded for Victor: *Dust Bowl Ballads,* Vol. 1, Victor P-27, and *Dust Bowl Ballads,* Vol. 2, Victor P-28. These have been reissued by Folkways as *Talking Dust Bowl,* FA2011 (FP11).

[80] Jerry Silverman, *Folk Blues: One Hundred and Ten American Folk Blues,* p. 12.

[81] *Ibid.*

urban folk movement had assumed in the United States. Guthrie was the most quoted and, to many urban enthusiasts, the greatest folk poet the United States had produced.[82]

Guthrie's relationship to commercial country music is seen in the influences that shaped his own particular style. Despite his urban orientation after 1938, Guthrie's vocal and instrumental styles were firmly within the southern hillbilly tradition. In fact, as Dick Reuss had indicated, Guthrie never used the word "folk" or "folksinger" to refer to himself before he made his move to New York. The Woody Guthrie of the pre-1938 period was a hillbilly singer who sang for hillbilly audiences.[83] His guitar accompaniment was a modification of that of Maybelle Carter,[84] and the lyrics of his songs, in many cases, were set to older melodies of commercial and noncommercial origin. His ballad "Tom Joad" (based on the John Steinbeck creation) was set to the melody of "John Hardy"; his popular "The Philadelphia Lawyer" was set to the melody of "The Jealous Lover";[85] and, evidencing further Carter Family influence, Guthrie used the melody of "The Wildwood Flower" in "The Reuben James" and that of "Little Darling, Pal of Mine" in "This Land Is Your Land." The list of Guthrie's melodic borrowings is much more extensive than this.[86]

Some of Guthrie's compositions gained wide popularity among hillbilly enthusiasts. These include such numbers as "So Long, It's Been Good to Know You," "The Philadelphia Lawyer," and the very popular "Oklahoma Hills," recorded by his cousin Jack Guthrie in the 1940's.[87] Although Woody Guthrie acknowledged his debt to the

[82] Alan Lomax, in discussing Guthrie's songs, said "they have a truth, an authenticity, and a punch which no other poet of this age can match" (*The Folk Songs of North America*, p. 431).

[83] Dick Reuss, student of folklore at Indiana University, is doing a major study of Woody Guthrie; he has made part of his research available to me.

[84] Greenway, *American Folksongs of Protest*, p. 285.

[85] Sometimes called "Fair Eyed Ellen" (see the Blue Sky Boys recording, Bluebird B-6808-B).

[86] Alan Lomax said that "Woody has never tried to be original . . . Like all folk poets, he uses familiar tunes, re-works old songs, adding new lines and phrases out of the folk-say of the situation" (*The Folk Songs of North America*, p. 431).

[87] Jack Guthrie's recording of "Oklahoma Hills," (Capitol 201), has become a standard in commercial country music. It has been reissued by Capitol on *Jack Guthrie and His Greatest Songs*, Capitol T-2456.

Carter Family and freely borrowed from hillbilly sources, it is doubt-ful whether he identified himself with the hillbilly performers of the post-1938 period. After that date he became associated with the urban folk movement and never thereafter had anything but remote connections with hillbilly music. He began a series of recording ventures with Folkways,[88] a company then catering only to a limited, sophisticated audience, and his concerts were given usually to East-ern college groups and sophisticates. Guthrie was well known, but not among the rural folk who had spawned both him and his music. The course of Guthrie's career was roughly equivalent to what was hap-pening to folk music as a whole. "Folk" music was becoming the province of intellectuals and sophisticates and was becoming farther and farther removed from the "folk." In the following decades Woody Guthrie's disciples would create a public image of folk music that generally would have no room for hillbilly music.

Apart from Guthrie, hillbilly singers responded to the rigors of the depression with a variety of songs.[89] Some of the singers joked about their predicaments; others made perceptive comments about the social scene; a few rejoiced at the changes wrought by the New Deal; and some engaged in self-pity and expressed longings for a land beyond the grave where no depressions would come. The southern United States was hard hit by the depression. In fact, the southern farmer had suffered throughout the 1920's while the remainder of the nation experienced a general prosperity. Whereas in preceding years the South had been generally characterized by a net loss of migration, the trend was reversed from 1930 to 1940 and the bulk of migrations tended to be internal. Southerners, in general, remained at home or moved into southern cities.[90]

Despite the population stability of the greater part of the South, a substantial, and socially important, exodus occurred from the South-west: the states of Oklahoma, Arkansas, and Texas. Dispossessed

---

[88] His album *Talking Union* (FA5284), recorded along with Pete Seeger, has been termed by Alan Lomax "the classic recording of American folksongs of protest" (*The Folk Songs of North America*, p. 610).

[89] The New Lost City Ramblers have recorded a representative selection of these songs, complete with printed notes, in *Songs From the Depression*, Folk-ways FN 5264.

[90] John Maclachlan and Joe S. Floyd, Jr., *This Changing South*, pp. 7–8; see also Rupert B. Vance, *All These People*, pp. 120–124.

farmers of this region, made homeless by automation, dust storms, and the depression, trekked westward, lured by the fabled promises of California as a land of hope for the migrants and an area of material abundance. This concept, graphically described in John Steinbeck's Grapes of Wrath, was later pictured in humorous fashion in a hillbilly song[91] that described jobs as being so abundant in California that all a man needed was a shovel—to pick up the gold.

California was not the Garden of Eden that the migrants expected. Jobs were scarce, wages were incredibly low, and California public opinion was bitterly hostile to the migrants. The Okies were resented because of their religious, speech, and cultural differences, and because of their poverty. The southwestern migrants carried with them to California their inherited store of beliefs, values, attitudes, and institutions. This included hillbilly music.[92]

In the Farm Security Administration camps, where the majority of the migrants temporarily resided, the dwellers amused themselves at night by singing and playing the old songs which eased their minds or reminded them of their former homes. One observer remarked that in his meanderings through the camps he heard "fragments of tunes that a more prosperous America has forgotten in the process of growing up and getting rich."[93] These songs ("Going Down the Road Feeling Bad" was said to be the most popular) included both the traditional songs and the newer ones produced by the commercial hillbillies. Songs popular among the Okies included "The Great Speckled Bird," "The Convict and the Rose," and "Carter Blues." The Okies' choice of songs was resented by many staid, respectable Californians who looked upon the music as one long wailing, nasal lament,[94] but the dispossessed southern migrants made their songs a permanent part of California musical life. Southern California, in particular, remained a stronghold of hillbilly music. The California migration was representative of the process which in the forties spread hillbilly

[91] See Greenway, American Folksongs of Protest, p. 205.
[92] By 1950 over half (51.4%) of California's residents had been born in other states. Texas was the largest contributor, followed by Illinois and Oklahoma. In addition, Arkansas and Louisiana had contributed over 100,000 each (Warren S. Thompson, Growth and Changes in California's Population, p. 68).
[93] Charles Todd and Robert Sonkin, "Ballads of the Okies," The New York Times Magazine (November 17, 1940), 6.
[94] Ibid., pp. 7, 18.

music all over the United States—the transplantation of a musical culture through population migration.

The surprising feature of commercial hillbilly protest songs was not necessarily their existence but the fact that the phonograph companies allowed them to be recorded. But it has been said that white southerners who suffered from the hard times demanded songs that spoke to them of their difficulties. The record companies, therefore, had no choice but to comply with the demand.[95] Okeh released a record by Bill Cox, entitled "Franklin Roosevelt's Back Again," applauding Roosevelt's re-election in 1936. Because of FDR's great personal popularity the existence of partisan songs is not surprising.[96] Cox, who has recently been rediscovered in West Virginia and re-recorded on Kanawha Records,[97] had an acute, partisan Democratic way of viewing society. Although he wrote some of the great perennials of country music, such as "Sparkling Brown Eyes" and "Filipino Baby,"[98] his most interesting compositions of the thirties were those which dealt with social problems. His "NRA Blues," for example, extolled the efforts of one of the major New Deal agencies to alleviate unemployment and to improve working conditions. Some of the depression songs, like Slim Smith's "Breadline Blues," were partisanly political; others, like Roy Acuff's "Old Age Pension Check,"[99] poked good-natured fun at some of the social legislation of the time. The Acuff song related how "poor old grandma" would suddenly become like a frivolous sixteen-year-old when the social security payments started rolling in. Uncle Dave Macon, always a perceptive and witty critic of the social scene, recorded a few songs that at least bordered on the "protest" category. They were, however, more in the nature of

[95] This was pointed out by John Cohen in the notes to the New Lost City Ramblers, *Songs from the Depression*, Folkways FH5264.

[96] Cox recorded another song on the same day (November 28, 1936) entitled "The Democratic Donkey Is in His Stall Again" Okeh 05896.

[97] Billy Cox, *The Dixie Songbird*, Kanawha 305.

[98] A Billy Cox discography, compiled by Eugene Earle, is in the *Disc Collector*, No. 13, 2–5; No. 14, 9–13; and No. 15, 2–7. Cox's songs, often recorded with Cliff Hobbs, include some of the most interesting titles found in hillbilly music; for example, "Electric Chair Blues," Vocalion 04924; and "The Trial of Bruno Richard Hauptmann," Parts I and II, Melotone 13344.

[99] Roy Acuff's "Old Age Pension Check" was first released on Okeh 05244. It has also been recorded, along with "NRA Blues," and "Breadline Blues," by the New Lost City Ramblers in *Songs from the Depression*, Folkways FH 5264.

commentaries than denunciations. They included such songs as "All I've Got's Gone" (Vocalion 14904), which described what had happened to the people who had lived beyond their means during the twenties, and "All in Down and Out Blues" (Bluebird 7350), which showed that for millions of Americans "Wall Street's propositions were not all roses."[100]

One of the richest, but as yet incompletely documented, bodies of industrial and protest songs on hillbilly records are those from the textile-mill villages of the Carolina piedmont region.[101] The existence of the textile factories—with their regimentation, long hours, low pay, and child labor—provide a grim refutation of the idea that the South has had no industrial tradition. The textile mills were brick- and stone testimonials to those "New South" propagandists who sought to bring progress to the South by ending its economic colonial dependence on the North. They sought to "bring the factory to the field."[102] The textile mills did bring progress to the South, and prosperity to some, but they also brought misery to many. Thousands of mountain- and hill-country people willingly left their farms to seek the promise of a better life, only to find that they had merely traded rural deprivation for an industrial poverty which robbed them even of their independence. Kept close to economic penury, depressed by a burdensome regimentation, and ostracized by middle-class southerners who called them "lintheads" and "factory trash," the textile operatives found solace in old-time religion, protection through the trade-union movement, and comfort in their age-old tradition of ballad-making.

The textile mills produced not only an important body of folksongs, they also spawned a high percentage of commercial country singers,

---

[100] Uncle Dave Macon recorded a number of songs that contained social criticism. One of the most significant was his "Governor Al Smith," (Brunswick 263), which called for the election of the New York governor and the repeal of prohibition.

[101] Archie Green has done the most significant work on the textile song tradition; for example, see his "Born on Picketlines, Textile Workers' Songs are Woven into History," *Textile Labor*, XXII, No. 4 (April, 1961), 3–5; and his notes to *Babies in the Mill*, Testament T-3301.

[102] One of the best case studies of a southern textile society is Liston Pope, *Millhands and Preachers.*

such as David McCarn, Henry Whitter, Fiddlin' John Carson, Jimmie Tarlton, Kelly Harrell, and the Dixon Brothers, all of whom worked full or part time in the mills, and the Bolick Brothers (the Blue Sky Boys) whose parents had been mill operatives. While many of the textile songs of the period were performed by well-known entertainers such as the Dixon Brothers (of "Weave Room Blues" fame),[103] some important songs were recorded by individuals who have a more obscure place in country-music history. Two important protest items, "The Marion Massacre" and "The North Carolina Textile Strike," were recorded on Paramount Records by Frank Welling and John McGhee under the name of the Martin Brothers.[104] Another fine example of the unsung balladeer is the case of David McCarn, who, after leaving the North Carolina mountains to gain employment in a textile mill, composed ballads and songs for the amusement of his fellow workers. Six of these songs were recorded for Victor, including "Cotton Mill Colic" and the sardonic "Serves 'Em Fine," which poked fun at the mountaineers foolish enough to leave their placid homes for the material lure of the textile mills.[105]

The textile songs and the other socially-conscious hillbilly songs of the thirties were continuations of the broadside tradition in that they commented on the social and political events of the time and were intended only for temporary circulation. But imprinted on phonograph records they become important social documents of the period. Commercial phonograph discs, produced by the folk, can provide useful commentaries on both their originators' social milieu and that of the nation.

Regardless of the particular style conveyed, social protest or otherwise, country music by the end of the thirties had gained a firm enough footing in American musical life to ensure its endurance. Although it had lost many of the characteristics it possessed in the twenties, country music had developed through an evolutionary process, and even its most sophisticated performers had emerged out of a folk past. Some country entertainers, such as the Blue Sky Boys,

---

[103] On *Babies in the Mill*, Testament T-3301.

[104] Letter to the author from Bob Pinson, September 4, 1966.

[105] Green, "Born on Picketlines, Textile Workers' Songs are Woven into History," *Textile Labor*, XXII, No. 4 (April, 1961), 3–5.

leaned heavily upon traditional material, while others, such as the Delmore Brothers, borrowed from many musical sources. Nevertheless, despite the persistence of tradition within country music, the music (and its performers) were becoming more sophisticated and complex. And while the musicians of the Southeast and deep South were perpetuating certain styles and modifying others, musical winds were blowing in from the Southwest—particularly from Texas— which would have far reaching and dynamic effects upon the future course of the music.

CHAPTER 5

The Cowboy Image and the Growth of Western Music

BEFORE THE 1930's, the term "western" was seldom applied to the commercial country music that was developing in the United States. The terms usually employed were "folk," "hillbilly," "rural," "old-time," "mountain," or "country." The connotations of the West, and of the cowboy, did not become fastened upon country music until the 1930's, when the change was wrought by musical currents in the Southwest.

The emergence of the western image in country music was perhaps inevitable, because throughout the twentieth century the cowboy has been the object of romantic adulation and interest. For the country singer to don cowboy clothing and inject western themes into his music and capitalize on the western popularity was, therefore, not a difficult transition.

The increased emphasis on western themes and attitudes came unsurprisingly in the western tier of the southern states: Louisiana, Oklahoma, and Texas. In this region country music assumed forms differing from those in the more easterly southern states. The pioneer hillbilly recording artists of the twenties, with some exceptions, had come from the southeastern states, and their styles and repertories revealed a traditional background. There is good reason to believe, however, that the Southeast may have been overemphasized in the early period because of the allurement of the romantic mountain image or, as Archie Green has suggested, because the New York-based recording firms found it easier to get to the Southeast than to the West.[1] Despite the excessive attention paid to southeastern performers, the role played by southwesterners was impressive. One of the earliest hillbillies to record was Eck Robertson of Amarillo, Texas. One of the first persons to record cowboy songs was Carl T. Sprague from Alvin, Texas. And the first person to realize and demonstrate how profitable hillbilly music could be was a Texan: Vernon Dalhart of Jefferson. It is significant, however, that in each of these cases the performer went to the recording studios on his own initiative. None was discovered by a field-recording unit. Robertson and Sprague went to New York and asked for auditions. Dalhart was already there as a light-opera singer. In the early thirties, as recording companies began sending their field units in increasing numbers into the Southwest, a multitude of new country artists appeared who revealed the musical richness and diversity of that area's folk culture.

The Southwest—particularly the states of Oklahoma and Texas—was part of the southern tradition, yet different. These states had, in general, been populated by former residents of the older southern states, who had brought with them their values, traditions, and institutions. Immigrants brought slaves and the cotton culture to Texas to make the state part of the southern economic and political orbit. They also transplanted their evangelical protestantism to southwestern soil and brought many features of their folk heritage. The early Texas settlers brought folksongs and ballads to Texas and composed new ones. Some of the old British ballads survived the westward migration, although they had lost many of their former characteristics.[2] In some Texas communities, particularly in remote East Texas areas such as the Big Thicket, the old ballads and the old style of singing remained well into the twentieth century. Many of the East Texas communities were, and are, replicas of the older southern environment. And, in many of them, folk traditions died hard.[3]

[1] Letter to the author from Archie Green, Champaign, Illinois, February 6, 1967.

[2] Alan Lomax, notes to *Texas Folksongs*, Tradition Records, TLP 1929; see also Norman L. McNeil, "The British Ballad West of the Appalachian Mountains," unpublished Ph.D. dissertation (Austin, The University of Texas, August, 1956), pp. 161–169.

[3] William A. Owens, *Texas Folk Songs*, pp. 13–14.

Texas' musical culture, therefore, prior to the urbanization of the post-1920's period, was produced by the southern heritage. Texas rural dwellers used substantially the same instruments common in the rest of the South and sang in a manner similar to other rural southerners. But despite its close cultural affiliation with the South, Texas had a culture all its own—a culture produced by the mingling of diverse ethnic strains: southern white, Negro, German (in the south-central Texas region), Mexican, and Louisiana Cajun. In this heterogeneous society musical styles flowed freely from one group to another, modifying the old southern rural style. Rural music was prevalent and pervasive, but it was not necessarily equivalent to the music produced in the Southeast or in the deep South.

Early in the twentieth century Texas experienced a series of developments which further served to make it unique in the southern environment. In the late twenties the oil boom and the rapid growth of industrialization set Texas apart from her sister states. These factors become increasingly important when superimposed upon the fact that, although Texas was part of the southern heritage, it was also part of the West. In fact, to most Americans Texas was and is the West. And this West was a glorious land peopled by cowboys.[4]

The romantic concept of the West, shared by many easterners, has a rather long history and is exemplified by the novels of Bret Harte, by the western "dime novels," and by such books as Owen Wister's *The Virginian*. The cowboy and the West had been subjected to the romanticizing process long before Hollywood and the television industry began their exploitations of the theme. And too, the American people had long demonstrated a general interest in the songs of the cowboy.[5] Not until the thirties, however, did the western theme make any significant impact on American music. But, when it did, even Tin

[4] For a discussion of the effects of the western and cowboy image on American life, see George Bluestone, "The Changing Cowboy: From Dime Novel to Dollar Film," *Western Humanities Review*, XIV, No. 3 (Summer, 1960), 331–337; David B. Davis, "Ten Gallon Hero," *American Quarterly*, VI, No. 2 (Summer, 1954), 111–126; Kenneth Munden, "A Contribution to the Psychological Understanding of the Cowboy and His Myth," *American Image*, XV, No. 2 (Summer, 1958), 103–147; and Joe B. Frantz and Julian Ernest Choate, Jr., *The American Cowboy: The Myth and the Reality*.

[5] Nathan Howard Thorp's *Songs of the Cowboy* and John A. Lomax's *Cowboy Songs and Other Frontier Ballads* were two of the earliest folksong compilations of any kind to be published in the United States.

Pan Alley reverberated with the melodies of the range. The farther Americans became removed from the cowboy past, the more intense became their interest in cowboy songs and lore. Hillbilly singers and musicians did much to implant the romantic cowboy image in the minds of their listeners.

Before the thirties a few individuals in their song offerings genuinely reflected the cowboy heritage. Some of them, like Charles Nabell (whose Okeh recordings of November, 1924, mark him as possibly the first westerner to record a traditional cowboy song[6]), came from states other than Texas; others, such as Carl T. Sprague, the Cartwright Brothers, Goebel Reeves, and Jules Verne Allen, were from Texas. Furthermore, the traditional songs they sang were authentic cowboy products.[7] Of these singers, Carl Sprague may have done most to generate an immediate interest in the recorded songs of the cowboy. Sprague grew up on a South Texas ranch near Alvin, where he learned many of the songs (most of them from his cowboy uncle) that he later recorded for Victor. His 1925 recordings of cowboy songs—topped off by the immensely popular "When the Work's All Done this Fall"—mark him as one of America's first singing cowboys. While attending Texas A&M he became convinced, through Vernon Dalhart's success as a singer of mountain songs, that a similar market for cowboy songs might exist. He traveled to New York, and had a successful audition with Victor Records. Singing, however, was never more than a hobby with Sprague, and aside from his recordings he made few commercial appearances. For many years he was on the coaching staff at Texas A&M and, in addition, attained the rank of major in the United States Army. He now lives in retirement at Bryan, Texas.[8]

Jules Verne Allen, who rivaled Nabell and Sprague for the title of the Original Singing Cowboy, had spent several years as a cowboy and had experienced the rugged life he sang about. Born in Waxa-

[6] Archie Green, while doing research on early gospel recordings, found material on the early Charles Nabell recordings; this information was made available to the author in a letter, February 6, 1967.

[7] Many of the early recorded cowboy singers, including Carl Sprague, Jules Verne Allen, and the Cartwright Brothers, can be heard on one of the most important reissues yet released by a major company, *Authentic Cowboys and their Western Folksongs* (RCA Victor Vintage Series LPV-522 [notes by Fred G. Hoeptner]).

[8] Interview with Carl Sprague, Bryan, Texas, August 4, 1963.

hachie, Texas, Allen began working cattle in Jack County at the age of ten. From 1893 to 1907 he worked as a rough string rider and bronco buster from the Rio Grande to the Montana line. Unlike Sprague, he used cowboy music as the basis for a professional career. During the twenties and thirties Allen sang over numerous radio stations, including WOAI in San Antonio, where he performed as "Longhorn Luke."[9] Neither he nor Sprague were drugstore cowboys, and, in fact, most of the pioneer cowboy recording stars of the twenties were much closer to the authentic traditional repertory than were the performers of the next decade.

Two early recording stars of the twenties, important for other material as well as cowboy songs, were Goebel Reeves and Harry McClintock. Goebel Reeves (the Texas Drifter) is one of the more interesting, legendary, and, until recently, unknown performers in country-music history. Modern country-music enthusiasts and researchers are heavily indebted to Fred Hoeptner, California collector and western-music authority, who has researched the relevant details of Reeves' life. The story that Hoeptner has disclosed is one of the most fascinating that country music affords.[10] Goebel Reeves was born in Sherman, Texas, on October 9, 1899, and before his death in California in 1959 he had enjoyed a varied career which led him across the United States and around the world. Although coming from a respectable middle-class family (his father served in the Texas Legislature), Reeves deliberately chose the life of a hobo. He was only one of many early country entertainers who bummed across the nation and lived the lives of hobos. Cliff Carlisle, Jimmie Tarlton, Kelly Harrell, and Harry McClintock were included in this group. When these men sang of dank prison cells, brutal cops, rattling freight trains, and lonely and hungry hours, they spoke with authoity and assurance. Nowhere does the authentic voice of the folk experience stand out more clearly than in the recordings of these singers.

During the course of Reeves' wanderings, he enlisted in the army, saw front-line service in World War I, worked as a merchant seaman, became active in the Industrial Workers of the World, re-

[9] Jules Verne Allen, *Cowboy Lore*, pp. viii–ix.

[10] Hoeptner's findings are discussed in Robert Shelton, *The Country Music Story*, pp. 149–151. A shorter discussion of Goebel Reeves is John Edwards, "The Mystery of the 'Texas Drifter,'" *Country and Western Spotlight* September, 1962), 31.

corded for such companies as Okeh and Brunswick, toured the vaudeville circuit, and performed on radio stations all over the nation. In his recording career as a singer and yodeler—he claimed to have taught Jimmie Rodgers the yodeling style—Reeves introduced some of the most interesting examples of both cowboy and hobo songs found in American music. These included the well-known "Hobo's Lullaby," "The Hobo and the Cop," "Railroad Boomer," and the cowboy songs "Bright Sherman Valley" and "The Cowboy's Prayer."

Harry McClintock is significant because of his recorded repertory of cowboy tunes and because of his authorship of a number of famous hobo songs. Born in Knoxville, Tennessee, he traveled over most of the United States and became a member of the Industrial Workers of the World in the early twentieth century. Because of his musical talents, McClintock was a welcome addition to the I.W.W., which had a well-known fondness for singing. His famous compositions "Hallelujah, Bum Again" and "Big Rock Candy Mountain" moved into oral tradition. He had a radio show on KFRC in San Francisco as early as 1925 and recorded for Victor from 1927 to 1931. Along with such cowboy songs as "Sam Bass," "Jesse James," and "Texas Rangers," McClintock's western labor songs of the 1920's make him one of the important progenitors of western music.[11]

Another important precursor of western music—particularly because of his commercial techniques—was Otto Gray of McGinty, Oklahoma. According to *Billboard* accounts, Gray organized a cowboy string band in about 1923. The Gray organization, the Oklahoma Cowboys, has the distinction of being one of the few country groups publicized in *Billboard*, although most of the advertising was paid for by Gray himself. From 1928 to 1932 Gray and his group made a tour of radio stations throughout the country and performed in the northeastern RKO vaudeville circuit.[12] The Oklahoma Cowboys were a highly professional group that possessed most of the characteristics of slick show-business organizations. A special publicity man traveled in advance of the group, and their appearances on radio stations aug-

---

[11] Letter to Joseph Nicholas from Harry McClintock, February 2, 1953, printed in *Disc Collector*, No. 12, 1–2; and *ibid.*, No. 13, 11–13.

[12] *Billboard* XL, No. 1 (January 7, 1928), 24; *ibid.*, XLII, No. 36 (September 6, 1930), 25; *ibid.*, XLIV, No. 21 (May 21, 1932), 16.

mented their advance publicity. Two agencies, the Weber-Simon agency in New York and the William Jacobs Agency in Chicago, handled the group's RKO bookings.[13] The Gray performers, dressed in plain, western-style clothing, traveled in Gray's $20,000 custom-built automobile. The car was equipped and wired for sound reproduction and had a radio receiver and transmitter.[14] Evidently, at least some of the country-music groups in the late twenties and early thirties enjoyed considerable prosperity.

Largely responsible for the growing "western" trend of the thirties was the Mississippi Blue Yodeler, Jimmie Rodgers. Rodgers spent the last few years of his life in Texas and conducted many of his most successful tours there. As has been described in Chapter 3, he took great pride in the Texas heritage and the romantic cowboy past. The modern concept of the "singing cowboy" and of "western" music may very well date back directly to Rodgers.

Scores of singers who modeled themselves after Jimmie Rodgers emerged in the thirties, and it is significant that many of them gave themselves "cowboy" titles and dressed in western attire. Young Hank Snow, for example, in far off Nova Scotia, dressed in cowboy regalia and called himself "the Yodeling Ranger." Others, like Ernest Tubb, included few cowboy songs in their repertories but wore cowboy boots and ten-gallon sombreros. The western attraction was very strong, and even young hillbilly singers from the deep South or from the southeastern mountains, whose only associations with cowboys were through story and song, became involved in the western image and imagined themselves "Out on the Texas Plains."[15]

Perhaps because of Rodgers' close association with Texas, many of the successful Texas hillbilly performers—Ernest Tubb, William Orville (Lefty) Frizzell, Tommy Duncan—credit Jimmie Rodgers as their inspiration. One of the most important of these individuals, and the one who completed the "romantic westernizing" process begun by Rodgers, was Gene Autry.[16] Autry owed most of his initial success to the fact that he could perform the Rodgers' repertory in the

[13] *Ibid.*, XLI, No. 36 (September 7, 1929), 34.
[14] *Ibid.*, XLIV, No. 21 (May 21, 1932), 16.
[15] Title of a song written and recorded by Stuart Hamblen in 1934 (Decca 5001).
[16] Linnell Gentry, *A History and Encyclopedia of Country, Western, and Gospel Music*, p. 182.

Rodgers' yodeling style. Autry was born on a tenant farm in Tioga, Texas, in 1907, and his upbringing in northeast Texas contained little that reflected the cowboy heritage; instead, the formative musical influences of his youth were substantially the same as those that affected most southern rural people. After his family moved to Oklahoma, Autry worked as a railroad telegrapher on the Frisco Railroad at Sapulpa, Oklahoma. To pass the lonely hours, he strummed his guitar and sang country melodies, many of them from the Jimmie Rodgers' repertory. Autry's early style, a soft, nasal tenor, was much like that of Rodgers, and he perfected a reasonable facsimile of Rodgers' yodel.

A much repeated story, confirmed by Autry himself, was that his chief encouragement to become a professional came from Will Rogers. The great humorist stopped off in Sapulpa one day in 1925 and upon hearing Autry sing encouraged him to go to New York and become a professional. With the onslaught of the depression in 1929, Autry lost his job and therefore decided to take Rogers' advice. Using a free railroad pass, he rode a chair car from Tulsa to New York and, carrying his guitar, walked up and down the streets, inquiring in various promotional offices about the possibility of a recording contract. He finally persuaded the American Record Corporation to allow him to make a number of records, which were released on a variety of labels. In the fall of 1929, he made his first records for Victor, and alive to the allurement of the western image, the company billed him as "Oklahoma's Singing Cowboy."[17]

For a short time Autry had his own radio program over KVOO, Tulsa, and the popularity gained there, along with his growing recording fame, landed him a spot on the WLS Barn Dance in Chicago in 1930.[18]

In Chicago Autry was an immediate success. His appearances on the Barn Dance and on his own radio program, "Conqueror Record Time," made him one of the most popular performers in the Barn Dance's history. His records, released on Sears' labels, were those most prominently displayed in the Sears-Roebuck catalogue. As a result of his growing popularity, a number of Gene Autry songbooks

[17] Testimony by Gene Autry on S. 2834, 451–452.
[18] Testimony by Gene Autry on S. 2834, 447.

and guitar instruction books began to appear in the early thirties. A Gene Autry "Roundup" Guitar, advertised for $9.95, reminded the reader that Autry had become a famous performer "simply because he learned to play a guitar while on the ranch."[19] It is not certain just how much of a "ranch" there had been in northeast Texas, or on the Frisco Railroad, but Autry's promotional mentors capitalized on the "western" motif and made him a singing cowboy long before the bulk of his recorded repertory came to include western numbers.

In his years on the WLS Barn Dance, from 1930 to 1934, Autry sang and recorded melodies typical of the hillbilly performers of the time. Only rarely did he sing anything of a western variety. In song selection and in style of performance he was strictly in the southern rural tradition. He sang many of Jimmie Rodgers' compositions, and his own numbers included such songs as "A Gangster's Warning," "A Hillbilly Wedding in June," "My Old Pal of Yesterday,"[20] and, in 1931, one of the biggest-selling hillbilly records of all time, "Silver Haired Daddy of Mine," recorded as a duet with the song's co-composer, Jimmie Long. Autry's recorded selections, which were many and varied, even included at least one labor song. This was "The Death of Mother Jones," recorded on at least seven labels, which chronicled the story of a famous and radical labor leader.[21] This recording was rather far away from the type of song one would expect from a cowboy singer.

His success on the Chicago radio stations and on record labels gained for Autry in 1934 the position that was to make him the best-known cowboy in the United States and one of the most famous hillbilly singers. In that year he went to Hollywood and began his career as the "Nation's Number One Singing Cowboy." In the following decades he made over one hundred feature movies for Republic and Monogram.[22] Not only did he become quite wealthy, but he created the stereotype of the heroic cowboy who was equally adept with a

[19] *Sears-Roebuck Catalogue* (Fall and Winter, 1933–1934), 535.

[20] These selections were taken from the Sears-Roebuck Catalogue listings, *Sears-Roebuck Catalogue* (1933–1934), 543; and *ibid.*, (Fall and Winter, 1934), 490.

[21] Archie Green, "The Death of Mother Jones," *Labor History*, I, No. 1 (Winter, 1960), 1–4.

[22] Testimony by Gene Autry on S. 2834, 447.

gun and guitar. Autry was not the first individual to sing in a western movie—Ken Maynard had done so as early as 1930[23]—but he was the first to attract any national attention. With Autry ensconced as a singing movie cowboy, hillbilly music now had a new medium through which to popularize itself. The Silver Screen romanticized the cowboy and helped to develop the idea of western music. After signing his Hollywood contract, Autry made a radical shift in his repertory from "country" themes to "western" motifs. Instead of performing songs about the mountains, he came increasingly to perform songs with such titles as "Riding Down the Canyon" and "Empty Cot in the Bunkhouse." The subject matter was different, but the style of presentation and the instrumentation were substantially the same as those of most hillbilly bands of the time.

Autry's popularity stimulated other movie companies to present their own versions of the singing cowboy. In searching for likely candidates, the companies usually delved into the ranks of country music. They acquired individuals who had already established themselves on hillbilly radio shows or on record labels. Some of them, like Johnny Bond, who began radio work in Oklahoma City in 1934, and Jimmy Wakely, who organized a trio in the same city in 1936, went to Hollywood as members of Gene Autry's musical organization.[24] Others, such as Tex Ritter and Roy Rogers, gained recognition because of the precedent set by Autry.

Throughout the late thirties and early forties Hollywood became a mecca for country entertainers.[25] Some groups, like the Sons of the Pioneers or Bob Wills' Texas Playboys, appeared in numerous movies as the accompaniment for the featured performer. A few, such as Ernest Tubb and Jimmie Davis, made only rare appearances in western films featuring actors like Charles Starrett and Johnny Mack Brown. As a result of Hollywood exploitation, the concept of "western music" became fixed in the public mind. After the heyday of

[23] According to Billboard, Maynard sang four original songs in a production called "Songs of the Saddle" (XLII, No. 5 [February 1, 1930], 19).

[24] Check the biographical account of Bond and Wakely in Gentry, A History of Country, Western, and Gospel Music, pp. 188, 332; see also (for Wakely) Hillbilly Hit Parade of 1942, p. 54.

[25] Veteran cowboy actor Buck Jones in 1941 decried the rise of "drug store cowboys." He said he was afraid that kids would grow up "with the wrong idea that all you need to stop an Indian or a rustler is a loud voice accompanied by a hillbilly band" Movie-Radio Guide, XI, No. 3 [October 25–31, 1941], 6).

Gene Autry the term "western" came to be applied to southern rural music by an increasing number of people, especially by those who were ashamed to use the pejorative term "hillbilly." Not only did the public accept the projection, but the hillbilly singers as well became fascinated with the western image and eventually came to believe their own symbols. Autry was the first of a long line of hillbilly singers who clothed themselves in gaudy, elaborate cowboy paraphernalia. The trend was to continue during the following decades, and eventually most country performers, whether they came from Virginia or Mississippi, adopted cowboy attire—usually of the gaudy, dude cowboy variety.

Along with the acquisition of western clothing, country bands and singers—particularly in the Southwest—adopted cowboy titles. Typical of these were The Cowboy Ramblers, The Riders of the Purple Sage, The Lone Star Cowboys, The Girls of the Golden West (Dolly and Milly Good), and Red River Dave McEnery. Many of them performed cowboy songs, usually highly romanticized, but more often their titles and attire were the only ties they had with the "West." There were, however, a number of groups who stayed rather close to the cowboy repertory. Some of them had been in existence long before Gene Autry achieved Hollywood fame, and many of them had made their headquarters on the West Coast, presumably because of the lure of Hollywood. These groups stressed the performance of western songs and differed from their southwestern counterparts in that they placed less emphasis upon instrumentation. Among the early California groups were Len Nash and his Original Country Boys, broadcasting from KFWB, Hollywood, as early as March, 1926; Sheriff Loyal Underwood's Arizona Wranglers; Charlie Marshall and His Mavericks; and perhaps the most important of all, the Beverly Hillbillies. The Beverly Hillbillies, originating in 1928, broadcast from the Hollywood-Los Angeles area. Led by Zeke Manners, the accordionist, the group featured country fiddling and western songs. Over the years, the Hillbillies attracted certain individuals who later became top-ranking country performers. These included Stuart Hamblen, from Texas, in 1930, and yodeler Elton Britt (James Britt Baker), from Arkansas, in 1932.[26]

[26] Bob Healy, "The Beverly Hillbillies," *Country Directory*, No. 3 (1962), 30–31.

The western group that was ultimately to become the most famous, and the one most frequently emulated, was The Sons of the Pioneers. This organization sang every type of country song and even ventured into popular music, but the majority of their melodies dealt with western themes. Perhaps more than any other group, they held on to the western repertory and exploited the romantic western image. More "western" than any other group, they were among the least western in terms of origin. Bob Nolan, a gifted songwriter, was from Canada; Tim Spencer was born in Missouri; and Roy Rogers (Leonard Slye) came from southern Ohio.[27]

The three original members of the Sons of the Pioneers traveled to California in the early 1930's and worked at various occupations and performed with several musical groups. Roy Rogers, the lead singer of the organization, was born in Cincinnati, Ohio, on November 5, 1911. He grew up on a small farm near Portsmouth, in southern Ohio. Here he garnered his earliest musical training from his Kentucky-born mother and his mandolin-and-guitar playing father. In 1931 he and his father went to Tulare, California, and worked as migratory fruit pickers. In the following five years, beginning with a group called the Slye Brothers (Roy and a cousin), he worked with different groups until the Sons of the Pioneers was organized. He appeared briefly with Uncle Tom Murray's Hollywood Hillbillies, The Rocky Mountaineers, the International Cowboys, The O-Bar-O Cowboys, and The Texas Outlaws. The Sons of the Pioneers (first called the Pioneer Trio) was organized in 1934 when Spencer and Nolan, who had also worked with some of the previously mentioned groups, joined with Rogers. With the acquisition of fiddler Hugh Farr in 1935, the group began to resemble most of the country bands of the period. The Pioneers, performing on an early-morning radio program over KFWB in Los Angeles, by 1936 had gained enough popularity to be invited to appear with Will Rogers and at the Texas Centennial.

Rogers left the Pioneers in 1937 after signing a movie contract with Republic Studios. It was at this point that his name was changed, first

[27] Both Nolan and Spencer, however, grew up in the Southwest: Nolan in Arizona and New Mexico, and Spencer in Oklahoma, Texas, and New Mexico (John Edwards, "The Sons of the Pioneers," *Country and Western Spotlight* (September, 1962), 34.

to Dick Weston and later to Roy Rogers.[28] Thereafter, his performances were made on an individual basis, and he eventually rivaled
Gene Autry as America's most popular singing cowboy. The organization he left continued to gain in popularity and expanded its
personnel. The Sons of the Pioneers became noted for their close,
smooth harmony and for their introduction of melodious numbers,
written usually by Tim Spencer and Bob Nolan. Nolan composed
some of the classics of country and western music, including the famous "Tumbling Tumble Weeds" and "Cool Water."[29]

The interest in western music during the 1930's was not limited to
hillbilly performers and their supporters. Songwriters from popular
music's Tin Pan Alley reacted to the western theme, and soon the
whole nation was humming western-styled tunes such as "Gold Mine
in the Sky," "Home in Wyoming," and "I'm An Old Cowhand."[30]
Most of these tunes were written by easterners who had never been
near a cow, yet were adept at devising songs that captured the public's interest. The most successful of the western-oriented popular
songwriters was a Bostonian, William J. (Billy) Hill. Although country music has always had a preponderance of southern-born writers
and entertainers, there have always been a few individuals from outside the culture who were able to master its genre and prosper within
it. Billy Hill's birth and musical training gave no indication of his
future success as a western songwriter. Born in Boston in 1899, he
studied violin at the New England Conservatory of Music, and for a
short while performed with the Boston Symphony Orchestra. In
1916, however, he began a western tour, riding the rails and working
at diverse occupations which ultimately carried him through most of
the western states. He returned to New York in the late twenties

[28] The data on Roy Rogers and the Sons of the Pioneers has been garnered
from a biography of Rogers by Elise Miller Davis (*The Answer is God*, pp.
9–34).

[29] The first records made by the Sons of the Pioneers were on Decca in 1934.
The group changed to the American Record Company in the late 1930's (John
Edwards, "The Sons of the Pioneers," *Country and Western Spotlight* [Septem-
tember, 1962], 34.)

[30] "Gold Mine in the Sky" was written by Nick and Charles Kenny; "Home
in Wyoming" was a Peter DeRose-Billy Hill composition; "I'm an Old Cowhand" was a western spoof written by Johnny Mercer (Sigmund Spaeth, *A
History of Popular Music in America*, pp. 494, 512, 515).

after receiving a thorough acquaintanceship with western life—
everything from camp cooking to cowpunching. In New York he
worked as a doorman at a fashionable hotel and composed songs
from time to time. Over the years his written repertory ranged from
popular melodies like "The Glory of Love" to hillbilly songs like
"They Cut Down the Old Pine Tree." His chief success, however,
came from the composition of western-styled songs like "Call of the
Canyon," which were distinguished for their beautiful melodies, and
were couched in rhythms suggestive of the gait of a horse. He experienced his most spectacular success in 1933 with "The Last
Roundup."[31] This song really awakened the general public to the
romantic West, and it became the most popular tune in the country.
The song was performed by both hillbilly and popular groups, and its
appeal perhaps stimulated a greater interest in the more "authentic"
country and western material and ensured a greater national following for country music.

Billy Hill's New York songwriting ventures were directed primarily
to big-city popular-music audiences, although most of the western
bands in California and the Southwest used his material. In general,
country music has always encountered its coolest reception in the
Northeast, particularly in the city of New York. In New York, when
country music has been performed it has usually been under the
more acceptable and "respectable" name of "folk" music. In the
thirties, however, and even in the pioneer days of the twenties, a few
groups were able to gain some success in that area. Bob Miller, from
Tennessee, went to New York in the twenties to become one of the
most successful writers of hillbilly songs. In the thirties such people
as Texas Jim Robertson[32] from Batesville, Texas, and Zeke Manners
and Elton Britt, who transferred their operations from California,[33]
provided a nucleus for country music's acceptance in New York.

The first performer to obtain any real recognition for country music

[31] David Ewan, *Panorama of American Popular Music*, p. 51; Daniel I.
McNamara, ed., *The ASCAP Biographical Dictionary of Composers, Authors,
and Publishers* (Second edition), p. 233. An untitled article by Jack Burton in
Billboard has both biographical information on Hill and a list of his most popular compositions (LXII, No. 23 [June 10, 1950], 41, 52).

[32] Foreword, *Texas Jim Robertson's Collection of Favorite Recorded Songs.*

[33] Bob Healy, "The Beverly Hillbillies," *Country Directory*, No. 23 (1962),
31.

in New York, however, was Woodward Maurice "Tex" Ritter. Ritter's success is an interesting commentary on the western legend. Born in Panola County in deep East Texas,[34] far removed from the scene of any cowboy activity, he attended The University of Texas for five years, and Northwestern Law School for one year. Throughout his youth he had collected western and mountain songs, which he used as the basis of his repertory when he began singing on KPRC in Houston in 1929. In 1930 he joined a musical troupe on a series of one-night stands through the South and Midwest. The tour was financially unsuccessful, so he journeyed to New York hoping to gain some success there. He joined the Theatre Guild of New York and in 1931 was given a featured role in "Green Grow the Lilacs." With his thick Texas accent, and his storehouse of cowboy lore, Ritter was a New York sensation. After his appearance in this play, he became greatly in demand for lecture recitals in eastern colleges on the cowboy and his song. During the fall of 1932 he was the featured singer with the Madison Square Garden Rodeo, and the success gained in this capacity won him a program slot on WOR entitled "The Lone Star Rangers," one of the first western radio programs ever to be featured in New York City. In the next four years Ritter performed on other New York radio shows, including a Barn Dance over WHN. Eventually, he reached the pinnacle that most country performers sought: he obtained a Hollywood movie contract in 1936.[35] Thus, to New Yorkers, Tex Ritter embodied the Texas cowboy. He came from rural East Texas and was part of the southern rural music tradition, but, since he came from Texas, to eastern urban dwellers he had to be a cowboy. And he tried to live up to the part. Tex Ritter's exploitation of the western theme was typical of what was happening all over the United States in the mid-thirties. From New York to California individuals were responding to the western myth, and "cowboy" singing groups were springing up in all sorts of unusual places. Steadily, the term "western" came to rival and even supplant "hillbilly" as the proper appelation for country music. "Hillbilly" suggested a back-

[34] A short biographical sketch of Ritter is in Gentry, *A History of Country, Western, and Gospel Music*, p. 299.

[35] Foreword, *Tex Ritter, Mountain Ballads and Cowboy Songs;* a brief biographical sketch of Ritter, including a valuable listing of his most popular recordings, is in John Edwards, "Old Time Singers—Tex Ritter," *Country and Western Spotlight* (September, 1962), 40–41.

woods, hayseed music, while "western" seemed to connote a music that had been developed by cowboys out on the Texas Plains. The growing use of the word "western" as a designation for country music was completely inaccurate if viewed in the light of a cowboy-produced music. With the exception of a few cowboy songs recorded by country entertainers, and the employment of cowboy titles and dude cowboy clothing, the cowboy has had no appreciable influence on American popular or country music. No particular vocal or instrumental style, or musical form or rhythm, was contributed by the cowboy. The "western music" that became fashionable during the thirties was not produced by the cowboy.

By the mid-thirties, however, a "western" music definitely was becoming dominant, but it was a music that was not even remotely connected with cowboy origins. A modification of the older southern rural music, it was a music that had developed in the western tier of the southern states: Louisiana, Texas, and Oklahoma.

This newer style of music was a product of both the southwestern cultural heritage and of the new social and economic forces that were developing in the region. The thirties was a time of tremendous and rapid change in Texas. Texas was undergoing a process which would transform it from a heavily rural region to a basically urban state. This transformation naturally exerted terrific pressure upon traditional country music. The music, arising from older southern sources, had to adapt to the changing conditions of the Southwest. Early Texas string bands, although performing much traditional material, tended also to employ rhythms and techniques borrowed from southwestern musical sources. It was natural, too, that songs originating in the Southwest would not necessarily employ the same themes as those produced in other parts of the South.

Texas' growing rate of urbanization, later accelerated by World War II, produced a population of city dwellers who were still basically rural in their values and attitudes. Urbanization (this aspect was to be true of the remainder of the South as well) did not kill country music, it merely transformed it. And the country musicians, placed in an urban atmosphere, performed their traditional music and adopted the newer styles and instruments that struck their fancy. In the Southwest there was an abundance of musical influences from which the country musician could borrow: the Mexicans in South Texas, jazz and Cajun music from Louisiana, southern traditional and gospel music, the cowboys, popular music, and the Negroes. When the rural dweller moved to town, he sought out the people and pleasures with which he had always been most closely identified. In fact, many country people who moved to town became more closely attached to country music in an effort to hold on to at least part of the way of life they had left.

The social flux of the thirties (and this can be applied to the entire history of country music) created an understandable confusion of values, a yearning for some sort of social stability, and a desire to maintain as many of the old values as possible. These attitudes explain, in part, the great number of nostalgic and sentimentally religious hillbilly tunes that have been produced since the twenties ("Detroit City" and "The Green, Green Grass of Home" are recent examples). In the thirties a multitude of songs depicted the security symbols of the vanished past. One of the best examples of these nostalgic melodies, and one of the classics of country music, was "Lamp-Lighting Time in the Valley," written by Herald Goodman and first performed by a smooth-singing trio called the Vagabonds: Herald Goodman, Dean Upson, and Curt Poulton (who in 1932 became the first professional group to join the Grand Ole Opry). Breathing with nostalgia, the song told the story of the departed but remembered valley, the mother who patiently waited for the return of her wandering boy, and of the boy who knew that he could never return except in dreams.[36]

Many of the security patterns of an older rural existence seemed to be decaying. The country person in the increased mobility of the decades following 1930 experienced the breakup of home, family, and church relationships. As Alan Lomax has said, the rural southerner was the last to know "the sorrows of divorce and unstable love affairs, and to discover the loneliness of a society in which the village, the clan and the family were in dissolution."[37] His songs reflected his changing status. Not only did they express yearnings and remembrances of the vanishing past, but they also discussed the new environment and the problems it contained. Country songs discussed

---

[36] Information about the Vagabonds' recording of "Lamp-Lighting Time in the Valley" was taken from Texas Jim Cooper, "Cousin Herald Goodman," *Country Song Roundup Annual*, No. 5 (Winter, 1967), 76–77, and from an interview with Herald Goodman in Carrollton, Texas, December 29, 1967.

[37] Alan Lomax, *The Folk Songs of North America*, p. 281.

life in a franker, more realistic manner than popular songs and tended toward less idealization of love and more discussion of the problems of romance: infidelity, divorce, and unrequited love.

The factors which produced new forms and styles within country music were in evidence all over the South. It was in Texas, however, that conditions proved to be most fertile for new developments. Since the thirties Texas has contributed many of the most spectacular stars to country music, and most of them received their basic musical training in a common school. This was a social institution, springing up in the chaotic ferment of the depression, designed for the needs of rural dwellers: the honky-tonk.[38] Saloons and taverns, of course, were not new to the American scene, but they assumed a new significance in the thirties. The Texas oil boom created a number of frontier-like areas where wide-open taverns, selling illegal liquor, catered to the desires of oil workers.[39] With the repeal of prohibition in 1933 the taverns were given a confirmed status. These taverns usually were situated on the outskirts of town for a variety of reasons. In this location tax rates were lower, police supervision was apt to be more lax, and it was relatively easy for both city and rural dwellers to reach the place.[40] In Texas, with some counties "dry" and others "wet," the county-line tavern developed. This convenient location could attract customers from both wet and dry areas. These wayside taverns were sometimes only small, dingy bars, but quite often contained a dance floor. Here, farmers, laborers, truck drivers, and displaced rural dwellers gathered to relax and drink beer or to work off their frustrations (or add to them) by an occasional round of merriment or "hell-raising." Many of the honky-tonks, particularly in Texas' German communities, were family affairs where everyone

---

[38] This is one of those obscure terms in the American language for which one can find definitions but nothing about its origin. Harold Wentworth and Stuart Flexner called it "a cheap saloon featuring gambling games and dancing by or with women of questionable repute" (*Dictionary of American Slang*, pp. 265–266). This definition, which in turn was taken from Alan Lomax's biography of Jelly Roll Morton, *Mr. Jelly Roll*, has obvious limitations.

[39] The problems of the oil boom have been discussed by William W. Sterling in *Trails and Trials of a Texas Ranger*, p. 227.

[40] The trend toward out-of-the-way taverns and cabarets was manifest before prohibition was repealed (President's Research Committee on Social Trends, *Recent Social Trends in the United States*, p. 942).

could gather for merriment, and where special places were set aside for the children.[41]

In the honky-tonk atmosphere, with its lower-class air of unrespectability, musical entertainment normally would not be provided by the "popular" music bands. The dance music, therefore, was provided by local string bands or occasionally by a touring country organization. Then, by the late thirties, much of the musical accompaniment came to be dispensed by the automatic phonograph, or "juke box."

When country music entered the honky-tonk, it had to change, both in lyrics and style. Songs about "Poor Old Mother at Home" and "The Old Country Church" seemed somewhat out of place in the honky-tonk environment. Instead, songs reflecting the problems and changing social status of the erstwhile rural dweller became paramount. Songs took on a franker and more socially realistic quality. The following titles are indicative of country music's changing nature: "Driving Nails in My Coffin" ("every time I drink a bottle of booze"), "Stompin' at the Honky Tonk," "Honky Tonk Blues," "I Ain't Goin' Honky Tonkin' Anymore," and "Headin' Down the Wrong Highway." The listener, if not interested in dancing, wanted to hear lyrics that reflected his own interests and problems.[42]

The music, too, had to change in its style of performance. Possibly in this respect—the modification of certain rhythms and instrumental styles—honky-tonk music had its greatest impact. In the honky-tonk, with its laughter and merriment, clinking of glasses, and shuffling of dancing feet, the instrumentation changed to accommodate the environment. Amidst the din and revelry there had to be, for both the dancer and passive listener, a steady and insistent beat which could be felt even if the lyrics could not be heard. The music became louder: "Sock rhythm"—the playing of closed chords, or the striking of all six strings in unison in order to achieve a percussive effect—

[41] Country-band leader Ted Daffan has attested to the conviviality of South Texas German dances in the 1930's (interview in Nashville, Tennessee, August 21, 1961).

[42] Throughout country-music history songs of this nature had existed, but in the decades following 1930 they began to appear more frequently. Songs depicting the "wild side of life" have never completely monopolized the country music repertory, but they appear much more often here than they do in popular music.

was applied to the guitar; the string bass became a firm fixture in the hillbilly band; and in rare cases drums were used. By the end of the thirties, hillbilly bands were steadily adopting that bane of tradition-minded enthusiasts, the electric guitar.

Honky-tonks of one variety or another became the "schools" in which hundreds of country musicians gained invaluable experience. The honky-tonk was a hard, but instructive, school. The entertainer who worked there, often with only a small band of fiddle and guitar, had to contend with competing noise, fights, and low income. The average country-music hopeful worked at some outside occupation during the day and then performed at honky-tonks until midnight, or on weekends when attendance would be best. Quite often the performers would try to appear in as many honky-tonks in a single night as possible. Not being established stars, the entertainers could not command a percentage of the house's financial intake. The established practice, therefore, was to set up a box, or "kitty," in which the customers could drop nickles and dimes if they enjoyed the performance. After entertaining for awhile in one location, the group would go elsewhere in an attempt to add to their earnings. This practice of "busting honky-tonks"[43] lasted well into the night until perhaps five or ten dollars had been accumulated.

If an entertainer were successful, or if he desired to make country music his profession, he worked at perfecting his style, obtained a spot on a radio station, began making small tours, and finally received a recording contract and a position on a respectable barn-dance show. But the honky-tonk gave him his first training. It taught him how to conduct himself in front of a noisy crowd that was not necessarily easy to please. In the environs of a tavern, the hillbilly singer quite often had to be just as tough and brawling as the customers. Fights between hillbilly singer and customer were not infrequent. It is not surprising either than many hillbilly singers became afflicted with drinking problems, since they were in such a constant association with beer and liquor. For those who decided to dedicate their lives to the music profession, the experience was filled

---

[43] The writer learned this term, also called "busking," from country musician Tommy Hill, who busted honky-tonks all over Texas as a bandleader and side-man for several country singers. He is now the recording director for Starday Records in Nashville (interview in Nashville, Tennessee, August 23, 1961).

with one kind of pressure or another: drink, late hours, and arduous and dangerous travel from one show to another.

The honky-tonk ultimately created a particular style of country music, a style which has become dominant. Conditions which existed all over the South, but most extensively in the Southwest, produced a new breed of hillbilly singers who sang about the new society in which rural southerners were living. Many singers emerged from the whirling world of the honky-tonk, but the one who best exemplified it and proved to be the most influential was Ernest Tubb. Tubb gained his greatest success during World War II and afterwards, but his earliest and most formative experience came during the thirties. Tubb was born on a farm near Crisp, Texas, in 1914, and was inspired at the age of thirteen to become a country singer by hearing a recording of Jimmie Rodgers' "T for Texas." He tried to model his style completely after that of Rodgers, and he practiced diligently for months trying to perfect a yodeling style.[44] Tubb's family moved to San Antonio during the early thirties, just at the precise period when Jimmie Rodgers was living there. It has been one of Tubb's greatest regrets that he did not meet Rodgers personally.[45]

During these depression years, while working for the Work's Progress Administration and at temporary occupations, Tubb visited the radio stations and asked to be placed on a program free of charge. Eventually, he persuaded KONO, a 250-watt station in San Antonio, to give him a fifteen-minute program twice a week at 5:30 A.M. His career actually took a turn for the better, however, when Jimmie Rodgers' widow took him under her tutelage, gave him one of her husband's guitars, and obtained a theater tour for him.[46] At this point in his career, Tubb was capitalizing on Rodger's popularity by singing the Blue Yodeler's songs in Rodger's singing-and-yodeling style. He did not gain any real success until he gave up the Rodgers style and developed his own unique approach. In the late thirties Tubb

[44] Norma Barthel, "Ernest Tubb," *Country and Western Spotlight,* No. 20 (October–December, 1957), 8. A brief biography of Tubb, including the Texas radio stations on which he has played, is found in Gentry, *A History of Country, Western, and Gospel Music,* p. 326.

[45] Interview with Ernest Tubb, Austin, Texas, March 24, 1962.

[46] Barthel, "Ernest Tubb," *Country and Western Spotlight,* No. 20 (October–December, 1957), 8–9.

received his training in the school of experience—going from one radio station to another, obtaining sponsors who sent him on small tours advertising their products, and singing in honky-tonks. After an unsuccessful recording venture with Victor in the late thirties, he finally obtained in 1940 a recording contract with the relatively new Decca Company, which, under the leadership of David Kapp, led in the exploitation of southwestern talent. From his first recording of "I'll Get Along Somehow" Tubb went on to become Decca's most successful country artist.[47] His own composition, "Walking the Floor Over You," became a national hit and was subsequently recorded by Bing Crosby. In the following years, marked by his signing with the Grand Ole Opry, Tubb became the inspiration for thousands of young country singers, and thus did much to create a new tradition in country music.

The development of Ernest Tubb's career is suggestive of what was happening to country music as a whole. In his earliest appearances he accompanied himself, à la Jimmie Rodgers, on the guitar. Later, another musician joined him as lead guitarist, while Tubb provided the rhythm. Therefore, as his success increased so did the size of his band. In the early forties, as the juke box became a firm fixture in roadside taverns, some of the honky-tonk operators complained to Decca that it was difficult to hear the Ernest Tubb records after business picked up at night. Prior to this time, the Tubb instrumentation had consisted of two unamplified guitars. At his next recording session, he was accompanied by an electric guitar played by Fay "Smitty" Smith, the staff guitarist at KGKO in Fort Worth. Tubb then instructed his regular guitarist, Jimmie Short, to attach an electric pick-up to his conventional Martin guitar.[48] Ernest Tubb thus became one of the first country performers to feature an electric guitar, and his reasons for doing so were the same as those of many other entertainers.

Whereas the juke box caused tavern operators to desire a louder type of music for the machine, hillbilly performers were deciding among themselves that the honky-tonk conditions necessitated an amplification of their instruments. The string bass, or "bass fiddle,"

[47] An Ernest Tubb discography (complete up to July I, 1956) is in *Disc Collector*, No. 10 (n.d.), 2–3.
[48] Interview with Ernest Tubb, Austin, Texas, March 24, 1962.

was instituted to provide a heavy beat,[49] and, most revolutionary of all, the guitar was electrified. Most of the changes were made in response to the honky-tonk environment, but, after the new developments were accepted, further changes were effected through the natural experimentation and improvisation of the performers.

Electric instruments have been much maligned by folklorists, music critics, and tradition-minded country enthusiasts, and occasionally one gets the impression that electrification has been foisted upon the country performers against their wills by the conspiratorial world of technology. Music professor Charles F. Bryan, in an attack on hillbilly music in 1949, said that the steel guitar represented a "pseudo stage of development" and was not, therefore, an authentic facet of folk culture.[50] This is a strange statement indeed. No instrument (not even the dulcimer or fiddle) developed as an inherent part of folk culture. All instruments were added periodically as they suited the people's fancy. In fact, the banjo and guitar were relatively late acquisitions. The folk readily accepted steel guitars when they became available, and they electrified them when technology made such a phenomenon possible. There were no electric guitars in the pioneer period because there was no electricity.

Electric instruments were not common before the late thirties, because of their expense and unavailability. Their acquisition is an indication of both the advances in electronic development and of country music's growing financial success. Rather than rejecting the electric guitar as the symbol of repudiation of the folk heritage, the typical country entertainer acquired such an instrument as quickly as he could afford it. His enthusiastic acceptance of the electric guitar must have been similar to the reaction experienced by Jim Boyd, of the Cowboy Ramblers, when he obtained his first electric instrument. To Boyd, the acquisition symbolized the ultimate in material accomplishment. It seemed to signify his accession to the ranks of professionalism.[51]

---

[49] The string bass was borrowed from jazz; Bill Johnson, the first organizer of the Original Creole Jazz Band, has been credited as the first man to play (as early as 1911) such an instrument in a jazz orchestra (Joachim E. Berendt, *The New Jazz Book; a History and Guide*, p. 196).

[50] Charles F. Bryan, "The Folk Music Enigma," *Tennessee Folklore Society Bulletin*, XV, No. 2 (June, 1949), 30.

[51] Interview with Jim Boyd, Dallas, Texas, April 20, 1962.

The steel guitar probably was electrified shortly before the standard guitar in an effort to attain greater volume and flexibility.[52] The steel guitar had long been a favorite instrument among country musicians, and can be heard on recordings dating back to the beginnings of commercial country music. Before commercialization, country musicians—both white and Negro—had often tried to get a sliding, wailing effect by pressing a knife blade or broken bottle along the strings of the guitar. The real popularity of the steel guitar among American musicians, however, can be traced directly to the appearance of touring units from Hawaii who took the country by storm at about the time of World War I and for over a decade thereafter.[53] The guitar had originally been transported by Portuguese and Spanish seamen to the Hawaiian Islands, where it was taken up by native musicians who used it in war and tribal dances. Instead of playing the instrument in the conventional upright style, the Hawaiian musicians—while maintaining the old Spanish tuning—turned the guitar flat and fretted it with some kind of hard substance, presumably bone or metal. Probably because of the growing interest in the Hawaiian Islands engendered by the Spanish-American War and our imperialistic phase at the turn of the twentieth century, Hawaiian bands became stellar attractions in American vaudeville and theater circuits. It was here in the first two decades of the twentieth century that an interest in Hawaiian melodies was kindled which has never com-

[52] The story of electric instruments has not yet been written. No one can with complete assurance identify the first person to play such an instrument. But from available accounts it appears that the electrification of instruments took place in the period between 1935 and 1940, and the steel guitar appears to have preceded the standard guitar in this development. Bob Dunn, of the Milton Brown aggregation, was playing an electric steel guitar by 1935. The electrification of the standard guitar was a jazz phenomenon which was copied by country musicians. Eddie Durham, guitarist, trombonist, and arranger in Count Basie's jazz organization, began playing an electric guitar as early as 1937. The electrically amplified guitar was made popular, however, by Charles Christian, who was Benny Goodman's guitarist from 1939 until his death in 1942. See Leonard Feather, *The Book of Jazz*, pp. 112–115; and Berendt, *The New Jazz Book: A History and Guide*, pp. 190–193.

[53] Most of the information on the history of the Hawaiian steel guitar was obtained from Bob Dunn, who not only was one of the most influential steel guitarists in the field of country music, but has also been a music teacher and a life long student of musical instruments (interview with Bob Dunn, Houston, Texas, July 17, 1966).

pletely died in this country. The Hawaiian musicians introduced an instrumental style and an instrument which have exerted profound and lingering influences upon country music.

The early Hawaiian recording stars—for example, Frank Ferara, who sometimes accompanied Vernon Dalhart; Pali Lua, who toured internationally with a group called the Bird of Paradise Trio; and Sol Hoopii, who played background music for Paramount movies— inspired hundreds of imitators. When a Hawaiian unit visited an American town or hamlet, it was certain to leave behind a number of enthralled partisans and at least one young boy who began badgering his parents to buy him a guitar and enroll him in a steel-guitar correspondence course. In like fashion, American bands featuring the Hawaiian guitar and playing both Hawaiian and native American tunes began to spring up throughout the country.

In the days before electrical amplification, the American enthusiast either converted a conventional guitar by elevating the strings or bought one of the specially constructed amplified guitars which the manufacturers began placing on the market. Among these items two brand names predominated: National, which was probably the first, and Dobro, which was the most popular. Both guitars were equipped with metal vibrating discs (the National had three and the Dobro one) which amplified them without benefit of electrification. The Dobro— first manufactured in 1925 by the Dopera Brothers of California[54]— after experiencing great popularity in the thirties, suffered a temporary eclipse in the late forties and early fifties but has come back strong in the modern period as a favorite instrument among old-time and bluegrass performers. Kept alive by Beecher Kirby of the Roy Acuff organization during the forties, the Dobro (which has become a generic term) has in the sixties been revitalized by Buck Graves (Uncle Josh) of the Flatt and Scruggs group.

In the absence of definitive research on early country recordings, it would be fruitless to speculate on the first specific appearance of the steel guitar in recorded country music. However, the research

[54] For a short discussion of the dobro's history and of the styles associated with it, see Russ Hooper and Randy Slocum "The Dobro Guitar and Bluegrass," *Bluegrass Unlimited,* I, No. 11 (May, 1967), 2–4. Although relatively inactive during the 1940's, the Dobro Company (located in Gardena, California) now advertises regularly in the leading folk music magazines. For example, see *Sing Out: The Folk Song Magazine,* XVI, No. 4 (September, 1966), 63.

that will ultimately provide the answer is now being done by collectors and by folklorists with a collecting bent. In a letter to the author, California collector Bob Pinson provided the results of his own
labors and those of Archie Green and Eugene Earle. Green's and
Earle's nomination for the first steel-guitar recording is the April 29,
1927, recording of the West Virginia singer and musician Frank
Hutchison on Okeh 45114. While Pinson is in general agreement with
Green's and Earle's conclusion, he thinks that another possibility
might be the Victor 20661 recording by the Johnson Brothers (Charles
and Paul). This recording had a release date of June 10, 1927, but,
according to Pinson, "since at least a couple of months span of time
exists between recording and release dates, the Johnson Brothers
item might well pre-date even the Hutchison item."[55] Although they
were certainly not the first, the November 30, 1927, recordings of
Tom Darby and Jimmie Tarlton on Columbia were among the most
influential of the early country steel recordings.[56] The instrument
gained additional popularity through the recordings of Jimmie
Rodgers, who was often accompanied by steel guitarists Joe Kaipo, a
gifted musician from Honolulu, and Cliff Carlisle, who made many
solo recordings through which he helped to popularize the Dobro
throughout the southeastern states.

By the end of the thirties the steel guitar, electrified and otherwise,
had become a fixture in southwestern country bands and was slowly
being adopted by groups in the Southeast. In Houston, Ted Daffan,
who began as a performer of Hawaiian songs, was achieving popularity as a country band leader and steel guitarist.[57] In Louisiana,
Charles Mitchell, whose early musical interests resembled those of
Daffan, gained recognition for his steel-guitar playing and for leading the band which backed Jimmie Davis in his rise to fame.[58]

The date of the steel guitar's first electrification and the performer
who first used such an instrument are not conclusively known. Bob
Dunn, however, was certainly one of the first of these performers.

[55] Letter to the author from Bob Pinson, Santa Clara, California, September
4, 1966.
[56] Letter to the author from Bob Pinson, October 21, 1963.
[57] Bob Healy, "The Ted Daffan Story," *Country Directory*, No. 4 (n.d.),
27–32.
[58] Untitled article on Charles Mitchell, *Hillbilly Hit Parade of 1942*, p. 42.

Dunn was well acquainted with traditional country music, which he had long heard from his father, who played the hoedown fiddle in his home near Braggs, Oklahoma. But Dunn did not become interested in the steel guitar until he heard it used by a group of Hawaiians who played a stage show in the World War I boom town of Kusa, Oklahoma, in 1917. During the next several years Dunn obtained a steel guitar, took lessons through correspondence with a native Hawaiian, Walter Kolomoku, and finally in 1927 became a professional by joining an Oklahoma group called the Panhandle Cowboys and Indians. For seven years (1927 to 1934) Dunn played with several groups on vaudeville tours and on radio stations in the Midwest and on XEPN on the Mexican border. His real involvement with country music, however, came in late 1934 when he joined the extremely popular Milton Brown and his Musical Brownies in Fort Worth. Dunn converted a standard round-hole Martin guitar into an electric instrument by magnetizing the strings and raising them high off the box. He then attached an electric pickup to the guitar, which in turn was connected to a Vol-U-Tone amplifier that Milton Brown had purchased at the Woodward Music Company in Mineral Wells, Texas. Since the electrical amplifier was already being commercially distributed by 1934, it is highly possible that somewhere someone had already attached a guitar pickup to it. But in January, 1935, when Dunn used the electrical amplifier in a recording session in Chicago, he probably became the first country musician to do so. Although no one realized it at the time, that recording session symbolized a turning point in country-music history.[59]

Bob Dunn performed with southwestern groups who played a type of music ultimately designated as "western swing."[60] Western swing, although not nationally popular until the late thirties, had roots running deeply into the country past. In part, it was a stage in the development of the southern string-band tradition and was performed by rural musicians whose ancestors had emigrated from the southeastern cotton states. But western swing, in its later manifesta-

[59] Interview with Bob Dunn, July 17, 1966.

[60] A good introduction to early western swing is *Western Swing*, Old-Timey OT-105. This important reissue contains selections by such performers as Milton Brown and Bill Boyd.

tions, reflected the diverse mingling of musical cultures existent in the Southwest. Before and during the twenties there were a host of small combinations, usually composed of fiddle and guitar, that performed all over the Southwest at barn dances, house parties, and fiddlers' contests, and a few of these groups gained recording contracts. They were the ancestors of the later western-swing organizations. One of the more important of the early groups was Prince Albert Hunt's Texas Ramblers. Hunt—a highly respected old-time fiddler from a state which has produced many—came from Terrell, a musically-rich area to the southeast of Dallas. This area also produced other fine fiddle and guitar combinations, such as Oscar and Doc Harper, and Solomon and Hughes—groups well known in the early thirties and to modern collectors. Recording briefly for Okeh, Prince Albert Hunt performed old-time country numbers with melodic variations that presaged western swing.[61] Hunt performed at house parties, in taverns, and at occasional fiddlers' contests throughout Texas until he was shot to death in Dallas on March 21, 1931.

Another group that anticipated western swing was the East Texas Serenaders of Lindale, Texas, who recorded a few songs for Columbia, Brunswick, and Decca in the late twenties. The Serenaders was basically a fiddle band with a guitar and tenor banjo used for rhythm. In its instrumental style the band was little different from the average hillbilly string band of the period, but in its choice of songs the Serenaders pointed the direction in which western swing would travel. All of the group's songs were instrumentals of either a waltz or breakdown nature, for example, "McKinney Waltz," "Mineola Rag," "Beaumont Rag," and "Arizona Stomp."[62]

Farther to the north, in Greenville, Texas, Bill and Jim Boyd had organized in 1928 a similar instrumental group called "The Cowboy Ramblers." The Ramblers, after their first recording date for Bluebird in 1934, performed few traditional numbers, with the exception of some cowboy songs like "The Strawberry Roan." Many of their songs were of an instrumental nature, and were taken from diverse sources: country music, jazz, and popular music. Their most successful recording was "Under the Double Eagle," a fiddle and guitar

---

[61] Interview with Bob Pinson, Dallas, Texas, August 23, 1963.
[62] Fred G. Hoeptner, "The Story of an Early Fiddle Band: East Texas Serenaders," *Disc Collector*, No. 17 (May, 1961), 8–11.

rendition of an old German march. This song came to rival "The Wildwood Flower" as the favorite number in the country guitarist's repertory.[63] Many similar groups arose in the Southwest during the late twenties and early thirties. Most of them were of country origin and featured the fiddle as the lead instrument, but in their employment of rhythm instruments (the tenor banjo, for example) they revealed a definite jazz influence. Southwestern musicians had revealed a tendency to improvise and experiment with melodic variations much earlier than their counterparts in the other southern states. This experimentation may have developed because of the diversity of cultures in the Gulf Coast region.[64] Knocky Parker, one-time piano player for the Light Crust Doughboys, gave an insight into the diverse cultural origins of southwestern string-band music when he remarked in a 1961 interview with Ed Kahn that western swing was essentially a mixture of Mexican mariachi music from the south with jazz and country strains coming in from the east.[65] Although no conclusive proof has been ascertained for the statement, at least one critic—Harry Smith—has suggested that southwestern string-band music, strongly influenced by Louisiana jazz, may have taken on its peculiar regional stylings when oil workers moved from Louisiana to Texas during the twenties.[66]

Western swing began its real development in the late twenties when Bob Wills and Herman Arnspiger began playing house parties in the Fort Worth Area as Wills' Fiddle Band. Wills, the fiddler, and Arnspiger, the guitarist, originally were the only members of the band, but when they were joined by vocalist Milton Brown in 1931 they became known as the Aladdin Laddies and performed over

[63] Interview with Jim Boyd, April 20, 1962. A complete discography of Bill Boyd and his Cowboy Ramblers, compiled by Brad McCuen, is in *Country Directory*, No. 3 (1962), 15–21.

[64] Suggested by Harry Smith in his notes (p. 6) to the *Anthology of American Folk Music*, Folkways FA 2951–3. Evelyn Kendrick Wells said that the folk song of the pioneer Southwest was conditioned by "its miscellaneous cultural strains and the shifting quality of its life" *The Ballad Tree*, pp. 297–398).

[65] Letter to the author from Ed Kahn, Los Angeles, California, February 1, 1967.

[66] Smith, notes to *Anthology of American Folk Music*. Smith's assertion has been disputed, however, by western-swing collector and authority Bob Pinson (interview with Bob Pinson, Dallas, Texas, August 23, 1963).

WBAP in Fort Worth. Later in 1931 they obtained a job with Burrus Mills advertising Light Crust Flour over KFJZ. In addition to their singing job, they worked for the flour company in other capacities, performing such jobs as loading and unloading and driving trucks. By early 1932 Arnspiger had left the group and had been replaced by Sleepy Johnson, who could play the guitar, tenor guitar, and tenor banjo. This group, joined by Milton Brown's younger brother Durwood, recorded two songs for Victor on February 9, 1932. Known first as the Fort Worth Doughboys and later as the Light Crust Doughboys, the organization became one of the important parent groups of western swing. Many of its members went on to found their own musical aggregations, and the Doughboys' popularity on various radio stations, including WBAP after 1933, gave Fort Worth the reputation of "the cradle of western swing."[67] The Burrus Mills executive who hired them and served as their original master of ceremonies was Wilbert Lee O'Daniel. He wrote some of the hillbilly hits of the period, including "Put Me In Your Pocket" and "Beautiful Texas," and later used hillbilly music in his successful campaign for the Texas governorship and for the United States Senate. After O'Daniel left Burrus Mills in 1935 he began pushing his own brand of "Hillbilly Flour." He had a performing group called the Hillbilly Boys who helped him sell flour and campaign for political office. O'Daniel's featured vocalist was the highly respected Leon Huff, who remained with him from 1935 until 1940.[68]

The Light Crust Doughboys personnel changed drastically during the years immediately following the group's founding, and by 1933 none of the original members were still associated with the group. Some of the individuals who performed with the Doughboys from time to time later became more important with other groups. The list included vocalist Leon Huff, one of the finest singers and yodelers of the late thirties, and steel guitarist Leon McAuliffe. The Doughboys' repertory was varied, including sacred and sentimental songs, but the bulk of their material tended to be instrumental, ranging all

---

[67] Basic information on the Light Crust Doughboys has been obtained from two sources: Bob Healy, "The Light Crust Doughboys," *Country Directory*, No. 3 (1962), 21–29; and Bob Pinson, "The Musical Brownies," *Country Directory*, No. 4 (n.d.), 11–17.

[68] Bob Healy, "W. Lee O'Daniel and His Hillbilly Boys," *Country Directory*, No. 4 (n.d.), 6–11. This article contains a complete discography.

the way from "Old Joe Clark" and "El Rancho Grande" to jazz-oriented melodies. From the early nucleus of fiddle, guitar, and tenor banjo the instrumentation steadily grew with the additions of steel guitar, accordion, and piano.[69]

By 1933 Bob Wills and Milton Brown had left the Doughboys to form their own musical organizations. Brown organized in September, 1932, a group called the Musical Brownies, and the group performed over Fort Worth Station KTAT. Brown's group, in its instrumentation and repertory, strongly reflected Louisiana jazz tendencies. The original members of the band include Jesse Ashlock on fiddle, Ocie Stockard on tenor banjo, Wanna Coffman on bass, Durwood Brown on guitar, and Milton Brown as vocalist. But when they added fiddler Cecil Brower and pianist Fred "Papa" Calhoun, the Brownies acquired jazzier tendences. Brower was a trained musician, and Calhoun had previously played in jazz bands.[70] The jazz trend was accelerated in late 1934 when steel guitarist Bob Dunn joined the organization. Dunn's style was virtually unique in steel-guitar circles. He played the steel guitar like a horn, with his short notes resembling the bursts of a trumpet.[71] Dunn, who had played in jazz bands earlier, was involved then as now in a personal campaign to make the steel guitar a jazz instrument, or what he terms a "modern instrument."

The Brownies' recorded repertory, found on Bluebird and Decca, only rarely touched conventional country music (as in "My Mary," and "Little Betty Brown"). More often, the Brownies' recordings were direct copies of current "popular" hits such as "The Object of My Affection," or old jazz standards like "Joe Turner Blues," "St. Louis Blues" (Brown's most popular recording), and "Memphis Blues."[72]

---

[69] Healy, "The Light Crust Doughboys," *Country Directory*, No. 3 (1962), 23–28.

[70] Pinson, "The Musical Brownies," *Country Directory*, No. 4 (n.d.), 12.

[71] Roy Lee Brown, a younger brother of Milton and a country musician, said that the members of the Musical Brownies were amazed when Dunn tried out with the organization; no one had ever seen a steel guitar played in such an unusual fashion before (interview with Roy Lee Brown in Fort Worth, Texas, May 24, 1963).

[72] Bob Pinson's article on the Musical Brownies includes a complete discography (*Country Directory*, No. 4 (n.d.), 14–17).

Before Brown's tragic death as the result of an automobile accident on April 18, 1936,[73] Brown and his Musical Brownies became the most popular southwestern musical organization[74] and inspired various fledgling organizations. In its inception the music that Brown and similar groups were creating was called "southwestern swing," and occasionally, after it spread to Oklahoma, "Okie jazz."[75]

The number of groups inspired by the Brown rhythm after 1934 reached uncountable proportions. Some of them recorded and gained a wide degree of success; others performed in taverns and never got beyond their native locale. Not all of them could properly be labeled "western swing" groups, but they all went far beyond the limits of traditional country music and performed in a jazzy style. There were so many southwestern groups performing in the Milton Brown style that it was common to hear of "hot Texas rhythms." Some of the new groups were organized by people who had played with Brown: for example, Ocie Stockard,[76] who organized a group in 1937 called the Wanderers; and Bob Dunn,[77] who called his group the Vagabonds. Others were strongly influenced by Brown. These included violinist Shelly Leé Alley, who had played in jazz and pop-music bands over Texas radio stations since the early twenties but had shifted to country music in the mid-thirties;[78] pianist Roy Newman, who performed

[73] The Fort Worth *Star Telegram*, April 18, 1936, estimated that the attendance at Brown's funeral was as high as 3500. He was interred at the Smith Springs Cemetery near his birthplace in Stephenville, Texas.

[74] Letters and business records in the possession of Roy Lee Brown indicate that the demand for personal appearances in the Southwest by the Musical Brownies was too large to fulfill. Milton Brown continually had to turn down requests for appearances because of prior commitments. The records also indicate that Brown was seriously considering moving his base of operations to Houston when he died. There had also been some talk of merging the Milton Brown and Bob Wills organizations.

[75] The terms were used by Fred G. Hoeptner in "Country or Western—It's a Choice of Words" (*Country and Western Jamboree*, IV, No. 1 [Summer, 1958], 37), and in "The Story of an Early Fiddle Band: East Texas Serenaders" (*Disc Collector*, No. 17 [May, 1961], 8).

[76] Bob Healy, "Ocie Stockard and the Wanderers," *Disc Collector*, No. 18 (n.d.), 19–20.

[77] There is a mention of Dunn's Vagabonds in Bob Healy, "The Ted Daffan Story," *Country Directory*, No. 4 (n.d.), 31.

[78] Interview with Mrs. Shelly Lee Alley, Houston, Texas, September 10, 1966.

with a group called Roy Newman and his Boys;[79] Leon "Pappy" Selph and his Blue Ridge Playboys (really a Texas group); the Bar-X Cowboys; and Ted Daffan and his Texans.[80]

The western-swing influence was manifested far beyond the borders of the Southwest. The organization most affected by the Texas rhythms was a Kentucky group known as the Prairie Ramblers. When first organized in 1932, the Ramblers (Charles Hurt, Jack Taylor, Shelby Atchison, and Floyd "Salty" Holmes) called themselves the Kentucky Ramblers. But the western image exerted itself, and in 1934 they added "Prairie" to the title.[81] In their long tenure on the National Barn Dance, from 1933 to 1948, they were joined by a Hot Springs, Arkansas, girl named Patsy Montana; in 1936 she became the first female singer and yodeler in country music to record a song which sold a million copies: "I Want to Be A Cowboy's Sweetheart."[82]

The Prairie Ramblers' repertory, one of the most diverse in country-music history, included mountain tunes ("Feast Here Tonight"), cowboy tunes ("Ridin' Ole Paint"), gospel songs ("What Would You Give in Exchange for Your Soul?"), and "pop" tunes ("Isle of Capri"). It was in their instrumentation, however, that the "swing" influence was most apparent: on their recordings they used, in addition to the conventional country instruments, the piano, clarinet, and saxophone.[83]

Western swing assumed many forms, and could be heard on radio and on phonograph records, but its natural habitat was the dance hall. In part, these southwestern country organizations were influenced by the popular swing orchestras of the time in their employment of a featured vocalist, in their adaptation of many popular and jazz-oriented melodies, and in their occasional use of brass. The use of horns was not universal among western-swing groups, and many

---

[79] Bob Healy, "Roy Newman and His Boys," *Country Directory*, No. 4 (n.d.), 24–26.

[80] All these groups are included in Healy, "The Ted Daffan Story," *Country Directory*, No. 4 (n.d.), 27–31.

[81] Bob Healy, "The Prairie Ramblers," *Country Directory*, No. 3 (1962), 4–14.

[82] Letter to the author from Dave Wylie, Wilmette, Illinois, March 24, 1967.

[83] Healy's article on the Prairie Ramblers contains a complete discography (*Country Directory*, No. 3 [1962]).

of them discarded brass after a temporary experimentation. The Musical Brownies never used brass on recordings, but some of the groups that sprang from them did. Ocie Stockard's Wanderers, for example, used the trumpet and clarinet in addition to the basic instruments. By 1938 Bob Wills and his Texas Playboys numbered fourteen members, including three fiddlers, two saxophone players, a trumpet player, and a drummer.[84] This was indeed a radical departure from the primitive string bands of the twenties.

Despite the popularity of other groups, Bob Wills from Limestone County, Texas, became synonymous with western swing, and became one of the dominant influences in country music. In the years before and during World War II, Bob Wills became one of the best-known names in country music, not only through his tours, but because of his popular phonograph recordings. At first operating out of Fort Worth, he moved his operations to Tulsa, Oklahoma, in 1934,[85] where he broadcast over 50,000-watt station KVOO. Wills was first brought to the attention of Okeh Records (by then a Columbia subsidiary) by Arthur Edward Satherly.

Satherly, born in Bristol, England in 1891, and the son of an Episcopalian minister, rivals Ralph Peer as one of the most important discoverers of hillbilly talent. Beginning in 1925 as a field talent scout for Columbia, Satherly roamed the byways and backwoods of the South searching for white and Negro entertainers. Among his more important acquisitions were Gene Autry in 1930 and Roy Acuff in 1938. He was responsible also for the signing of most of Okeh's western swing talent, including Bob Wills and the Light Crust Dough-

[84] Phillip Fortune, "Who the Old Time Western Bands Consisted Of," *Disc Collector*, No. 12 (n.d.), 11.

[85] The paucity of written material on Wills is amazing in light of his popularity and influence as a western band leader. Linnell Gentry gives a very brief biography of Wills in *History of Country, Western, and Gospel Music*, (p. 343). The dearth of printed material promises to be resolved eventually because collectors Bob Pinson, Bob Healy, and Glenn White have been at work on a combination biography and discography of Wills and his Texas Playboys. Two relevant articles which have information about Wills' early professional career are Bob Healy, "The Light Crust Doughboys," *Country Directory*, 21–30; and Bob Pinson, "The Musical Brownies," *Country Directory*, No. 4, (n.d.), 11–17. The writer is personally indebted to Bob Pinson for information on both Brown and Wills.

boys.[86] Satherly, of Okeh Records, and David Kapp, of Decca, made their companies the leading popularizers of western-swing music and, in fact, of country music as a whole.

At KVOO Wills built an hour-long noontime program into one of the most popular Oklahoma radio shows and thereby became the best-known country entertainer in the Southwest. His popularity gained him the sponsorship of Red Star Milling Company, which offered him a percentage of the profits from all the flour sales promoted on his show. In November, 1935, a special "Playboy Flour" was introduced and it sold well.[87] Through his increased wealth, Wills bought his own flour mill and began advertising the flour by appearing at grocery stores in towns and villages throughout Oklahoma. In addition, he and The Texas Playboys appeared at locations within the listening range of KVOO and at a ballroom in Tulsa owned by Wills. Each ballroom appearance drew between two thousand and four thousand people, young and old alike. Bob Wills enjoyed a success that "popular" swing-band leaders could well envy.[88]

Although Bob Wills and his Texas Playboys used brass occasionally, they did not make their most lasting contributions in this area. The featured instrument in the Wills organization was the fiddle, the instrument that Wills played himself. The Bob Wills variety of western swing was characterized by a heavy, insistent beat, the jazz-like improvisations of the steel guitar, and the heavily bowed fiddle. It was a rhythmic, infectious music designed for dancing, but it also stressed lyrics, rendered usually by a vocalist such as the late Tommy Duncan, who also had countless imitators.[89] The Wills repertory was wide and varied and reflected the wide range of influences that came to bear on southwestern musicians. Illustrating Wills' tie with the southern rural past were such oldtime fiddle pieces as "Beaumont Rag," sometimes called "White River Stomp"; "Lone Star Rag," once known as "Stone Rag"; and "Prosperity Special," known by old-time

[86] *Time*, XXXVI, No. 10 (September 2, 1940), 45; Maurice Zolotow, "Hillbilly Boom." *The Saturday Evening Post*, CCXVI (February 12, 1944), 39.

[87] Letter to the author from Bob Pinson, September 4, 1966.

[88] *Billboard*, LIII, No. 35 (August 31, 1941), 18.

[89] Modern country music fans can hear the Bob Wills-Tommy Duncan combination on *Together Again*, Liberty LRP 3173; *A Living Legend*, Liberty LRP 3182; *Mr. Words and Mr. Music*, Liberty LRP 3194.

devotees as "Rat Cheese Under the Hill."[90] Another indication of Wills' basic rural orientation was his recording of certain traditional numbers that emphasized both lyrics and breakdown instrumentation. These included the very popular "Cotton Eyed Joe," "Ida Red," and "Take Me Back to Tulsa." Although no exhaustive study has yet been attempted (and one is certainly needed), Bob Pinson, through a study of his own immense record collection, has become convinced that Bob Wills' debt to traditional country music, in the form of melodic borrowing, is quite extensive.

Traditional rural music, however, was only one source that contributed to the Bob Wills catalogue. Indicative of the jazz influence were "Basin Street Blues" and "St. Louis Blues," while "Trouble in Mind" came from the Negro country-blues repertory. "Steel Guitar Rag," copyrighted and made famous by Wills' steel guitarist Leon McAuliffe,[91] became a country-music standard and revealed the popularity that instrument would attain. "Steel Guitar Rag" was essentially a reworking of an old "race" number called "Guitar Rag," recorded by Sylvester Weaver on Okeh 8109 on November 2, 1923.[92]

Along with the borrowed material came a large number of compositions, written by members of the Wills organization and others, that differed little from the typical country melodies of the day: ballads, love songs, and novelties. Many of these songs—such as "My Confession," "Whose Heart Are You Breaking Now," "Roly Poly," "Time Changes Everything," and "Rose of Old Pawnee"—have continued to be popular and are known by nearly all of the western-style bands and singers.[93] The majority of Wills' national hits did not come until the war years, but one composition early in 1941 forecast the future popularity that both Wills and country music would attain. This was "The San Antonio Rose." It was first recorded as a country instrumental on November 28, 1938, and on April 16, 1940, was re-

[90] Letter to the author from Bob Pinson, September 4, 1966.

[91] Leon McAuliffe now vies with Billy Gray and Hank Thompson for the position of number one western-swing band leader in the United States. Examples of his instrumental work can be heard on *Mister Western Swing*, Starday SLP 171.

[92] Letter to the author from Bob Pinson, September 4, 1966.

[93] One of the best collections of Bob Wills' songs, and one of the best tributes to his work, is the Ray Price album, *San Antonio Rose*, Columbia CL-1756.

corded with the addition of lyrics performed by Tommy Duncan.[94] The Duncan recording achieved wide popularity, but in 1941 the song as recorded by Bing Crosby sold over 84,000 copies in the month of January alone.[95] The Bob Wills style, if not the Bob Wills name, was now being given national distribution.

Bob Wills left his brand on country music not merely through the spawning of imitative western-swing bands but in the introduction of certain songs and instrumental rhythms that were adopted by other musicians. Long after the large western-swing band had declined in popularity, the Bob Wills "beat" and style of fiddling continued to attract the attention of country musicians. All through the southwestern states, in literally hundreds of taverns, dance halls, and country night clubs, countless groups, in their choice of songs and styles, are a testament to the pervasive Bob Wills influence. And a phenomenon which folklorists should begin to ponder—because it provides clues to the future directions that folk music will take—is the influence exerted by Bob Wills upon participants at the old fiddlers' contests. In these contests, long acknowledged as arenas for authentic old-time music, many of the performers (usually the younger ones) practically duplicate old Bob Wills recordings.[96]

Bob Wills' influence is only one example of the influence exerted by Texas singers and musicians. In the years following 1940 the country-music styles emanating from Texas, the honky-tonk sound and western-swing rhythms, exerted a powerful influence on country music as a whole, until the majority of southeastern and deep southern rural bands adopted the bulk of the techniques and styles originated by southwestern groups.

In the years immediately preceding the outbreak of World War II, country music was still—in terms of its personnel and most intensive popularity—a distinctly regional phenomenon. Although attracting much attention in the Midwest, it gained its greatest adherents in the South and Southwest. Many of its performers were unknown in the

[94] Letter to the author from Bob Pinson, September 4, 1966.
[95] "Songs from Texas," *Time*, XXXVII, No. 12 (March 24, 1941), 36.
[96] Although I have noted this phenomenon at such old-time fiddle contests as the one held each summer in Athens, Texas, my contention has been supported by Bob Pinson.

northern United States but were household words all over the South and commanded a dedicated and loyal following.

The phonograph companies still looked upon country music as a stepchild of the entertainment industry, and usually shunted it off on minor, subsidiary labels. They neglected to exploit it with the same promotional devices that characterized popular music, and as a result, country music was left on its own to build up a following in the best way it could. The country musician, therefore, obtained a spot on a radio station and toured within its listening range, usually handling the promotional work himself. Then he worked to obtain a recording contract, hoping that a successful record would make him more widely known.

In the exploitation of country records, and other records as well, the automatic coin-operated phonograph was becoming an important force by the end of the thirties. The juke box, so called because of its popularity in southern roadhouses called "juke joints,"[97] experienced a heavy sale after 1934 when prohibition repeal opened up thousands of beer halls and taverns that needed some kind of musical entertainment. By 1940 more than 300,000 juke boxes were in operation.[98] Juke box operators began to notice that, especially in the South, hillbilly records experienced a long popularity. Long after a "popular" record diminished in popularity, a hillbilly song like Jimmie Davis's "Nobody's Darling but Mine" continued to attract the customers' nickels. By early 1941 operators noticed, too, that hillbilly records were becoming popular in the areas well outside the South—even in the taverns of Detroit.[99] Some juke box operators deliberately moved toward the inclusion of a few hillbilly songs, because they felt that the customers preferred something fresh and novel, or "a relief from the overworked sentimental ballads."[100] Hillbilly songs, then, were showing up in areas traditionally alien or hostile to country music.

Despite an occasional glimmer of interest elsewhere, hillbilly music

---

[97] Lewis Nichols, "The Ubiquitous Juke Box," *The New York Times Magazine* (October 5, 1941), 22.
[98] *Supplement to the Billboard*, LII, No. 39 (September 28, 1940), 3–5.
[99] *Ibid.*, 59.
[100] *Billboard*, LIII, No. 14 (April 5, 1941), 72.

continued to attract its greatest following throughout the Southland. Attendance at hillbilly roadshows and at barn dances, like the Renfro Valley Show and the Grand Ole Opry, continued to be high, and hillbilly performers could be heard on radio stations, large and small, everywhere in the South. Gene Autry and his cohorts popularized "western" music through the medium of Hollywood movies, and in the Southwest western-swing bands gained new adherents for country music through their performances in dance halls and ballrooms. In the recorded repertory of country performers one could find almost any type of song and style.

There were the "mountain-style" offerings of the Monroe Brothers and the Blue Sky Boys; the country blues renditions of the Delmore Brothers; the cowboy ballads of Tex Ritter; the honky-tonk songs of Ernest Tubb; the danceable rhythms of Bob Wills. Scores of songs were being issued which would become country-music standards. In its choice of song favorites the country-music audience revealed, despite the diversity of material within the music, just how deeply ingrained the old attitudes were. In these prewar years the songs that made the deepest impressions were the songs of doleful love: Floyd Tillman's "It Makes No Difference Now," Ted Daffan's "Born to Lose," and Rex Griffin's tragic song of unrequited love, "The Last Letter." In another vein, "You Are My Sunshine," written and first recorded by Jimmie Davis, became a national favorite when recorded by popular favorite Bing Crosby. In 1941 it was, according to *Billboard*, "the taproom and tavern classic of the year."[101] Its popularity was an indication that, given proper promotion and stimulus, country music could become an important part of the entertainment industry all over the United States.

[101] *Billboard*, LIII, No. 34 (August 23, 1941), 13.

CHAPTER 6

The War Years — The National Expansion of Country Music

THE JAPANESE ATTACK on Pearl Harbor abruptly ended American isolation. The war that followed accelerated the tempo of American life and disrupted the country's social fabric. The war made demands upon the energies and resources of the American people but at the same time brought a general rise in the level of material prosperity. The conflict also produced mass population shifts in the country as young men marched off to training camps and civilians moved into defense occupation centers. World War II, more than any single event, signaled the end of American rural supremacy over the urban way of life. In a very real sense, America's rural population was liberated by the war, especially in the South where impoverished white and Negro tenant farmers and sharecroppers left their meager farms and trekked to the urban areas in quest of more lucrative occupations. Southern migration, relatively static during the depression except for some movement into southern cities, now began to pour into the urban regions. The migration flowed not only into southern cities, but penetrated into such northern cities as Detroit and Chicago as well.[1]

[1] There are several studies of war-time population movements in the United States. These include Homer L. Hitt's "Peopling the City: Migration," in Rupert B. Vance and Nicholas J. Demerath, eds., *The Urban South*, pp. 45–77; John M. Maclachlan and Joe S. Floyd, Jr., *This Changing South*; Ronald Freedman, *Re-*

The population movements of World War II brought Americans into closer contact with each other, intermingled differing cultures, and served to break down regional differences. World War II, and the prosperity it produced, ensured that American society would thereafter be much more mobile and dynamic. The pressures upon rural Americans to conform with the new society were correspondingly increased.

Just as the war enlarged the scope and magnitude of American life, so did it affect the character and popularity of country music. The music, which had shown signs of increased national interest in the late thirties but was still basically regional in its approach, became a national phenomenon during the war. Expanded popularity brought increased attention from the commercial fraternity—the recording companies, promotional agencies, and associated endeavors—whereas augmented incomes caused an increased activity among the performers themselves. Together, these influences exerted terrific pressure upon country musicians to modify their styles and repertories in an effort to win more adherents and in order to maintain popularity.

To many folklorists and country enthusiasts the year 1941 marked a definite, and dismal, turning point in hillbilly-music history. The war, with its breakdown of American regionalism, brought to a close the "Golden Age" of hillbilly music.[2] The closing, symbolized by the cessation of recording by the Carter Family in 1941, brought the emergence of a more complex, highly commercialized form of music that was controlled by northern capitalists more interested in profit than in ethnically pure music. Some of the Golden Age devotees' comments seem to imply that the capitalists were solely responsible for the changes in country music—in a "conspiracy" to destroy the pure, traditional music in the interests of higher profits. It is doubtful, however, that the country musicians, for the most part, ever presented any serious opposition to modifications of their music. It has always been a rather painful fact that the "folk" do not always act in the manner in which some people think they should. It is an equally

---

cent *Migration to Chicago*; and Lewis M. Killian, "The Adjustment of Southern White Migrants to Northern Urban Norms," *Social Forces*, XXXII, No. 1 (October, 1953), 66–70.

[2] See discussion in Chapter 2; this term was evidently the creation of John Edwards of Australia.

painful fact that the folk, in our mobile society, easily succumb to the middle-class ethic of respectability and success. Although it was highly regrettable that the number of traditional songs in the hillbilly repertory declined and that the old, simple, unaffected ways of performing them were disappearing, it must be remembered that the conditions that had produced these responses were also disappearing. The South of the twenties was not the same as that of the forties, and new generations, who were unfamiliar with the traditional songs of an earlier period, had arisen. Modern generations had been reared instead on the commercial country music produced during the twenties and thirties. Nevertheless, despite the amalgamating trends of the forties, country music consisted of many varied and differing styles—some traditional and some not. There was still much about country music that could appeal to the "old-time" devotee. Although John Edwards and the other Golden Age advocates can build a strong case for their point of view, in many respects the year 1941, rather than marking the decline of the music, signaled the beginning of country music's golden era.

If juke-box popularity and heightened road-show activity are any real indications, country music was achieving a national footing before the war. But events during the war, some of them independent of the conflict, further served to strengthen the music's position. Country music's commercial rise parallels, in part, the development of a new, and eventually powerful, music licensing corporation, Broadcast Music Incorporated. Before the establishing of BMI, an organization called ASCAP (American Society of Composers, Authors and Publishers) had functioned as a semimonopolistic licensing concern. Founded in 1914, ASCAP was designed to protect composers from unwarranted use of their material. Anyone using music for public consumption was required to pay ASCAP a stipulated royalty or fee. ASCAP provided an important and useful function for composers at a time when sheet music was steadily ceasing to be important.[3] Country music, however, was relatively unprotected by the licensing concern. Since ASCAP's membership committee looked askance at hillbilly composers, very few were admitted. Those permitted to join complained about the delays involved in ob-

[3] David Ewen, *Panorama of American Popular Music*, pp. 191–193.

taining compensation. The performance of hillbilly songs was, on the whole, unprotected.[4]

The diminution of ASCAP's power, which opened the way for the recognition of hillbilly composers, came as a result of a conflict between that organization and American broadcasters. A five-year contract between ASCAP and the radio networks expired on December 31, 1940. In negotiations for a new contract ASCAP demanded about $9,000,000 a year, or twice what it had been receiving. The National Association of Broadcasters was angered at the increased rates but had anticipated the difficulty and had established a rival licensing concern on October 14, 1939.[5] The new organization, Broadcast Music, Inc., was at a great disadvantage in its competitive struggle with ASCAP, because ASCAP controlled most of the music written and published in the United States after 1884. The only exceptions were the songs in the public domain and a small number held by a noncompetitive performance-rights society, SESAC (Selected Editions of Standard American Catalogues).[6] On January 1, 1941, the broadcasters imposed a ban on all material controlled by ASCAP and determined to use only those songs protected by other licensing organizations. BMI, however, originally had few songs in its musical reservoir. Most music publishers were hesitant about joining the fledgling organization because they believed that it would ultimately collapse. BMI, therefore, had to rely upon new and inexperienced songwriters. In July, 1940, the fortunes of BMI began to rise when the established publishing firm of Edward B. Marks, with its extensive catalogues of popular and Latin material, became a member. The Marks acquisition established a precedent which

---

[4] This was a major complaint of those country singers who testified in committee hearings in Washington, D.C., in 1958. Hearings Before the Subcommittee on Communications of the Committee on Interstate and Foreign Commerce, United States Senate, Eighty-Fifth Congress, Second Session, on S. 2834. (A Bill to provide that a license for a radio or television broadcasting station shall not be granted to, or held by, any person or corporation engaged directly or indirectly in the business of publishing music or of manufacturing or selling musical recordings). March 11 through July 23, 1958.

[5] Ewen, *Panorama of American Popular Music*, pp. 194–195. The founding of BMI is also discussed in Renfro Cole Norris, "The Ballad on the Air" (unpublished M.A. thesis [Austin, The University of Texas, 1951]).

[6] Hazel Meyer, *The Gold in Tin Pan Alley*, p. 89.

other publishing firms followed. Important in the furthering of hill-billy music were Ralph Peer's Southern Music and M. M. Cole of Chicago, both of which had extensive country-music catalogues.

During the first ten months of 1941, BMI steadily expanded its catalogue until it included over 36,000 copyrights from 52 publishers.[7] As the sole source of music for broadcast purposes during that period, BMI attracted a number of composers who had been thrown out of work because of the ban. Hillbilly music owes much of its success in the forties to the protection granted it by BMI. During the ten-month ban hillbilly songs were given increased airplay because of the country-song catalogue acquisitions, and because of the increased reliance upon public-domain melodies. When ASCAP and the radio networks resolved their differences in October, 1941, BMI had se-cured a firm footing in the entertainment world and was well on the way to success. It provided a measure of competition for ASCAP and contributed to the economic security of beginning songwriters. BMI was instrumental, therefore, in breaking New York's, or Tin Pan Alley's, monopoly on songwriting. As a result of BMI's activity, the American music industry became more decentralized. Songwrit-ers were encouraged all over the United States, and producers of the so-called grass-roots material (country and race music) were given a decided boost. Although critics argue that the emergence of BMI led to a cheapening of American music,[8] it also led to a greater democratization, and Tin Pan Alley can now be found all over the United States.[9]

Less than a year after the settling of the ASCAP-broadcasters feud, a new controversy erupted in the music industry. This was the strike called by James C. Petrillo and his American Federation of Musicians, a phenomenon that gave a further impetus to the development of country music. Petrillo argued that juke boxes, which now numbered over 400,000, and broadcasting stations which used phonograph records were driving musicians out of work. Asking for the establish-ment of a fund for unemployed musicians, payable by the recording companies, the American Federation of Musicians went on strike on

[7] *Billboard Music Week* (January 30, 1961), 14, 22.

[8] Vance Packard, maintaining that country music had been foisted upon the American public, called it a "lode of cheaply mined music" (Testimony by Vance Packard in Hearings . . . on S. 2834).

[9] *Billboard Music Week* (January 30, 1961), 13.

August 1, 1942, declaring that there would be no more recording.[10] Having been warned on July 25 that such an event was imminent, the record companies had built up a heavy backlog of records by operating their studios on a round-the-clock schedule. By the fall of 1943, however, the companies began to feel the pinch, and they noticed too that their reservoir was inadequate in one important respect: it did not contain the new songs that caught the public's fancy in musicals and movies. When these songs were asked for at a record store, they were not available.[11]

Of the major record companies Decca was the most adversely affected, because its revenue came almost entirely from popular music. In September, 1943, faced with possible bankruptcy, Decca signed a contract with the American Federation of Musicians. The other phonograph companies came into line in November, 1944, when Columbia and Victor concluded similar agreements with the musicians' union.[12]

The musicians' strike was a great boon for numerous small and independent record firms. Most of these signed contracts with Petrillo immediately, and the others followed when Decca came to terms. Of the newer and smaller firms, Capitol Records, a West Coast company headed by Johnny Mercer, proved to be the most important. Organized shortly before the ban went into effect, Capitol achieved a strong position which might not have been achieved so quickly had the ban not been in progress.[13]

The record ban was important in furthering hillbilly music because many of the small record companies specialized in hillbilly and race music. This fact, along with the shortage of "popular" tunes, created a demand for specialized types of recordings, which the record companies were quick to supply. Hillbilly records began to attract attention all over the country, and hillbilly singers began to produce records of hit proportions. The burgeoning popularity of hillbilly music inspired the major companies to capitalize on the music's success. Decca's first release after the resumption of recording was Bing Crosby's and the Andrews Sisters' version of "Pistol Packin' Mama,"

[10] Roland Gelatt, *The Fabulous Phonograph*, pp. 278–279; *The Billboard Music Year Book* (1943), 81.
[11] Gelatt, *The Fabulous Phonograph*, p. 279.
[12] *Ibid.*, pp. 280–281.
[13] *The Billboard Music Year Book* (1944), 147.

a hillbilly song first written and recorded by Al Dexter. Crosby, in fact, recorded many of the country and western favorites of the period.[14]

While the strike was in progress BMI suffered because of the lack of depth of its catalogue. Most of the older recordings were songs listed in the ASCAP catalogue. In 1942, however, at the height of the strike, songwriter Fred Rose withdrew from ASCAP and signed with BMI. He and country singer Roy Acuff organized the publishing firm of Acuff-Rose, with headquarters in Nashville, Tennessee. This event strengthened BMI and heralded the beginning of Nashville's pre-eminence as a country-music center. The most important publishing house developing out of the increased interest in hillbilly music was Hill and Range, organized in 1945 when Julian Aberbach, a natural-ized American of German birth, returned to the United States after his army duty determined to capitalize on the widespread popularity of country music. He had heard the music often during his army duty and decided that the country was ripe for a hillbilly-music boom. Along with his brother Gene he organized two country music firms, Hill Music and Range Music, which were eventually merged into one organization. It became one of the largest BMI firms.[15]

The phonograph industry, which suffered from the ASCAP-BMI controversy and the recording ban, languished also because of the pressures of the war effort. At the outset of the war shellac, important in the manufacture of records, was frozen by government order. Al-though the restrictions were later relaxed, records did not regain their prewar levels until after the war's end. Recording studios could not operate at full capacity, because new machinery was unobtainable and trained personnel was scarce. Under these pressures only about fifty per cent of previous record quotas could be filled, but the enter-tainment-hungry public was eager to obtain anything that could be produced.[16]

Because of the pressures of shellac-rationing, hillbilly record re-leases were limited. Some hillbilly entertainers temporarily stopped recording either because of the shellac scarcity or because of induc-

14 *Ibid.*, 145–147.
15 *Billboard Music Week* (January 30, 1961), 22.
16 *The Billboard Music Year Book* (1943), 81.

tion into the armed forces. Companies released an average of only three hillbilly records a week, and at one critical point only one a week.[17]

But even at the most critical points of shellac-rationing, the companies continued without interruption to release hillbilly records— an illustration of the importance attached to country music by the recording companies. And the public bought the records or played them on juke boxes. Although few songs were released, juke-box operators and record-retailing firms found that the tunes experienced a strong and enduring popularity. Long after a popular song had declined in popularity, melodies like Ted Daffan's "Born to Lose" or Roy Acuff's "Great Speckle[d] Bird" continued to attract the nickles of juke-box patrons.[18]

By 1942 there was a general awareness of country music's growing national popularity. *Billboard,* the leading music trade magazine, after decades of neglect, began to devote some attention to country performers. At first this was done with considerable hesitation, for no one was quite certain how permanent the popularity would be. *Billboard's* first accounts dealt primarily with the astonishing spread of country music, and it was some time before the periodical devoted an entire column to the music. *Billboard* did not quite know what to do with the music, or what to call it. In its first cautious ventures into the exploitation of hillbilly music, the periodical lumped the country tunes in a category along with foreign numbers.[19] In January, 1942, *Billboard* inaugurated a column entitled "Western and Race," which featured current releases of everything from Tex Ritter to Louis Armstrong.[20] Then in February, 1942, the designation was changed to "American Folk Records,"[21] and that title remained throughout the war years. In 1944 *Billboard* began a brief listing of the most popular hillbilly songs found on juke boxes and included them along with popular race recordings.[22] It was not uncommon to see a song like

[17] *Billboard,* LIV, No. 20 (May 23, 1942), 63.
[18] *Ibid.,* LV, No. 3 (January 16, 1943), 59; *ibid.,* LV, No. 9 (February 27, 1943), 93.
[19] *Ibid.,* LIII, No. 48 (November 29, 1941), 91.
[20] *Ibid.,* LIV, No. 1 (January 3, 1942), 66.
[21] *Ibid.,* LIV, No. 9 (February 28, 1942), 61.
[22] *Ibid.,* LVI, No. 2 (January 8, 1944), 18.

Floyd Tillman's "They Took the Stars Out of Heaven" included with
a song like "When My Sugar Walks Down the Street" performed by
Ella Fitzgerald.[23]

Country music flourished in some northern urban areas simply
because southern rural people had moved there during the late
thirties and early forties in search of defense work. Cities like Baltimore, Detroit, Cincinnati, and Chicago reported heightened country
music activity as southern migrants—particularly from the border
states—poured into the areas and demanded a music of their own
tastes.[24] The southern migrants sought out their own kind and fre-
quented the churches and taverns that most reflected their socio-
economic backgrounds. The proprietors of these "hillbilly" taverns,
as well as the juke-box operators, found it advantageous to feature.
songs by Jimmie Davis, Ernest Tubb, and other country singers.[25]
Hillbilly tunes were said to be especially popular at places patronized
by former West Virginians and North and South Carolinians. The demand for country music in Baltimore became so enormous that the
juke boxes were inundated with hillbilly selections.[26] Detroit juke-
box operators reported in 1943 that hillbilly recordings were the most
popular single class of music present on their machines. Hillbilly
popularity was explained as a result of the influx of defense workers
from the South.[27] The West Coast, which had experienced the Okie
migration in the mid-thirties, reported a tremendous growth in
country-music popularity as southerners and midwesterners—both
civilians and servicemen—poured into the area. In Los Angeles, as
many as five to ten hillbilly songs were appearing on coin machines
that formerly had no more than one. Popular bands that normally
featured only swing and jazz music began adding country tunes to
their repertories in response to demands from their audiences. Crowds

[23] *Ibid.*, LVI, No. 12 (March 18, 1944).

[24] *The Billboard Music Year Book* (1944), 343.

[25] The social nature of the hillbilly taverns has been discussed by Lewis M.
Killian in "The Adjustment of Southern White Migrants to Northern Urban
Norms," *Social Forces*, XXXII, No. 1 (October, 1953), 66–70.

[26] *Billboard*, LV, No. 10 (March 6, 1943), 60.

[27] *Ibid.*, LVI, No. 37 (September 9, 1944), 63; *ibid.*, LV, No. 27 (July 3,
1943), 62.

in Southern California wanted the popular swing bands to perform in the Bob Wills style.[28]

The intermingling of servicemen was an important factor in the spread of country music. Servicemen, seeking the cheapest possible form of entertainment, were the main source of the juke-box boom in the early forties.[29] Young southerners, many of whom had never been more than a few miles from the place where they were born, marched off to training centers carrying their musical tastes with them. Barrack rooms reverberated with the sounds of guitars, nasal country voices, and the current hillbilly songs.[30] Quite often, these same rooms echoed with arguments between soldiers as to whom was the better singer, Roy Acuff or Frank Sinatra. Country music was transported all over the United States by servicemen who listened to the professional singers and by those who formed their own amateur bands. And, ultimately, the music was carried around the world. By 1943 the Special Services Division of the European Theatre of Operations included at least twenty-five hillbilly bands.[31]

In order to satisfy the musical hunger of servicemen, the Grand Ole Opry in October, 1941, had organized a traveling unit of twenty entertainers called the "Camel Caravan." Sponsored by the R. J. Reynolds Company, the unit (composed of such entertainers as Pee Wee King and his Golden West Cowboys, Eddy Arnold, and comedienne Minnie Pearl) toured army camps, giving a performance climaxed by a public square dance. By late 1942 the Camel Caravan had traveled more than 50,000 miles in 19 states and had played 175 shows in 68 army camps, hospitals, air fields, and naval and marine bases.[32]

The popularity of the Camel Caravan was only one example of the striking success exhibited by traveling hillbilly units during the war. Throughout the United States country entertainers were drawing

[28] *Ibid.*, LV, No. 22 (May 29, 1943), 25.

[29] *The Billboard Music Year Book* (1943), 26–27.

[30] *Billboard* quoted unnamed Army Special Service officers as saying that country music was "the most popular of all music with the services" (LVII, No. 10 [March 10, 1945], 29).

[31] *Billboard*, LV, No. 21 (May 22, 1943), 62.

[32] *Movie-Radio Guide*, XI, No. 1 (October 11–17, 1941), 1; *Billboard*, LIV, No. 18 (May 2, 1942), 7.

larger crowds and larger box-office receipts than they had ever drawn before. The personal-appearance field, now becoming highly developed, was based primarily on the established radio barn dances such as the Grand Ole Opry, the National Barn Dance, Cincinnati's WLW Barn Dance, and the Renfro Valley Show in Kentucky. These programs sent their touring units on an ever widening arc depending on the appeal and range of the radio show.

Chicago's WLS National Barn Dance continued to be an important source of the personal appearances made in the midwestern and southern border states. Conducted by such individuals as Clyde (Red) Foley, and Lulu Belle and Scotty (Myrtle Eleanor and Scott Wiseman), the WLS road shows, which had played more than six thousand personal appearances since 1932, grossed over $500,000 in the period from 1939 to 1942.[33] These performances, as was true of the other hillbilly shows of the period, were conducted with a minimum of initial investment. Their profits, then, were that much more astounding. The Hoosier Hot Shots, a small instrumental combination featuring home-made instruments, frequently grossed between $3,000 and $5,000 on one-day stands. Lulu Belle and Scotty, who performed periodically over WLS in Chicago and WLW in Cincinnati, were in constant demand for public appearances, for which they commanded $500 a day and transportation.[34]

Other barn dances experienced similar financial successes. The WLW Boone County Jamboree on occasion grossed as much as $12,-000 on one-day stands.[35] The Renfro Valley Show, conducted by folk-music authority John Lair, kept on the road two tent shows which averaged around $5,000 a week. Biggest one-day grosses for the Renfro Valley organization were a $5,500 matinee and night show in Indianapolis, and a $4,000 gross in Dayton, Ohio. These road shows, plus radio performances, won an extensive popularity for the Renfro Valley Show. Renfro Valley (near Mt. Vernon, Kentucky) is a small village sixty miles from Lexington and two and a half miles from any railroad station, but the paid attendance at the regular Saturday night show averaged about 5,000 and was sometimes as high as 10,000.[36]

[33] *Billboard*, LV, No. 10 (March 6, 1943), 7–9.
[34] *The Billboard Music Year Book* (1943), 102.
[35] *Billboard*, LV, No. 10 (March 6, 1943), 9.
[36] *The Billboard Music Year Book* (1944), 344–345.

Despite the success experienced by the barn dances and their road-show units, it became increasingly evident during the war years that Nashville's Grand Ole Opry was becoming the most important country-music show. The program, which boomed out all over the southland over the clear-channel, 50,000-watt WSM, became nationally-known when it gained network status in 1939. For thirty minutes every Saturday night the National Broadcasting Company carried a segment sponsored by Prince Albert Tobacco. The thirty-minute program, representative of the larger four-and-a-half-hour show, featured a top performer supported by other acts, including comedians such as Lazy Jim Day or Minnie Pearl (Sarah Ophelia Colley). The Grand Ole Opry had advanced far beyond its earlier format, and, although it held rigidly to the traditional styles, it was not until the forties that the show became famous because of its vocalists. Before America's entry into the war in 1941, the Grand Ole Opry had already begun sending its units far beyond the bounds of middle Tennessee. Opry units, performing often in huge tents, had attracted thousands of supporters throughout the South.[37] Then, with the outbreak of war, Opry groups, exemplified by the "Camel Caravan," began carrying country music throughout the United States.

The Grand Ole Opry's upsurge in popularity was attended, as was true in the case of other country-music shows, by the rise of independent promoters who were quick to notice the financial possibilities of the country-music business. At the beginning of the war the most important promoters were individuals like Earl Kurtze, George Ferguson, and Dick Bergen, who gained success through their associations with the WLS Artists' Bureau. By 1943 they were being rivaled by independent promoters such as Larry Sunbrock and, in the South, Oscar Davis, Tom Parker, Hal Burns, and J. L. Frank, who capitalized on the wealth of southern hillbilly talent, particularly that found on the Grand Ole Opry. J. L. Frank, the father-in-law of Pee Wee King, was instrumental in the careers of both Gene Autry and Roy Acuff, and, because of his pioneering efforts on behalf of expanded country road shows, he was called the "Flo Ziegfeld of Country Music

---

[37] Information on the Grand Old Opry's acquisition of network status and information on the southern tent tours was obtained from Harry Stone (one-time director of the Grand Ole Opry) in an interview in Nashville, Tennessee, August 28, 1961.

Show Business." In October, 1967, Frank was named, as a deceased nonperformer, to the Country Music Hall of Fame.

In promoting hillbilly performances, all of the promoters used similar techniques. Little billing, or newspaper advertising, was employed. Chief emphasis was placed instead upon radio announcements. Davis' and Burns' units played to what *Billboard* referred to as "phenomenal business."[38] Out on the West Coast on June 26, 1942, Foreman Phillips converted the ballroom on Venice Pier, California, into a country-music haven when he opened the "Los Angeles County Barn Dance." Phillips brought big-name country performers to Venice Pier periodically. The two most successful appearances were those of Bob Wills, who attracted 8,600 customers, and Roy Acuff, who set an attendance record of 11,130. The Los Angeles County Barn Dance attained such popularity that Phillips extended his promotional activities to other California cities.[39]

Further evidence of country music's burgeoning popularity was the growth of "Folk Music Parks." These resort areas, which featured country-music units on weekends, were located chiefly in the border states and in some northeastern states.[40] Country music was especially popular in Pennsylvania. In fact, Arthur Satherly, veteran talent scout for Columbia, estimated that country music had a greater following in that state than in any other.[41]

Many individuals and groups participated in country music's great wartime surge. By 1944 more than six hundred hillbilly radio programs could be heard on stations ranging from the tiny 100-watt WAGM, at Presque Isle, Maine, to a score or more of powerful 50,000-watt stations such as WSM.[42] The number of recording performers was also extensive. In a list prepared by *Billboard* in 1943, a total of 608 recording artists was led by hillbillies, with a total of 198.[43] The entire aggregate of hillbilly performers, ranging from the professionals to the amateurs who struggled for success in the honky-

---

[38] Information on J. L. Frank was obtained from *Music City News*, V, No. 4 (November, 1967), 32. The Davis and Burns promotions are described in *The Billboard Music Year Book* (1943), 102.

[39] *The Billboard Music Year Book* (1944), 344.

[40] *Billboard*, LIV, No. 21 (May 30, 1942), 101.

[41] *Ibid.*, LVII, No. 10 (March 10, 1945), 29.

[42] *The Billboard Music Year Book* (1944), 349.

[43] *Ibid.*, (1943), 102.

tonks, must have been enormous. Of the total, only a small percentage rose to the heights of financial success. By the mid-forties, Bob Wills was well known far beyond the range of KVOO, and through the popularity of such songs as "San Antonio Rose" could command large audiences as far away as Venice Pier, California.[44] Wills' records were consistently among the top sellers during the war years. Ernest Tubb had advanced far beyond the realm of a struggling honky-tonk singer to become the leading performer in Decca's country category. Ernest Tubb songs like the very popular "Walking the Floor Over You," also recorded by Bing Crosby, became juke-box favorites all over the United States.[45] Wiley Walker and Gene Sullivan, transplanted Alabamians, moved to KVOO in Tulsa and became not only territorial favorites but national stars as well through their Columbia recordings of "Live and Let Live" and "When My Blue Moon Turns to Gold Again."[46] Some of the popular singing stars of the period, like Roy Rogers and the Sons of the Pioneers gained their greatest success through motion-picture promotions, while others, like Lulu Belle and Scotty and the Hoosier Hot Shots, earned popularity through their connections with radio barn dances.

At the onset of the war Gene Autry was the most financially successful and possibly the most popular country performer.[47] Autry's movie appearances kept him in the public eye, and shrewd business activities made him a wealthy man. His phonograph records were among the nation's top sellers, and he was more popular in northern areas than any other country performer.[48] Autry might have gained even greater success had he not been inducted into the army in 1942. At the time of his induction he commanded $1,000 a performance and was said to be a profitable investment at that figure.[49] Autry's popularity suffered a gradual decline after his induction, and he was never able to regain his former recording popularity. He even lost to Roy Rogers his title of "America's Number One Singing Cowboy."

As far as the country songs themselves were concerned, their character during the war years reflected increasingly the honky-tonk

[44] *Ibid.*, (1944), 345.
[45] Bing Crosby's version was issued in 1942 on Decca 18371.
[46] *Hillbilly Hit Parade of 1943*, p. 2.
[47] *Billboard*, LIV, No. 34 (August 22, 1942), 69.
[48] *Ibid.*, LIV, No. 12 (March 21, 1942), 65.
[49] *Ibid.*, LV, No. 10 (March 6, 1943), 7.

and western-swing styles of the Southwest. Mountain-style groups still performed, but they rarely made records of hit proportions. They were, however, firm fixtures on the radio barn-dance programs. In general, the country songs were performed with traditional instrumentation, marked by the growing acceptance of the electric steel guitar. Although the country-music repertory continued to contain a wide variety of themes and styles, interest in patriotic songs was growing. In their discussions of the problems of war, the hillbillies demonstrated their links with the "event" balladeers of the twenties and with the earlier ballad-making tradition. The hillbilly singers and composers were chroniclers of the war years who told of the experiences, sufferings, and death of the departed soldier, and of the anxieties and sadness of his loved ones. Patriotic songs and related war songs were among the most popular numbers in the hillbilly repertory from 1941 to 1946. Carson Robison's "1942 Turkey in the Straw" was, according to Billboard, the most popular hillbilly song during the first year of the war.[50] The one song that surpassed all the other patriotic numbers in popularity, and the one that revealed the national interest in hillbilly music, was Elton Britt's "There's a Star Spangled Banner Waving Somewhere." Written by the prolific songwriter Bob Miller, the song was first released in May, 1942, as the "B" side of a Bluebird record.[51] Recounting the story of a crippled mountain boy who yearned to do his part in the war effort, the record gained astounding success because it attracted not only hillbilly enthusiasts but popular-music fans as well. Britt's recorded version sold over a million and a half copies, while almost as many copies of sheet music were sold.[52] Remaining popular well into 1943, the song was eventually recorded by many groups, popular and hillbilly. In his recorded version, however, Elton Britt, billed as "the highest yodeler in the world," became the first hillbilly singer since Vernon Dalhart to record a song of national hit proportions which transcended the bounds of most musical categories.

Some of the songs, like Roy Acuff's "Cowards Over Pearl Harbor," expressed Americans' shock and anger at their sudden and undesired entry into the war. Red Foley's "Smoke on the Water" breathed a defiant tone as it recounted what would happen "when our army and

[50] Ibid., LIV, No. 18 (May 2, 1942), 67.
[51] Ibid., LIV, No. 20 (May 23, 1942), 63.
[52] The Billboard Music Year Book (1944), 46.

navy overtake the enemy." Other songs told of the anxieties felt by both the serviceman and his loved ones during the long months of separation, and of the soldier's desire to know whether his sweetheart was remaining faithful:

> Are you waiting just for me my darling,
> While I'm far across the deep blue sea,
> Or have you found someone else my darling?
> Tell me are you waiting just for me?[53]

Frank Loesser, a "popular" songwriter capitalizing on hillbilly popularity, wrote a similar song, "Have I Stayed Away Too Long,"[54] which attained wide success when recorded by Gene Autry and Tex Ritter. Hillbilly songs expressed also the yearnings of the people back home for their loved ones, as in Gene Autry's "I'll Wait for You," and Bob Wills' "Silver Dew on the Bluegrass,"

> Soldier boy, so far from me,
> How I wish that you could see,
> Silver dew on the bluegrass tonight.[55]

The most poignant wartime songs dealt with the tragedy of war. Tex Ritter's "Gold Star in the Window" told of "the price a mother paid to keep us free." Songs like "Stars and Stripes on Iwo Jima" and "White Cross on Okinawa," both recorded by Bob Wills, told of American sacrifices for the cause of freedom. "The Soldier's Last Letter," written by Ernest Tubb and Sergeant Henry Stewart, told of a mother's sorrow upon receiving word that her son had been killed in action. The song which expressed more than any other the sorrow and real meaning of the conflict for so many people was "Searching for a Soldier's Grave," written by Roy Acuff at the conclusion of the war.[56] The song tells of a person who travels abroad to find the final resting place of a loved one, and it universalizes the individual trag-

[53] Ernest Tubb, "Are You Waiting Just For Me," Decca 6110. Words and music by Ernest Tubb. © Copyright 1946 by Noma Music, Inc., New York. Used by permission.

[54] *Billboard*, LV, No. 43 (October 23, 1943), 66.

[55] "Silver Dew on the Bluegrass Tonight," words and music by Ed Burt. © Copyright MCMXLIII by Duchess Music Corporation, 445 Park Ave., New York, New York 10022. Used by permission. All Rights Reserved. The Wills recording is on Columbia 20425.

[56] Bailes Brothers, Columbia 36932.

edies produced by the war when it remarks that beneath the white crosses lie buried the hearts of thousands of Americans back home across the ocean.

Apart from the patriotic songs, wartime country music continued in substantially the same vein as before—unrequited love and tragedy, dance music and gospel music. Except for the songs composed for motion pictures, however, "cowboy" melodies ceased to be an important part of the hillbilly repertory. The western myth nevertheless remained in the wearing of gaudy, cowboy paraphernalia. The honky-tonk had definitely come to exert a powerful and dominating role in country music. Among songs of the honky-tonk variety, Ted Daffan's "Heading Down the Wrong Highway" and "No Letter Today," and Floyd Tillman's "Driving Nails in My Coffin" attracted considerable popularity, but the one that gained the greatest success was "Pistol Packin' Mama." Inspired by the violence and turbulence of East Texas oil-field days, the song was written and recorded by Al Dexter (Albert Poindexter) of Jacksonville, Texas, and released in March, 1943.[57] The rollicking novelty tune succeeded "There's a Star Spangled Banner" as the country's most popular hillbilly song and reached even greater heights when Bing Crosby and the Andrews Sisters performed it as their first post-ban recording. Within six months of its issuance over one million copies of the record had been sold, and the song ranks as one of the two or three most popular songs of the war years. The song was not placed on CBS' Lucky Strike Hit Parade, then the chief means of denoting America's most popular melodies, until October, 1943. As a result, the publishers sued the program. The reasons for the song's long rejection were unknown, but *Life* magazine suspected that it might be because of the sponsor's dislike or because Frank Sinatra, the show's star vocalist, could not sing it.[58] The song sold more than three million records in less than two years, and Dexter was still receiving royalties as late as April, 1962.[59]

Many singers and many songs earned national popularity in those turbulent war years, but one individual dominated and symbolized country music in that period. He was a mountain boy from East

[57] Maurice Zolotow, "Hillbilly Boom," *The Saturday Evening Post,* CCXVI (February 12, 1944), 22–23.

[58] *Life,* XV, No. 11 (October 11, 1943), 55.

[59] Al Dexter, quoted in Weldon Owens, "Cross Country," Dallas *Times Herald,* April 22, 1962.

Tennessee, Roy Acuff. There may have been some who made more "hit" records, and there may have been many who had better singing, though not more easily recognizable, voices. None, however, became as well known as Acuff, and none could attract the tremendous crowds that he did. Roy Acuff's career is significant in that, as a mountain singer of traditional derivation, he gained his greatest success at a time when the newer "western" styles and influences were becoming dominant. His success came largely as a result of his choice of songs and because of his showmanship.

Roy Claxton Acuff was born on September 15, 1903, in Maynardsville, Tennessee, the son of Neill Acuff, a lawyer and a Baptist minister.[60] The family, however, was not well-off financially, and Acuff spent his early life on a tenant farm in the foothills of the Smoky Mountains. When he was sixteen, his family moved to a Knoxville suburb, Fountain City. During his attendance at Central High School in Knoxville, Acuff became a star athlete and won a total of thirteen athletic letters. He was so proficient at baseball that the New York Yankees invited him to attend their summer training camp in Florida. While in Florida he suffered a serious sunstroke which, ironically, came during a fishing trip and not at the baseball training camp. The stroke ended his hopes for a baseball career and turned his interests toward music.

Acuff had always shown an aptitude for music and probably received his greatest inspiration from his father, who played the fiddle in the wee hours of the morning before the chores were done. A recurrence of his illness kept Acuff in Knoxville for two years, a period in which he practiced both the fiddle and his singing style. He had always sung during church services and, along with the influence exerted by his father, this early religious training proved to be the dominant influence in his musical career. Additional influences were the hillbilly records to which he often listened and a sister who had taken voice lessons. He first entered the world of show business in the early thirties when he became an entertainer for Doc Hower's medicine show which toured eastern Tennessee. It was here that he de-

[60] The basic biographical information has been obtained from Elizabeth Schlappi (compiler), *Roy Acuff and His Smoky Mountain Boys Discography* (Country Research Series, Disc Collector, No. 23, 1966), pp. 1–6. Additional information was obtained in an interview with Roy Acuff, Nashville, Tennessee, August 26, 1961.

veloped the ease and showmanship that have remained with him throughout his career.[61]

By 1933 Acuff had become a radio performer, first on WROL and later on WNOX, both in Knoxville. He organized a band called the "Crazy Tennesseans" and by 1936, largely through the efforts of Arthur Satherly, had obtained a recording contract with Columbia Records. In his early career Acuff had not yet developed a set style and a few of his recordings, including "Yes Sir, That's My Baby" (performed by other members of the band), were of a "popular" variety. When he finally discarded these attempts at musical eclecticism, he settled on the mournful, wailing style that was traditional in his musical heritage. And this made him famous.

In 1938 Acuff moved to the Grand Ole Opry in Nashville. The move was to make him nationally known, and the Opry the most famous radio barn dance in the United States. Accompanied by his string band, now called "The Smoky Mountain Boys,"[62] he became the first singing star of the Grand Ole Opry. Thereafter, the trend was away from emphasis on the old-time string bands and toward the individual vocalist. During the late thirties and the war years, "Roy Acuff" and "Grand Ole Opry" became almost synonymous.

As the leading star of the Opry, Roy Acuff performed a repertory heavily weighted with sacred and traditional mountain-style melodies,[63] all rendered in a plaintive and utterly sincere manner. Like all great country singers, Acuff felt strongly the sentiments he was expressing and was able to communicate his feelings to his listeners. On some of his most plaintive numbers he became so emotionally involved with the lyrics that he wept openly. His intense delivery and graceful stage presence made him a crowd-pleaser and a great drawing card.

Oddly enough, Acuff's first recording, in 1936, was the one with which he was always most strongly identified. This was "The Great Speckle[d] Bird," a faintly metaphysical tune written by a Rev. Gant

---

[61] The star of the medicine show was veteran country performer Clarence Ashley, who taught Acuff valuable show business techniques (Ralph Rinzler, notes [p. 2] to *Old-Time Music at Clarence Ashley's*, Folkways FA2355).

[62] Acuff changed the name from the Crazy Tennesseans because he thought this title was "derogatory toward his native state" (interview, August 26, 1961).

[63] The most valuable discographic study of Roy Acuff is Schlappi, *Roy Acuff and His Smoky Mountain Boys Discography*.

and set to the melody of "I'm Thinking Tonight of My Blue Eyes."[64] The song, which pictures the church as a group of persecuted individuals who ultimately will gain eternal salvation as a reward for their earthly travail,[65] is based upon the ninth verse of the twelfth chapter of Jeremiah: "Mine heritage is unto me as a speckled bird, the birds round about are against her." The song was popular not only as a recording hit but as a favorite in some of the Pentecostal Holiness churches as well. Vance Randolph heard it sung in Pawhuska, Oklahoma, as an official "Assembly of God" hymn,[66] and W. J. Cash claimed that it was "the official hymn of the Church of God."[67]

Also from Acuff's first recording session came a song which probably proved to be more lucrative than "The Great Speckle[d] Bird"—this was "The Wabash Cannon Ball." In this recording Acuff delved deeply into the traditional lore of the hobo and sang about a mythical train that would carry the hobo to the land of fantasy.[68] Acuff's recording, which sold well over a million copies, was marked by his imitation of a train whistle, reminiscent of that of Jimmie Rodgers. Both "The Wabash Cannon Ball" and "The Great Speckle[d] Bird" could still be found on juke boxes throughout the war years, and they remain Acuff's most widely requested songs.[69]

After experimenting with various instrumental combinations, Acuff by 1940 had developed the band pattern which, with some exceptions, he still employs. Lacking confidence in his ability to play the fiddle (which he actually played rather well), he left the bulk of the instrumentation to the other band members. The instrumentation, with few of the western-swing flourishes, was typically that of a mountain string band: fiddle, string bass, rhythm guitar, five-string banjo (played in the old-fashioned frailing style), and the Hawaiian dobro guitar. Occasionally, the mandolin, harmonica, accordion, and

[64] "I'm Thinking Tonight of My Blue Eyes" has been attributed to A. P. Carter and the Carter Family. The melody is surely one of the most famous and durable in country music history. In 1952 it was used as the melody for "The Wild Side of Life," recorded and made nationally famous by Hank Thompson.

[65] See W. J. Cash's discussion in *The Mind of the South*, p. 297.

[66] Vance Randolph, *Ozark Folksongs*, IV, 59.

[67] Cash, *The Mind of the South*, p. 297.

[68] There are many versions of "The Wabash Cannon Ball." George Milburn, in *Hobo's Hornbook*, prints six stanzas of what might be the original version (pp. 189–191).

[69] Interview with Roy Acuff, August 26, 1961.

the piano were featured, but the most frequently featured instrument, and the one heard most prominently on Roy Acuff recordings, was the dobro. This instrument was played on the early recordings by James Clell Summey (now a popular comedian known as Cousin Jody) and after 1938 by Beecher Kirby ("Oswald"), who sang one of the highest and most easily recognized harmonies in country music and provided the comedy routines for the group. Kirby, who is still with the Acuff organization, made the unelectrified dobro the most prominent feature of the Smoky Mountain Boys' instrumentation at the very time when electric instruments were becoming the rage in other country music groups.[70]

Instrumentation was only one aspect of Acuff's effort to keep his music as traditional as possible. His singing style and choice of songs suggested the mountain country churches. When his entire group joined him on gospel numbers no attempt was made to achieve close harmony, for Acuff wanted to keep the style similar to that heard in his boyhood church.[71] The Smoky Mountain Boys were unaffected by the western image. Acuff wore sport clothes during his stage appearances, while his band members dressed in overalls or other country uniforms. There is not a single "cowboy" or western-style song in Roy Acuff's repertory. It is heavily weighted with sacred numbers like "The Great Judgment Morning"; sentimental songs of unrequited love like "Come Back Little Pal" or "All the World Is Lonely Now"; old-time novelty numbers like "Ida Red"; or tragic numbers like "Unloved and Unclaimed,"[72] co-authored by the long-time floor manager of the Grand Ole Opry, Vito Pellettieri.

Acuff was the composer or co-composer of many of his most popular songs, including "The Streamlined Cannon Ball," "Beneath that Lonely Mound of Clay," and "The Precious Jewel."[73] In popularity

[70] Acuff believed that his style was unsuited for electric instrumental accompaniment. He was not opposed to electric instruments as such, feeling that they did have a place in certain country styles (interview with Roy Acuff, August 26, 1961).

[71] *Ibid.*

[72] Columbia 20425.

[73] The interested reader can consult any one of several available Roy Acuff albums that contain his most popular songs. These include *Songs of the Smoky Mountains*, Columbia HL 9004; *Roy Acuff and His Smoky Mountain Boys*, Capitol T 1870; and *King of Country Music, Hickory* LPM 109.

and record sales, "The Precious Jewel" rivaled "The Great Speckle[d] Bird" and "The Wabash Cannon Ball" as Acuff's most famous song. Borrowing the melody from a mournful mountain ballad, "The Hills of Roane County,"[74] Acuff wrote the words that every country partisan immediately recognizes: "Way back in the hills where a boy I once wandered . . ."

Roy Acuff gained success as a "mountain" singer when the majority of country singers and groups seemed to be discarding the traditional melodies and accepting "western" styles and techniques. His great success came partly because he presented a musical alternative to the country-music fans who were being deluged with the newer musical styles and because (and this might help to explain country music's over-all popularity) the war "caused people to turn to simpler and more fundamental things."[75] When Roy Acuff raised his voice in his mournful, mountain style, he seemed to suggest all the verities for which Americans were fighting: home, Mother, and God.

Regardless of the source of his appeal, Americans packed any place in which Roy Acuff appeared, whether it was Nashville's Ryman auditorium, for the Saturday night Grand Ole Opry, or the site of one of his numerous touring appearances. A capacity crowd at Constitution Hall in Washington paid as much as $6.60 each to see him;[76] at Cincinnati's Music Hall a country-music show starring Acuff and Ernest Tubb attracted 13,000 people for two performances;[77] and at Venice Pier, California, Acuff drew the largest crowd that had ever gone to a Foreman Phillips promotion. There were 11,130 paid admissions, and it seemed that the pier was going to fall from the weight.[78]

Acuff's income, which over the years has been among the highest in the country-music business, was estimated at well over $200,000 in 1942.[79] Largely through the business acumen of his wife, Mildred,

[74] "The Hills of Roane County" is one of the great prison ballads in American music and has been recorded many times. Two of the better recordings are those of the Blue Sky Boys (Bluebird B-8693-A) and of the Stanley Brothers (on *Folk Concert*, King 834).

[75] This quote has been attributed to popular songwriter, Frank Loesser (*Billboard*, LV, No. 43 [October 23, 1943], 66).

[76] North Callahan, *Smoky Mountain Country*, p. 137.

[77] *Billboard*, LV, No. 8 (February 20, 1943), 65.

[78] *The Billboard Music Year Book* (1944), 344–345.

[79] *Billboard*, LV, No. 10 (March 6, 1943), 7.

Acuff built an immense personal fortune through adroit business dealings, through his co-ownership of Acuff-Rose Publishing House, and, after 1947, through the ownership of Dunbar Cave Resort near Clarksville, Tennessee.[80]

His popularity was not confined to native American audiences. A two-week popularity contest held on the Armed Forces Network's "Munich Morning Report" gave Roy Acuff, out of 3,700 votes cast, a lead of 600 votes over popular crooner Frank Sinatra. As a result, the AFN instituted a new show, Hillbilly Jamboree, directed from Munich at American occupation forces in Europe.[81]

An incident that reveals the world-wide significance of Roy Acuff's name, and is probably the greatest tribute he ever received, occurred on the remote island of Okinawa. Upon attacking a marine position, a Japanese banzai charge used a battle cry which it thought would be the ultimate in insults: "To hell with Roosevelt; to hell with Babe Ruth; to hell with Roy Acuff."[82]

An important figure in Acuff's career was Fred Rose, who grew up outside the country-music world and spent his early career as a popular-music entertainer. Despite his "nonrustic" origins, he became the most successful country songwriter and was among the first three individuals elected to the Country Music Hall of Fame. Fred Rose was born in Evansville, Indiana, on August 24, 1897. Before the forties, he had had little connection with country music, but had pursued a career as a pianist and popular songwriter in Chicago. Elected to ASCAP in 1938, Rose had gained considerable success as the writer of such songs as Sophie Tucker's "Red Hot Mama," "Deed I Do," and "Honest and Truly."[83]

His first venture into the writing of country-style songs came on

[80] Ben A. Green, "Dunbar Cave Always Reflects Roy Acuff's Love for People," Country and Western Jamboree, III, No. 5 (August, 1957), 34.

[81] Billboard, LVII, No. 38 (September 29, 1945), 87.

[82] This is a statement of unknown origin which is often quoted: see Eli Waldron, "Country Music: The Squaya Dansu from Nashville," The Reporter, XII, No. 11 (June 2, 1955), 41; Dickson Hartwell, "Caruso of Mountain Music," Colliers, CXXIII, No. 10 (March 5, 1949), 26; and North Callahan, Smoky Mountain Country, p. 135. In a Nashville interview on August 26, 1961, Acuff declared that the original source of the story was war correspondent Ernie Pyle. The writer, however, has as yet been unable to corroborate Acuff's contention.

[83] The ASCAP Biographical Dictionary of Composers, Authors, and Publishers, p. 421.

the West Coast in 1940 when he wrote sixteen songs for Gene Autry, including the very popular "Be Honest With Me." In the next decade Rose wrote hundreds of songs that were recorded by most of the country performers. When Rose moved to Nashville and became the staff pianist for Station WSM, he first became associated with Roy Acuff—an association that proved mutually profitable and beneficial. Rose commented that he never truly understood the real meaning of country music until he stood backstage one night at the Grand Ole Opry and watched Roy Acuff, with tears streaming from his eyes, sing a tragic song about a dying child, "Don't Make Me Go to Bed, and I'll Be Good." Writing often under assumed names, such as Floyd Jenkins and Bart Dawson, Rose composed many of the most popular songs of the forties and fifties. He was one of the few individuals emerging from a non-Southern or noncountry origin who was able to adapt himself to the country music genre. He produced a steady stream of songs—marked by beautiful, melancholy melodies —that country fans enthusiastically accepted: "Be Honest With Me," "No One Will Ever Know," "Pins and Needles," "Blue Eyes Crying in the Rain."[84]

In 1942, along with Roy Acuff, Rose organized the first exclusive country-music publishing house in the United States, Acuff-Rose Publications.[85] This firm provided the nucleus for Nashville's later rise to eminence in the music industry and brought further financial success to each of its founders. In December, 1945, Fred Rose turned the operation of the business over to his son Wesley and began devoting most of his time to the aid and encouragement of prospective young songwriters, the most famous being Hank Williams.[86]

The success of hillbilly radio shows, recordings, and road tours augured well for the future of country music when the nation settled down after the disruption of the war years. When the music industry once again achieved normality, and was no longer beset with a labor shortage, shellac rationing, jurisdictional fights, and recording bans, the prosperity that country music had once achieved could only be multiplied. Country music had gained a foothold in the entertainment world during the hectic war years and could no longer be neglected

---

[84] Interview with Wesley Rose, Nashville, Tennessee, August 28, 1961.
[85] *Billboard*, LIV, No. 52 (December 26, 1942), 64.
[86] Interview with Wesley Rose, Nashville, Tennessee, August 28, 1961.

by either the public or by the commercial purveyors of music. Southerners had demanded it wherever they migrated, and southern servicemen had transported it to different parts of the globe. The names of Jimmie Davis, Ernest Tubb, Ted Daffan, Bob Wills, and Roy Acuff had become known, in varying degrees, all over the United States. People outside the southern rural tradition had become attracted to the music because of its novelty or infectious rhythms. This was especially true when the songs were recorded by a popular singer of the caliber of Bing Crosby. Throughout the late thirties and the war years songs had occasionally transcended the bounds of country music to become national favorites, as did "You Are My Sunshine," "There's A Star Spangled Banner Waving Somewhere," and "Pistol Packin' Mama." At the end of the war Dick Thomas's "Sioux City Sue," released in September, 1945,[87] was attracting the same sort of attention and in the following year became a national favorite when recorded by Crosby and the Andrews Sisters. At any rate, the music industry took note of country music's great gains during the early forties. *Billboard* noted prophetically that "it has shown by its work against adverse conditions that when the war is over and normalcy returns it will be the field to watch."[88]

[87] *Billboard*, LVII, No. 38 (September 29, 1945), 29.
[88] *Ibid.*, LV, No. 9 (February 27, 1943), 94.

The Boom Period of Country Music — The Growth of Big Business

THE UNCERTAIN PEACE that followed World War II ushered in a period of unparalleled prosperity. Anxious Americans, freed from wartime restraints, now longed for the stability and material abundance that had been denied them in previous eras. The pursuit after pleasure and amusement proceeded apace, and country music profited as a result. In some respects this period was the real "Golden Age" of country music. Future decades would produce greater material wealth for country musicians, but for a time when the music, still characterized basically by its old forms, achieved national popularity and profitability, no era equals that of the immediate postwar years. The music was still "country" in its themes and styles and in the maintenance of the fiddle and steel guitar as basic instruments.

As the nation converted successfully to a civilian, domestic economy, the music industry, unhampered by wartime restrictions, geared itself for a highly prosperous period. Records could now be produced in quantities above their prewar levels, and an entertainment-hungry public was ready to buy them. Country music, which had prospered despite (or perhaps because of) defense regulations, was already giving signs of increased national recognition. Songs like "The Oklahoma Hills," performed by Jack Guthrie (soon to die in a veteran's hospital from tuberculosis, the same grim disease that killed Jimmie Rodgers),[1] were earning lucrative sums for their com-

[1] *Billboard*, LX, No. 6 (February 7, 1948), 112.

posers and performers. The nation's most popular song in early 1946 was "Sioux City Sue," catapulted to success by Bing Crosby,[2] who periodically crossed into the country pasture to feed at its commercial trough.

At the conclusion of the war at least sixty-five recording companies, fifteen of them on the West Coast, were releasing country records.[3] Radio continued to be an indispensable means of exploiting hillbilly talent. By 1949 at least 650 radio stations used live hillbilly talent.[4] In the early commercial years most of the hillbilly shows had been broadcast during the early morning hours, since program directors felt that only early-rising farmers listened to the shows. But with their newly discovered popularity country programs were scheduled at more advantageous hours and were produced with the same care given to other musical offerings. In addition to established shows like the Grand Ole Opry, the period saw the emergence of regional barn dances like Dallas' "Big D Jamboree," Los Angeles' "Town Hall Party," and, most important of all, Shreveport's "Louisiana Hayride."[5] In addition to providing local entertainment, these shows started many successful country musicians on the road to fame.

Country music, therefore, was in the midst of a burgeoning commercial success that was most evidenced, perhaps, by the growth and development of the personal-appearance field. *Billboard* claimed that country performers were major box-office attractions almost anywhere in the United States, even in "sedate New England." The South, as usual, was a lucrative area for hillbilly entertainers, but Pennsylvania, Ohio, and Michigan were recorded as important markets for country music.[6] Country music was doing booming business on the West Coast, where major emphasis was placed on ballroom performances and square-dancing. Western swing bands, such as those led by Bob Wills, Spade Cooley, and Tex Williams, continually broke West Coast box-office records. Capitalizing on the western demand for country music, Bob Wills kept his base of operations in Cali-

[2] *The Billboard Encyclopedia of Music*, Eighth Annual Edition (1946–1947), 538.

[3] Paul S. Carpenter, *Music, an Art and a Business*, pp. 72–73.

[4] *Billboard*, LXI, No. 43 (October 22, 1949), 97.

[5] A listing of radio barn dances can be found in Linnell Gentry, *A History and Encyclopedia of Country, Western, and Gospel Music*, pp. 168–175.

[6] *Billboard*, LIX, No. 52 (December 27, 1947), 18.

fornia from 1945 to 1948. California was dotted with ball-rooms bearing such names as Riverside Rancho and specializing in country and western music. In Santa Monica, for example, Spade Cooley operated his own ballroom, which drew between five thousand and six thousand customers every Saturday night.[7] An indication that country music had advanced far beyond the provincial days of its origins came in October, 1947, when a Grand Ole Opry unit, headed by Ernest Tubb, became the first country group to be featured in concert at Carnegie Hall. The two-night concert grossed well over $9,000.[8]

The postwar period also saw a further development of folk-music parks. These parks were distinguished from regular parks in that they contained large outdoor stages and seating areas in which weekly country-music performances were given. By 1949 at least sixty of these parks were in operation. Originating in New England during the mid-thirties and spreading throughout New York, Pennsylvania, and the Midwest, they included such resorts as Buck Lake Ranch, at Angola, Indiana, and Ravine Park, at Blairsville, Pennsylvania. Strangely enough, the South had no folk-music parks until 1948, when Roy Acuff opened his Dunbar Cave Resort near Clarksville, Tennessee.[9]

In the postwar years country music was characterized not only by commercial success but by the entertainers' growing awareness that they were involved in a highly complex commercial form of activity. Country entertainers were also becoming good businessmen. Many of them, like Gene Autry, owned radio stations. A few, like Roy Acuff, owned publishing houses. (This activity would increase tremendously during the next decade).[10] And, universally, country performers had learned how to manage their own promotional and contractual affairs. No longer, as was often true before 1940, was the

---

[7] *The Billboard Encyclopedia of Music* (1946–1947), 530.

[8] *Billboard*, LIX, No. 52 (December 27, 1947), 18.

[9] *Ibid.*, LXI, No. 43 (October 22, 1949), 97.

[10] Since country musicians' investments in broadcasting and publishing became more widespread in the late 1950's and early 1960's, this phenomenon will be discussed more fully in Chapter 8. Specific data on investment—Gene Autry's radio holdings, for example—can be found in Hearings Before the Subcommittee on Communications of the Committee on Interstate and Foreign Commerce, United States Senate, Eighty-Fifth Congress, Second Session, on S. 2834.

hillbilly easy prey for the crafty businessman who ventured into an area laden with portable recording apparatus, made some quick recordings, paid a small sum, and then dashed off again. Hopeful country entertainers everywhere evidenced a growing understanding of contract manipulations. By 1946 performers were demanding from $150 to $200 for each record side, asking for advances against royalties, and exhibiting a familiarity with copyright laws and American Federation of Musicians regulations.[11] With the rise of BMI, hillbilly songwriters had begun to receive greater protection and profits in the performance rights of their songs. ASCAP had come to recognize the legitimacy of country music and was becoming more favorably disposed to the admission of hillbilly songwriters. Conceding that hillbilly songs had been inadequately covered in previous surveys, ASCAP in 1947 promised to improve its logging surveys of independent radio stations, where the majority of hillbilly songs were played.[12]

As the number of professional country musicians increased, and the number of entertainment outlets with them, a new group of personal managers and bookers emerged. Until the end of the war, most country-talent promotions were handled by radio-station talent bureaus, such as those of WSM and WLS. Under this arrangement the scheduling of personal appearances was often limited to the immediate territory blanketed by the station's transmitter. After the war a number of major talent offices concerned with cross-country touring became interested in country music. Such booking agencies as Jolly Joyce in Philadelphia, Stan Zucker in New York, American Corporation in Hollywood, and Gene Johnson in Wheeling, West Virginia, by 1949 had expanded their touring operations to the forty-eight states. In addition, personal managers such as Oscar Davis and Colonel Tom Parker had gained great profits through fostering country talent.[13]

If some doubts had existed in previous years, there was now no question that the Grand Ole Opry had become "king" of barn-dance radio shows and that Nashville had become the leading country-music center. The Opry, with its wide radio coverage on WSM aug-

[11] *Billboard*, LVIII, No. 7 (February 16, 1946), 20.
[12] *Ibid.*, LIX, No. 3 (January 18, 1947), 13.
[13] *Ibid.*, LXI, No. 43 (October 22, 1949), 97.

mented by the thirty-minute NBC segment, had become universally known as the hillbilly heaven. Roy Acuff's immense popularity had transformed the Grand Ole Opry from a localized barn dance to a national program featuring "star" talent. His success inspired young country talent everywhere to emulate his career. Regardless of their commercial origins—honky-tonk or small radio shows—every hillbilly performer dreamed of someday being invited to become a member of the Opry cast. An appearance on the Grand Ole Opry meant that one had finally reached the pinnacle of success. The Grand Ole Opry brought additional prestige and an augmented income to the individual fortunate enough to capitalize on the program's name. An individual was willing to appear on the Opry for a modest fee on Saturday night and then tour with an Opry unit during the week in the knowledge that his over-all income would be increased.

By the late forties many country fans had come to look upon the Grand Ole Opry, perhaps unfortunately, as synonymous with country music. Every rabid country enthusiast felt that before he died he must make at least one trip to the citadel of country music. As a result, every Saturday night people from all over the United States and from Canada gathered in Nashville to view the program.[14] Those without reserved seats gladly stood in line outside the Ryman Auditorium for hours and then sat inside for hours more to view their favorites. The Grand Old Opry was carried over WSM from 7:30 P.M. until midnight.

As the Grand Ole Opry grew in size and popularity, it gradually added most of the big-name stars to its roster. By 1950 the show had a cast, including sidemen and comedians, of about 120 individuals.[15] The program was divided into fifteen- and thirty-minute segments which featured a leading performer supported by other acts. Throughout the war and immediate postwar years the Opry had added such individuals as Ernest Tubb, Lloyd "Cowboy" Copas, and Eddy Arnold. It was no longer a middle-Tennessee barn dance, but

---

[14] The Grand Ole Opry was known far beyond the bounds of the United States. After a series of tornadoes hit Tennessee in the spring of 1952, WSM received a number of letters from Japanese citizens inquiring whether any of the hillbilly stars had been injured (Rufus Jarman, "Country Music Goes to Town," *Nation's Business*, XLI [February, 1953], 45).

[15] Don Eddy, "Hillbilly Heaven," *The American Magazine*, CLIII (March, 1952), 121.

was a super-show devoted to the national furtherance of country music. The National Barn Dance had declined to regional insignificance. Shreveport's Louisiana Hayride threatened occasionally to rival the Opry in popularity, but as soon as a Hayride performer gained national recognition he left to join the Grand Ole Opry. This happened with such frequency—for example, in the cases of Hank Williams, Webb Pierce, Slim Whitman, Jim Reeves, Kitty Wells, Faron Young, and Johnny and Jack (Johnny Wright and Jack Anglin)—that the Hayride gained the sobriquet of "the Cradle of the Stars."[16] No other radio barn dance could equal the appeal of the Grand Ole Opry.

With the assembling of top-ranking country talent, who in most cases made their permanent homes in the city, Nashville became a leading music center. As the singers moved in, so did the musical entrepreneurs—the booking agents, the artists and repertory men, the promoters. With the evident emergence of Nashville as the ranking country-music center, the commercial fraternity flocked there to be near the performers. Acuff-Rose was the first of many—and in most cases, smaller—publishing houses to congregate in Nashville. Sheet music had ceased to be an important part of the music industry, and, instead, the typical publishing house depended on phonograph recordings for its existence. After a song was copyrighted and published, the publishing house, if it expected a financial return, had to get the song recorded by some performer. In effect, the publishing house became a vehicle for the recording of a written composition. Small publishing firms, often operated by country performers themselves, sprang up all over Nashville.[17]

In writing country songs, country singers had traditionally played a preponderant role. Although there occasionally had been professional composers like Bob Miller and Billy Hill, hillbilly singers usually had written their own songs. Matters had changed very little in the mid-forties. With increasing regularity, however, professional songwriters began to supply songs for the country entertainers. Some of the professionals were also entertainers: the highly respected Floyd Tillman, Johnny Bond, Jenny Lou Carson, and Cindy Walker, for example. But others devoted their time exclusively to song com-

[16] This was the sub-title of the souvenir album, *KWKH's Louisiana Hayride*.
[17] For statistics on Nashville music publishers, see Hearings . . . S. 2834.

position and tried to create songs that would fit the styles of specific singers. These included Vaughn Horton, who wrote "Teardrops in My Heart" and "Mockingbird Hill"; Cy Coben, who wrote many songs for Eddy Arnold and Hank Snow; and Felice and Boudleaux Bryant, a husband and wife team, who were among the most successful of the professional songwriters.[18]

Nashville's pre-eminence as a country-music center led also to a concentration of booking agencies there. The Grand Ole Opry's personnel had formerly been handled by the WSM Talent Bureau under James Denny. When Denny left the Opry in 1954, he carried much of the talent with him. This led to a decentralization of talent handling and the consequent development of numerous independent agencies.[19]

In the highly commercial world of the fifties, recording had ceased to be the primitive affair that it had been in the past. No longer did the recording men venture into back-country southern areas carrying portable equipment and searching for hillbilly talent. Now the country performer had to journey to the recording studio—in New York, or some regional office—to place his songs on wax or tape. Nashville's emergence as a recording center, and, in fact, much of its trend toward musical pre-eminence, is directly attributable to Paul Cohen. Cohen, who had been connected with Decca since the thirties, became that company's country artists and repertory director in the mid-forties. Under Cohen, the Decca Company began in the spring of 1945 to record its hillbilly artists in Nashville, first in WSM's Studio B, and later in the Castle Studios. These early recordings (of such people as Red Foley, Ernest Tubb, and Kitty Wells) marked the beginning of Nashville's rise to recording eminence.[20] Decca's move was emulated by other phonograph companies, which began recording much of their country talent in Nashville. Capitol Records in July, 1950, became the first major company to locate its country director in Nashville.[21]

[18] A short account of country songwriters, past and present, can be found in *The World of Country Music*, pp. 146, 162–163.

[19] Interview with James Denny, Nashville, Tennessee, August 25, 1961; see also "Jim Denny Lived Country Music," *The World of Country Music*, p. 216.

[20] Interview with Paul Cohen, Nashville, Tennessee, August 29, 1961; see also Robert Shelton, *The Country Music Story*, p. 126.

[21] *Billboard*, LXII, No. 30 (July 29, 1950), 12.

The growing prosperity and national recognition of country music brought increased respectability, something country performers had always yearned for. Country singers and their fans had always bridled at any suggestion that their music might be cheap or inferior. Some country entertainers felt that the pejorative nature of the word "hillbilly" repelled some people who looked upon the music as of low-class origin and beneath their dignity, and a movement developed in the late forties to replace "hillbilly" with "country." The effort was directed first at the recording companies by leading singers. Eddie Kirk and Cliffie Stone, West Coast musicians, persuaded Capitol executives to adopt the new term, while Ernest Tubb and Red Foley similarly influenced Decca.[22] Country musicians did not necessarily resent the term "hillbilly" or feel that it was degrading, but they were convinced that other people reacted to it adversely. By June, 1949, *Billboard* had begun to list country-music popularity charts under "country" or "country and western."[23]

Apart from its evident financial growth, country music exhibited its amazing vitality in this period through the general popularity of its songs and singers. This was country music's "high" period, a time when its personnel achieved a popularity and recognition approaching that given to rock-and-roll performers in a later period. It was a time when thousands of cafes, drugstores, and bars reverberated with the sounds of "Bouquet of Roses," "There Stands the Glass," "Let Old Mother Nature Have Her Way," "Jole Blon," "Poison Love," and "Love Song of the Waterfall."[24] Throughout the nation well over a thousand disc jockeys poured out a daily stream of country renditions.[25] Record retail stores did a flourishing business, and the personal-appearance field continued to be a very lucrative enterprise. Almost every country performer had a fan club, composed of dedicated fans who bought his records and were well informed about

[22] Fred G. Hoeptner, " 'Country' or 'Western'—It's a Choice of Words," *Country and Western Jamboree*, IV, No. 1 (Summer, 1958), 38; interview with Ernest Tubb, Austin, Texas, March 24, 1962.

[23] *Billboard*, LXI, No. 26 (June 25, 1949), 117.

[24] A listing of those songs which made Billboard's Top Ten from 1948 to 1963 can be found in *The World of Country Music*, pp. 187–199.

[25] One estimate set the figure as high as 1,400 (*Billboard*, LXIII, No. 37 [September 15, 1951], 61).

his activities.[26] It was a time when an annual income of $100,000 and ownership of two or three Cadillacs ceased to be an uncommon thing for a country entertainer. Country music was becoming big business. No longer would it be neglected in the trade magazines or shunted onto the minor or subsidiary record labels.

Once looked upon as primitive practitioners of their art, country musicians in the late forties had become highly professional. Masters of their respective instruments, the "sidemen" who assembled in Nashville and in other country music centers could play any type of music in a style that would have made their hillbilly precursors either envious or contemptuous. Building upon the styles and techniques of the past while also borrowing from other sources, the new breed of country musicians continually strived to perfect their art and carry it on to further developments. The simple dobro gave way to a conventional, single-necked electric steel guitar (often called the "biscuit board") which in turn was abandoned for double and triple-necked instruments bedecked with foot pedals and various gadgets designed to create greater flexibility and resilience. Unsatisfied with a simple, unobtrusive accompaniment, the steel guitarist experimented in a constant effort to create new sounds and stylings. His ability to do so determined his future success. The steel guitar had become the dominant country instrument, and its wailing, "blues" sound provided an excellent complement for the mournful, heart-broken laments of the period.

The honky-tonk sound, in its many variations, dominated the country music of the mid-forties. A style created in the tavern atmosphere was transplanted to the auditorium, recording studio, and broadcasting station. The "western" styles were now commonly accepted throughout the South. The western style had been brought to the Grand Ole Opry, first by Ernest Tubb in 1942 and later by Cowboy Copas and Pee Wee King and the Golden West Cowboys during the war years. King's organization is historically important in that it brought not only the western style but an alien instrument, the drum, to the Grand Ole Opry stage (a move bitterly resisted by tradition-

[26] Fan-club listings, along with club officers and mailing addresses, were usually carried in popular country-song magazines such as the *Country Song Roundup*.

alists).[27] By the end of the forties almost all of the Grand Ole Opry units had adopted some facet of the western approach, whether style, instrument, name, or clothing.

Still, within the commercially expanding world of country music, if one knew where to look, almost every conceivable type of music existed. With accelerating commercialism, however, the old-time string bands were finding it much more difficult to survive. One could occasionally find an old record by Mainer's Mountaineers or the Monroe Brothers in an old record store, in a junk shop, or in the files of a radio station. Only a rare country disc jockey such as Wayne Raney, Esco Hankins, or Lee Sutton played records of this type or vintage. Of the mountain singing groups of the thirties, only the Blue Sky Boys remained. Never compromising with the newer material, the Blue Sky Boys continued to sing their mournful, traditional-style songs right up to the time of their retirement in 1951.

Numerous newer groups, however, stressed the traditional songs and styles. Many of these were religion-oriented performers who had followings that, although loyal and ardent, were limited and localized. Among the more important of the tradition-oriented groups were the Bailes Brothers (Johnny, Walter, and Homer) of West Virginia, who performed first over WSM but later over Station KWKH in Shreveport, Louisiana. Performing with guitar and mandolin (and sometimes the dobro), the Bailes Brothers sang in an emotional, heartfelt style and maintained a musical link with the family singing styles of the thirties. With a repertory strongly reminiscent of that of the Blue Sky Boys, but with a vocal style strongly suggestive of Pentecostal Holiness singing, the Bailes Brothers wrote and sang gospel tunes and sentimental love songs, some of which attained lasting and national popularity: "Dust on the Bible," "Give Mother My Crown," "I Want to be Loved (But Only By You)," and "Oh, So Many Years."[28]

A number of groups might be placed in the "mountain-style" category. For example, Wilma Lee and Stoney Cooper, a husband and

[27] Shelton, *The Country Music Story*, p. 125.

[28] There is a brief sketch on the Bailes Brothers in George D. Hay, *A Story of the Grand Ole Opry*, p. 31. A sampling of the Bailes Brothers' style can be heard on *Avenue of Prayer*, Audio Lab AL-1511.

wife team from West Virginia, performed with fiddle, five-string banjo, and other old-time instruments; in 1950 the Library of Music, Harvard University, named them "the most authentic mountain singing group in America."[29] The Coopers were certainly rivaled, however, by other groups just as authentic and important. No group, in fact, had a purer or more old-time flavor in their singing style than the Louvin Brothers and the Stanley Brothers. Ira (now deceased) and Charles Louvin (born Loudermilk) learned old-time country and gospel songs at their home in Henegar, Alabama, and used them as the basis for a commercial career. Beginning as gospel singers, the Louvin Brothers performed with mandolin and guitar and sang in a very close, but high-pitched harmony. They gradually expanded their repertory to include every kind of song in the country category, and they added electric guitar instrumentation. They nevertheless remained one of the "purest" country groups in the entertainment business and, in their choice of songs and styles, revealed a debt to the Monroe Brothers, Delmore Brothers, and Blue Sky Boys.[30]

Ralph and Carter Stanley, widely known as outstanding practitioners of bluegrass music until Carter's death on December 1, 1966, learned their music in the Clinch Mountains of Dickinson County, Virginia. After completion of their World War II military service, they formed a band in Norton, Virginia, in 1946. Featuring the five-string banjo (played at that time in the claw-hammer style by Ralph Stanley) and high harmony singing (generally performed by mandolinist Pee Wee Lambert), the Stanley Brothers possessed the most tradition-oriented repertory in country music and a vocal style that was heavily influenced by the Monroe Brothers and Mainer's Mountaineers. In an era of increasing electrification and urbanity in the country-music world, the Stanley Brothers (first recorded on

---

[29] Gentry, *A History of Country, Western, and Gospel Music*, p. 208. A representative sampling of the Coopers' work is found in *Sacred Songs*, Harmony HL 7233; and *Family Favorites*, Hickory LPM H106.

[30] "The Louvin Brothers" (no author listed), *Country and Western Spotlight*, No. 21 (January–March, 1958), 6–7. The Louvin Brothers have recorded many albums for Capitol, but three of them most vividly illustrate their traditional orientation: *The Family Who Prays*, Capitol T1061; *Tribute to the Delmore Brothers*, Capitol T1449; and *Tragic Songs of Life*, Capitol T769, which Alan Lomax has described as "fine folk hillbilly" (*The Folk Songs of North America*, p. 611).

Rich-R-Tone records) suggested an earlier and more rustic phase of development.[31]

In a musical style dominated by men, a few female entertainers gained recognition in the immediate postwar years. Among these entertainers, Molly O'Day was the most tradition-oriented. Miss O'Day, who is now a Church of God evangelist who will sing nothing but religious songs, might be considered the female equivalent of Roy Acuff because of her mournful, emotional style. Performing with a group called the Cumberland Mountain Folks (led by her husband Lynn Davis) Molly O'Day sang a variety of songs spiced with the old-time flavor; for example, sacred numbers like "Tramp on the Street," and old ballads such as "Don't Sell Daddy Any More Whiskey" and "Poor Ellen Smith," a North Carolina murder ballad found in the repertories of many modern folk and country entertainers. Veteran Columbia talent scouts Arthur Satherly and Don Law were quoted as saying that Molly O'Day was the greatest woman country singer of all time.[32]

Other tradition-based female singers with a wider commercial appeal and more eclectic repertories were Rose Maddox and Kitty Wells. Alabama-born Rose Maddox performed with her brothers in a group billed as "the most colorful hillbilly band in the land." Dressed in gaudy, western costumes, the Maddox family featured electric instrumentation and uptempoed rhythms. Featured singer Rose Maddox, however, performed in an old-fashioned emotional style suggestive of country camp meetings.[33] Kitty Wells (Muriel Deason) sang in a similar, yet more restrained, fashion. Beginning as a gospel singer traveling with the Johnny and Jack team (she was the wife of Johnny Wright), Kitty Wells emerged in the fifties as not only the highest-ranked female country singer but as a strong rival to the male

[31] Basic biographical information on the Stanley Brothers was obtained in an interview with them in San Marcos, Texas, February 6, 1964. For further information on their styles and recordings, see Chapter 10. Their important Rich-R-Tone recordings have been reissued on *The Stanley Brothers: Their Original Recordings*, Melodeon MLP 7322.

[32] *The World of County Music*, p. 61. Columbia has released many of her best numbers on *The Unforgettable Molly O'Day*, Harmony HL7299.

[33] Gentry, *A History of Country, Western, and Gospel Music*, p. 269. For examples of her style see *The One Rose* (Capitol T132) and *Rose Maddox Sings Bluegrass* (Capitol T1799).

leaders. Her Decca recordings, exemplified by "It Wasn't God Who Made Honky Tonk Angels," consistently placed in the Top Ten category and earned her the title of "Queen of Country Music."[34]

In the perpetuation of traditional forms, Kentucky entertainers played a vital role. And none proved to be more influential or lastingly popular than Marshall Louis "Grandpa" Jones. Not only was he a faithful partisan of traditional country songs and styles, he was also a first-rate stage comedian and entertainer. Dressed in the garb of an old man and sporting false whiskers, Grandpa Jones beguiled his listeners with expert banjo-playing and his store of old-time stories, songs, and jokes. In a sense, Jones might be considered the successor to Uncle Dave Macon through his maintenance of mountain banjo songs and styles. But in another sense he was a real throwback to an older tradition embodied in the medicine show, minstrel show, and vaudeville performance. Jones was first and foremost a showman and through his forays into northern territory helped to attract a larger audience to country music.[35]

Grandpa Jones was not the only Kentuckian who helped to preserve the traditional flavor in country music. Others who made significant contributions were Merle Travis, Jimmie Osborne, and Bill Monroe. Travis cannot easily be placed in any one category. Born in the coal region of Muhlenberg County, Kentucky, he based his professional career in California and gained his greatest success through the performance of western and honky-tonk country songs. He was, however, deeply influenced by traditional music. His highly intricate and complex guitar style, among the most accomplished in country music, was nonetheless derived from folk sources in western Kentucky, particularly from the playing of such home-grown talent as Mose Rager, Ike Everly, and Arnold Schultz. Travis's style, in turn, has been imitated by countless American musicians. His album *Folksongs from the Hills* (Capitol AD50), recorded in 1949, contained traditional songs, like "Nine Pound Hammer," and original compositions which had a traditional flavor, such as "Dark As a Dungeon," "I Am a Pilgrim," and "Sixteen Tons." Each of these songs gained na-

[34] In the period from 1952 to 1963 Kitty Wells recorded nineteen songs which placed in *Billboard's* Top Ten Category (*The World of Country Music*, p. 190).

[35] George D. Hay, *A Story of the Grand Ole Opry*, p. 52; and WSM's Official *Grand Ole Opry History-Picture Book*, I, No. 3 (1957), 24.

tional popularity and has become widely known in folksinging circles throughout the world.[36]

Jimmie Osborne is remembered in folk circles, not because of his over-all career, but because of his authorship of one song: "The Death of Little Kathy Fiscus." This tragic song told the true story of a little girl who died of suffocation in an abandoned well in San Marino, California. Performed with typical honky-tonk instrumentation, the song attained considerable national popularity. Yet, despite its modern flourishes, the song contained strong echoes of the event ballads of the 1920's:

> On April the 8th, the year '49,
> Death claimed a little child,
> So pure and so fine.
> Kathy they called her met her doom that day.
> I'm sure it was God that called her away.[37]

One of the most striking and unnoticed developments in the country-music field, in terms of its future course, was brought about by Bill Monroe. As one of the last remaining links between the modern styles and those of the thirties, Monroe exerted a strong influence upon a new generation of country musicians. When the Monroe Brothers disbanded in 1938, Charlie and Bill organized separate units emphasizing unamplified string-band music. With his own group, the Blue Grass Boys, Bill Monroe became one of the favorite acts of the Grand Ole Opry. With his high tenor singing and virtuoso mandolin-playing, Bill Monroe created a new style of music, based on traditional styles, which was ultimately to create a national sensation in the mid-fifties. This style would become known as "bluegrass." But in the glittering, highly commercial world of country

---

[36] Brief biographical notes on Travis are found in Gentry, *A History of Country, Western, and Gospel Music*, p. 325. D. K. Wilgus has commented on the sources of the Travis guitar style in "On the Record," *Kentucky Folklore Record*, VII, No. 3 (July–September, 1961), 126. John Greenway has called Travis "one of the better hillbilly singers" (*American Folksongs of Protest*, p. 271).

[37] "The Death of Little Kathy Fiscus," words and music by Jimmie Osborne. © Copyright 1949 by Lois Publishing Co., Cincinnati. See Gentry, *A History of County, Western, and Gospel Music*, p. 235. This song has been released by King Records on a subsidiary label (*Jimmie Osborne*, Audio Lab AL1527).

music right after the war, none but a few enthusiasts noticed the consequences of Monroe's work. At a time when numerous country performers were achieving fortune and national distinction through the acceptance of western styles and the acquisition of more "modern" sounds, a growing aggregation of bluegrass performers were carrying the unamplified, string-band tradition to its farthest development and were falling back on the traditional repertory for many of their songs.[38]

While the bluegrass bands moved toward the perpetuation and refinement of old-time styles, urban folk enthusiasts endeavored to create a stronger public following for folk music within the ranks of popular-music fans. These people, aiming at a more sophisticated audience, generally considered themselves apart from and superior to the country musicians. The urban folk performers only rarely came from a rural or "folk" background, and they endeavored to present the pure folksongs of tradition, or their imitations, in a manner that could be appreciated by musically sophisticated middle-class audiences.

Urban folk music, which became a national "craze" in the early sixties, was represented in the postwar period by a variety of performers who ranged from the "art singers" such as John Jacob Niles and Richard Dyer-Bennett to the "popular folk singers" like Burl Ives. The one group, however, that contributed most to the urban folk-music boom during the mid-fifties was the Weavers, so called because the name suggested "the qualities of rhythm and work." Composed of three men and one woman (Pete Seeger, Fred Hellerman, Lee Hays, and Ronnie Gilbert), the Weavers produced an exuberant, infectious type of music that included American and foreign material. They performed folk-flavored material with banjo and guitar accompaniment and created a style that was neither "country" nor "popular." With their hybrid style and material the Weavers gained extensive popularity in academic communities and nightclub circles. They achieved the distinction, never before attained by "folk-music" practitioners, of placing some of their songs high on the lists of popular music ratings. These included "Tzena, Tzena," "Goodnight, Irene," and "Kisses Sweeter than Wine." The Weavers pre-

---

[38] For a fuller discussion of Bill Monroe and Bluegrass music, see Chapter 10.

sented much material of a country origin in a style palatable to an audience that did not grow up in the rural tradition.[39]

While urban folk enthusiasts were culling songs from the traditional depository and performing them before nonfolk audiences, country musicians, who sprang directly from the folk tradition, were developing their own styles, largely oblivious to whether they conformed to older patterns or not. This was no different from the manner in which folk musicians had always acted. The country performer sang a song, not because it was in the "folk" tradition, but because it conformed to his own standards and tastes or was a familiar remembrance of his childhood. Many singers appeared during country music's "high" period who reached the pinnacle of success, remained there for a few years, and then leveled off in popularity and made way for another star.

Eddy Arnold, who came from Madisonville, Tennessee, and billed himself as "The Tennessee Plowboy," was the most prominent country performer during the late forties. Although he had served as a vocalist in the mid-forties for Pee Wee King and the Golden West Cowboys, he did not make his first record until December, 1944.[40] As a featured Grand Ole Opry artist and as a maker of "hit" records, Eddy Arnold superseded Roy Acuff as the nation's best-known hillbilly. In the early years of his career, Arnold exhibited a style reminiscent of that of Gene Autry, but without the nasality. He was a country "crooner" with a smooth, yet plaintive, delivery. In his early recordings of "Mommy, Please Stay Home With Me," "It's a Sin," and "Chained to a Memory," Arnold sang in a simple, plaintive, and affecting manner. As the years passed and as his success mounted, Arnold's singing style changed. By 1947, when he recorded the very popular "Bouquet of Roses," Arnold had adopted a more sustained and more forceful approach. His career is representative of that of many country singers who, after a period of initial success, become dissatisfied with their original rural style and strive to achieve a more polished and smoother approach. In so doing, they may become more accomplished, self-conscious vocalists, but with an attending loss of rustic simplicity and sincerity. By the mid-fifties Eddy Arnold could no longer be pictured as strictly a hillbilly singer. He had greatly

[39] Lee Hays, et al., eds., The Weaver's Song Book, pp. v–xii.
[40] Billboard, LXVII, No. 3 (January 15, 1955), 26.

modified his vocal delivery and was making a determined effort to attract attention as a "popular" singer.[41]

Eddy Arnold's popularity, in terms of hit records, began to level off by 1950, but he had had a long string of record successes in the late forties. With the recording of such songs as "That's How Much I Love You," and "Don't Rob Another Man's Castle," Arnold became the best-selling Victor recording artist. In one of the rare statements about record sales, Victor announced that in 1947 over 2,700,000 Eddy Arnold records had been sold.[42] Even without his recording success, Arnold had enough additional interests to ensure a very substantial income. In addition to his regular Grand Ole Opry appearances, he had his own daily show for Purina Mills carried on at least three hundred Mutual stations. He achieved also a distinction seldom attained by country singers—a series of guest appearances on big-time radio shows. A half page ad in *Billboard* announced the following Arnold appearances: RCA Victor Show, We the People, Spike Jones Show, Hayloft Hoedown, Luncheon at Sardi's, Paul Whiteman Club, the Breakfast Club, Sunday Down South, and Western Theatre.[43]

So many singers achieved recording success in the years immediately following Arnold's heyday that it is difficult to label any one individual as the top-ranking star. They represented a wide variety of styles. A few like George Morgan, Eddie Kirk, Wesley Tuttle, Wally Fowler, Leon Payne, and Zeke Clements sang in the soft, smooth style of Eddy Arnold. Payne, in addition, revealed a marked aptitude for song composition and produced many of the successful tunes of the period, including "I Love You Because," "Lost Highway," and "They'll Never Take Her Love From Me."

The period witnessed also the occasional blending of country and "pop" talent. Ernest Tubb and the Andrews Sisters recorded "Don't

[41] Arnold's career since 1944 has witnessed a progressive movement away from the rustic image. By the early 60's the former "Tennessee Plowboy" had discarded his cowboy uniform and, dressing in casual or business attire, was appearing in sophisticated supper and night clubs throughout the country.

[42] *Billboard*, LX, No. 9 (February 28, 1948), 106. There is no question about Arnold's commercial appeal. From 1948, when *Billboard* first began its Top Ten listings, until 1963 he led all country performers with a total of fifty-three "top ten" tunes, thirteen of which reached the number one position (*The World of Country Music*, p. 190).

[43] *Billboard*, LX, No. 21 (May 22, 1948), 18.

Rob Another Man's Castle" and "Biting My Fingernails"; Tennessee Ernie Ford and Kay Starr recorded "I'll Never Be Free" and "Nobody's Business." Jimmie Wakely and Margaret Whiting, who achieved the widest success with this kind of styling, produced such favorites as "One Has My Name, The Other Has My Heart," "Slipping Around," and "The Gods Were Angry With Me."

Sacred songs provided a very popular type of musical offering in the mid-fifties. Although all country singers included such numbers in their repertory, two performers—Clyde "Red" Foley and Stuart Hamblen—managed to place sacred songs on the popularity charts. Foley, who had been a country entertainer since the early thirties, had such a versatile vocal style that he could perform, with equal facility, novelty songs like "Chattanoogie Shoe Shine Boy" or gospel tunes like "Just a Closer Walk With Thee," "Peace in the Valley," and "Steal Away." Another veteran of country music, Stuart Hamblen, began writing and recording sacred songs after his conversion in a Billy Graham Revival Crusade. These included such popular melodies as "It Is No Secret" and "This Old House."

The honky-tonk tradition was well represented by several singers. William Orville "Lefty" Frizzell, of Corsicana, Texas, achieved national fame through the recording of such numbers as "Always Late," and "If You've Got the Money, I've Got the Time." "Little" Jimmie Dickens recorded novelty tunes like "Take an Old Cold Tater" and "Country Boy." Moon Mullican, a country pianist, achieved recognition with "Jole Blon," "Sweeter than the Flowers," and "I'll Sail My Ship Alone." Lloyd "Cowboy" Copas introduced "Filipino Baby," "Signed, Sealed, and Delivered," and "Tragic Romance." Floyd Tillman, a highly regarded singer and composer, first recorded the country standards "Slipping Around" and "I Love You So Much It Hurts." Carl Smith, like Roy Acuff from Maynardsville, Tennessee, sang in a style not far distant from Eddy Arnold's but was accompanied by the basic honky-tonk instrumentation in his recording of such songs as "Let Old Mother Nature Have Her Way." From Louisiana, Webb Pierce became Decca's top country star; he produced a steady stream of best-selling records, including, in 1952, "Wondering" and the country classic, "Back Street Affair":

> You didn't know I wasn't free
> When you fell in love with me,

And with all your young heart
You learned to care.
I brought you shame and disgrace;
The world has tumbled in your face,
And yet they call our love a back street affair.[44]

Another durable honky-tonk exponent was Henry "Hank" Thompson of Waco, Texas. Beginning with a small honky-tonk band, Thompson, through the recording of hit songs like "Humpty Dumpty Heart" and "Wild Side of Life" ("I Didn't Know God Made Honky Tonk Angels"), eventually increased the size of his aggregation until he emerged in the mid-fifties as the leader of the nation's top western-swing band.[45]

The most versatile country entertainer of the mid-fifties, when judged by both vocal ability and instrumental proficiency, was Clarence E. (Hank) Snow. A native of Nova Scotia, Hank Snow had been a popular Canadian singing star since 1936. With his mellow, resonant voice and faultless articulation, Snow could ably perform both slow and fast songs. Hank Snow, a loyal Jimmie Rodgers' devotee with strong roots in traditional country music, was the ablest exponent of the train-song tradition. His first big hit after he became a permanent resident of the United States was a rhythmic train song, "I'm Moving On." His other popular numbers included "The Golden Rocket," "With This Ring I Thee Wed," "Nobody's Child," and "The Gold Rush Is Over."[46]

In a different category was Otis Dewey (Slim) Whitman, from Tampa, Florida.[47] Whitman had a high, clear tenor voice and a yodeling style that was virtually unique in the fifties. Whitman was

[44] "Back Street Affair," words and music by Bill Wallace. © Copyright 1952 by Valley Publishers, Inc., New York. Used by permission. Pierce's recording is on Decca 28369.

[45] For the multitude of singers who achieved recording fame in the mid-1950's, and naturally the list above is not exhaustive, one might consult any of several sources for biographical and discographical information; see, for example, Gentry, *A History of Country, Western, and Gospel Music; The World of Country Music* (for the hit songs of the period); and the issues of *Billboard* for the period 1945 to 1954.

[46] See *The Hank Snow Twenty-Fifth Anniversary Album* for biographical and discographical information.

[47] Gentry, *A History of Country, Western, and Gospel Music*, 339.

unusual in that he rarely recorded a novelty song or one of the raw honky-tonk variety. His specialty was the sentimental or sad love song. He even delved into the popular field for material. Whitman's personal hero was the Canadian country star of an earlier period, Montana Slim.[48] In his yodeling style and in his selection of sentimental and nostalgic melodies Whitman exhibited his debt to the Canadian. Some of his recordings, like "I'm Casting my Lasso Toward the Sky," were western. Some, like "Danny Boy," were old standards. A few, like "Tears Can Never Drown the Flame," were melodies of unrequited love. "The Indian Love Call" (his most successful recording) was taken from a Broadway musical. Whitman, whose recordings were characterized by a "crying" steel guitar, attained a popularity not confined to this country. He was the most popular country singer in England, where he became the first hillbilly to appear in the London Palladium.[49]

Regardless of the style presented, the country singers who made the popularity charts were almost universal in their use of the electric steel guitar. Western-swing bands had declined in national popularity and were now confined largely to the West Coast, Las Vegas, and Oklahoma. Many of their styles and improvisations, however, had become standard features of the smaller country bands. The honky-tonk beat was widely accepted, and the steel guitar was commonly used as the lead instrument. Most of the leading country stars had a particular style or "sound," which their supporters immediately recognized. The extent of one's success quite often depended upon the uniqueness of his sound. This sound was sometimes produced by the singer's vocal mannerisms, as in the case of Lefty Frizzell's drawl or Hank Snow's deep nasal resonance, and often by a distinctive instrumental technique of one of his musicians, as the steel-guitar stylings of Roy Wiggins in Eddy Arnold's organization and the lead guitar work of Billy Byrd with the Ernest Tubb group.

By 1950 many of the features that had been in only embryonic form during earlier periods now had become stereotyped. Some type of western clothing, regardless of the singer's origin, had become the accepted form of stage costume. The steel guitar, with a variety of

---

[48] Asserted in *Billboard*, LXVII, No. 13 (March 26, 1955), 146.
[49] Gentry, *A History of Country, Western, and Gospel Music*, p. 339.

instrumental techniques, had become the dominant instrument. The use of electric instruments was becoming more widespread. It was now not uncommon to find electric string basses and electric fiddles. Drums, too, were frequently employed.

Some features, however, had been abandoned. With rare exceptions, no one sang cowboy songs. Except for the bluegrass bands, no one sang mountain-style melodies. Country songs were less nostalgic. After thirty years of commercial existence and a comparable period of change in American rural life, country music had abandoned much of the romanticism of an earlier period and had come to reflect the changing social and economic patterns of American society.[50] Of the thousands of country songs written during the postwar years there were many that were banal and worthless, some that attracted temporary popularity and then declined, never to be heard again. But a few would stand the test of time. Country-song lyrics dealt with universal themes—love in all of its manifestations, hate, happiness, sorrow, religion, and death. This explains, in large part, the popularity of country music. The simplicity and commonality of its expressions made it easily understandable to the average person. It is true that, in the last analysis, the major difference between country and "popular" songs has been their instrumentation. But, apart from the mode of accompaniment, country songs differed in that their lyrics dealt with subjects that other forms of music would not touch. More than any other form, country music became the naturalistic mode of expression within American music, dealing with the problems of drink, divorce, infidelity, marital problems, and tragedy. The country song, more than any other American musical expression,

[50] Continuing to be America's most topical music, the country repertory included a spate of songs on the Korean War and the Cold War: for example, Harry Choate's "Korea, Here We Come," Bill Monroe's "Rotation Blues"; Ernest Tubb's "Missing in Action" and "A Heartsick Soldier on Heartbreak Ridge"; Roy Acuff's "Doug MacArthur"; Bud Messner and Don Abrams' "Are There Angels in Korea"; the Louvin Brothers' "From Mother's Arms to Korea"; Jimmie Osborne's "Thank God for Victory in Korea"; Jimmie Dickens' "They Locked God Outside the Iron Curtain"; Louvin Brothers "The Great Atomic Power"; F. Kirby's "When That Hell Bomb Falls"; Elton Britt's "The Red That We Want Is the Red We've Got (in the Old Red, White, and Blue)"; and Luke the Drifter's "No, No Joe" (anti-Stalin). See *Billboard* (the late 1940's through early 1950's) for many other examples.

dealt with the tragic element in life, and the sad song was the type which prevailed and predominated.[51]

The increasing popularity of country music was bound to have an effect upon "popular" music. Astute entrepreneurs, always alive to the commercial possibilities of an idea, recognized the financial increment that a country song might bring if recorded by a popular vocalist with lush accompaniment. The noncountry audience, although unwilling to accept the country singer and the basic fiddle and steel guitar accompaniment, would listen to a country song if it was produced under "respectable" and palatable circumstances. Country songs in the past, as in the case of "The Prisoner's Song" and "Pistol Packing Mama," occasionally had passed beyond the limits of strict rural acceptance and become national favorites. They were to do so with great frequency in the modern period. The period witnessed the gradual breakdown of the lines that existed between the various types of music, and the beginning of a closer amalgamation of the different forms. The country song was accepted first; later, the singer himself, if he modified his style, would be accepted.

The year 1950 probably marked the highpoint of country music's postwar surge. By this time songs like Floyd Tillman's "Slipping Around," Moon Mullican's "Jole Blon," Hank Snow's "I'm Moving On," Hank Williams' "Lovesick Blues," Leon Payne's "I Love You Because," and Red Foley's "Chattanoogie Shoe Shine Boy," had brought country music its greatest recognition and prosperity. Jimmie Dickens' "Hillbilly Fever," released in 1950, expressed the heightened interest in country music all over the nation:

> When you step up to a juke box and you slip a nickel in,
> You can bet your bottom dollar when that record starts to spin,
> You'll hear a fiddle and a guitar with that honkytonkin' sound,
> It's that hillbilly breakdown that's spreading all around.[52]

[51] The lyric content of country music is an area worthy of separate attention. Although the folk background has been analyzed by D. K. Wilgus, Archie Green, and others, no one has yet probed the relation between modern country music and its social-economic-cultural milieu. There have been, however, a few articles which briefly touch upon the problem; see, for example, "Realistic View of Life is Implicit in Country Song Material," *The World of Country Music*, pp. 23–24.

[52] "Hillbilly Fever," words and music by George Vaughn. © Copyright 1950 by Cherio Corp., New York. Dickens' recording is on Columbia 20677.

In addition to the typical country favorites, Tin Pan Alley became caught up in the country or folk-style craze and produced a number of best-selling favorites such as "Riders in the Sky," "Mule Train," and "Cry of the Wild Goose."[53] The popular-music favorite charts in *Billboard* also began to see the appearance of country tunes such as "Slipping Around" and "Chattanoogie Shoe Shine Boy."

The song which really signaled the arrival of country music's prosperity—and became one of the largest selling records of all time—was "The Tennessee Waltz." This song had an unusual career in that it was released in 1948 strictly as a hillbilly song,[54] enjoyed considerable popularity, and then was seemingly forgotten. Resurrected in November, 1950 by popular vocalist Patti Page and considered, strangely enough, as the "B" side of her record,[55] the song had become the nation's favorite by December of that year. "The Tennessee Waltz" was written by western-swing band leader Pee Wee King and his vocalist Redd Stewart, who received the inspiration for the song after noting the popularity of Bill Monroe's "Kentucky Waltz" in 1948.[56] "The Tennessee Waltz" was a typical country song in its depiction of a broken romance, but its simplicity and haunting melody made it a national favorite.

"The Tennessee Waltz" alone must be given much of the credit for country music's great commercial surge and the future integration of America's popular music forms. By May, 1951, 4,800,000 records of the song had been sold, and it had earned its writers and publishers (Acuff-Rose) a gross of $330,000. These totals did not include foreign-language recordings or rhythm-and-blues and minor country recordings. It was generally believed that "The Tennessee Waltz" was the biggest hit in modern popular-music history, and it was certainly the top song ever licensed by BMI. The song brought extensive financial profit to its composers, and launched Acuff-Rose on the road to publishing success. Acuff-Rose actually had been surprised by the song's popularity, and had neglected, or was unable, to exploit it nationally. The Nashville publishing firm had no contact men or

[53] See *The World of Country Music* for a listing of the 1950 favorites (p. 189).

[54] *Billboard*, LX, No. 9 (February 28, 1948), 106.

[55] *Ibid.*, LXII, No. 45 (November 11, 1950), 13.

[56] Pee Wee King, Testimony quoted in Hearings . . . on S. 2834.

business representation in the three traditionally accepted music centers, New York, Los Angeles, and Chicago.[57]

The spectacular success of "The Tennessee Waltz" ensured that the music industry in the future would give close attention to country songs as possibilities for national exploitation. This opened the way for country-music's further expansion and for its greater national acceptance. In future years country composers and publishing houses would devote more conscious efforts toward breaking down the barriers between popular and country music in hopes of emulating "The Tennessee Waltz" success.

The individual who most successfully spanned the gulf between country and popular music was King Hiram "Hank" Williams, who along with Jimmie Rodgers and Fred Rose constituted the triumvirate first elected to country music's Hall of Fame.[58] Williams was the symbol of country music's postwar upsurge, and his sudden death in 1953 signified the ending of the boom period. His early death solidified the legend that had already begun during his lifetime.

It is paradoxical that Hank Williams, whose compositions were more readily accepted by popular-music practitioners than any other country writer's, was more firmly grounded in the rural tradition than most other hillbilly performers. In the influences that worked upon him, in his early upbringing, and in his mode of musical expression, Williams reflected the inherited traditions of the rural South and the forces that have strived to urbanize it. He is, therefore, an interesting fusion of the old with the new; he was a rural singer who had the talent (or knack) to create compositions acceptable to people outside the rural tradition. But, at the same time, his career came at a fortuitous moment when country music was gaining wider public acceptance and when the commercial entertainment world was devoting greater attention to country songs. Despite his talents, Williams would not have gained fame as a popular songwriter had he lived during an earlier period. The preceding decades had not been propitious for such a development. As it was, Williams rode to prosperity and fame on the crest of the postwar wave that spread country music throughout the nation, and, as much as any one man, he in-

---

[57] *Billboard*, LXIII, No. 20 (May 19, 1951),1, 13.
[58] The "official" Hall of Fame created by the Country Music Association (see Chapter 10).

George D. Hay, founder of the Grand Ole Opry.

Left to right: Al Hopkins, John Hopkins, Elvis Alderman, John Rector, Uncle Am Stuart, Fiddlin' John Carson. Photographed at old-time fiddler's convention, Mountain City, Tennessee, 1925.

The Carter Family (left to right): Maybelle, Sara, and A. P. Carter.

Charlie Poole (seated) and the North Carolina Ramblers.

Above left: Carson Robison.

Above right: Henry Whitter, 1923.

Right: Rev. Andrew Jenkins.

Al Hopkins and the Hillbillies, "The Band that Named the Music" (left to right): Tony Alderman, John Hopkins, Charlie Bowman, Al Hopkins.

Uncle Dave Macon and his son Dorris.

Vernon Dalhart

Bradley Kincaid

Bill Cox, composer of "Filipino Baby."

Jimmie Rodgers

Left to right:
Jimmie Rodgers, Mrs. Ralph Peer,
Ralph Peer, Mrs. Jimmie Rodgers,
Anita Rodgers (center).

Left to right:
Jimmie Rodgers, Maybelle, A. P., and
Sara Carter.

Jimmie Rodgers

Prince Albert Hunt

Jimmie Tarlton, 1963

Rex Griffin, composer of "The Last Letter."

The Callahan Brothers: Bill (left) and Joe.

The Blue Sky Boys: Bill (right) and Earl Bolick, 1964.

The Cumberland Ridge Runners (standing, left to right): Slim Miller, Karl Davis, Red Foley, Harty Taylor; (seated) John Lair, Linda Parker.

The Prairie Ramblers (left to right): "Happy" Jack Taylor, Charles "Chuck" Hurt, Shelby "Tex" Atchison, Floyd "Salty" Holmes—and Patsy Montana.

Grace Wilson

Left, Carl T. Sprague in the 1920's; above, Carl T. Sprague in 1964.

The Light Crust Doughboys, original group (left to right): Sleepy Johnson, Bob Wills, Milton Brown, W. Lee "Pappy" O'Daniel.

The Light Crust Doughboys, 1933 (left to right): W. Lee "Pappy" O'Daniel, Henry Steinbarth (the driver), Sleepy Johnson, Raymond DeArman, Leon McAuliffe, Leon Huff, Clifford Gross, Herman Arnspiger.

Roy Acuff as a young man.

Gene Autry, about 1930–before Hollywood.

Roy Acuff in movie still from *Smoky Mountain Melody*.

Milton Brown and His Musical Brownies, 1935 (left to right): Ocie Stockard, Fred Calhoun, Wanna Coffman, Milton Brown, Cecil Brower, Bob Dunn, Durwood Brown.

Ralph (left) and Carter Stanley, 1966.

The Blue Grass Boys (left to right): Art Wooten, Bill Monroe, Billy Borum, Jim Holmes.

The Blue Grass Boys (left to right): Birch Monroe, Lester Flatt, Bill Monroe, Earl Scruggs, Chubby Wise.

Bill Monroe

Ernest Tubb

Buck Owens

Hank Williams

augurated the movement that, despite his own immersion in the rural tradition, served to becloud country music's unique identity.

Hank Williams was born on September 17, 1923, on a tenant farm in Mt. Olive, Alabama, where he remained until the age of five, when his family moved to Georgiana, near Montgomery.[59] As a small boy he helped to supplement the family income by selling peanuts and newspapers and by shining shoes. Williams had a serious, sensitive nature and very early displayed a strong love for music. His earliest musical influence was derived from attendance at fundamentalist Baptist churches, where he learned to love the spirited hymns and gospel tunes. In his later recording career, Williams made the gospel song, both original and otherwise, an important part of his repertory. His favorite song was "Death Is Only a Dream," an indication of his musical tastes and his own particular way of viewing life.[60]

Another musical influence on Williams was an old Negro street-singer named "Teetot," who first taught him the guitar. This influence is a further example of the musical acculturation that existed among southern Negroes and whites. Williams gained fame as a "country blues" singer, and much of his style could have been derived from Negro sources.[61] By the time Williams was twelve years old, he had developed a strong compulsion to be a professional singer. At Montgomery's Empire Theatre, he won an amateur night contest singing his own composition, "The WPA Blues."[62] Encouraged by this recog-

[59] Although short biographical sketches on Williams can be found in many places, primary reliance has been placed on the following sources: Eli Waldron, "Country Music: The Death of Hank Williams," *The Reporter*, XII, No. 10 (May 19, 1955), 35–37; Waldron, "Country Music: The Squaya Dansu from Nashville," *The Reporter*, XII, No. 11 (June 2, 1955), 39–41; *Country Song Roundup* (Special Hank Williams Memorial Issue), I, No. 24 (June, 1953), 5–14; interview with Mrs. Hank (Audrey) Williams, Austin, Texas, July 2, 1962; interview with Wesley Rose, Nashville, Tennessee, August 28, 1961.

[60] Interview with Audrey Williams, July 2, 1962.

[61] An interesting resemblance to the Williams style, and one that might suggest his debt to Negro blues, is John Dudley's rendition of "Cool Water Blues." Dudley was a sixty-year-old Negro prisoner in the Mississippi Penitentiary at Parchman, Mississippi. Dudley used a semi-yodeling style similar to that used by Williams on such songs as "Long Gone Lonesome Blues," "Moaning the Blues," and "Lovesick Blues." Both singers came out of the same deep south environment. Dudley's performance is found on *The Blues Roll On*, Southern Folk Heritage Series, Atlantic Records, No. 1352 (recorded by Alan Lomax).

[62] Interview with Audrey Williams, July 2, 1962.

nition of his talents, he began performing at any affair that might be willing to listen to him. At the tender age of thirteen he had become well acquainted with the honky-tonk environment and, reflecting the omnipresent western image, had formed a band called The Drifting Cowboys. This Alabama tenant farmer's son, steeped in the southern rural tradition, called himself the Drifting Cowboy. Except for "The Happy Roving Cowboy," which he sometimes used as a theme song, and "Cool Water,"[63] which was taken from a home tape recording and posthumously placed on a long-play album, Williams never recorded a western song. His creations were realistic depictions of his own social environment and of the deep-South culture from which he came.

In 1937, when he was fourteen years old, he set out on the road traveled by thousands of previous hillbilly entertainers: he obtained a singing job on a radio station, in his case WSFA in Montgomery. During the following five years he struggled for recognition and financial success, playing honky-tonks, schoolhouses, and medicine shows. Williams, who at the age of seventeen married Audrey Shepherd, lived an existence typical of the struggling hillbilly aspirant: working at various occupations and singing during his off hours, always looking for the big break. Williams might well have abandoned his musical aspirations had it not been for the loyalty of his mother. During the war years he temporarily gave up singing and took a job in a Mobile shipyard. Concerned because of his disappointment, his mother began inquiring at clubs and honky-tonks and secured him a long string of entertainment dates. Thereafter, he was never unemployed for long periods.[64]

In 1946, he signed his first recording contract with a minor label, Sterling. At this point in his career Williams' style revealed a strong Roy Acuff influence, and his earliest recordings were of a tragic or gospel nature. When *Billboard* reviewed "Wealth Won't Save Your Soul" and "When God Comes and Gathers His Jewels," it made the following revealing comments: "It's the backwoods gospel singing— way back in the woods—that Hank Williams sings out for both of

---

[63] "The Happy Roving Cowboy" can be heard on *On Stage*, MGM E3999; "Cool Water" is on *The Lonesome Sound of Hank Williams*, MGM E3803.

[64] Waldron, "Country Music: The Death of Hank Williams," *The Reporter*, XII, No. 10 (May 19, 1955), 36–37.

these country songs taken at a slow waltz tempo. Both the singing and the songs entirely funereal."[65]

Both melodies, heavily steeped in tradition, were Williams' own compositions, as were most of his later recordings. During 1946 several of his songs were accepted by Acuff-Rose publishing company and some of them, like "When God Comes and Gathers His Jewels" and "Six More Miles to the Graveyard," were recorded by Molly O'Day. A story often repeated, but possibly apochryphal, concerns Williams' first meeting with Fred Rose. According to the story, when Williams visited Fred Rose in Nashville in an effort to get his compositions accepted, Rose was interested but somewhat skeptical about the songs' authorship. In an effort to test Williams' creative ability, Rose gave him the hypothetical situation of a haughty girl in a fine mansion who rejected the love of her poor suitor who dwelled in a humble cabin. Williams supposedly took the situation and made it into one of his most popular songs, "Mansion on the Hill." Impressed by both his singing and writing ability, Rose helped Williams to obtain a recording contract with MGM, where he was directed by veteran talent scout Frank Walker. His first recordings were "Move It On Over" and "I Heard You Crying in Your Sleep."[66]

Hank Williams' association with Acuff-Rose and MGM served to ensure the success of those organizations. In the following five-year period Hank Williams became the best known and most emulated country entertainer in the United States. After an initial series of moderate successes, he recorded the most popular song of 1949,[67] and one of the most famous of the postwar period. This was "Lovesick Blues," an old country-blues item and in its progressions one of the most difficult songs in the country repertory. This country-blues classic dates at least to a 1925 recording by yodeler Emmett Miller on Okeh 40465. A recording from the thirties, however, may have directly inspired Williams' recording: Rex Griffin's rendition on Decca 5770-A was de-

[65] *Billboard,* LIX, No. 14 (April 5, 1947), 123. The journal added further that the songs were "not for music machines."

[66] Interview with Wesley Rose, August 28, 1961; interview with Audrey Williams, July 2, 1962. The "Mansion on the Hill" legend, according to Ed Kahn, is not true (letter to the author from Ed Kahn, Los Angeles, California, February 1, 1967).

[67] Listed in *The World of Country Music,* p. 189. For confirmation see *Billboard,* LXII, No. 2 (January 14, 1950), 18.

livered with almost the identical yodeling technique later used by Williams.[68] When performed by Williams the song brought encore after encore and established him as a distinctive blues singer. It also earned him a position on the Grand Ole Opry, which he joined in June, 1949, after a two-year stint with the Louisiana Hayride.[69]

After this date Hank Williams never again had financial problems. From his recordings and personal appearances, he earned an average of $200,000 a year until his death in 1953.[70] In October, 1951, he signed a five-year movie contract with MGM,[71] which, because of his death, did not result in a motion picture. If it had, his income probably would have been much more fabulous.

A man's income is no real measure of his worth, but in reference to the country performers who achieved financial success in the mid-fifties, it is an indication that they were able to communicate with thousands of listeners. And no one communicated as well as Hank Williams. He had a small, light voice capable of all sorts of peculiar twists and turns. He had a versatile vocal style and could perform equally well fast novelty tunes, blues numbers, religious melodies, and sad love songs. Hank Williams approached every song with complete seriousness, as if the lyrics expressed his individual, personal experience. He sang with the quality that has characterized every great hillbilly singer: utter sincerity. He "lived" the songs he sang— he could communicate his feelings to the listener and make each person feel as if the song were being sung directly to him. On one occasion when asked to explain the success of country music, Williams replied: "It can be explained in just one word: sincerity. When a hillbilly sings a crazy song, he feels crazy. When he sings, 'I Laid My Mother Away,' he sees her a-laying right there in the coffin. He sings more sincere than most entertainers because the hillbilly was raised

---

[68] Letter to the author from Bob Pinson, Santa Clara, California, September 4, 1966.

[69] *Billboard*, LXI, No. 24 (June 11, 1949), 30.

[70] Bernard Asbell, "Simple Songs of Sex, Sin, and Salvation," *Show: the Magazine of the Performing Arts*, II, No. 2 (February, 1962), 89.

[71] *Billboard*, LXIII, No. 41 (October 13, 1951), 16. MGM did, however, produce an unsatisfactory screen biography of Williams in the 1960's. George Hamilton starred in the title role, while Hank Williams Jr. performed his father's songs.

rougher than most entertainers. You got to know a lot about hard work. You got to have smelt a lot of mule manure before you can sing like a hillbilly. The people who has been raised something like the way the hillbilly has knows what he is singing about and appreciates it."[72]

When a heart attack brought a sudden and tragic end to Hank Williams' glittering career on New Year's Day, 1953, he had become the best known and most financially successful country singer in the United States. Material success, however, had not brought peace of mind to the twenty-nine-year-old entertainer. In fact, the last several months of his life were clouded by heartbreak and tragedy. Continually beset by a spinal ailment that forced him to walk in a slightly stooped position and which necessitated the periodic employment of drugs and medical attention, Williams lived a tortured physical existence. Physical suffering, combined with mental anguish provoked by marital problems, produced a lonely, unhappy individual who poured out his feelings in a steady stream of melancholy and tragic songs.[73] The last few months of his life were financially profitable[74] but emotionally tragic. Fired from the Grand Ole Opry in August, 1952,[75] because of chronic drunkenness and instability, Williams returned to the scene of his earliest barn-dance triumph, the Louisiana Hayride. During this short period he divorced his first wife, Audrey, and quickly married Billie Jones, the daughter of the Bossier City, Louisiana, police chief.[76]

Death came to Williams in Oak Hill, West Virginia, while he was en route to a New Year's performance in Canton, Ohio. His funeral, held at Montgomery, Alabama, amid a background of gospel singing performed by Ernest Tubb, Carl Smith, Roy Acuff, and Red Foley,

[72] Quoted in Rufus Jarman, "Country Music Goes to Town," *Nation's Business*, XLI (February, 1953), 51.

[73] Frank Walker, Williams' MGM recording director, believed that Audrey Williams "was undoubtedly the inspiration for many of his great songs and records" (*The World of Country Music*, p. 43).

[74] Williams placed five songs on *Billboard's* country popularity chart in 1952, two of which reached the number one position: "Jambalaya" and "I'll Never Get Out of this World Alive" (*The World of Country Music*, p. 192).

[75] *Billboard*, LXIV, No. 35 (August 31, 1952), 19.

[76] *Ibid.*, LXV, No. 11 (March 14, 1953), 49.

drew one of the largest gatherings in the city's history. An estimated crowd of twenty thousand people[77] gathered in and outside the city auditorium to catch a last glimpse of the young singer. The event, termed the "greatest emotional orgy"[78] in Montgomery's history, provoked an outburst of weeping, wailing, and fainting spells.

On the day of Williams' death and periodically thereafter, country radio shows devoted major segments of their air time to songs that he made famous. Almost immediately, songs describing his death or commemorating his career made their appearances on juke boxes and radio shows: Jack Cardwell's "The Death of Hank Williams," Jimmie Skinner's "Singing Teacher in Heaven," Johnny and Jack's "Hank Williams Will Live Forever," and, perhaps prophetically for the future of country music, Ernest Tubb's "Hank, It Will Never Be the Same Without You."

[77] *Newsweek*, XLI, No. 3 (January 19, 1953), 55; *Country Song Roundup* (Special Hank Williams Memorial Issue), I, No. 24 (June, 1953), 5.

[78] Waldron, "Country Music: The Death of Hank Williams," *The Reporter*, XII, No. 10 (May 19, 1955), 35.

CHAPTER 8

The Development of Country-Pop Music and the Nashville Sound

THE YEARS FOLLOWING Hank Williams' death witnessed a series of far-reaching developments which made country music a firmer part of the nation's commercial scene and yet threatened to becloud its unique identity. Country music would probably have followed the course that it did even had Williams lived, but, coming as it did at the beginning of a new era, his death symbolized the closing of country music's "high" period. It is ironic that Williams, whose style was so firmly grounded in rural tradition, did more than any other individual to modify the traditional music forms and broaden the music's base of acceptance, thereby diluting its rural purity. Williams' success at song composition gained a wider acceptance for country music and, furthering the advances made by "The Tennessee Waltz," served to batter down the tenuous walls between popular and country music. With increasing regularity country songs made their appearances on the popular-song charts.[1] And as the number of

---

[1] The Hank Williams compositions recorded by pop singers include "Cold, Cold Heart" by Tony Bennett, "Jambalaya" by Jo Stafford, "I Can't Help It" by Guy Mitchell, "You Win Again" by Tommy Edwards, "Hey, Good Looking" by Frankie Laine and Jo Stafford, "Kawliga" by Frankie Laine, "Your Cheating Heart" by Joni James, and "Honky Tonkin'" by Teresa Brewer. Mitch Miller, television personality and one-time pop artists- and repertoire-man for Columbia, is credited with having aided the popularization of country music in general, and Hank Williams' songs in particular. Through Miller's encouragement Tony Bennett recorded "Cold, Cold Heart," which sold a million and one-half copies (*The World of Country Music*, p. 145).

songs accepted by popular vocalists increased, so did the desires of country performers to be recognized by the popular audience. Country singers wanted to place themselves as well as their songs on the popular-music charts. This was achieved in the following years, but not without radical changes in the stylistic structure of country instrumentation. Country musicians and singers adapted their styles to fit the tastes of popular-music devotees who refused to accept the traditional country styles. These changes, which brought grief to many supporters and joy to others, made country music a billion dollar industry and completely "revolutionized" the popular-music world.

For approximately one year after Williams' death, country styles did not change materially. The songs played on radios and juke boxes still were characterized by the honky-tonk beat and the sounds of the fiddle and steel guitar. New singers continued to appear, to earn hefty incomes, and to gain glittering success. Some of them, like Ray Price and George Jones (both from Texas), received their inspiration from Hank Williams.[2] A few, like Marty Robbins of Arizona and Jim Reeves from Texas, used a soft, semi-crooning style somewhat suggestive of Eddy Arnold. The most successful country performer in the year immediately following Williams' death was a wailing honky-tong singer from Monroe, Louisiana, Webb Pierce. Recording for Decca, Pierce produced twenty-one consecutive "hits," or songs that sold over 100,000, including the modern numbers "More and More" and "That Heart Belongs to Me"; an old country favorite, "Wondering," first recorded in 1937 by the Riverside Ramblers; "I'm in the Jailhouse Now," an old Jimmie Rodgers' tune; and "Sparkling Brown Eyes," from the Bill Cox repertory. Using standard honky-tonk instrumentation featured by a "crying" steel guitar, Pierce occupied the position vacated by Williams and catapulted himself first to the Louisiana Hayride and later to the Grand Ole Opry.[3] In short, Pierce

---

[2] Both singers have acknowledged their debts to Williams (interview with Ray Price, Austin, Texas, March 2, 1962; interview with George Jones, Austin, Texas, August 16, 1962).

[3] Information on Pierce was obtained from Linnell Gentry, *A History and Encyclopedia of Country, Western, and Gospel Music*, p. 288; *Billboard*; *The World of Country Music*, 192–199; interview with James Denny (of Cedarwood Publishing Company), Nashville, Tennessee, August 25, 1961; and a letter to the author from Bob Pinson, Santa Clara, California, September 4, 1966.

was only one of several country entertainers who continued to produce hit records and attract large followings. But no one could capture the public imagination as Williams had.

The year 1954 saw the emergence of a new musical force which completely engulfed the other musical forms, dominated American popular music for several years, and shattered the existing conceptions of what a popular song should be. The rock-and-roll phenomenon was triggered largely by a revolution in the record-buying habits of America's teenage population. Postwar prosperity had placed more money in the hands of greater numbers of young people, who had expended an increasing proportion of it for amusement, particularly the buying of records. The teenage market had, in fact, accounted for much of the success of country music after the war. In the mid-fifties this market, taking in the ever-increasing youthful segment of the population, turned toward another product of grassroots America. This was a form of music that, in point of ultimate origin, was as old as country music but of a much more hybrid nature. One line of ancestry, of course, ran through Negro musical history. The country blues of the twenties had evolved into the loose category of Negro commercial music known as "race" music, which by the early fifties had come to be known as "rhythm-and-blues."

Although rhythm-and-blues was a music produced for Negroes by Negroes, the walls dividing the musical forms had never been strong enough to keep individual songs and styles from crossing the musical barriers. Throughout the late forties and early fifties young white juke-box devotees became increasingly acquainted with such legendary rhythm-and-blues names as Muddy Waters, Howlin' Wolf, and Joe Turner. It was perhaps inevitable that country music would be affected by the popularity of this music, because southern Negroes and whites had promoted a vigorous musical interchange ever since the two races had been thrown together. When the two cultural traditions fused their musical chemistries in the mid-fifties, they created an explosion that still reverberates throughout the popular-music world.

Rock-and-roll, a term coined by Cleveland disc jockey Alan Freed in 1951,[4] has been a continuingly controversial musical phenomenon.

[4] Alan Freed's influence has been discussed by Carl I. Belz in one of the best articles yet written on rock-and-roll ("Popular Music and the Folk Tradition," *Journal of American Folklore*, LXXX, No. 316 [April–June, 1967], 131).

Although rock-and-roll is detested by many (usually adults),[5] Alan Lomax summed up the attitude of many observers when he termed rock-and-roll "the healthiest manifestation yet in native American music."[6] Lomax considered the music to be authentic grass-roots material, and the furthest intrusion of Negro folk music into popular music. It was this, and much more, however. Rock-and-roll was a conglomeration of musical forms. In part, with its heavy, monotonous beat and electric guitar instrumentation, it suggested the noisy raucous environs of a Negro juke joint. On the other hand, the wailing vocal styles and rolling piano chords (such as those of Fats Domino) were reminiscent of Negro country church services. Although Negro influence was obvious, rock-and-roll became essentially a music performed by white people for white audiences. Even the wide variety of Negro performers (such as Chuck Berry, Fats Domino, or the Platters) who worked with the rock-and-roll idiom generally presented smoothed-over or toned-down versions that would be palatable to white audiences.[7]

Country music had long demonstrated its affinity for the stepped-up rhythms of Negro music, as evidenced in the success of the Delmore Brothers in the thirties and the boogie and blues guitar stylings of Arthur "Guitar Boogie" Smith in the forties.[8] White guitarists, and such important country pianists as Moon Mullican, had developed long before the fifties a variety of instrumental styles that would fit readily into the rock-and-roll genre. The musical deluge that had been anticipated by the independent work of Negro and white musicians came in 1954 when Bill Haley, who had directed a country organization with little success for several years, recorded the extremely popular "Rock Around the Clock."[9] To many observers, this was the real beginning of rock-and-roll. Bill Haley, with his rock-and-roll unit, the Comets, became the first country entertainer to

[5] Vance Packard asserted that rock-and-roll, which in his opinion had been foisted upon an unwilling public by BMI, was designed to "stir the animal instinct in modern teenagers" (testimony on . . . S. 2834).

[6] Alan Lomax, *Esquire*, LII, No. 4 (October, 1959), 88.

[7] For this view of rock-and-roll see Tony Glover, "R & B," *Sing Out: The Folk Song Magazine*, XV, No. 2 (May, 1965), 7.

[8] *The Little Sandy Review*, II, No. 1 (July, 1966), 31.

[9] *Billboard*, LXVI, No. 20 (May 15, 1954), 17; *The World of Country Music*, p. 194; Belz, "Popular Music and the Folk Tradition," *Journal of American Folklore*, LXXX, No. 316 (April–June, 1967), 131.

anticipate the coming spectacular success of the new musical phenomenon. Many others, recognizing the financial possibilities, followed his example.

The performer who most ably illustrated the intermingling of country and rhythm-and-blues music, and the one who achieved the most fabulous success, was Elvis Presley. Presley, a farm boy from Tupelo, Mississippi, journeyed to Memphis, Tennessee, in 1954 and obtained a contract with Sun Records—a company, headed by Sam Phillips, that played a major role in the rock-and-roll boom.[10] At this stage in Presley's career, no one was quite sure to what musical category he belonged. Throughout his life, he had been exposed to the various forces that shaped the southern musical repertory. Brought up on commercial country music and Pentecostal gospel songs (he was reared in the Assembly of God faith), Presley early became addicted to the rhythmic music of the southern Negro. Like many rural Mississippi youth, Presley journeyed to Memphis to find employment and, after a short stint as a truck driver, gained a recording contract. His original string band became the prototype of the rock-and-roll organizations: electric guitar, rhythm guitar, and string bass. His repertory included many country songs, but they were performed in a fashion roughly equivalent to that of the rhythm-and-blues aggregations. It is significant, as an indication of the mixed nature of his style, that his first recordings included an old "race" number first recorded by Arthur Crudup, "That's All Right, Mama," and a hillbilly tune written by Bill Monroe, "Blue Moon of Kentucky."[11] As his records attracted attention, country disc jockeys realized that he was a hybrid phenomenon. Although his early tours were made with country organizations, his appeal was much wider than that, and his popularity was most intense among teenagers.

The reasons for Presley's popularity are not difficult to gauge. To a certain degree he capitalized on the newly developing interest in rhythm-and-blues and with his extraordinary sense of rhythm could perform the music more ably than any of his white counterparts. But Presley's appeal did not derive solely from his musical abilities; it came primarily from his personality and showmanship, and it was in this respect that Presley exerted his strongest influence. His career

[10] Sam Phillips' role in promoting country and rock-and-roll music is discussed in *The World of Country Music* (p. 48).

[11] *Billboard*, LXVI, No. 43 (October 23, 1954), 42.

marked the beginning of a period when youth and stage color would be the essential hallmarks of success. The youthful record-buying population demanded handsome performers from their own generation who would sing about subjects with which they were familiar. The rock-and-roll fad was part of what sociologist David Reisman had earlier called a teenage rebellion against established musical forms and the people who performed them.[12] Presley, who combined sex appeal with a dynamic singing style, was the first of a myriad of entertainers who attracted a legion of followers as much because of their youth and vitality as for their talent. Among them were Gene Vincent, of "Be-Bop-Alulu" fame; Rick Nelson, teenage son of the radio family "Ozzie and Harriet"; Buddy Holley (later killed in a plane crash); Jerry Lee Lewis, a pianist in the Moon Mullican tradition; Roy Orbison, who is still experiencing success; Carl Perkins, performer of "Blue Suede Shoes"; and Conway Twitty (Harold Jenkins), who returned to the country-music field in 1965.[13]

Conway Twitty's career is a good capsule study of the influence exerted by Elvis Presley and the rock-and-roll revolution on southern country boys. He came from a little town in Mississippi named Friars Point, seventy miles south of Memphis and only forty miles from Presley's home town of Tupelo. When he first became interested in music he sang only the country music that he learned from his riverboat-captain father and from the recordings of such people as Red Foley, Ernest Tubb, and Roy Acuff. During his two year tenure in the army he organized a country band known as the Cimarrons. When he returned to the United States from Japan in 1955, he heard Elvis Presley's recorded version of "Mystery Train" and was immediately swept away by the excitement that was affecting young people everywhere. He formed a rock-and-roll band, changed his name from Harold Jenkins to Conway Twitty, and set out on a career that was to lead to millions of record sales.[14]

In the immediate post-Presley years the accent was clearly on

[12] Reisman, "Listening to Popular Music," *American Quarterly*, II, No. 4 (Winter, 1950), 363–364.

[13] The interested reader might consult issues of *Billboard* for accounts of other rock-and-roll performers. Carl Perkins, the most country-oriented of the group, is discussed in *Country and Western Jamboree*, II, No. 4 (June, 1956), 19.

[14] Dixie Deen, "Conway Rocks Right into Country Success," *Music City News*, IV, No. 8 (February, 1967), 3–4.

youth, and recording companies were always on the lookout for young performers who could equal the success of Presley or Twitty. Teenage buyers responded with the formation of fan clubs and the purchase of millions of records. Records were bought in such quantities that the figures denoting all-time sellers became meaningless, and records were often bought unheard simply because they were performed by a particular star. This increased musical interest on the part of teenagers coincided with a growing emphasis by the record companies on the issuance of the 33 1/3 rpm long-play albums. By 1958, the old 78 rpm disc had become almost a museum piece. In its place the record companies introduced the smaller, unbreakable 45 rpm disc, and the multiplay 33 1/3 item, both originally introduced in 1948.[15] With the issuance of long-play records the adult virtually ceased to be a buyer of single records. Rather than purchase individual discs, which had to be changed on the phonograph every few minutes, adults found it more advantageous and economical to buy a record that would provide several minutes of uninterrupted listening. Conversely, the youthful fans became the buyers of the single records, and the recording industry provided them with the type of music they wanted.

No phase of American popular music escaped unaffected from the rock-and-roll deluge. By 1956 rock-and-roll singers had flooded the music popularity charts,[16] and radio disc-jockey shows had come to be geared largely to the interests of teenage listeners. This period saw the introduction of "teenshows" and "the top 50" shows, which specifically catered to the interests of young people. The rock-and-roll appeal had become so strong that it was a rare entertainer who successfully avoided altering his style to conform to its dictates. The country musician was no exception. Just as country-oriented performers Bill Haley and Elvis Presley helped to trigger the rock-and-roll boom, many others helped to continue it. Some country musicians fought against the pressure to alter their styles, while others wholeheartedly accepted the changes. Although some country performers

[15] *Billboard Music Week, 1962–63 International Music Industry Buyers' Guide and Market Data Report* (August 4, 1962), 10.

[16] Although rock-and-roll inundated the pop music charts more rapidly than it did those denoting country songs, the *Billboard* country popularity chart in 1956 listed seven rock-and-roll tunes, four of them by Presley (*The World of Country Music*, p. 195).

prospered because of their willingness to compromise, for a period pure country music suffered, and, to many tradition-minded fans, the old music seemed to be on its way to destruction.[17]

Rock-and-roll did not immediately inundate country music. The process was gradual. Although a few performers like Elvis Presley and Carl Perkins performed rock-and-roll extensively, and prospered, the bulk of the stars tried to hold on to the older and more traditional styles. Throughout 1955 and much of 1956 Hank Snow, Ernest Tubb, Webb Pierce, and other "old-timers" continued to produce a steady stream of typical country songs. But the music was not faring as well as it had in previous years.[18] The youthful generation was being won over to the more rollicking rhythms of rock-and-roll.

Although country singers did not abandon the older musical styles in wholesale fashion, many of them modified these styles to a certain extent in an attempt to attract a larger following. As a result, a hybrid specimen developed: an individual who possessed characteristics of both the rock-and-roll and country singer, the rockabilly. And again the premium was on youth. That individual who could best combine youthful good looks with a bouncy style would climb the ladder of musical success. Some of the entertainers who emerged had roots deep in the country tradition. The Everly Brothers (Don and Phil), who eventually left the country-music field, were the sons of old-time country guitarist Ike Everly of Kentucky. They sang songs of the youthful generation, but in a style of harmony derived from such southern country singers as the Blue Sky Boys.[19] Sonny James (James

---

[17] For an example of the opposition to the rock-and-roll infiltration of country music, see the "letters to the editor" sections of the country song journals, particularly *Country and Western Jamboree*, III, No. 5 (August, 1957), 26–28; *ibid.*, II, No. 4 (July, 1956), 34. Of course, there were also letters praising rock-and-roll.

[18] In reporting the declining sale of country music in the South, *Billboard* quoted certain unnamed recording executives who attributed the decline to the "anti-progress" attitude of country disc jockeys who refused to play pop or rock-and-roll material (*Billboard*, LXVIII, No. 9 [March 3, 1956], 541).

[19] Ike Everly, "Father Calls Mother Secret of Amazing Success," *Country and Western Jamboree*, IV, No. 1 (Summer, 1958), 10–16, 33, 38. Also *ibid.*, III, No. 5 (August, 1957), 15, 34. For the Everly Brothers' country background see their album entitled *Songs Our Daddy Taught Us* (Cadence CLP 3016), which contains such songs as "Down in the Willow Garden" and "Lightning Express."

Loden), recognized as one of the most versatile country entertainers of the sixties and now billed as The Southern Gentleman, gained his first national popularity as a singer of teenage-oriented songs. Although he came out of a musical Alabama family which played the traditional hillbilly fiddle and five-string banjo,[20] James placed greatest emphasis on the modern sounds and styles. After the rock-and-roll boom developed, he modified his rural approach in an attempt to attract the popular audience. His boyish good looks proved to be an invaluable asset.

Even those singers who remained firmly within the country-music field seemed to prosper best when they jived up their rhythms and used a "hot" guitar. Johnny Cash from Arkansas, whose deep-voiced singing style suggested the honky-tonk influence of Hank Williams and Ernest Tubb, nevertheless won a large following among young people because of his sense of rhythm and lively instrumentation. Performing with a group called The Tennessee Two (Electric guitarist Luther Perkins and string bassist Marshall Grant), Cash produced a number of big selling records, including "Folsom Prison Blues" and "Hey, Porter," that were country in nature but rhythmic enough to attract the rock-and-roll audience. Luther Perkins' guitar technique helped to produce a distinctive, recognizable rhythm.[21]

Strong evidence of the impact of rock-and-roll upon American musical rhythm was shown in the amazing success of the country coal-mining song "Sixteen Tons." First recorded in 1947 by its composer, the brilliant country guitarist Merle Travis, the song did not gain national recognition until 1955, when it was recorded by Tennessee Ernie Ford. Ford, who by this time had left the country music field, recorded the song over a semi-rock-and-roll background. One of the fastest-selling records in history, it reached the number one position on the best-selling charts only sixteen weeks from its first issuance, and only three weeks after its first appearance on the *Billboard* charts.[22]

[20] Frieda Barter Gillis, "In the Spotlight—Sonny James," *Rustic Rhythm*, I, No. 4 (July, 1957), 19–24.

[21] Gentry, *A History of Country, Western, and Gospel Music*, 202; Gillis, "Johnny Cash," *Rustic Rhythm*, I, No. 2 (May, 1957), 23–26.

[22] *Billboard*, LXVII, No. 43 (October 22, 1955), 27; *ibid.*, LXVII, No. 49 (December 3, 1955), 21.

The steadily developing popularity of rock-and-roll and the evident power of the teenage buying public forced the recording executives to take a closer look at the offerings of country performers. It was a rare individual indeed who could enter a recording studio and withstand the pressure to modify his style. The artists-and-repertoire directors counseled their country artists to adopt certain techniques and styles of the rock-and-roll and popular performers in order to attract a wider following. The stage was set for a closer amalgamation of American musical forms, and for the emergence of "country-pop" music.

The rock-and-roll phenomenon merely accentuated a trend that had been in progress for several years. By 1953 country songs recorded by pop entertainers were making periodic appearances on the popular-music charts. Country songwriters, reflecting upon Hank Williams' glittering success, began to devote as much attention to catering to popular-music devotees as to hillbilly enthusiasts. The average songwriter hoped that his selections would be recorded by both country and popular performers. In the past, when a country song had been recorded by entertainers of a different genre, the selection had been carefully and selectively marketed.[23] And there were clear and well-defined lines between the musical forms. Popular vocalist Patti Page's rendition of "Tennessee Waltz" was seldom heard on a country disc-jockey program, and was marketed as a popular item. Renditions of the number by country performers, such as Pee Wee King or Cowboy Copas, were directed strictly at the country audience and no attempt was made to present these versions on popular-music programs. In the hectic years of the late fifties, however, when rock-and-roll was turning the popular-music world topsy turvy and new singers were becoming overnight sensations, the time was ripe for a major development within country music. With the popularity of country-style songs firmly established, the next step was to place the country singers on the popular-music charts.

Recording executives—and, later, performers—discovered that the chief stumbling block to the acceptance of country music by popular

[23] This, in general, remained true in the following years (as late as 1967). Country disc jockeys, on the whole, played only selections by country entertainers. However, country singers—Jim Reeves, Johnny Cash, Marty Robbins, Roger Miller, and others—could be heard quite often on pop shows.

fans was the instrumentation.[24] The hillbilly fiddle and the wailing electric steel guitar either repelled the musical sensitivity of listeners or created a "rural" or "tavern" image that urbanites wanted to avoid. If these instruments were replaced with more conventional items—an electric takeoff guitar and drums for the teenagers, or a piano and strings for the adults—even the country singer would be accepted (providing he did not sing in too nasal a fashion, or did not perform a song that was too "backwoodsy"). Country entertainers had long yearned for "respectability" and recognition and had thrilled when country songs such as "Your Cheating Heart" gained high ratings on popular-music charts. Many of the singers seemed to think that urban or popular-music acceptance was the highest distinction a country performer could achieve.[25] But in achieving this type of recognition, the country entertainer had to modify his style and approach. The major concessions came from him and not from his new-found audience. Viewed in this light, therefore, the acquisition of the new audience was not necessarily a victory, for it was gained at the expense of the diminution of traditional forms. It is questionable whether the country music being accepted by popular-music fans was really "country."

Historically important as the first recording by a country singer to achieve the number one position on the popular-music charts was Sonny James' "Young Love,"[26] and it signaled the beginning of the growing fusion of popular and country music. Although it was not necessarily of a rock-and-roll nature, the song did appeal to teenage listeners. Little in its instrumentation suggested traditional country music, and it was perhaps the first country song to feature a choral background. After the success of "Young Love" the number of coun-

---

[24] Even this factor would change to a limited extent. In the late 1950's country instrumentation of a much more subdued and sedate variety—for example, the Kingston Trio—began to capture the fancy of pop listeners.

[25] According to Mrs. Audrey Williams, Hank Williams was "thrilled" when his songs were recorded by pop singers (interview, Austin, Texas, July 2, 1962).

[26] There have been other songs which might challenge "Young Love" for this distinction. Vernon Dalhart's "The Prisoner's Song" was certainly a national favorite, but it was recorded at a time when there were no popularity charts. Other well-known country favorites, such as "Pistol Packin' Mama," "San Antonio Rose," "Sioux City Sue," and "Tennessee Waltz," gained their positions on pop charts when recorded by such entertainers as Bing Crosby and Patti Page.

try intrusions into the popular-music world increased. The most spectacular successes were Marty Robbins' "White Sport Coat" and Ferlin
Huskey's "Gone." In almost every example of the new string of
country-pop offerings there were a few recognizable characteristics:
the absence of the fiddle and steel guitar; the employment of some
type of choral backing; and the use of hybrid instrumentation that
was not solely country, popular, or rock-and-roll. In short, in many
cases the only tie a song had with country music was the fact that
its singer had once been known as a "country" singer. There seems,
however, to be an unwritten law in country music—"once a country
singer, always a country singer." Long after a performer leaves the
country-music field he carries with him a country identification which
his fans. will not let him forget. This, in part, is an evidence of the
loyalty of the country audience, but it also reveals an effort by the
country-music business to capitalize on whatever prestige or recognition the entertainer might gain in another area of music.

By May, 1957, country music had become inundated by the new
rash of hybrid performances as the singers, either independently or
through the prodding of recording men, rushed to profit from the
new-found audience. Billboard's country music best-seller chart amply demonstrated the new trend. In the May ratings[27] only one song
in the top ten featured the fiddle. This was Bobby Helms' "Fraulein,"
which prospered, in part, because it offered an alternative to the
plethora of rock-and-roll and country-pop offerings. The emergence
of country-pop music and the growing success of country songs on
popular charts were reflected in the amalgamation of the music ratings. This feature was inaugurated by Charles Lamb, editor of the
Music Reporter. The magazine was begun in Nashville, Tennessee,
on August 18, 1956, under the name Country Music Reporter.[28] Originally just a country journal with limited circulation, by 1964 the
magazine had achieved national circulation and had come to rival
such music trade publications as Billboard and Cashbox.

The growth of the Music Reporter and its change in format are illustrative of the major changes that occurred in country music during
the late fifties. When "Young Love" and "White Sport Coat" were
released in 1957, Lamb approached the Columbia and Capitol re-

[27] Billboard, LXIX, No. 21 (May 20, 1957), 146.
[28] Interview with Charles Lamb, Nashville, Tennessee, August 28, 1961.

cording executives and asked to run ads on the songs in the *Country Music Reporter*. He encountered opposition from both companies, including the performer of "White Sport Coat," Marty Robbins, who felt that both songs were popular and would be harmed by being placed in a country publication. Lamb thereupon dropped the word "country" from the title, and from that point on expanded the musical coverage of the publication. Lamb inaugurated the "One Big Chart," a popularity listing which included songs regardless of style or origin.

Lamb's de-emphasis of country music drew criticism from several quarters, especially from the veteran performers like Ernest Tubb and Hank Snow, who viewed the move as a betrayal of hillbilly music. Lamb, however, responded by saying that he was only a reporter of developments and not a maker of them. If country music had changed in its styles and techniques, it had not been because of the policies of magazine reporters, but because country entertainers had accepted the changes.[29] The drift of country entertainers into the popular-music field was not accepted unanimously by country fans or by all of the performers. The overriding complaint on the part of supporters was the loss of simplicity—exemplified by Eddy Arnold being accompanied on "Cattle Call" by Hugo Winterhalter and his orchestra.[30] Some performers resented the modern changes and reluctantly modified their instrumental accompaniment. Only a few in the mid-fifties, and Ray Price was the chief exception,[31] resisted the modern sound and maintained any sort of popularity. By the early sixties, most of the singers who yearned for hit-parade recognition had accepted at least some features of the new techniques. For those who resented the growing commercialization and sophistication of country music, the villains of the unfolding tragedy were the recording executives—the artists-and-repertoire men—who pressured the singers into dressing up their styles in order to gain higher profits.[32]

[29] *Ibid.*

[30] RCA Victor 447–0502.

[31] Price's hit tunes included such numbers as "Crazy Arms," "My Shoes Keep Walking Back to You," and "City Lights" (*The World of Country Music*, pp. 195–197).

[32] Be they "villains" or "heroes," the artists-and-repertoire men who led the breakthrough into popular music included Don Law of Columbia, Fred Foster of Monument, Ken Nelson of Capitol, Shelby Singleton of Mercury, Jim Vin-

In part correct, this assumption does not take into account the willingness of many performers to compromise when they became convinced of its economic feasibility. Neither does it take into account the natural proclivity of country musicians to experiment and perfect their instrumental skills. Much of what occurred in the late fifties came not from outside pressure but from within the music, as a result of the logical development and refinement of instrumental techniques.

The country-pop music of the late fifties and early sixties was primarily a product of Nashville. The emergence of the modern country sound had paralleled Nashville's rise to one of the three or four largest music centers in the United States. It had, in fact, been largely responsible for that rise. Working from the base provided by the Grand Ole Opry and publishing houses such as Acuff-Rose, Nashville had come to rival New York and Hollywood as a recording center.[33] The exact date of the first Nashville recording has not been pinpointed, but it may have been that of DeFord Bailey, the Negro harmonica player of the Grand Ole Opry, who recorded in the twenties. The modern era of Nashville recording, however, began in 1945 when Decca scout Paul Cohen recorded Red Foley in WSM's Studio B. These Decca recordings inaugurated a trend that accelerated in the fifties. Two engineers from WSM, Aaron Shelton and Carl Jenkins, opened a recording studio in the Tulane Hotel, and other independent organizations eventually established operations in the city.[34] By 1960 most of the major recording companies, in addition to several minor ones, recorded all of their country talent in Nashville. It was more convenient and economical to establish operations where the talent resided than to transfer the talent to New York. By the late fifties the musicians residing in Nashville could rival in proficiency and skill

neau of MGM, Paul Cohen and Owen Bradley of Decca, and Steve Sholes and Chet Atkins of RCA Victor. See *Billboard*, LXIX, No. 46 (November 11, 1957), 42; *ibid.*, LXXII, No. 28 (July 11, 1960), 29; *The World of Country Music*, pp. 58–72.

[33] *Billboard*, LXIX, No. 46 (November 11, 1957), 42; Goddard Lieberson, "Country Sweeps the Country," *The New York Times Magazine* (July 28, 1957); 13; Clarence B. Newman, "Homespun Harmony," *The Wall Street Journay*, XXXVII, No. 141 (May 3, 1957), 1, 6.

[34] Bernard Asbell, "Simple Songs of Sex, Sin, and Salvation," *Show: The Magazine of the Performing Arts*, II, No. 2 (February, 1962), 91; Shelton, *The Country Music Story*, p. 233.

musicians from anywhere else in the United States. Country musicians, in general, had reached an advanced stage of instrumental accomplishment far beyond the styles featured by rural musicians of previous decades. But Nashville musicians were in the vanguard.

Although most Nashville musicians were like their counterparts of previous decades in that they read little or no music, this lack generally worked to their advantage. The Nashville sidemen were improvisers—men of instrumental flexibility who could easily adapt themselves to any style. The Nashville coterie of musicians played together so frequently—at Grand Ole Opry performances and at recording sessions—that they became thoroughly familiar not only with each other's styles but with the singers for whom they played. They could thereby anticipate each other's moves, so that their sessions were characterized by inventiveness and informality. Many musicians congregated in Nashville, but only a small and recognized percentage could be heard on the country-pop recordings. The most eminent member of the group was Chester (Chet) Atkins, guitarist par excellence and chief of RCA Victor's country-music division, who directed the Victor sessions and performed on many of the hit records produced in Nashville. A guitarist in the Merle Travis tradition, Atkins had by 1960 moved out of country music and was performing only popular and jazz material. Periodically, he appeared with a few other musicians at a Nashville night club, the Carousel, where they played progressive jazz.[35] The group included pianist Floyd Cramer, drummer Buddy Harman, bassist Bob Moore, and guitarists Grady Martin and Hank Garland. This group of musicians, performing on most of the recordings aimed at popular audiences, produced a distinctive instrumental pattern widely referred to as the "Nashville Sound."[36]

This "Sound," characterized by a "relaxed, tensionless feeling and a loose, easygoing beat,"[37] had few resemblances to early country instrumentation. With the fiddle completely shunted aside, and the

[35] *Billboard,* LXXII, No. 26 (June 27, 1960), 4.

[36] Although the term is now commonly employed in articles and trade publications, the writer first heard it used by Tommy Hill, musician and recording engineer for Starday Records, (interview, Nashville, Tennessee, August 23, 1961).

[37] Richard Warren Lewis, "Thar's Gold in Them Thar Hillbillies," *Show Business Illustrated,* II, No. 2 (February, 1962), 35.

steel guitar abandoned until the early sixties, the music produced had a sedate quality designed to appeal to diverse tastes. The electric guitars provided a catchy beat not unlike that of rock-and-roll, while the tinkly piano provided a cool, uptown quality. Pianist Floyd Cramer, featuring a novel "slipnote" style of playing, made a few hit recordings of his own (including "Last Date"), sat in on most of the successful recordings made in the country-pop category, and was largely responsible for the distinctive quality of the Nashville Sound. Cramer was on an estimated twenty-five per cent of all the hit records produced in the late fifties, including Elvis Presley's "Heartbreak Hotel."

Vocally, the Nashville Sound was characterized by background choruses, most often provided by two vocal quartets, the Jordanaires (normally a gospel group) and the Anita Kerr Singers, and sometimes by the Glaser Brothers, who often accompanied Marty Robbins.[38] Although group singing had existed in country music before, none of it had been of the trained, professional variety. Country music had reached its most advanced state of sophistication.

Most of the country performers at one time or another recorded, with varying success, in the country-pop fashion, but only a few were consistent in achieving success on both the country- and popular-music charts. The most successful included Patsy Cline, Don Gibson, Ferlin Huskey, Marty Robbins, Faron Young, and Jim Reeves. All of these individuals were deeply grounded in traditional country music and had consistently performed the older styles until the late fifties. Patsy Cline (Virginia Patterson Hensley), after winning an Arthur Godfrey Talent Scout contest, moved to the Grand Ole Opry and became the highest-ranked female singer and the first woman to dethrone Kitty Wells from her position as "queen of country music." Her recordings of "Walking After Midnight" and "I Fall to Pieces" gained high positions on both pop and country charts. Her promising career was cut tragically short on March 5, 1963, by an airplane crash that also took the lives of Cowboy Copas and Hawkshaw Hawkins.[39]

Ferlin Huskey, a highly regarded showman, recorded first under the name of Terry Preston but gained little national recognition until

[38] *Ibid.*

[39] WSM's Official *Grand Ole Opry History-Picture Book*, I, No. 3 (1957), 15. *Country and Western Spotlight* devoted several pages to the entertainers who were killed in the crash (No. 42 [June, 1963], 7–9).

he reverted to his real name and recorded such pop-style favorites as "Wings of a Dove" (a gospel tune) and "Gone"; he had earlier recorded "Gone" with little success under the name of Terry Preston. Huskey was also a first-rate comedian and recorded several comic songs under the name of Simon Crum. Ironically, Huskey's alter ego, the hayseed Mr. Crum, often demonstrated greater popularity than Huskey.[40]

Don Gibson, the most rock-and-roll influenced of the group, came from the western North Carolina area that produced such tradition-based stars as banjoist Earl Scruggs. At one time a pure and simple practitioner of honky-tonk country music, Gibson evolved into perhaps the most sophisticated of the country performers; his emotional singing style was his strongest link with the past. A songwriter of note, Gibson wrote some of the better-known material of the period, including "I Can't Stop Loving You."[41]

Arizona-born Marty Robbins[42] had, until the mid-fifties, performed only standard country material with background instrumentation similar to that of the early Eddy Arnold recordings. His emotional renditions, illustrated by "At the End of a Long Lonely Day" and "Castle in the Sky," earned him the sobriquet of "Mr. Teardrop." But by 1960 the fiddle and steel guitar had been dropped from his band, and he had become a performer of diverse material ranging from rock-and-roll and calypso to sentimental pop ballads. His popularity—gained from the rendition of such numbers as "El Paso" and "Singing the Blues"—far transcended the limits of the country-music audience. He had probably the widest appeal of any country singer.

Faron Young, born in Louisiana,[43] had traveled the same musical route followed by most country performers, struggling on minor record labels and appearing on various radio stations until success beckoned. At first accompanied by the standard honky-tonk instrumentation of fiddle and steel guitar, Young moved from the Louisiana Hayride to the Grand Ole Opry. Possessed of a strong, virile

[40] Frieda Barter, "Ferlin Huskey—What's in a Name," *Country and Western Jamboree*, I, No. 12 (February, 1956), 8–9.

[41] WSM's Official *Grand Ole Opry History-Picture Book*, I No. 3 (1957), 21.

[42] Gentry, *A History of Country, Western, and Gospel Music*, p. 300; "Marty Robbins," *Rustic Rhythm*, I, No. 1 (April, 1957), 20–21.

[43] Gentry, *A History of Country, Western, and Gospel Music*, p. 349; Hubert Long, "Faron Young," *Rustic Rhythm*, I, No. 2 (May, 1957), 16–20.

voice and a style that ranged from rock-and-roll to an almost Frank Sinatra type of phrasing, Faron Young bore greater resemblance to the popular crooners than did most of the other country singers. By 1961, with his renditions of "Hello Walls" and "The Yellow Bandana," his appeal had gone far beyond the country audience.

Of all the country-pop singers of the late fifties and early sixties, Jim Reeves, before his death in an airplane crash in Tennessee on July 31, 1964,[44] had perhaps the greatest ability to appeal to popular audiences without at the same time losing his sense of country identity. Whatever the source and nature of his musical style, there was no question about the authenticity of his country credentials. He was born on August 20, 1923, in Galloway, Panola County, Texas, the same rural East Texas area that produced Tex Ritter.[45] Since his father, Tom Reeves, died when Jim was only ten months old, his upbringing was the responsibility of his mother, Mary Adams Reeves, and his eight older brothers and sisters. Reeves discovered very early, as farmboys have always done, that farm life could be an intolerable burden unless diversions were found. His diversions were baseball and country music.

Although Reeves had played the guitar since he was six and had often played in neighborhood sessions with Bill Price, a guitarist friend from Galloway, baseball initially seemed to hold the most promising future. After a successful athletic career at Carthage High School, he attended The University of Texas and played baseball there. He then became a pitcher in the St. Louis Cardinal system, playing for Marshall and later Henderson in the East Texas League. His baseball career ended, however, when he injured his leg in 1947.

With his fine speaking voice, Reeves obtained a position as announcer and hillbilly disc jockey on a Henderson radio station, KGRI, which he later owned jointly with popular disc jockey Tom Perryman. During the years immediately following 1947 Reeves began singing in the Henderson area and for a short period worked in Beaumont in a group headed by pianist Moon Mullican.[46] His earliest recordings were made in Houston in 1949 and were released on the

44 Austin *Statesman*, August 5, 1964.

45 Biographical information on Jim Reeves was obtained from an interview with Mrs. Mary Adams Reeves, DeBerry, Texas, September 7, 1966.

46 Interview with Mary Adams Reeves, September 7, 1966; interview with Tom Perryman, Henderson, Texas, September 7, 1966.

Macy label.[47] Success, however, was not to come until the early fifties when he signed a contract with Abbott Records (1952) and joined the Louisiana Hayride (1953). His second Abbott recording, "Mexican Joe," was his first big hit, and it proved to be only the beginning of a long string of successful recordings which would eventually take him to the Grand Ole Opry, earn him a contract with RCA Victor, and make him a popular favorite in places as far away as Norway and South Africa.

In the early years of his career, Reeves used honky-tonk instrumentation and performed songs of the Hank Williams or Eddy Arnold variety. His voice, however, was never necessarily of the honky-tonk variety but had, instead, a mellow, resonant quality which his supporters like to describe as "a touch of velvet."[48] When the country-pop trend set in, Reeves' style of delivery was well suited for the new genre, and when he dropped the traditional country instrumentation, he attracted numerous adherents from the popular-music audience.

In lyric content the songs performed by Reeves were no different from those produced by other country singers with different instrumental accompaniment. And they were little different from the country songs of previous years. His two most successful songs, "Four Walls," and "He'll Have to Go," were honky-tonk songs without the honky-tonk instrumentation, and both dealt with rejected or unrequited love. "Four Walls" depicted a man forsaken by a girl who preferred the gay night life:

> Out where the bright lights are glowing,
> You're drawn like a moth to the flame.
> You laugh while the wine's overflowing,
> While I sit and whisper your name.[49]

Reeves' success with this type of song with both country and popular audiences illustrates a general process going on in American music. Not only had popular music exerted a strong influence upon country

[47] Letter to the author from Bob Pinson, September 4, 1966.

[48] Used as the title of a Jim Reeves album—(RCA Victor LPM 2487) composed exclusively of pop songs.

[49] "Four Walls," written and composed by Marvin Moore and George Campbell, published by Travis Music Co. Copyright © 1957, Travis Music Co., Hollywood, California. Reeves' recording is on RCA Victor 447–0413.

music, but the converse had also been true. Types of lyrics and themes were now appearing in popular music that had appeared only rarely before. The "Tennessee Waltz" and Hank Williams' numbers such as "Your Cheating Heart" and "Cold, Cold Heart" had injected a theme of lost or rejected love seldom before found in pop music. The trend became much heavier in the late fifties. The most influential element that country singers and composers brought to American popular music was an emotionally frank and simple manner of viewing life. With basic and uncomplicated melodies and lyrics, the country-pop singers discussed the problems of the average man and talked about the subjects that pop singers had seldom discussed. Hank Locklin's[50] "Please Help Me I'm Falling," which in melody and lyrics could have been typical of most any country-music period, depicted a very common theme in country music: the temptations of illicit love. The theme was even more boldly expressed in Leroy Van Dyke's "Walk on By," a variation of the old "slipping around" theme:

> Just walk on by. Wait on the corner.
> I love you, but we're strangers when we meet.[51]

By the mid-sixties country music had backed off a bit from its earlier flirtation with rock-and-roll, but the amalgamation with pop music showed little sign of diminishing. Although fewer country entertainers appeared on the pop-music hit charts, country music itself had seemingly been permanently affected by the attempted marriage with popular music. The popular influence could be seen in the continued appearance of sophisticated performers—who might be labeled as "stylists"—who used vocal techniques more suggestive of rock-and-roll, pop, or jazz music than of country music.

The talented Johnny Cash—a purebred country boy if there ever was one—performed on stage as if he were a Harry Belafonte with white skin. Often dressed in skin-tight black clothing and ambling around the stage like a recent graduate of a school for method actors,

---

[50] Locklin was a native of McClellan, Florida, and a veteran of country music. His earlier hits, such as "Same Sweet Girl" and "Let Me Be the One," appealed exclusively to country audiences (Gentry, *History of Country, Western, and Gospel Music*, p. 263).

[51] Mercury MG 20862. "Walk on By," copyright © 1961 by Lowery Music Co., Inc.

Cash attracted a wide following who, like the singer himself, seemed to confuse dramatic reactions with authentic folksinging. The irony of Cash's situation lies in the fact that, of all the modern country singers, he probably has less reason to "act" the part of a folksinger. He was born into a poor country family in Kingsland, Arkansas, on February 26, 1932.[52] After the coming of the New Deal the Cash family moved to Dyess, Arkansas, as part of the Roosevelt Resettlement program for submarginal farmers. Cash escaped the cycle of rural poverty only through his induction into the army and through his eventual musical career.

If it is possible in this modern urban era for one to be of folk origin, then Johnny Cash definitely meets the requirements. Not only was his family socially and economically representative of those elements who had traditionally comprised the southern folk population, it was also a group in which the singing of gospel and folk tunes was almost second nature. Cash learned a large repertory of country melodies from his parents and from radio broadcasts and phonograph recordings of such entertainers as Ernest Tubb, Hank Williams, and the Carter Family, who were among his special favorites. In his performances before country and urban audiences Johnny Cash need only be himself in order to achieve a folk aura; he certainly does not need to adopt the techniques and mannerisms of the "urban folk" singers. It is possible that by consciously trying to be "folk," he ceases to be.

Dave Dudley, born in Spencer, Wisconsin,[53] is another "stylist" who often reflects both the influences of rock-and-roll and the method school of acting. In many songs, Dudley affects a hard-driving, virile style of singing replete with mumbles and slurred expressions which make him sound like an adult Elvis Presley. That this style is largely an affectation is evidenced by his recording of "Mama, Tell Them What We're Fighting For," a conventional and super-patriotic country song rendered in a straight-forward manner without vocal slurs or guttural growls. When this rendition is contrasted with his earlier recordings of "Six Days on the Road" and "A Pair of Cowboy Boots," the radical differences between the stylistic approaches become ap-

[52] The best discussion of Johnny Cash is Shelton, *The Country Music Story*, pp. 97–101.

[53] Dixie Deen, " 'Six Days on the Road' Puts Ravin' Dave Dudley on Country Music Map," *Music City News*, IV, No. 1 (July, 1966), 11.

parent.[54] Both Dudley and Presley, like many hundreds of American youth, visually and vocally give proof that they were influenced by the youthful symbols of rebellion immortalized by the Hollywood movie industry: James Dean and Marlon Brando.

Of the various stylists of the modern period, two names predominate not only because of their broad-ranging popularity but because of their radical divergences from conventional country stylings: Willie Nelson, a Texan, and Roger Miller, who claims both Texas and Oklahoma. Both Nelson and Miller had long been accomplished songwriters who experienced continued frustration in their personal singing ventures, yet repeatedly saw their own compositions earn high positions on popularity charts when performed by other singers. In the mid-sixties both entertainers, whose styles differed drastically, began receiving the recognition as vocalists for which they had always longed. And when the recognition came, their names became well known in households and areas where few country performers had been known before.

Willie Nelson is well acquainted with traditional country music, as his recording of "Columbus Stockade Blues" and an occasional Bob Wills tune would indicate, but the bulk of his repertory includes his own compositions rendered in a highly personal yet lackadaisical and almost conversational manner.[55] Nelson's songs, such as "The Party's Over" and "Night Life," tend to be more complex in their chordal structure than the typical country melody and, except for their lyrical content, veer close to the borders of pop and blues music.[56] Nelson's stylistic approach, with its subtle phrasings and employment of blue notes, actually makes his songs appear more complex than they really are.

Perhaps the most interesting song in his recorded repertory is one completely modern in melody and structure, yet age-old in theme: the modern murder ballad "I Just Can't Let You Say Goodbye." The

[54] Dudley's various approaches toward songs can best be heard on *There's A Star Spangled Banner Waving Somewhere*, (Mercury 21057) and *Greatest Hits* (Mercury 21046).

[55] "Here's Willie Nelson," *Music City News*, II, No. 7 (January, 1965), 10; "Willie Nelson the Songwriter, 'One in a Row,'" *Music City News*, IV, No. 6 (December, 1966), 24–25.

[56] The best introduction to both Willie Nelson's songs and his style is *His Own Songs*, Victor LPM-3418.

song, one of the most artfully written of the modern period, seems on first hearing to be merely a story of broken love, and only at the conclusion does the realization dawn on the listener that the narrator has been slowly choking his sweetheart to death!

Roger Miller, after spending several frustrating years recording unrecognized songs, has made the whole world of American show business sit up and take notice. His recordings have earned ratings on both the country- and popular-music charts; he has appeared regularly on national television programs such as the Johnny Carson show; and for a short period emceed his own thirty-minute television show on the NBC network, something which only two other country-oriented performers, Jimmie Dean and Tennessee Ernie Ford, had accomplished. His appeal to groups outside the usual country audience is unsurpassed by that of any other country performer. It is clear, then, that Miller's appeal cannot be traced exclusively to his country-music orientation. Miller's country credentials actually are as good as those of anyone in the business: he was born in Texas and grew up in Oklahoma amid rural and small-town surroundings; he listened to and was influenced by Bob Wills; he learned to play both the guitar and fiddle; and he wrote some of the more popular honky-tonk "heart" songs of the fifties, including George Jones' "Hearts in My Dream" and Ray Price's "Invitation to the Blues."[57]

Miller's personal appeal, however, is a result of his engaging personality (which borders on the "kooky"), his adroit skill at composing catchy and clever lyrics, and his highly original vocal style, which is reminiscent of the "scat" singing of jazz music.[58] The image that Miller evokes is not that of a rural singer, but that of a cool, urbanized hipster who can adapt himself to the most sophisticated of audiences. His recording of "Dang Me," one of the more remarkable examples of Miller's sense of rhythm and facility with the English language, demonstrates what one might call the country version of scat singing. But instead of vocally imitating the slides and wails of horns as Ella Fitzgerald and Louis Armstrong had sometimes done in their recordings, Miller imitates the twangs of the electric guitar. A more subdued

[57] Eva Dolin, "Does Roger Miller Know What He Wants?" *Country Song Roundup*, XVII, No. 87 (February, 1965), 28–29.
[58] The most representative selection of Roger Miller songs is *Golden Hits*, Smash 27073.

song, but one which provides an even better example of Miller's expert writing skill, was a national favorite, "King of the Road," a hobo song reminiscent of the "bum" songs of the twenties but at the same time radically different in its use of popular background instrumentation and in its central theme. The hero of "King of the Road" is a "cool cat" who gloried in his freedom, and not the harassed, impoverished, and police-driven character who dominated the story-line of so many of the older ballads. As an indication of the difference between Roger Miller and the composers of an earlier period, and as a clue to the changes that had taken place over a forty-year period in both country music and the nation, one should compare Jimmie Rodgers' "Hobo Bill's Last Ride" with Miller's "King of the Road." The contrast between the homeless and dying Hobo Bill and the hip hobo who exults in the fact that he pays "no union dues" is revealing indeed.

The big-city acceptance of Roger Miller and other country-pop music practitioners did much to lift country music in general from the financial doldrums. Whereas country music seemed to be declining in popularity in 1956–57,[59] by 1960 it had completely revived and had become a very lucrative part of American entertainment.[60] Nashville, of course, most reflected the country resurgence. The Nashville Sound (which by 1960 had almost lost definition and had come to be applied to any record produced in Nashville) lured to the city scores of pop and rock-and-roll artists who hoped to capitalize on the resurgence. Country publishing houses and recording companies poured an estimated $35,000,000 yearly into Nashville's economy.[61] Recording studios, clogged with both country and pop entertainers, hummed with activity. The two busiest studios were those of RCA Victor, with

[59] The country music "industry" was indeed prospering during this period. One source estimated that fifty million hillbilly records were sold in 1956 (Clarence B. Newman, "Homespun Harmony," *The Wall Street Journal*, XXXVII, No. 141 [May 3, 1957], 1). The statistics for the following two years may be just as high, but one might well question the authenticity of the "country" material being produced in that period.

[60] Country promoter Connie B. Gay was quoted in November, 1960, as saying that "from a dollar and cents viewpoint country music never had it so good" (*Billboard*, LXXII, No. 45 [November 7, 1960], 3).

[61] This was an estimate made by James Metcalfe, Chairman of the Nashville Chamber of Commerce's Public Relations Committee (*Billboard Music Week*, LXXIII, No. 21 [May 29, 1961], 5).

its multimillion-dollar facilities, and the independent establishment of Owen Bradley.[62] At one time a professional musician in both country and popular music, Bradley served as musical director for WSM in the late forties and then became assistant country-music director for Decca under Paul Cohen in 1947. When Cohen moved to Coral Records in 1958, Bradley became Decca's country artists-and-repertoire man. Through his capacity as artists-and-repertoire man, and as chief of the top recording studio in Nashville, Bradley became *Billboard's* choice for "Country and Western Man of the Year" in 1961.[63] By 1961, Bradley Studios was averaging about seven hundred recording sessions a year, and such pop singers as Jaye P. Morgan, Connie Francis, Guy Mitchell, and June Valli had availed themselves of its services.[64] They, along with Dean Martin, Perry Como, Nancy Sinatra, Burl Ives, Peter, Paul, and Mary and a stream of others who came to Nashville in the late sixties, were there in quest of the lucrative, but often elusive, hit sound. And according to reports from *Billboard*, the Nashville Sound paid off for the recording companies. For the first six months of 1960 Victor had fourteen sides in the top 50 of *Billboard's* "Hot 100." Of the fourteen, nine were recorded in Nashville, while Columbia, Mercury, Cadence, and Warner Brothers placed in the top 50 a scattering of songs that had their origins in Nashville.[65]

Nashville's burgeoning prosperity was also reflected in the increased activity of the city's talent agencies.[66] The Grand Ole Opry no longer dominated the booking of country artists emanating from the city. Independent agencies now monopolized this activity, and the most important agency was headed by James Denny. Born in Buffalo Valley near Cookeville, Tennessee,[67] Denny began his career

[62] *Billboard*, LXIX, No. 46 (November 11, 1957), 42; Lewis, "Thar's Gold in Them Thar Hillbillies," *Show Business Illustrated*, II, No. 2 (February, 1962), 35.

[63] *Billboard Music Week*, LXXIII, No. 42 (October 30, 1961), 20.

[64] *Ibid.*, No. 31 (August 7, 1961), 4.

[65] *Billboard*, LXXII, No. 28 (July 11, 1960), 29.

[66] These include the Hubert Long Agency, Acuff-Rose Artists Bureau, Hal Smith Agency, and the Wil-Helm Agency. For a listing of country promoters see *The World of Country Music*, p. 144.

[67] "Jim Denny Lived Country Music," *The World of Country Music*, p. 76.

as a computing clerk in the actuarial department of the National Life and Accident Insurance Company but became connected with show business when the company assigned him the extra job of answering the telephone at the Ryman Auditorium on Saturday nights. Later, he was appointed house manager for the Saturday night shows. This appointment led to his eventual promotion as general manager of the Grand Ole Opry, including the direction of the station booking agency, the WSM Artists Bureau.[68]

When Denny left WSM in 1956, he established his own talent agency, which came to represent many of the top stars in Nashville, including Webb Pierce. He also had previously opened a publishing house, Cedarwood Music, which was second only to Acuff-Rose. The Denny offices were strategically located between the two largest recording studios in Nashville, those of Owen Bradley and RCA Victor.[69] In 1961 James Denny Artists Bureau handled well over 3,200 personal appearances throughout the world.[70] Denny, in fact, has been referred to as "the biggest booker of one-night stands in the world."[71]

Denny's successful career is only one of many in the music city of Nashville, and his success exemplifies the big-business proportions of modern country music. With country music becoming an allied branch of popular music, and with its financial returns reaching an all-time high, many of its business-minded leaders felt a necessity for a trade association that would preserve and augment the music's economic status. The Country Music Association, first convened in November, 1958, grew out of an organization called the Country Music Disc Jockey's Association, organized in 1954.[72] The avowed purpose of the Country Music Association, or CMA, was to improve, market, and publicize country music "to the end that it would become an even greater industry." This chamber-of-commerce of country music,

[68] Asbell, "Simple Songs of Sex, Sin, and Salvation," *Show*, II, No. 2 (February, 1962), 90–91.

[69] *Ibid.*, p. 91.

[70] *Billboard Music Week*, LXXIV, No. 2 (January 13, 1962), 36.

[71] Asbell, "Simple Songs of Sex, Sin, and Salvation," *Show*, II, No. 2 (February, 1962), 90.

[72] *Billboard*, LXVI, No. 46 (November 13, 1954); 14; *ibid.*, LXX, No. 26 (June 30, 1958), 9.

with its headquarters in Nashville, strove to include in its membership "every possible individual or organization who has a part in
producing or performing country music."[73] The CMA, a commercial-
minded organization, endeavored to gain greater air-play and more
extensive advertising coverage for country music. One of the vigorous
ventures supported by the CMA was the establishment of country-
music radio stations. In the mid-fifties the number of country radio
shows had declined. Live country radio programs, with the exception
of major shows like the Grand Ole Opry, had all but vanished. The
early-morning record program was almost a thing of the past. Rock-
and-roll had dealt a damaging blow to country music as radio stations
moved to satisfy the desires of teenagers. To counteract this trend,
and with the active encouragement of the CMA, an increasing number of stations moved toward the inclusion of country music programming until the number doing so reached well over two thous-
and by 1967. The most novel feature of the country upsurge was the
all-country-music radio stations. In areas where other types of music
predominated on radio stations, a great desire for country music programming existed. The station that emphasized the country sound
therefore tapped an unexploited but eager audience. There appeared
throughout the United States scores of stations, many of them high-
powered, that played nothing but country music throughout the day.
Whereas in 1961 there had been a total of 81 full-time country radio
stations, by 1966 the figure had risen to 328. Advertisers discovered
that the country-music audience was large and loyal, and faithful to
the program's sponsors. Market analyses conducted during the mid-
sixties indicated that not only was country music nationally popular
but its clientele was now predominantly urban based. The Market
Research Department of Columbia Records in New York declared
that its study of marketing conditions in the mid-sixties revealed that
the typical country-music listener was a person between thirty and
forty; married, with two children; a homeowner; a skilled or semi-
skilled worker in or near a metropolitan area; and had an annual income of about $6,000.[74]

[73] Harry Stone, "The Country Music Association," *The Country Music Who's
Who* (First Annual Edition for 1960), 79.
[74] *CMA Close-Up* (February, 1967), 7.

The Country Music Association deserves much of the credit for country music's great commercial upsurge and world-wide expansion during the sixties. In its early years the CMA appeared to be wholly commercially-oriented and to be little concerned with the traditions and historical importance of the music. As one CMA brochure noted, "the 'C' in country music means cash."[75] The annual conventions held in Nashville (along with the business meetings held in places like San Juan, Puerto Rico)[76] demonstrate just how far removed from the rustic image country music has ventured and how much it has succumbed to the middle-class ethic of respectability and success. The yearly conventions remind one of a meeting of businessmen, replete with stockholders' reports, fancy banquets, cocktail hours, and a final formal dance with music provided by one of the sophisticated, pop-style country bands such as that headed by Leroy Van Dyke. If country music had not become a major industry by the late sixties, it was not because its leading trade organization—the CMA—was not making every determined effort to make it so.

An encouraging indication that the CMA was moving away from its emphasis on the present and its absorption with promotion and profit was the establishment of the Country Music Hall of Fame and Museum in Nashville, an effort to give recognition to the great historical figures of the music. Even here, however, the CMA (which still describes itself as "the world's most active trade association") demonstrated its reluctance or inability to veer away from an emphasis on the contemporary and the idea of success. And, too often, success has seemed to be equated with the accumulation of material wealth. Originally modeled on the Baseball Hall of Fame at Cooperstown, New York (but modified when it was discovered that these rigid rules allowed admission of only a very few individuals), the society in 1961 elected as its first members Jimmie Rodgers, Fred Rose, and Hank Williams. In November, 1962, the CMA abandoned its initial intention to select only deceased entertainers and chose Roy Acuff as the first living member of the Hall of Fame. Since that date Tex Ritter (1964), Ernest Tubb (1965), Uncle Dave Macon, George D. Hay, Eddy Arnold, and James Denny (1966), and Red

[75] *Behind the Record of the Country Music Association* (n.d.), 4.
[76] Advertised in *CMA Close-Up* (February, 1967), 1.

Foley, Jim Reeves, J. L. Frank, and Steve Sholes (1967) have been added.[77]

To house the beautiful plaques bearing the pictures and names of the honorees, the CMA, largely through the devoted work of people such as Roy Horton and Stephen Sholes, conducted a massive fund-raising campaign, which resulted in the construction of a million-dollar structure, ultra-modern in design, which would also contain the offices of the Country Music Association and a center for historical research. The dream which had been conceived as early as 1961 came to fruition on March 31, 1967, when the doors of the Country Music Hall of Fame and Museum officially opened in Nashville. The gala opening ceremony began when CMA Board Chairman Roy Horton and President Paul Cohen cut the ribbons before NBC television cameras, and continued with speeches by Tennessee governor Buford Ellington, Congressman Richard Fulton, and Nashville Mayor Beverly Briley.[78]

In this beautiful building in Nashville, which seems destined to become one of the major tourist attractions in the Music City, one can meander down the Walkway of the Stars, which is embedded with the names of those entertainers who have contributed at least $1,000 to the Hall of Fame, see the instruments, wearing apparel, and mementoes of the earlier stars, and top off the visit by watching a short film on the history of country music. The creation of the Hall of Fame and the consequent stressing of the historical record are objectives which all country-music enthusiasts can support, and the CMA deserves unqualified commendation for these worthwhile programs.

The selection of Hall of Fame honorees, however, which is entrusted to well over one hundred individuals who have at least ten years of active service in the country-music field, reveals tendencies that might be criticized: the choosing of modern stars who are still performing, and the almost-exclusive honoring of Nashville-based

[77] *Billboard Music Week* (November 6, 1961), 52; *ibid.*, (November 17, 1962), 5; *Music City News*, IV, No. 10 (April, 1967), 8, 15; *ibid.*, V, No. 4 (November, 1967), 32.

[78] An excellent history of the Country Music Hall of Fame and its official opening is Dixie Deen, "Country Music Hall of Fame Opens," *Music City News*, IV, No. 10 (April, 1967), 4, 8, 15–16.

performers. The CMA therefore becomes vulnerable to the charge that not only is it unaware or scornful of the music's pioneer entertainers but it is also almost exclusively a Nashville organization. Every member of the Hall of Fame to date, with the exception of Jimmie Rodgers, is or has been a Nashville-based musician or businessman. Even the pioneer performer Uncle Dave Macon was a Nashville musician. One cannot justly criticize the selections that have been made; Tex Ritter, Eddy Arnold, and Jim Denny, for example, deserve to be in the Hall of Fame—eventually. But whether they deserve admission now, before many of the old-timers, deceased and otherwise, have been chosen, is questionable. The selection of Eddy Arnold, in particular, has drawn more criticism than any other choice yet made.[79] A singer who since 1946 has moved consistently away from country music into the field of pop music, and who seems uncomfortable when anyone calls him a country singer, Arnold seemed to many to be a strange and unwise choice. The most relevant criticism that might be made of the CMA Hall of Fame concerns not the performers who have been named but those who have not been named. One might question for example, the naming of Tex Ritter and the omission of Gene Autry, whose success made it possible for the whole string of Hollywood singing cowboys to thrive. Similarly, modern executives such as Steve Sholes and Jim Denny are included, but not Ralph Peer, who did so much to inaugurate country music's commercial history. There will be plenty of time to name the modern superstars, but the pioneer performers who laid the groundwork for the modern industry should be recognized now. The Carter Family, Riley Puckett, Bill Monroe, Vernon Dalhart, and other influentials already should be in the Hall of Fame.

The CMA's modern orientation and stressing of commercial aspects to the exclusion of most other factors within the music was typical of the general attitude within the country-music industry at the beginning of the sixties. To many observers it appeared that promoters and recording executives, as well as performers, were willing to accept any modification—even destruction perhaps—of the music in order to achieve greater commercial success. In 1954 Steve Sholes,

[79] See the "letters to the editor" sections of the Music City News, IV, No. 5 (November, 1966); and ibid., IV, No. 6 (December, 1966).

country artists-and-repertoire man for RCA Victor, made a prediction which seemed ten years later to be close to fruition: "If the next ten years brings about developments in the country and western field as constructive and vital as in the past, I believe 1964 will find the country and western and pop fields of entertainment so closely allied that it will be impossible to tell the difference without a score card."[80]

In a nation that is so deeply committed to urban-industrial values, it is notable that country music was so long able to maintain its identity and resist change. The changes taking place within the music during the late fifties and early sixties, however, seemed to be driving it out of existence or making it an unrecognizable part of popular music. Not only did some members of the country-music profession appear to be so deeply involved in the day-to-day struggle for the acquisition of wealth, prestige, and success that they did not see or care what was happening to the music, some of them openly rejoiced at the music's growing urbanization. In describing the musical trends of the early sixties, entrepreneur Owen Bradley applauded the hybridization of American music: "Now we've cut out the fiddle and steel guitar and added choruses to country music. But it can't stop there. It has to always keep developing to keep fresh."[81]

Publisher James Denny even doubted whether there was still such a thing as country music. The purchasers of country-music records were primarily middle- and lower middle-class urbanites. To Denny's mind, actually very little in country song lyrics differentiated them from other type of lyrics.[82] If Denny's assumptions were correct, they seemed to signal the disappearance of rural music and the arrival of musical amalgamation.

Were the prophets and apostles of American musical homogenization correct? Can a music, or a people, so firmly rooted in rural values, attitudes, and traditions vanish so quickly after suddenly being thrust into an urban atmosphere? The South had urbanized at a rapid pace after World War II, until in the sixties rural isolation was virtually a nonexistent phenomenon. Southerners had also moved in tremendous numbers to northern metropolitan centers, and radio,

---

[80] *Billboard*, LXVI, No. 21 (May 22, 1954), 39.
[81] *Billboard Music Week*, LXXIII, No. 31 (August 7, 1961), 4.
[82] Interview with James Denny, Nashville, Tennessee, August 25, 1961.

television, Hollywood, and the phonograph had exerted their stand-
ardizing influences everywhere. But the question still remains: could
the older musical tastes, and those factors which produced them,
disappear so quickly? Could a music which thrived so vigorously in
the mid-fifties suddenly succumb to commercial blandishment and
pressures and become merely an undistinguishable facet of popular
music? Are American cultural tastes completely formed by commercial forces?

The "country" performers of the modern period may have emphasized profit and commercial gain to the exclusion of other factors, but
they could not completely escape their heritage. Singer and songwriter John D. Loudermilk was quoted as saying that "there's no
country music anymore because there is no more country. The hillbillies are all gone, man."[83] This statement, which has a certain degree of truth to it, completely overlooks the conservative nature of
inherited social patterns. Country people would not easily shake off
rural-spawned attitudes in a new environment, especially when that
new environment happened to be a southern city possessing strong
rural overtones. A love for the old music, and the associations it
brought to mind, still lingered in the hearts of many country or ex-
country people, a love which in fact deepened as the rural experience
receded into the mists of memory. An increasing number of performers were determined that the traditional musical forms would not
vanish.

[83] Quoted in Asbell, "Simple Songs of Sex, Sin, and Salvation," *Show*, II, No.
2 (February, 1962), 91.

The Reinvigoration of Modern Country Music — Honky-Tonk and Saga Song

AT THE BEGINNING of the 1960's there could be no doubt that country music as a commercial phenomenon was firmly implanted in the American cultural and entertainment fabric. Indeed, it had become a world-wide phenomenon. The music that had once been confined to the rural areas of the southern United States now penetrated into all sections of the country—even to cosmopolitan New York and Boston, where Grand Ole Opry units played to standing-room-only crowds in staid Carnegie Hall and Jordan Hall.[1] Nashville recording studios produced an estimated one-half of all the phonograph records released in the United States; furthermore, sixty per cent of all single records produced in the United States were said to have a "country influence."[2] At least two thousand radio stations (by 1967) programmed some country music each day, and many stations played nothing but country music.[3]

Country-oriented performers now made periodic appearances on

[1] The Carnegie Hall concerts have been previously noted; the Jordan Hall concert in Boston was given by Flatt and Scruggs (*Billboard Music Week* [December 18, 1961], 42). Other "prestige" concerts made by Flatt and Scruggs, the Stanley Brothers, and similar groups are discussed in Chapter 10.

[2] Country Music Association, *CMA Close-Up* (February, 1963), 1.

[3] *Ibid.*, (February, 1967), 7.

television extravaganzas, such as the Steve Allen and Jackie Gleason shows, while some country shows, such as that emceed by Roger Miller, even gained network status. The Grand Ole Opry for a short time appeared as a televised network segment, as did Red Foley's Ozark Jubilee in Springfield, Missouri. The most publicized and best-known country television performer, however, was Jimmie Dean, a young Texan from Plainview, who starred on two different network programs during the late fifties and early sixties. Dean conducted from Washington, D.C., in the late fifties an early morning variety show called "Country Style," which featured music and pungent country humor. Promoted by Washington entrepreneur, Connie B. Gay, the Jimmie Dean show was carried on the CBS network each morning from 7 until 7:45. It attracted wide recognition and even surpassed in popularity for a time Dave Garroway's venerable "Today" show, carried on the rival National Broadcasting Company network.[4] This show not only introduced the personable young Dean to a national audience, it also presented for the first time the expert guitarist and singer Billy Grammer. Although Dean's early morning show could not maintain its initial popularity, Dean was able to use the program as a stepping stone to greater advancement in show business. In the mid-sixties he emceed from New York a weekly one-hour special which, although oriented toward country-pop music, did give authentic country performers, such as Buck Owens and George Jones, an opportunity for national exposure when they appeared as featured guests.

Important as the network television shows were, an even more phenomenal indication of country music's expanding profitability was its growing acceptance in areas outside the United States. A music basically "Anglo-Saxon" in its origins and forms, it has demonstrated an amazing ability to worm its way into areas where the English language had never predominated, and even to rival or supplant the native musical forms. Country music, if research on Jimmie Rodgers is any indication, has always had a certain following in foreign countries, particularly in the English-speaking world. World War II intensified this interest as American soldiers took their musical heritage with them to remote corners of the globe. As American occupa-

4 *Variety*, CCVI, No. 3 (March 20, 1957), 35; *Billboard*, LXIX, No. 21 (May 20, 1957), 146.

tion continued during the postwar period, American musical tastes became solidly established in other lands. The appearance of "cowboys" in Japanese show business is no longer a rarity.[5]

The most obvious manifestation of country interest, however, came not in the Orient, but in Europe. European interest developed in general because of the presence of American troops, and in particular because of the influence of the United States Armed Forces Network. From its inception as a weak GI station using a borrowed transmitter, the AFN has grown to a mammoth broadcasting system catering not only to the needs of American troops but to a European audience estimated at well over fifty million. The AFN has received letters from every country in Europe, from North Africa, and even from behind the Iron Curtain, and is credited with generating interest in American musical forms of all kinds.[6]

The dispersal of country music in Europe grew out of the programming of the AFN. One of the more popular programs carried by the network was a hillbilly disc-jockey show called "Stickbuddy Jamboree," conducted by Sergeant Tom Daniels from Texas. The Jamboree was said to have the biggest listening audience of any European program on the air at that time (3:05 P.M.). In addition, Daniels conducted an early morning country show called "Hillbilly Reveille," which had a large audience.[7] In accordance with the growing popularity of country music with both servicemen and Europeans, the AFN steadily increased its country-music exposure until in 1961 such music accounted for over thirty-five per cent of the programming.[8]

European interest in country music was demonstrated by the emergence on the Continent and in England of fan-club journals and country-music periodicals,[9] by the popularity of country-music tour-

---

[5] "Country Music Goes International," *The World of Country Music*, 165–167, 171–173.

[6] Omer Anderson, "Fifty Million Europeans Can't Be Wrong," *Billboard*, LXXII, No. 28 (July 11, 1960), 1.

[7] Anderson, "Grass Roots Sprout," *Billboard*, LXXII, No. 31 (August 1, 1960), 4.

[8] *Billboard Music Week*, LXXIII, No. 33 (September 25, 1961), 3.

[9] Some of the more important journals devoted to country music are *Country and Western Spotlight*, edited by Garth Gibson in South Island, New Zealand; *Country and Western Express*, edited by George W. Tye in Bromley, Kent, Eng-

ing units, and by the appearance of native-born European entrepreneurs who promoted the music on radio and television. One of these native entrepreneurs was Martin C. Haerle, an executive in the export department of a Stuttgart, Germany, refrigerator manufacturing company. Haerle produced country-music shows on German radio and television and became such an active entrepreneur that he was hired in July, 1960, to head the newly formed international sales and exploitation department for Starday, an American record company. Haerle, who eventually came to the United States to work in Starday's Nashville offices, developed an interest in country music by listening to the Armed Forces Network.[10] Haerle's career is similar in some respects to that of Dixie Deen, the English-born assistant editor and columnist of the *Music City News*. Miss Deen toured England and Europe for several years as a trick rider for a wild west show but did not receive an intensive introduction to country music until she came to the United States in 1960 at the urging of Don Pierce of Starday Records. After coming to the United States, she became an award winning songwriter and a businesswoman who is acquainted with virtually every aspect of the country-music industry.[11] Although she did not grow up in the country-music tradition, her columns and interviews for the *Music City News* have contained the most incisive writing being done on the contemporary country-music scene. Future researchers and historians of country music will be heavily indebted to her.

According to Martin Haerle, European listeners seemed to prefer the more traditional forms of country music, and entertainers of the Roy Acuff and bluegrass variety were the most popular performers. (Jim Reeves' great popularity in Norway, however, would seem to call this statement into question.) Few of the European listeners could understand the lyrics of the hillbilly songs, but they could appreciate the feeling conveyed and the improvisation and intensity

land; *Western Songs*, edited by Lillies Ohlsson in Vasteras, Sweden; and *Country News and Views*, edited by Charles G. Newman in Lowestoft, Suffolk, England.

[10] *Billboard*, LXXII, No. 28 (July 11, 1960), 4; interview with Martin Haerle, Nashville, Tennessee, August 23, 1961.

[11] *Music City News*, IV, No. 4 (October, 1966), 1, 3; *ibid.*, III, No. 3 (September, 1965), 18.

of the music.[12] American country music exerted such a strong influence that it affected even indigenous German popular music. In September, 1961, for example, a hillbilly-style song entitled "Jacky Jones aus Oklahoma," performed by Caterina Valente, won first place at the Third Annual Song Festival, held under the auspices of Radio Luxembourg.[13]

If the interest in country music exhibited by Europeans seems surprising, the extent to which American servicemen stationed on the Continent patronized the music is even more remarkable. World War II experience had shown that country music was the favorite of thousands of American servicemen, but the late fifties and early sixties revealed that, if anything, such interest had intensified. Foreign-based servicemen exhibited a growing preference for rural rhythms in the period when civilians on the homefront were moving toward the acceptance of rock-and-roll and country-pop music. If record purchases are any indication, country music had a wide lead in popularity over other brands of music on American military bases. Throughout 1960 and 1961 country-record sales in base PX's accounted for about sixty-five per cent of the entire total, and even reached as high as seventy-two per cent on one occasion.[14] The high percentage would indicate that the music attracted many supporters who came from nonsouthern and nonrural backgrounds. Country music appealed to many servicemen, perhaps, as an authentic representation of the society they had left behind, and it seemed to suggest all the verities they were defending. Although a few musical sophisticates attempted to ban country music from the airwaves altogether, the Army steadily increased the music's exposure, feeling that it contributed to an uplift in morale. An Army record buyer was quoted as saying: "country and western strikes the troops as part of the American heritage, and the troops prefer it to sophisticated, schmalzy music."[15] And at Munich an American serviceman, a country-music fan, said, "We are all a little keyed up; we don't know what's ahead.

---

[12] Interview with Martin Haerle, August 23, 1961; interview with Tom Perryman, Henderson, Texas, September 7, 1966.

[13] *Billboard Music Week*, LXXIII, No. 39 (October 2, 1961), 11.

[14] *Billboard*, LXXII, No. 31 (August 1, 1960), 4.

[15] *Billboard Music Week*, LXXIII, No. 33 (September 25, 1961), 3.

We're thinking of home more than ever before, and country music is the music of home for all of us."[16]

Reacting to the world-wide country-music boom, American country singers began extensive tours of American military bases, not only in Europe, but in Africa and Asia as well. Everywhere the audience response was both large and enthusiastic. Lloyd Nelson, who managed Hank Snow's European tour in 1961, commented on the over-all military enthusiasm: "Americans overseas are starved for country and western music. The boys played to packed houses at every stop, and the footstomping and cheering applause was tremendous."[17] When the United States became bogged down in the Vietnam quagmire, country singers became part of the large contingent of American entertainers who toured the war zones of Southeast Asia. Hank Snow, who has made several professional tours of foreign countries during the sixties, spent eighteen days in Vietnam during the Christmas season of 1966. Snow's Asian tour was made not only to entertain American troops but to counteract the activities of antiwar demonstrators back home.[18]

Country-music's popularity among servicemen was only part of a general upsurge experienced by the music all over the world. Having suffered such a dismal decline in the mid-fifties, country music demonstrated a remarkable vitality only a few years later and gave evidence of becoming America's most lucrative musical form. Those country entertainers who survived the initial rigors of a professional career and established themselves as permanent stars could expect relatively lucrative careers thereafter. Country singers could now expect treatment equal to that of pop stars. No one who looked at the cold statistics of record sales, concert tours, and the rise of Nashville as a leading music center could question country music's vitality and prosperity or doubt its status as one of America's most vibrant entertainment forms. That the music was lucrative, no one could doubt. But whether it was still "country," many would question.[19]

---

[16] *Ibid.*, (December 25, 1961), 5.

[17] *Ibid.*

[18] *Music City News,* IV, No. 8 (February, 1967), 1.

[19] For the most biting criticisms of country-pop music in the late fifties, see the editorial and record review sections of *Country and Western Spotlight.* For later examples of criticism of the country-pop trend, see the "letters to the editor" section of *Music City News* in the mid-sixties. For criticisms by country

In the realistic business world of commercial country music in the late fifties and early sixties, few people questioned the course the music was taking. And few ever thought about the roots from which it sprang. In the last analysis, the factor that promoters, artists-and-repertoire men, and performers most considered was the commercial potentialities of their product. In other words, would it sell? And the greater the sales potentiality the more valued was the product. Too often a "great" country singer was considered to be one who sold the greatest volume of records and gained the greatest recognition from people outside the normal country music audience. He was not necessarily that person who had a strong sense of tradition and who had a good "country" voice filled with emotion and understanding. In fact, an old-time country singer like Hylo Brown,[20] who sang in the high-lonesome mountain manner, found it increasingly difficult to compete against the smooth, "hip" country singers of the modern period. More often than not, the old-time country singer would be shunted aside by the country disc jockey because he sounded a little too back-woodsy. Modern singers like Don Gibson, who combined sex appeal with rock-and-roll vocal techniques, became the darlings of disc jockeys and of much of the public.

In a determined effort to capture the noncountry music audience and attain respectability, country-music styles became blurred and often indistinguishable from popular forms. Adopting many of the techniques of noncountry musicians, country performers attracted a broader-based audience but created a hybrid form of music that quite often was neither good nor country. The Nashville Sound, in its inception a novel and fresh musical style, eventually became stereotyped, over-stylized, and over-used. The majority of records produced in Nashville were characterized by the same features: the background chorus, the Floyd Cramer piano style, and a paucity of country instruments.[21] The records distinguished by these features were commercial and profitable, but they eventually became bland and unimaginative, and many would argue that they were not country. In

---

disc jockeys of the trend toward pop music, see *Billboard*, LXX, No. 46 (November 17, 1958), 18–22.

[20] For an example of Brown's style see *Hylo Brown*, Capitol T1168, one of the best examples of pure country music ever recorded.

[21] See Chapter 8.

conjunction with the smooth commercial sound of the country-pop practitioners was the appearance of various "hot" rhythms, in part continuations of styles that had long been in existence, and in part adaptations of rhythms from the rock-and-roll era. In the new era, country music attracted many young performers who had received their first training, and indeed had first been attracted to music in general, from rock-and-roll performers. Young guitarists who first learned the instrument by listening to rock-and-roll musicians of the Elvis Presley and Chuck Berry variety later moved over to country music as they became older and as the general frenzy for rock-and-roll subsided. But they carried their instrumental techniques with them, and country music was affected by this development. Drums had become permanent additions to most of the country organizations, and with the addition of electric basses, "beat" became increasingly important. A great percentage of the audience, youthful and also deeply influenced by the rock-and-roll wave, demanded intensified beats and stepped-up rhythms. The performers and their commercial managers, alive to the possibilities of increased financial returns, responded to the demand.

The changes which came to country music might be interpreted by some as part of a natural, evolutionary growth which enabled the older music to survive in a modern, rapidly changing society.[22] The young people who became interested in the music as a career were influenced by the performers popular in their own generation, and not by the Buell Kazees and Uncle Dave Macons. Tradition, therefore, meant little to them. Whether the music remained close to a rustic base or whether it changed radically, or even became an indistinguishable facet of popular music, meant little to the emerging generations. Some argued that this was the way things had to be, and that no one should be restricted by a rigid reliance on the past.

Although there might be strong measures of truth in these assertions, many people, both performers and supporters, felt that their music was in danger. They were unwilling to abandon the old styles without a struggle. There was a movement, therefore—never in the form of an overt protest, but still vigorously active—to retain traditional styles and songs and rid country music of many of its commercial pop characteristics. The efforts of these people to keep their

[22] See Owen Bradley's statements, discussed in Chapter 8.

music as rustically "pure" as changed conditions would allow, as well as the consequent realization by commercial entrepreneurs that the more traditional forms could be profitable, helped to spark the country-music boom of the early sixties.

Developing in the midst of country music's growing sophistication and commercialization, therefore, and in large part in reaction against it, was a traditional renaissance. The rebirth of interest in older songs and styles was manifested in a variety of ways: the reinvigoration of honky-tonk music, the appearance of country historical, or saga, songs, an upsurge of interest in folk music in urban areas, and perhaps most important of all, the renewed development of bluegrass music.[23]

The style that suffered most during the rock-and-roll onslaught, and in fact, the one that seemed dangerously close to disappearing, was honky-tonk music.[24] Once a very vigorous style—the one that had dominated the immediate postwar period—honky-tonk music could rarely be heard on the juke boxes and disc-jockey shows. In the late fifties, the fiddle almost disappeared from country recordings, and the steel guitar suffered a similar decline in popularity. During the decline only a rare voice broke the heavy monotony of rock-and-roll and the Nashville Sound. Ray Price, with his husky, Hank Williams-style voice and a band that featured the heavily-bowed fiddle, provided hit after hit. His success, in large part a tribute to his talent, came also because he provided an alternative to the dominant styles.

The strong revival of honky-tonk music at the onset of the sixties was produced by men like Price who remained firmly attached to older styles and were able to resist most of the modernizing pressures of the times. Their success revealed that a large portion of the country audience also preferred the older rhythms. Although many individuals contributed to the honky-tonk resurgence, one of the most significant aspects of the revival was the preponderance of Texas-born singers who contributed to it. Honky-tonk music was, after all, a

[23] Urban folk music and bluegrass music are discussed in Chapter 10.
[24] The reader is reminded that "honky-tonk" is not used in a derogatory or pejorative sense. It is intended as a description of the country music that developed in the taverns and dancehalls of the Southwest. "Western" is a commonly-used synonym.

"western"-born and based style.[25] The men who in many ways were the fathers of that type of music, Ernest Tubb and Bob Wills, were native Texans and were still going strong. Ray Price, George Jones, Johnny Horton, Hank Thompson, Buck Owens, Charlie Walker, Sonny Burns, Warren Smith, Frankie Miller, and others of equal or lesser stature had either been born in Texas or reared there. And they learned their trade in the tavern and dance-hall environment of Texas.

Ray Price, who became one of Columbia's brightest stars in the late fifties and early sixties, was born on a farm near Perryville, Texas. Like most young Texas farmboys he grew up on a musical diet of country music of the Jimmie Rodgers and Ernest Tubb variety. While attending North Texas Agricultural College (now the University of Texas at Arlington) near Dallas, he began singing in the dance halls in that area. His early style revealed a strong influence from Hank Williams, whom he had met and from whom he received personal tutoring. Price made one recording for a minor label, Bullet, and then moved over to Columbia. He performed and recorded with a group called the Cherokee Cowboys, a group that originally contained remnants of Hank Williams' old organization, the Drifting Cowboys.[26] In the beginning a prototype and recognized successor of Williams, Price in the following decade evolved into one of the most individualistic of country singers, with a style heavily influenced by blues music. In fact, Price has been so individualistic that by the late sixties, when country music had shifted back radically toward the honky-tonk style, he began regularly performing songs in the country-pop style which he had so resolutely rejected in the late fifties. Whether performing a honky-tonk tune like "Crazy Arms" or a pop-style tune like "Burning Memories," Price has demonstrated a versatile vocal style that consistently places him in the upper echelons of country-music favorites.

Instrumentally (at least on personal appearances) the Ray Price style is heavily indebted to Bob Wills and western swing.[27] Price and

[25] The origin and early commercial exploitation of western music is discussed in Chapter 5.

[26] Interview with Ray Price, Austin, Texas, March 2, 1962. See also George D. Hay's *A Story of the Grand Ole Opry*, p. 57; and "Hit Maker—Ray Price," *Rustic Rhythm*, I, No. 2 (May, 1957), 11–15.

[27] For examples of the Price vocal and instrumental styles, and also of the Bob Wills' influence, listen to the following albums: *Ray Price Sings San Antonio*

his organization are representative of literally scores of organizations all over the country who draw their inspiration from the Wills brand of music. The bands in most cases are much smaller than the original swing units, are marked by an absence of brass, and employ only one fiddle, whereas the western-swing groups had sometimes used several. But in their selection of songs, in their style of vocalizing, in their use of the "walking" bass, and in their employment of the "hot" western-swing style of fiddling, they reveal a strong debt to Wills.

An individual who gave strong signs of becoming a star of great magnitude before his tragic death in November, 1960, was Johnny Horton. Born in California, Horton grew up in East Texas near Rusk.[28] Throughout the fifties Horton was a moderately successful honky-tonk singer who performed in dance halls and small radio stations in the East Texas area around Tyler. In the late fifties he began to acquire national stardom under the tutelage of his manager and bass player, Tillman Franks, who has shown a remarkable facility for taking relatively unknown performers, such as Claude King and David Houston, and molding them into superstars.

Performing as "The Singing Fisherman" (because of his highly acclaimed skill as an angler), Horton became one of the stars of Shreveport's Louisiana Hayride, where he revealed an ability to perform almost any kind of song. His "I'm a Honky Tonk Man" was one of the classic numbers of this particular melodic genre. Toward the end of his career, however, he had gained national recognition and had placed some of his songs on the popular hit parade. He became widely known as a singer of saga songs (not to be confused with event songs which depicted current happenings) and saw a few of them, such as "The Battle of New Orleans" and "Sink the Bismarck," attain first position on both country and pop charts.[29] It is significant that, although Horton achieved pop-music recognition, he did not gain such acclaim as a country-pop singer. His most popular recordings,

---

Rose, Columbia CL1756; *Ray Price Sings Heart Songs,* Columbia CL1015; *Talk to Your Heart,* Columbia CL1148; and *Ray Price's Greatest Hits,* Columbia CL1566.

[28] Linnell Gentry, *A History and Encyclopedia of Country, Western, and Gospel Music,* p. 245.

[29] *Billboard,* LXXI, No. 20 (May 18, 1959), 43; *ibid.,* No. 22 (June 1, 1959), 41.

such as "Springtime in Alaska," were performed with country string instrumentation. Country music suffered a tragic loss on the night of November 5, 1960, when Horton was killed in an automobile collision near the small town of Milano, Texas.[30] An ironic feature of the tragedy was that Horton's wife was left a widow for the second time; she had been the second wife of Hank Williams.

Johnny Horton was only one of many individuals who contributed to the revival of the honky-tonk or western country styles. The opponents of country-pop music and the devotees of the purer country styles owe a great debt of gratitude to the steadily growing band of performers such as Jack Greene, Charley Pride, and Merle Haggard who show a dedicated loyalty to authentic country music forms and a reluctance to accept such trappings of pop music as orchestras and background choral arrangements. The list of these performers is very long, and it is regrettable that not all of the relevant performers can be mentioned, and that the discussions of important performers, for the most part, must be brief.

One of the most valuable members of the country-music profession, both because of the quality of his singing and because of his commitment to genuine country styles and themes, is Porter Wagoner, a farmboy from the area near West Plains, Missouri.[31] By 1967 the Porter Wagoner syndicated television show was being carried on at least one hundred stations around the country,[32] and Wagoner, whose formal education ended with the seventh grade, was one of the most heavily booked country stars in the nation and the possessor of an RCA Victor contract that had spanned a seventeen-year period. His value to country music, however, lay not solely in his commercial success; it derived primarily from the fact that since the day he first performed the old Carter Family tune, "Jimmie Brown the Newsboy," as part of his audition test for RCA Victor,[33] he has never ventured into the fields of pop or country-pop music. Wealth and success have not made Porter Wagoner forget his rural origins and the people who had nurtured both him and his music.

---

[30] *Ibid.*, LXXII, No. 46 (November 14, 1960), 8.
[31] The best article on Porter Wagoner is Dixie Deen, "Purely Porter Wagoner," *Music City News,* IV, No. 9 (March, 1967), 3–4.
[32] *Ibid.*, p. 1.
[33] *Ibid.*, p. 3.

The Porter Wagoner repertory is diverse even though it stays within the realm of country music. On his recordings and television performances he ranges all the way from mountain-style numbers like Bill Monroe's "Uncle Pen" and Johnny Horton's "Ole Slewfoot" to gospel numbers like "If Jesus Came to Your House." The dominant theme of the Porter Wagoner repertory, however, seems to be what one of his most popular songs called the "cold hard facts of life."[34] With the possible exception of Merle Haggard, Wagoner has done most to chronicle in song the tragic foibles and failures of humanity: the condemned prisoner of the "Green, Green Grass of Home," the distraught husband who murdered his unfaithful wife and her lover in "The Cold Hard Facts of Life," and the pitiful creature who went insane as he watched his beautiful sweetheart "Julie" turn progressively wayward and wild.

Porter Wagoner's television show is sponsored by a firm long familiar to rural southerners: The Chattanooga Medicine Company,[35] the makers of Black Draught and Wine of Cardui and the distributor of the famous wall calendars that were once found in nearly all rural homes. Not only does the thirty-minute television segment present Porter Wagoner to a national audience, it also serves as a showcase for other talented performers. Norma Jean Beasler (known simply as "Miss Norma Jean") appeared regularly on the show until she was replaced by Dolly Parton in 1967. Norma Jean became one of the most highly regarded and authentic-sounding female country entertainers in the nation. Mack MaGaha, who earlier had been a member of Don Reno and Red Smiley's bluegrass band, has contributed some of the best old-time fiddling heard on any country show in the sixties. Buck Trent, a gifted instrumentalist, plays both the electric guitar and five-string banjo. Trent, in fact, probably made country-music history when he successfully converted the five-string banjo into an electric instrument—an electronic development that could only bring dismay to tradition-minded country enthusiasts. Trent's innovation had the dubious distinction of making the banjo sound like an electric guitar.

Television has become one of the most important media for the

[34] On *The Cold Hard Facts of Life*, RCA Victor LPM-3797. Another Porter Wagoner album containing this kind of material is *Confessions of a Broken Man*, RCA Victor LPM-3593.

[35] *Music City News*, IV, No. 9 (March, 1967), 1.

national circulation of country music, and several entertainers, including Buck Owens, Ernest Tubb, Bill Anderson, Arthur Smith, and those associated with Cincinnati's Midwestern Hayride, have been featured on their own nationally syndicated shows. One of the most important groups to have their musical wares distributed via television is a popular duo named the Wilburn Brothers. Although several of their recordings in the early sixties veered closely toward the borders of country-pop music, the Wilburn Brothers' performances on radio and television and in personal appearances have revealed how deeply their rural-fundamentalist background influenced their song choices and styles. Teddy and Doyle Wilburn came out of a Hardy, Arkansas, farm family that sang and played gospel and old-time country melodies. The entire Wilburn family, in fact, including the father, mother, and older brothers and sister, were musically inclined and performed professionally for several years in the deep South. The Wilburn Brothers formed their duo in 1954 and traveled extensively with Webb Pierce and Faron Young.[36] Their rise to musical fame began in 1955 with the recording of the very popular "Go Away With Me,"[37] and they are now not only the most popular singing group, but are one of the few remaining duet brother groups (along with Jim and Jesse McReynolds) still performing within country music. The great country duet tradition that has included the Monroe Brothers, Dixon Brothers, Callahan Brothers, and Bolick Brothers, has been virtually concluded by death. The Louvin Brothers had already dissolved their partnership when Ira Louvin was killed in an automobile crash in 1965, and the Stanley Brothers' career as a valuable old-time duo ended with the death of Carter Stanley in late 1966.

In addition to an occasional country-pop melody, the Wilburn Brothers repertory includes nearly every type of country song, traditional and otherwise. Their television format has revealed their commitment to genuine country music and, in fact, evokes a decidedly different image from that of their Nashville Sound recordings. Sponsored by such long-time country favorites as Garrett Snuff and Bull-of-the-Woods Tobacco, the Wilburn Brothers television show features the singing of the nation's most popular female country singer,

[36] Dixie Deen, "The Woman Behind the Man," *Music City News*, III, No. 10 (April, 1966), 5, 14, 19.
[37] *Music City News*, V, No. 2 (August, 1967), 9.

Loretta Lynn, the five-string banjo playing and comedy of Harold
Morrison, and the steel-guitar styling of Don Helms, who was largely
responsible for the distinctive instrumental sound of the original
Hank Williams recordings. In their own vocal performances, the Wilburn Brothers consistently delve into the depository of old-time music
to present songs like the honky-tonk favorite "Live and Let Live,"
gospel numbers like "Farther Along" and "Old Camp Meeting Days,"
Carter Family songs like "My Little Home in Tennessee," and an occasional ballad from the very early days of country music, such as
the British-derived "The Knoxville Girl."[38]

One of the more genuine country singers of the modern period is a
Columbia recording star with the unlikely name of Stonewall Jackson (his real name as far as can be determined). Although he was
born in North Carolina, Jackson opened a log-trucking business in
Moultrie, Georgia, after completing his navy service in the early
fifties. In October, 1956, he drove his logging truck to Nashville,
where, after a successful audition, he was given a position on the
Grand Ole Opry. Jackson is one of the few individuals to be added
to the Grand Ole Opry roster without benefit of a prior recording
contract.[39] Since 1956 Jackson has become one of the most successful
country recording stars and, although he occasionally has recorded a
country-pop song such as "Waterloo," his main forte is the performance of authentic country songs such as George Jones' "Life to Go,"
a prison ballad; "Black Sheep," a sentimental ballad from the 1890's;
and "Don't Be Angry," a modern love song complete with dobro accompaniment. Stonewall Jackson, regardless of the type of song performed, possesses a distinctive rural voice that not even the Nashville Sound can diminish.[40]

Another performer of the early sixties who came out of a background similar to Jackson's was the West Virginia-born Harold
"Hawkshaw" Hawkins.[41] Although coming from a mountain state,
Hawkins was heavily indebted for his vocal style to the western-
based styles of such performers as Ernest Tubb. Hawkins' early re-

[38] Examples of old-time songs in the Wilburn Brothers' repertory can be heard
in *Folk Songs* (Decca 4225) and *Take Up Thy Cross* (Decca 4464).

[39] Gentry, *A History of Country, Western, and Gospel Music*, p. 247.

[40] Representative albums by Stonewall Jackson are *Sadness in a Song* (Columbia CL-1770) and *Greatest Hits* (Columbia CL-2377).

[41] Gentry, *A History of Country, Western, and Gospel Music*, p. 239.

cordings on the King label, in fact, strongly resembled both the vocal and instrumental styles of Ernest Tubb, and his physical appearance and dress evoked an apparent cowboy image. The deep-voiced Hawkins was always a respected singer, and his early recording of "Sunny Side of the Mountain" has become a country classic. Real success did not come, however, until his recording stint with RCA Victor.[42] Before his death in 1963 Hawkins gave promise through the recording of such tunes as "Lonesome 7–7203" (written by Ernest Tubb's son, Justin) of being one of the most successful performers of the contemporary period.

If the mountain image did not exert itself in the case of Hawkshaw Hawkins, it certainly did in the career and style of Carl Butler of east Tennessee.[43] In many respects Butler was just as affected by western themes as any other modern country entertainer, particularly in his wearing of gaudy cowboy costumes and in the employment of honky-tonk instrumentation, but in his vocal approach he revealed an obvious debt to country gospel music and the rural styles of the southeastern United States. His intense emotional style was suggestive of both Roy Acuff and the Bailes Brothers.[44] Butler did much to reinvigorate the honky-tonk style of music when he recorded, along with his wife Pearl, the top country song of 1963, "Don't Let Me Cross Over," a number made conspicuous by its lack of modern "popularizing" influences.

In the country-music resurgence women singers have played a role as decisive as that of the male singers. The growing recognition of women country singers is a relatively new phenomenon, dating back, with a few exceptions, to no earlier than World War II. Women had always participated in the country-music profession, but generally, as in the cases of Maybelle and Sara Carter, as part of a group; only rarely, as witnessed by the success of Patsy Montana, did women gain success on an individual basis. The path of individual stardom for women country singers was broken in the forties by such performers as Rosalie Allen, Jenny Lou Carson, Cousin Emmy, and Molly O'Day. In the prosperous years following World War II, pos-

---

[42] Samples of the Hawkins style can be heard on *Country Gentleman* (Camden 931) and *Hawkshaw Hawkins Sings* (Camden 808).

[43] Gentry, *A History of Country, Western, and Gospel Music*, p. 193.

[44] Carl and Pearl Butler have recorded an album of Bailes Brothers songs on *Avenue of Prayer*, Columbia CL-2640.

sibly as a manifestation of the general liberation of American women and of the breakdown of rural social patterns that had relegated country women to a position subordinate to that of the male, such important female singers as Kitty Wells and Rose Maddox began to place their songs consistently on the popularity charts.

In the sixties several female entertainers have vied for the title of "Queen of Country Music": Jan Howard (the wife of songwriter Harlan Howard), Wanda Jackson, Jeannie Seely, Marion Worth, Tammy Wynette, Jean Shepard (wife of Hawkshaw Hawkins), Norma Jean (of the Porter Wagoner television show), Dottie West (whose beauty would challenge that of any Hollywood movie queen), Connie Smith (who, unlike most of the other female singers, comes from a northern state, Ohio), Skeeter Davis, Melba Montgomery, Loretta Lynn, and numerous others. Some of these singers, such as Wanda Jackson, Norma Jean, Jean Shepard, Bonnie Owens, Melba Montgomery, Dolly Parton, and Loretta Lynn, have unmistakably country voices that contain echoes of earlier great singers like Molly O'Day and Kitty Wells. Other singers, like Jan Howard, Tammy Wynette, and Dottie West, sing country songs in styles obviously influenced by such pop vocalists as Doris Day and Patti Page.

Although it is difficult to identify any one entertainer as the leading female vocalist (and very risky considering the fleeting nature of modern show-business stardom), a few names have predominated during the sixties. The Kentucky-born Loretta Lynn,[45] with a style similar to that of Kitty Wells, has recorded with honky-tonk instrumentation such songs as "Before I'm Over You" and "You're Not Woman Enough to Get My Man" and probably comes closest to being the top female country singer. Providing a worthy challenge, however, are at least three other entertainers: Connie Smith, Melba Montgomery, and Skeeter Davis.

Connie Smith literally became a sensation overnight in 1964 when her initial recording of "Once a Day," written by the prolific songwriter Bill Anderson, became the nation's number one country song.[46] Connie Smith's meteoric rise had almost been equalled earlier by

---

[45] Ginger Willis, "A Day with Loretta Lynn," *Country Song Roundup*, XVII, No. 90 (October, 1965), 20–21. Two of Loretta Lynn's most representative albums are *Before I'm Over You* (Decca 4541) and *Blue Kentucky Girl* (Decca 4665).

[46] *Music City News*, II, No. 6 (December, 1964), 4.

Melba Montgomery, whose songs began appearing on the country popularity charts in 1963. Melba Montgomery's recordings are distinctive not solely because of her singing style, which is one of the most genuine in its country phrasing, but also because of the featured use of the dobro. In addition to her solo recordings, she has recorded several best-selling duet numbers with George Jones, including "We Must Have Been Out of Our Minds" and "Let's Invite Them Over," two excellent examples of country songs denoting the temptations and heartbreaks of illicit love.[47]

The most widely popular of the female country singers in her appeal to groups outside the country music audience, and the possessor of the most eclectic repertory, is Skeeter Davis (Mary Frances Penick). She seems to be moving persistently toward country-pop music, but earlier her recordings generally had been performed in the older, genuinely country styles. Her recording career began in 1953 when, along with her schoolmate Betty Jack Davis, she performed as part of a duo called the Davis Sisters. Their recording of "I Forgot More Than You'll Ever Know" (also recorded by Sonny James) was one of the most popular country songs of 1953. After the death of Betty Jack Davis in an automobile accident in August, 1953, Skeeter Davis retired from show business and did not resume her career until the late fifties when she recorded such popular favorites as "Set Him Free" and "Optimistic."[48]

Of all the singers in the honky-tonk resurgence, two individuals with styles deeply rooted in country tradition give greatest promise of achieving the kind of fame earlier won by such country music giants as Jimmie Rodgers, Hank Williams, and Roy Acuff. They are George Jones and Buck Owens. George Jones, of Sarasota, Texas,[49] near Beaumont, has been influenced by a variety of earlier country styles, and his devotion to the country tradition is so

[47] The Melba Montgomery-George Jones combination can be heard on *What's In Our Heart* (United Artists UL3301) and *Bluegrass Hootenanny* (United Artists UAL3352).

[48] The best series of writings on Skeeter Davis are four articles by Dixie Deen: "Skeeter Davis: Born to Sing," *Music City News,* IV, No. 7 (January, 1967); *ibid.,* IV, No. 8 (February, 1967); *ibid.,* IV, No. 9 (March, 1967); *ibid.,* IV, No. 10 (April, 1967).

[49] Interview with George Jones, Austin, Texas, August 16, 1962: see also Dixie Deen, "The Crown Prince of C-W Music," *Music City News,* IV, No. 2 (August, 1966), 1, 31.

strong that he has resisted most of the modern commercializing pressures. He is so firmly imbedded in the country tradition that even the addition of popular choral backgrounds cannot diminish the distinctive country sound of his voice. George Jones is an excellent example of the thesis that traditional styles and sounds die very slowly. He was reared in an industrial-urban center of Texas at a time when the old rural ways were declining and the state was being transformed into a heavily populated industrial area. He was born into a working-class family heavily steeped in fundamentalist religious attitudes. His family was typically southern and rural in its outlook despite the fact that his father was not a farmer but a log-truck driver.[50] The Jones family, in fact, was typical of the rural Texas family that moved into the urban centers during the immediate prewar and war years and remained rural in everything but residence and occupation. The old rural values and attitudes, built up through the decades, would be a long time a-dying.

Jones grew up during the exciting war years when rural Texas families were pouring into cities like Beaumont, Port Arthur, and Houston in search of defense work. Hundreds of taverns and dance halls poured out a steady stream of hillbilly music, while juke boxes and radio stations did likewise in an effort to satisfy the ever increasing market. The youthful Jones heard the singers of the time—the Floyd Tillmans and Ernest Tubbs—and, like many young Texans of the period, was both thrilled and influenced by them. His personal favorites of the war period were Roy Acuff and Bill Monroe, whom he heard over Grand Ole Opry broadcasts.[51] If one listens closely to Jones' recordings, the Acuff influence can be detected, especially in his phrasing on the high notes. After the war Jones came under the spell of Hank Williams, and, in his earliest professional jobs in the taverns and dance halls of Beaumont, he affected a style very close to that of Williams.

Jones began his recording career in 1954 with Starday, a company then located in Beaumont and named after the two individuals who founded it, H. W. "Pappy" Dailey and Jack Starnes.[52] The year 1954

[50] Deen, "The Crown Prince of C-W Music," *Music City News*, IV, No. 2 (August, 1966), 31.

[51] Interview with George Jones, August 16, 1962.

[52] Deen, "The Crown Prince of C-W Music," *Music City News*, IV, No. 2 (August, 1966), 31.

was a most inopportune time for a dedicated country singer. Jones and Ray Price were among the lonely few who maintained the traditional country sound during the rock-and-roll period. Jones, however, did not gain the success that Price enjoyed and, although his 1955 recording of "Why Baby Why" made the country popularity charts, his prosperous period did not come until the late fifties and early sixties. In 1962 and 1963 the nation's country disc jockeys voted him the nation's number one country singer,[53] a position attained without benefit of membership in the Grand Ole Opry. His success came because of his unique style, personal and intense, and because of his choice of songs, many of which he wrote himself. Jones' voice sometimes takes on the wailing quality of Roy Acuff or the plaintive tone of Hank Williams, and he occasionally lets his voice slide and bend around notes in a manner reminiscent of Lefty Frizzell or Floyd Tillman. But despite the numerous influences that have worked upon his style, Jones has a manner of presentation that is original, and it has come to be copied as much as that of earlier singers. Jones has the mark of an authentic country singer, the quality of sincerity, which he conveys to the listener through his intensity of style. His recordings of "Don't Stop the Music" and "Just One More" are excellent examples of both the honky-tonk style and of Jones' own personal emotional style. His deeply implanted rural style, tempered by the atmosphere of industrial East Texas, is evident even when backed with modern instrumentation. On "The Window Up Above" and "She Thinks I Still Care," both employing choral backgrounds, the essentially country voice and phrasing of Jones still stands out.[54]

When Jones' popularity declined from its dominant position in 1964, the commanding leadership of country music was assumed by another Texas-born singer, Alvis Edgar "Buck" Owens, whose continuing popularity seems to indicate that he will eventually emerge as one of the most successful country singers of all time. Although he was born in 1929 in Sherman, Texas, Owens grew up in Arizona, where he learned to play the mandolin and guitar at an early age.

[53] *The World of Country Music*, p. 176.

[54] To hear the diverse styling of George Jones, listen to the following albums: *My Favorites of Hank Williams*, United Artists UAL3220; *George Jones' Greatest Hits*, Mercury MG20621; and *George Jones Sings the Hits of His Country Cousins*, United Artists UAL 3218.

When he was only seventeen, he began as a guitar player on a show carried over KTYL in Mesa, Arizona. He later moved to Bakersfield, California, where he bought a ranch and began playing guitar on country shows in the Southern California region.[55]

Owens was one of many fine entertainers who made their base of operations on the West Coast during the post-World War II years. Ever since the Okie migrations of the thirties and the boom period of World War II, California has been a thriving center for country music. Long a haven for western night clubs, California did not have its major radio barn dance—the Town Hall Party in Compton—[56] until the late forties. The Town Hall Party featured a nucleus of established performers such as Tex Ritter, Tex Williams, Joe and Rose Maphis, Eddie Kirk, Cliffie Stone, Wesley Tuttle, Johnny Bond, and Merle Travis, but the show also served as a launching ground for future stars such as Freddie Hart and Tommy Collins. It was as a lead guitarist for such performers as Tommy Collins that Buck Owens first gained invaluable show-business experience. Although he is one of the most accomplished guitarists in country music, Owens, perhaps like the majority of sidemen, always harbored the desire to be a featured vocalist.

When he made his first solo recordings, Owens became associated with a type of music that might be called the "West Coast Sound" or the "California Sound." This "sound" was a product of several performers, both instrumentalists and vocalists, and was essentially a modification of older country styles. In part, this recognizable style owed its originality to the inventiveness of such pedal-style steel guitarists as Ralph Mooney who played in an uptempoed, supercharged manner with their instruments tuned to an almost ear-splitting pitch. Vocally, the style was much the same. The singers—and Wynn Stewart and Merle Haggard are representative—sang in a dynamic, vibrant, and often strident manner heart-rending songs of unsuccessful love and barroom romances. Wynn Stewart, whose band did much to popularize the California Sound, is a singer whose value and influence has far outstripped his commercial recognition. He oc-

---

[55] Harris Martin, "Buck Owens Riding All Time Height of Popularity," *Music City News*, II, No. 12 (June, 1965), 4.

[56] Gentry, *A History of Country, Western, and Gospel Music*, p. 175.

casionally records songs which earn hit parade recognition. These include the poignant love song "The Keeper of the Key"; one of the hits of 1967, "It's Such a Pretty World Today"; and several tunes employing traditional melodies which reveal Stewart's acquaintance-ship with old-time country music: for example, "Another Day, An-other Dollar" (to the melody of "Greenback Dollar"); and "Wishful Thinking" (to the melody of "Little Rosewood Casket").[57]

Merle Haggard, who got his first real start playing bass with the Wynn Stewart band, is an unusual member of the California fra-ternity of country musicians. He, unlike most of them, is a native Californian. He was born into a working-class family in the oil and farming town of Bakersfield, an area so heavily populated by former southwesterners that it can almost be called "the Oklahoma of the West." Haggard learned his first songs and guitar styles by listening to records by Bob Wills, Lefty Frizzell, and Jimmie Rodgers. Al-though he made a few moderately successful recordings, such as Wynn Stewart's "Sing Me a Sad Song," for Tally Records, he gained little success until he recorded a very popular favorite written by Liz Anderson, "All My Friends Are Gonna Be Strangers."[58] By 1967 Haggard had been voted the number one country singer by the Academy of Country and Western Music (an organization composed of singers and musicians on the West Coast).[59] Performing as a soloist, and sometimes as part of a duet combination with his wife Bonnie Owens, he has produced a steady stream of hit recordings, some of which are classic examples of the story song and of the honky-tonk genre: "The Bottle Let Me Down," "The Fugitive," "Branded Man," and "I Threw Away the Rose."[60]

Although Stewart and Haggard are outstanding examples of both the honky-tonk style and the California Sound, neither has equalled the glittering success won by Buck Owens during the period since 1964. In some respects, Owens' sound reflects the California style

[57] Many of Stewart's best songs can be heard on *Its Such a Pretty World To-day*, Capitol T-2737.

[58] Dixie Deen, "Merle Haggard: 'Someone Told My Story In a Song'," *Music City News*, IV, No. 11 (May, 1967), 9–10.

[59] *Music City News*, IV, No. 10 (April, 1967), 28.

[60] A representative sampling of the Haggard style and repertory is on *Swinging Doors/Bottle Let Me Down*, Capitol T-2585.

of Wynn Stewart and the Texas approaches of Ray Price and George Jones. But as is generally true of accomplished artists, Owens' success is directly attributable to his own originality and distinctiveness. Possessing a clear, ringing tenor voice and an earnest, almost-pleading style, Owens has contributed a seemingly never ending succession of hit songs such as "Above and Beyond," "Foolin' Around," "Excuse Me" ("I Think I've Got a Heartache"), "Crying Time," and "Together Again," which are firmly within the honky-tonk genre and absolutely devoid of country-pop influences.[61]

Owens' meteoric rise to success as a Capitol recording artist has done much to reinvigorate western honky-tonk music and is strongly applauded by those country fans who had feared that their music was about to be hopelessly submerged by rock-and-roll and the Nashville Sound. Owens has resolutely rejected background choruses and pop-style instrumentation and adhered closely to the use of the steel guitar and electric take-off guitar as lead instruments. One of the closest ties to country tradition possessed by the Buck Owens unit is the high, piercing style of harmony—performed by Owens' lead guitarist and occasional fiddler, Don Rich, who is one of the most versatile entertainers in the country-music field. Another interesting link with rural tradition in the Buck Owens band, the Buckaroos, is steel guitarist Tom Brumley; his father, Albert Brumley, is one of the most highly regarded composers of gospel songs in the United States and is the writer of such well-known songs as "I'll Fly Away" and "If We Never Meet Again."[62]

Employing a fast-tempoed, heavily-accented brand of instrumentation, Owens has produced songs that are easily admired, but in a style that is not easily imitated. After attempting to sing the songs themselves, many admirers quickly discovered that it was the Buck Owens style, and not his songs, that had captivated them. Although some of his songs are admittedly clever and comical—such as "Act Naturally," "I've Got a Tiger By the Tail," and "Sam's Place"—it is the dynamic Owens style that made them popular. To the tradition-

[61] Albums which contain representative samplings of Owens' work include *Buck Owens* (Capitol T-1489), *Carnegie Hall Concert* (Capitol T-2556), and *Dust on Mother's Bible* (Capitol T-2497).

[62] Albert Brumley deserves a full-length study. He is the subject of a short article in *Music City News*, III, No. 1 (July, 1965), 18.

minded enthusiast Owens gained recognition at a fortuitous time, for he may have done much to divert country music from its headlong and foolish rush toward amalgamation with, and annihilation by, pop music. Owens proved that a singer, if he possesses talent, can be both country and successful. In the spring of 1965 he published a full-page ad in the trade journals— his "Pledge to Country Music"—which served as a veritable battle-cry for those who sought to preserve the purity and distinctiveness of country music:

> I shall sing no song that is not a country song.
> I shall make no record that is not a country record.
> I refuse to be known as anything but a country singer.
> I am proud to be associated with country music.
> Country music and country music fans have made me
>   what I am today.
> And I shall not forget it.[63]

Although honky-tonk singers occasionally have employed modern, sophisticated instrumentation, they tend to place greater reliance upon traditional instruments and modifications of them. Some performers, like Buck Owens, have not wavered in their loyalty to the older styles and sounds, while some of them occasionally add a country-pop feature such as a choral background. It should be stressed, however, that the recording sound of these performers is not necessarily the same as that heard in their concerts. If a performer succumbs to commercial pressure and uses an orchestra or choral background on his records, he cannot very well use these features on his tours because of the expense and the nature of the places in which he plays. The natural habitat of this kind of music, the dance hall, is usually not equipped for elaborate backgrounds and settings. Therefore, when the honky-tonk singers go before the public in person, their instrumentation is considerably more traditional than it is on many of their records.

The instrumentation of honky-tonk music is a major reason for the success of the music. The instrumentation is traditional in that most of the instruments have been used since the beginnings of commercial country music: the guitar, fiddle, string bass, and steel guitar. The only modern intruder in the honky-tonk band is the drum, used to

[63] *Ibid.,* II, No. 9 (March, 1965), 5.

provide a consistent danceable beat. Although the instruments are traditional, they have changed radically from the simple instruments of earlier years. Now it is highly probable that every instrument in the band, with the exception of the vocalist's rhythm guitar,[64] is electrified—even the fiddle. While the drum provides a steady, hard beat, the electric bass sets up a walking, rhythmic pattern and the electric takeoff guitar, fiddle, and steel guitar take the lead passages. They produce an instrumental style that draws heavily on western swing, jazz (much of it from the Benny Goodman-Glenn Miller era), rock-and-roll, and traditional country music. When a vocalist like George Jones steps back from the microphone and permits his band to do an instrumental break, they more often than not choose a jazz number like "One O'Clock Jump" in which the steel guitar and electric lead guitar take passages formerly reserved for trumpets and clarinets.

The instrument that has experienced the biggest comeback in the honky-tonk music revival is the electric steel guitar. No longer the simple, one-necked instrument of prewar days, the steel guitar has risen from the obscurity of the rock-and-roll phase to a position of commanding interest and popularity. Its renewed popularity came partly through technological change and partly through new stylistic techniques developed by the musicians. Instead of one-necked six-stringed instruments with a simple amplification system, the modern steel guitars are three and four-necked devices equipped with foot pedals, resonators, and complicated control panels capable of making the guitar sound like anything from a Hammond organ to a diesel locomotive. Modern steel guitars, therefore, are capable of producing a much louder and more resilient sound than earlier ones.

Many individuals have contributed to the revitalization of the electric steel guitar. They range from the "old-timers" like Jerry Byrd, Don Helms, Leon McAuliffe, and Roy Wiggins, who play in subdued Hawaiian-influenced styles, to newcomers like Pete Drake, Jimmy Day, Buddy Emmons, Bobby Garrett, Buddy Charlton, Ralph Mooney, and Tom Brumley, who play in styles heavily influenced by jazz techniques. At the beginning of the sixties the steel guitar had attracted so much attention that record companies were releasing

---

[64] Occasionally, vocalists played electric guitars. Buck Owens, for example, was for a time his own lead electric guitarist.

albums devoted solely to that instrument[65]—something that companies had seldom done before.

Although instrumental technique has played an important role in honky-tonk music's upsurge, the lyric content of the song material also has exerted a strong influence. Honky-tonk song lyrics tend to be more reflective of modern social patterns and cultural attitudes than are other varieties of country music. The dominant theme, of course, is love in its various manifestations. But there is less idealization of love than usually is found in popular music, and the more tragic and unfortunate aspects of the relationships between men and women are depicted. That lost and unrequited love are two of the predominant themes illustrates the basic continuity between the country music of modern times and that of the early period.

Song lyrics of today seldom rhapsodize about the old country home or the rural heritage. Instead, they describe the problems and dreams of a generation that no longer lives on the farm, but works as truck drivers, common laborers, factory workers, and salesmen. A generation only shortly removed from agriculture, it now makes up a large part of America's lower-middle and middle-middle-class urban population, and it has responded to that music best equipped to depict its thinking. An example of country music's adaptation to changing economic conditions is the appearance of a relatively new, but growing, body of occupational songs describing the perils and attractions of truck driving. The truck driver—fighting the hazards of sleep, curving mountain roads, and faulty air brakes—has become one of America's new folk heroes, and the songs written about him seem destined to rival the popularity of the railroad songs. A genre that began probably with the 1939 Decca recordings by Cliff Bruner and Moon Mullican of Ted Daffan's "Truck Drivers' Blues" has flourished until it now provides many of the nation's country juke-box favorites. Although several performers, such as Red Simpson, the Willis Brothers, Red Sovine, and Dick Curless, have contributed to the steadily growing catalogue of trucking songs, the genre's ablest spokesman is obviously Dave Dudley, the half honky-tonk, half rockabilly performer,

[65] These include Jimmy Day's *Golden Steel Guitar Hits*, Phillips PHM200–016; Speedy West's *Guitar Spectacular*, Capitol T-1835; Buddy Emmons' *Steel Guitar Jazz*, Mercury MG20843; and an extensive listing on Starday: *e.g.*, Leon McAuliffe's *Mister Western Swing*, SLP171; Roy Wiggin's *Mister Steel Guitar*, SLP188; and *Steel Guitar Hall of Fame* (by assorted artists), SLP233.

whose "Six Days on the Road" set off the modern "truck-driving" boom.[66]

Despite its world-wide growth, country music continues to be largely a southern-produced music, both in reference to performers and songwriters.[67] The country songwriters, particularly those who cater to the honky-tonk style, are predominantly southerners who come from small towns or once lived on farms. An investigation of modern country songs will disclose, too, that a great percentage were written by the singers themselves—as 'has always been the case. In the list of songwriters who have contributed material to the honky-tonk singers many names could be included: Mel Tillis, Wayne Walker, Jack Rhodes, Red Hayes, Merle Kilgore, Justin Tubb, John D. Loudermilk, Jack Clement, Dallas Frazier, Hank Cochran, Tom T. Hall, Darrell Edwards, Liz Anderson, Alex Zanetis, and numerous others.[68] Two writers, however, who seem to surpass the others in writing consistent hit material are Bill Anderson and Harlan Howard.

These two writers have been successful because of their ability to capture moods and expressions of common occurrence with which a country audience could readily identify. Anderson, who came from Georgia, is also a singer of note; he wrote and recorded one of the biggest hits of 1962 ("Mama Sang a Song") and of 1963 ("Still").[69] In contrast to most country singers and composers, Anderson is a college graduate. He attended the University of Georgia, where he majored in journalism, but throughout his college career he sang

[66] Robert Shelton, "Meet a New Folk Hero, the Truck Driver," *The New York Times*, December 4, 1966. "Six Days on the Road" can be heard, along with other examples of modern occupational songs, on Dudley's *Songs About the Working Man*, Mercury MG20899. Other representative albums which reflect the changing status of the erstwhile ruralite now dwelling in the city include Dick Curless' *Tombstone Every Mile*, Tower T5005; Ray Price's *Night Life*, Columbia CL1971; *Diesel Smoke, Dangerous Curves* (assorted artists), Starday SLP250; and *Bright Lights and Honky Tonks* (assorted artists), Starday SLP239.

[67] For confirmation of this assertion check the artists' listings in any country music publication; for example, in Gentry, *A History of Country, Western, and Gospel Music*, pp. 176–349; and *The World of Country Music*, pp. 201–215.

[68] *The World of Country Music*, p. 162. A good vignette of one outstanding songwriter, Tom T. Hall, the composer of "Tell Them What We're Fighting For" and "I Washed My Face in the Morning Dew," is Dixie Deen, "Tom T. Hall's Touch of Greatness," *Music City News*, V, No. 2 (August, 1967), 3–4.

[69] *The World of Country Music*, p. 199.

298 *Country Music, U.S.A.*

professionally and worked as a country disc jockey.[70] The first public awareness of his ability came in 1958, when one of his compositions, "City Lights," was recorded and made into a national hit by Ray Price. "City Lights," also recorded by Anderson and many others, is one of the best-written songs of the modern era and vividly depicts the temptations and frustration that come to many heartbroken souls who venture into the big city in quest of some kind of solace:

> A bright array of city lights as far as I can see;
> The great white way shines through the night
> For lonely souls like me.
> The cabarets and honky tonks flashing signs invite
> A broken heart to lose itself in the glow of city lights.[71]

Harlan Howard, born in Lexington, Kentucky, is the acknowledged "king" of country songwriters. Although he had written songs from the age of twelve, he did not gain acceptance for any of them until 1959. At that time he was employed as a $90-a-week apprentice bookbinder in Huntington Park, California. He approached several publishers but none before Tex Ritter and Johnny Bond would give him a fair hearing.[72] His first accepted composition, recorded by Bond, was a failure, but he now had the opportunity he had been seeking. Success came to him in 1958. His first major hit, "Pick Me Up on Your Way Down," was written for Ray Price, who, however, passed it on to his friend Charlie Walker, San Antonio singer and disc jockey, who recorded it and saw it achieve national recognition. "Pick Me Up on Your Way Down," based on an actual event,[73] was Howard's impression of a man's displeasure with an ex-sweetheart who had rejected him for someone with more money and sophistication:

> You were mine for just awhile
> Now you're putting on the style,
> And you never once look back

---

[70] Interview with Bill Anderson, Nashville, Tennessee, August 22, 1961.

[71] "City Lights," words and music by Bill Anderson. Copyright © 1958 by TNT Music, Inc., San Antonio, Texas. "City Lights," Columbia 41191, made the No. 1 position on the country popularity charts (*Billboard* [November, 1958]).

[72] Interview with Harlan Howard, Nashville, Tennessee, August 24, 1961; also Richard Warren Lewis, "Thar's Gold in Them Thar Hillbillies," *Show Business Illustrated*, II, No. 2 (February, 1962), 38.

[73] Interview with Harlan Howard, August 24, 1961.

> At your friends across the track.
> You're the gossip of the town,
> But my heart can still be found
> Where you tossed it to the ground.
> Pick me up on your way down.[74]

This song's attainment of popularity coincided with the success of two other Howard songs, "Heartaches by the Number," recorded by Ray Price, and "Mommy for a Day," recorded by Kitty Wells. From this point on, working as a freelance writer, Howard rose to the top ranks of country music by writing songs that were recorded by a multitude of performers: "A Guy Named Joe," recorded by his boyhood idol, Ernest Tubb; "I Fall to Pieces," a national best-seller recorded by Patsy Cline; and "Excuse Me" ("I Think I've Got a Heartache"), recorded by Buck Owens. His most successful composition, "Heartaches by the Number," recorded in both popular and country music, grossed well over fifty thousand dollars for the writer's share alone.[75] Howard's songwriting abilities earned him ten citations (awards of merit) from BMI in 1961 (a record) and well over $100,-000 in that same year.[76]

The compositions of Howard and of the other country songwriters were, of course, not traditional, and many of them would not survive the year of their recording. They were, however, in traditional styles and reflected the thoughts and aspirations of the average man. By exploiting the universal themes common to humanity—lost love, death, religion, suffering, rejection—they ensured their popularity and strengthened country music's role as the music of the common man. Students of folklore, many of whom are still imprisoned by the mountain image or by a romanticized concept of rural culture, rarely give the honky-tonk musicians and writers a second glance. Indications do exist, however, as evidenced by the writings of Mayne Smith for *Sing Out* magazine and of Robert Shelton for the *New York Times*, that students and scholars are finally giving modern country music

---

[74] "Pick Me Up on Your Way Down," words and music by Harlan Howard. Copyright © 1959 by Pamper Music, Inc., Goodlettsville, Tennessee. Used by special permission of the copyright owner. This song is recorded on Columbia 41211.

[75] Interview with Harlan Howard, August 24, 1961.

[76] *Billboard Music Week* (November 6, 1961), 52.

the critical recognition that it is due.[77] The honky-tonk coterie, instead of employing traditional mountain songs and themes, are extraordinarily present-minded and base their songs on personal experiences and emotions of current significance. Instead of attempting to perpetuate old-time styles and songs, the modern generation wants to create its own styles and contribute something new.

Despite their innovations and urbanized sophistication, the country singers of today are the cultural and musical descendants of the rural folk of earlier centuries who had perpetuated the ancient ballads and eventually created commercial country music. Just as earlier generations of country people had sung and created songs that reflected their own social patterns and culture, so have the honky-tonk singers of the sixties. Instead of being neglected because of their commercialization and emphasis on the present, the offerings of the honky-tonk musicians should be studied as valid indicators of modern society and culture. Despite the vapidness and banality of much of their lyrics and the raucousness and excessive electrification of much of their instrumentation, the honky-tonk performers have produced a music well attuned to the times. These performers are neglected as were the hillbilly musicians of the twenties, but in generations to come folklorists and sociologists may find that the musical offerings of such people as Ray Price and George Jones most closely chronicled the despairs and aspirations of their contemporaries. The honky-tonk songs of the fifties and sixties may very well be collected some day as folksongs, after age has given them respectability.

Regardless of the status honky-tonk songs may achieve in the future, there was a body of songs produced beginning in late 1958 and reaching a peak of production in 1959 that resembled in stylistic construction the old-time folk ballads. This type of song, known variously as the saga or historical ballad, produced a flurry of imitative excitement and played an important role in the reinvigoration of country music. Although similar in some ways to the event ballad of the twenties, the saga song was greatly different in its depiction of com-

[77] Mayne Smith, "A Reply to John Cohen," *Sing Out*, XVI, No. 3 (July, 1966), 31, 33. Aside from his occasional columns on country music in *The New York Times*, Robert Shelton has applauded "honky-tonk" music (with which he sees a kinship with rockabilly music) in "Country from Another Country" (*Cavalier*, XVII, No. 11 [September, 1967], 18–19) and in *The Country Music Story*, p. 200).

pletely fictional episodes or remote historical events. Only rarely did the saga song describe events of current significance. It sounded, not like the natural folk-moulded ballads of the past, but like the creation of a professional composer who had one eye on the past and the other on the commercial market.[78] The song was written with a conscious effort to recreate the sound or style of an earlier time. As a result, despite its stylistic excellence, it could never be more than an imitation. Regardless of its artificiality, however, the saga song was a welcome relief from the over-commercialization of country-pop music and signaled at least a temporary trend toward more traditionally-styled music.

The saga song emerged and drew much of its popularity from the success gained by similar songs in popular music. The year 1958 witnessed the beginning of a so-called urban folk revival, and the song which signaled the appearance of the folk boom was an old mountain murder ballad, "Tom Dooley," recorded by the Kingston Trio. The success of this ballad, which made the number one position on popular hit charts,[79] inspired the recording of similar ballads, fake and otherwise, by countless other performers. For several months the airwaves were filled with songs about mythical and real heroes who gained fame or notoriety during the American pioneer period.

In the recording of the saga songs Columbia Records played a preeminent role. In late 1958 and early 1959 there appeared a variety of saga songs, most of them in Columbia's 41300 Series,[80] which suggests that someone in the Columbia offices was alive to the immediate commercial advantages of the pseudo-historical song. The series was inaugurated by Johnny Horton's "Springtime in Alaska," a ballad in the Robert Stewart Service tradition, which related the story of a prospector killed in a tavern brawl in the Klondike.[81] To the delight

---

[78] It must be remembered, however, that the ballad mongers who peddled their broadsides on English street corners in the seventeenth and eighteenth centuries also had an eye on the commercial market. And more of their songs entered tradition, and made the jump across the Atlantic, than any other kind of British folksong.

[79] It first appeared in *Billboard*, LXX, No. 46 (November 17, 1958), 50.

[80] The record numbers were obtained from various issues of *Billboard*.

[81] Although it was released in December, 1958, "Springtime in Alaska" did not reach the number one position until April 6, 1959 (*Billboard*, LXX, No. 50 [December 15, 1958], 83; *ibid.*, LXXI, No. 14 [April 6, 1959], 77).

of dyed-in-the-wool country fans, this ballad, performed with simple, country accompaniment, attained the number one position on the country-music charts and remained for several weeks against the competition of country-pop numbers.

"Springtime in Alaska" was followed soon after by the release of Johnny Cash's "Don't Take Your Guns to Town,"[82] an account of a young cowboy who disregarded his mother's warnings and was killed when he ventured into town. An equally popular song, and another example of the pseudo-western ballad, was Marty Robbins' "Hanging Tree,"[83] which gained recognition on the pop charts, as had Cash's number.

The most notable national recognition for a country saga song came in 1959 when Johnny Horton recorded "The Battle of New Orleans," a tradition-based ballad which gained the number one position in both popular and country music. The ballad first appeared in a 1958 album recorded by Jimmie Driftwood (James Morris), an Arkansas schoolteacher and folklorist, for the RCA Victor company.[84] Driftwood had composed his own lyrics about Andrew Jackson's famous victory and had set them to an old hillbilly fiddle tune, "The Eighth of January," which commemorated the event. Horton's version, considerably shorter than Driftwood's, first appeared on a Columbia record in April, 1959, and by June of that year had vaulted to the position of number one song in the nation. Horton was, therefore, the performer par excellence of the saga song. In the year and a half preceding his death he recorded a variety of songs, the contents of which are indicated by some of the titles: "Sink the Bismarck," "Johnny Reb," and "The Battle of Bull Run."[85]

Several historical, or folkish, songs which had varying degrees of success were issued in 1959, but none approached "The Battle of New Orleans" in popularity. They included Carl Smith's "Ten Thou-

[82] In the *Fabulous Johnny Cash*, Columbia 1253. Other Cash albums with this kind of material are *Songs of Our Soil* (Columbia 1339) and *Ride This Train* (Columbia 1464).

[83] "The Hanging Tree" was the theme of a Warner Brothers' movie of the same name (*Billboard*, LXXI, No. 5 [February 2, 1959], 35).

[84] *Jimmie Driftwood Sings Newly Discovered Early American Folk Songs*, RCA Victor RPM 1635.

[85] These and similar songs are on *Johnny Horton Makes History*, Columbia 1478.

sand Drums" (a pseudo-revolutionary war song), Eddy Arnold's "Tennessee Stud," and Hawkshaw Hawkins' "Soldier's Joy," another revolutionary war song. Of all the folkish ballads of the period "The Long Black Veil," recorded by Lefty Frizzell, gave evidence of the strongest durability and most widespread appeal. Written by Mary John Wilkin and Danny Dill, the song was eventually recorded by a diverse group of performers ranging all the way from the Country Gentlemen, a bluegrass group, to Joan Baez, an urban-folk performer.[86]

In late 1959 the saga-song craze subsided somewhat, but the trend continued spasmodically with the appearance of albums devoted to ballads or historical events and the release of an occasional single. Marty Robbins wrote and recorded a song in late 1959 which rivaled the success gained earlier by "The Battle of New Orleans." This was "El Paso";[87] a well-written ballad with a Mexican flavor, it tells of a man who was killed fighting for the love of his border-tavern sweetheart. "El Paso," only one of many "western" songs, real and fake, recorded by Robbins, was a unique recording in modern American music, because it lasted well over four minutes, a rarity among commercial recordings.

Saga songs have continued to appear occasionally and, in fact, sometimes resemble event ballads in their depiction of contemporary incidents. One of the most popular songs in 1961 was a semi-recitation by country singer Jimmie Dean entitled "Big John," the story of a big miner who gave his life to save his fellow workers. Dean followed the success of that song with a similar recording called "PT 109," which chronicled the wartime exploits of John F. Kennedy.[88]

Under the onslaught of the Vietnamese war, country singers responded as they always had in similar situations. They wrote and recorded songs about the war. These, strictly speaking, are not saga

---

[86] *John Baez in Concert*, Part 2, Vanguard VRS-9113; The Country Gentlemen, *On the Road*, Folkways FA 2411.

[87] Robbins has recorded both genuine and pseudo-cowboy songs. For examples listen to the albums *Gunfighter Ballads* (Columbia 1349) and *More Gunfighter Ballads and Trail Songs* (Columbia 1481).

[88] The popularity of these two songs in both pop and country music helped to earn Dean *Billboard's* "Country Music Man of the Year" award for 1962. He was the first performer to win the award, the others—such as James Denny—having been executives (*Billboard Music Week* [November 17, 1962], 5).

songs but are continuations of the broadside and event-song traditions. Although the conflict in Vietnam has been one of the most unpopular wars in American history, country songs universally have defended the actions and motives of the United States. This record of defense points up one of the most striking contrasts between country and urban folk music. Urban folksingers have contributed a large body of material protesting American involvement. Country singers, on the other hand, not only have defended the war but have done so in a downright jingoistic fashion. There are, it is true, several conventional, nonpolitical songs such as Loretta Lynn's "Dear Uncle Sam," which describes a woman's sadness at the loss of her sweetheart in battle, but there are others which are heavily political and nativistic in nature. Dave Dudley's "Tell Them What We're Fighting For" is based on the idea of a perplexed soldier writing home to complain about the widespread demonstrations and protests. Roughly on the same theme, but aggressively ultra-conservative in its orientation, is Johnny Sea's "Day of Decision," a super-patriotic monologue which purports to show that the country is rapidly going to the dogs. Even more blatant in its political overtones is the ludicrous "The Minute Men Are Turning in their Graves." Recorded by Stonewall Jackson, the song claims that the peace demonstrations indicate that the Spirit of '76 has died in the United States. Although the song demonstrates a type of patriotism, it shows a less than perceptive understanding of history. Perhaps the greatest irony of the song lies in the fact that its singer was named after a southerner who had not only protested against the United States government but had waged war against it during the Civil War. Jackson, who went so far as to name his band "the Minute Men," has recorded some of the best songs of the sixties, including "Don't Be Angry," but his pro-war song is not one of his finer efforts.[89]

Valid or not in their comments about the American war effort, the Vietnam war songs demonstrate that country music has not lost its propensity for story songs. These songs, along with the historical-saga tunes, have served to keep country music as least partially implanted in tradition.

[89] Examples of country war songs can be heard on Dave Dudley's *There's A Star Spangled Banner Waving Somewhere* (Mercury 21057) and on Stonewall Jackson's *All's Fair in Love and War* (Columbia CL2509).

CHAPTER 10

Bluegrass and the Urban Folk Revival

HONKY-TONK MUSIC and the saga ballads have exerted influences upon country music that help to divert it somewhat from the headlong rush toward amalgamation with popular music forms. But neither of these forms is free from modifications (or contamination) by other musical styles, and the tradition-minded country partisan can decry much in both of them. This is not true, however, of another musical phenomenon which became apparent in the late 1950's. This was a country music style (or sound) that seemed novel and fresh, yet was as old as the hills from which it came, and its full effect upon American music has not yet been determined. It became known as "bluegrass" music.[1]

Strangely enough, bluegrass music did not come from the bluegrass region of Kentucky. Although that area has contributed entertainers to the genre, most of the well-known bluegrass performers have come from the hill-country sections of North Carolina, Tennessee, and

---

[1] The two most significant scholarly works on bluegrass music are L. Mayne Smith, "An Introduction to Bluegrass," *Journal of American Folklore*, LXXVIII, No. 309 (July, September, 1965), 245–256 (cited hereinafter as Smith); and Neil V. Rosenberg, "From Sound to Style: The Emergence of Bluegrass," *Journal of American Folklore*, LXXX, No. 316 (April–June, 1967), 143–150 (cited hereinafter as Rosenberg). Both articles can be obtained as reprints from the John Edwards Memorial Foundation.

Virginia. The term "bluegrass" does not refer, then, to a music specifically situated in a geographic area; it was derived from the name of Bill Monroe's string band, the Blue Grass Boys, who created a musical sound that has been widely copied throughout the United States. Exactly when and how the appellation came to be applied to similar types of music is not known, although critics are generally agreed that the term came into use sometime in the late forties or early fifties when both fans and disc jockeys noticed the similarity that certain string bands, such as those of Flatt and Scruggs and the Stanley Brothers, had to the sound usually associated with Bill Monroe. Like all musical styles, bluegrass has been affected by commercial pressures, by other styles that grew up around it, and by the experimentation and inventiveness of its own performers. Such a style that has spawned modifications and sub-styles is therefore difficult to define.

Although its vocal style is generally recognizable and distinctive— a high-pitched, often strident style, characterized by two, three, and four part harmony—bluegrass is essentially a type of instrumentation, and this is what has been responsible for its amazing spread around the country. One of bluegrass music's marked features is the absence of electric amplification, although occasionally a few of the bands have used an electric guitar.[2] In the employment of an unamplified style, five instruments make up the standard bluegrass band: fiddle, guitar, mandolin, string bass, and five-string banjo. Other instruments, such as the dobro, harmonica, accordion, or a second guitar occasionally have been used. Some bluegrass bands, such as the Country Gentlemen, have dispensed with the fiddle; a few, like Flatt and Scruggs, do not use a mandolin;[3] and occasionally, at least on concerts, a few, like the Stanley Brothers, do not employ a string bass.[4] Two instruments, however, that are always found in a bluegrass unit are the guitar and the five-string banjo. Conceivably a bluegrass band could function without a guitar with the rhythm and bass runs supplied by the mandolin and string bass. And though some would argue that the bluegrass style would still be intact if the banjo

[2] These include Charlie Monroe, Reno and Smiley, the Osborne Brothers, and Jim and Jesse McReynolds.

[3] The mandolin was, however, a prominent feature of the early Flatt and Scruggs recordings on Mercury and Columbia.

[4] By 1967 the Stanley Brothers had also discarded the fiddle; see *Country Folk Music Concert*, King 864.

were omitted, bluegrass music attracted little attention, and in fact did not exist in its present form, until the five-string banjo was revolutionized and made into a lead instrument of technical brilliance. Regardless of the origin of bluegrass music, and of the rhythms and styles that gave it cohesion, it is my contention that a musical organization cannot be truly labeled "bluegrass" unless it contains a five-string banjo, and that instrument must be played in a particular style: the three-finger, or Scruggs' style.

The development of bluegrass music cannot be attributed to any one man, although certain individuals have played decisive roles. It did not assume its present fully developed form until the post-World War II period, particularly from 1945 to 1948. There is little in it, however, that cannot be traced back, at least in some form, for several generations. Bluegrass music is new in so far as its development as a complex, standardized ensemble style. The various techniques which merged to create the general bluegrass pattern were continuations or modifications of country styles long in existence, and were the results of borrowing, improvisation, and inventiveness by the individual performers.

The guitar, for example, is played in the open-chord manner (in contrast to the "sock" rhythm[5] associated with most western country styles), and is used primarily for background rhythm. During the formative years of the bluegrass style the guitar was seldom heard as a lead instrument, except for a few important exceptions such as the outstanding instrumentation of Bill Monroe on "Mule Skinner Blues."[6] During the fifties Bill Clifton and Earl Scruggs performed songs using techniques suggestive of both Carter Family and finger-picking styles, and Don Reno occasionally put down his banjo to pick out guitar melodies in a rapid, flat-picking style. By the mid-sixties the guitar was assuming a more prominent lead role and seemed destined to supplant the mandolin in some bluegrass organizations. Bill Napier, normally a mandolin player, adapted his mandolin tremolo style to the guitar and, on such songs as "Good Old Mountain Dew,"[7] helped to give the Stanley Brothers a more distinctive sound. After Napier left the Stanley organization, he was replaced by the gifted guitarist George Shuffler, who played a flat-picking,

[5] See Chapter 5.
[6] Bluebird 8568 and Victor 20-3163.
[7] Heard on *The Stanley Brothers,* King 772.

semi-mandolin style that made him one of country music's best guitarists.

Despite its periodic usage as a lead instrument, the guitar was more often depended upon for rhythmic effect and for a dramatic touch supplied by the bass runs. The bass runs—one of the most distinctive features of bluegrass music—came at the end of fiddle, mandolin, or banjo sequences and added a dramatic note of emphasis or finality to the over-all mood of intensity created by the supercharged music. The runs were not new in country music; in fact, they could be found in an almost infinite number of variations in the several hillbilly styles existent during the twenties and thirties. But they were never used so often and so insistently as by the bluegrass bands; produced by a resonant, unamplified instrument (often a big D28 Martin guitar), their tones sounded fresh and clear in comparison with the brash, strident notes of electric guitars. The most famous run of all, the so-called Lester Flatt G-run,[8] preceded Flatt by possibly two decades, and can be heard on recordings of other country styles. To identify any one person as the inventor of this particular run would be hazardous, since it probably sprang from several sources. Among early recording stars Riley Puckett,[9] of Skillet Lickers fame, was prominent in his use of this and similar runs. In the thirties Charlie Monroe,[10] of the Monroe Brothers, made this and other runs a distinctive part of his style while playing guitar accompaniment for his brother Bill.

The other bluegrass instruments demonstrate a similar type of development in that they are traditional yet marked by the improvisations of musicians down through the years. At a time when the fiddle seemed to be disappearing from country units (with the occasional exceptions of those headed by entertainers like Buck Owens, Porter Wagoner, Ray Price, and Hank Thompson), the old-time instrument was given a new prominence by the bluegrass bands. The fiddle was played in a number of styles ranging all the way from old-

[8] As far as I have been able to determine the term was coined by Mike Seeger in the notes to *Mountain Music Bluegrass Style,* Folkways FA2318.

[9] Puckett can be heard on an album produced by the Folksong Society of Minnesota entitled *Gid Tanner and His Skillet Lickers* (FSSMLP 15001-D). For biographical information see Chapter 2.

[10] The modern listener can most readily hear the Charlie Monroe guitar stylings on an RCA Victor reissue entitled *Early Bluegrass Music* (Camden 774).

fashioned hoedown fiddling to the heavily-syncopated, almost jazz-like styles of a musician like Chubby Wise or Mack MaGaha.[11] Along with the five-string banjo, the fiddle carried the heaviest brunt of lead instrumentation in the bluegrass bands. The mandolin, on the other hand, was used as both a lead and percussive instrument. Some modern groups have abandoned the mandolin, but in the early years of the developing style nearly every band featured the instrument and, moreover, played it in a style almost directly derivative of Bill Monroe. Monroe's intricate jazz-influenced style has continued to be a challenge to modern mandolinists, and many of them, such as Frank Wakefield and John Duffy,[12] have carried the instrument even closer to the borders of jazz. Not only is the mandolin used in a lead solo capacity, it also serves as a percussive rhythmic instrument and, in the hands of a dominant musical personality like Bill Monroe, it probably did much to create the distinctive rhythms and beat of bluegrass music. In the establishment of beat and rhythm, which may be the decisive components of bluegrass music,[13] the string bass has contributed almost as much as the guitar. Although the walking bass patterns common to honky-tonk and western-swing music are seldom heard in bluegrass instrumentation, examples of highly complex and intricate bass playing, such as that of John Shuffler in the Stanley Brothers band and Tom Gray of the Country Gentlemen,[14] have enlivened the performances of several bluegrass groups. Most often, the bass sets up a conventional rhythmic pattern and leaves the intricacy to the lead instruments. Rounding out the list of the most commonly used bluegrass instruments is, of course, the five-string banjo. Bluegrass musicians rescued this instrument (which will be discussed in more detail later) from the relative obscurity of the thirties and forties; such musicians as Earl Scruggs, Ralph Stanley, and Don

[11] Both Wise and MaGaha have now left the bluegrass field. Wise has long been a fiddler for Hank Snow's Rainbow Ranch Boys, while MaGaha is a member of Porter Wagoner's Wagonmasters.

[12] Frank Wakefield has played for several units, including the Greenbriar Boys, while Duffy is one of the leaders of the Country Gentlemen.

[13] L. Mayne Smith, "First Bluegrass Festival Honors Bill Monroe," *Sing Out: The Folk Song Magazine*, XV, No. 6 (January, 1966), 69.

[14] For example, the bass work of Shuffler on "A Voice From on High," heard on the Stanley Brothers' *Country Pickin' and Singin'* (Mercury MG20349), and the bass playing of Gray on "Grandfather's Clock," on the Country Gentleman's Folkways album, *On the Road* (FA2411).

Reno gave the instrument an exciting, vibrant sound which did much to create the distinctive quality of bluegrass music.

The bluegrass style was the direct descendent of the hillbilly string bands of the twenties and thirties, as were most other modern country styles (ranging from honky-tonk to western swing) which used the fiddle as the dominant instrument. Bluegrass, however, resisting electrical amplification, used some instruments, such as the five-string banjo, which the "western" bands ignored, and harked back to the employment of traditional country melodies like hoe-downs and play-party songs. Bluegrass music was the refinement and modification of the instrumentation developed by several organizations, including Gid Tanner's Skillet Lickers, Al Hopkins' Buckle Busters, the Piedmont Log Rollers, Charlie Poole's North Carolina Ramblers, and Mainer's Mountaineers, and it is probably no accident that, with the exception of the Georgia-based Skillet Lickers, all of these groups were of North Carolina origin. Bluegrass is definitely a southeastern brand of country music. The bluegrass musicians of the modern period heard and learned from these and similar organizations by seeing them in concert or hearing them on records or radio broadcasts. When the bluegrass style coalesced in the late forties, it was created by a host of musicians who had absorbed techniques from a multitude of sources. And the more talented of these musicians made the music distinctive and ensured its success.

Of all the musicians associated with the development of this style none looms higher than Bill Monroe, the "father of bluegrass music."[15] One of the most influential performers in country-music history, Monroe's role as creator of the bluegrass style is almost universally accepted, and Mayne Smith, in an interesting modification of views he had earlier held, went so far as to say that "bluegrass is the intimate, personal music of a single man, Bill Monroe."[16] No question involving country music has been more debated than that involving

[15] This has been a commonly applied designation for Monroe and has been used as the title of one of his albums (*Father of Bluegrass Music*, Camden 719).

[16] Smith's views in "First Bluegrass Festival Honors Bill Monroe" (*Sing Out*, XV, No. 6 [January, 1966], 65) should be compared with those of his *Journal of American Folklore* article, "An Introduction to Bluegrass" (LXXVIII, No. 309 [July–September, 1965], pp. 245–246, 251), in which he emphasizes the role of Earl Scruggs.

the origins of the bluegrass style, and the problem can be crystallized into one specific question: Whose influence has been most decisive, that of Bill Monroe or Earl Scruggs? My own position on this question—though admittedly evasive—can perhaps best be summed up in the following manner: If there had been no Bill Monroe, there would be no bluegrass music; but, on the other hand, if there had been no Earl Scruggs, the music would not have become nationally popular and Bill Monroe would not have gained the widespread recognition that he had long deserved.

Monroe was born in 1911 on a farm in western Kentucky, near Rosine and far from the bluegrass district.[17] He showed an interest in music almost from infancy and received training and inspiration from a host of sources. His mother, who died when he was ten, was an old-time fiddler and singer who deeply influenced her eight children. Monroe began playing his first instrument, a guitar, when he was about twelve years old, and his first actual experience as a performer came when he accompanied the well-known Negro guitarist and fiddler, Arnold Schultz, who played for country dances in the area around Rosine. Monroe always admitted a great liking for Negro music, and he received extensive musical training not only from Schultz but from other Negro musicians and singers who worked as laborers in western Kentucky. The blues style, which was an important ingredient of Monroe's musical approach, came to him from Negro sources and from the recordings of Jimmie Rodgers, who was also one of Monroe's all-time favorites. Despite these various influences, Monroe's singing style was derived largely from attendance at church singing schools, the descendants of the old New England shape-note schools and training ground for thousands of rural white and Negro southerners.

Probably the greatest noncommercial influence in Monroe's musical life came from one of his mother's brothers, Uncle Pen Vanderver,[18] an old-time fiddler and inspiration for one of Monroe's most

---

[17] Although brief biographical citations on Monroe can be found in both Smith and Rosenberg, the writer has leaned most heavily upon an interview between Monroe and Ralph Rinzler (made available in an interview with Ralph Rinzler, Austin, Texas, October 7, 1962).

[18] Interview with Ralph Rinzler, October 7, 1962.

popular songs, "Uncle Pen."[19] Uncle Pen played for country dances while his young nephew backed him up on the guitar. These country dances, which often devolved into all-night sessions, were gay, exuberant affairs attended by young and old alike.

Monroe dabbled with several country instruments before finally settling on the mandolin as his favorite. This decision eventually made him the leading exponent of that instrument in country music. His style, which has changed greatly through the years and is largely the result of his own improvisation and experimentation, was initially based on fiddle styles. In his mandolin playing Monroe tried to emulate the continuous flowing notes of the fiddle, but he was always an experimentalist and improviser and his style became jazzier as his commercial career progressed.

His professional career began in 1927 when, along with his brothers Charlie and Birch, he organized a band that toured throughout the midwest and upper South. In 1930 the trio began performing first on WWAE in Hammond, Indiana, and later on WJKS in Gary, Indiana. (Monroe has always maintained a musical connection with Indiana. Today he owns a country-music park in Bean Blossom where Sunday afternoon concerts are given.) In 1936, with Birch no longer performing with them, Bill and Charlie began their recording career for Bluebird records as the Monroe Brothers.[20] In their brief three-year recording period (1936–1938), they recorded sixty songs,[21] both gospel and secular, that in style of performance stand as important precursors of the modern bluegrass style. During this brief commercial span the Monroe Brothers became well known in the upper South and mountain states. In hundreds of country homes youngsters who would later become accomplished musicians sat by phonographs or battery radios and were enthralled by the hard-driving style of the two brothers.

The Monroe Brothers, featuring only Bill's mandolin and Charlie's guitar, was similar to the many duet combinations of the time, but smaller than the typical country string band. Many of the elements of bluegrass music—the high harmony singing (performed by Bill),

---

[19] Decca 46283.

[20] Interview with Ralph Rinzler, October 7, 1962.

[21] For the Monroe Brothers discography (compiled by Pete Kuykendall) see *Disc Collector*, No. 15 (n.d.), 30; and Brad McCuen, *Country Directory*, No. 2 (April, 1961), 14–16.

the bass guitar runs, the hard-driving mandolin style, and the inclusion of traditional songs—could already be heard.[22] In these formative years Bill Monroe always sang harmony; he did not sing lead or solo until he joined the Grand Ole Opry in 1939 with his own band.[23] Always an individualistic performer, his singing style, like his mandolin playing, has changed radically through the years.

When the Monroe Brothers disbanded in 1938, Charlie and Bill organized separate units. In honor of his native state of Kentucky, Bill named his group the Blue Grass Boys, unaware that like Al Hopkins and his string band of the twenties, the Hillbillies, he had coined a title that would one day become a generic term for a specific type of country music. This original group, which included Cleo Davis on guitar, Art Wooten on fiddle, and Amos Garin on bass,[24] was the first of many similar groups that would bear the bluegrass title. In 1939 Bill and his organization joined the Grand Ole Opry, and Bill is still with the show. Monroe's early band style was much like that of other string bands—for example, Mainer's Mountaineers —in that it featured much instrumention, particularly of the fiddle breakdown variety. On most of his recorded numbers the entire instrumentation was based on Bill Monroe himself. His expert mandolin style set the tempo and rhythm for the band and took most of the lead passages while his high tenor voice did the vocal solo parts and the harmony on the gospel numbers. The dominant personality in each song was always Monroe. The listener was always aware that, despite the particular instrumental style conveyed, Monroe was the main cog and all other musicians revolved around him.

In the years since 1939 the personnel of the Blue Grass Boys has changed often, and the list of individuals who played with Bill Monroe and then went on to found their own organizations reads like a Who's Who of Bluegrass Music: Lester Flatt, Earl Scruggs, Don Reno, Gordon Terry, Carter Stanley, Mac Wiseman, Jimmie Martin, and Sonny Osborne.[25] Until approximately 1945, however, the Monroe style, although distinctive, was not radically different from the

[22] RCA Victor has reissued some of the Monroe Brothers' tunes in *Early Bluegrass Music*, Camden 774.
[23] Interview with Ralph Rinzler, October 7, 1962.
[24] *Ibid.*
[25] Rinzler, "The Nashville Scene: The Roots of Bluegrass," *Hootenanny*, I, No. 2 (March, 1964), 55.

string bands of earlier decades,[26] so that a form of music known as "bluegrass" was not yet officially recognized. But after 1945 a radical addition was made to the band, and all the elements now commonly associated with bluegrass music became fully integrated into the band style.

Before 1945 one of the striking characteristics of Bill Monroe's unit had been the conspicuous absence of the five-string banjo—conspicuous in light of the later prominence of that instrument in bluegrass music. In the earliest recordings made by Bill Monroe's Blue Grass Boys there had been no banjo at all, and when that instrument was finally added in 1942 (played by David "Stringbean" Akeman), it played no prominent role but was used exclusively for rhythmic purposes.[27] The five-string banjo's neglect by Monroe's organization was paralleled by its general neglect in country music. The instrument that had been so popular in the twenties almost disappeared from records in the following decades and was maintained only by an occasional individual like Uncle Dave Macon or Grandpa Jones. With the advent of electric instruments in the forties the banjo fell into further disuse and came to be looked upon as a comedian's instrument, to be played by people like Bashful Brother Oswald of Roy Acuff's musical unit. The banjo suffered, in part, because no one had as yet demonstrated that its use in a band could be much more than as a background rhythm instrument, even though it had always been an effective solo instrument in the hands of such diverse stylists as Clarence Ashley, Buell Kazee, Uncle Dave Macon, Dock Boggs, Cousin Emmy, and Molly O'Day. Unlike the mandolin, the banjo seemed incapable of providing lead passages for a musical ensemble. But when Earl Scruggs joined Bill Monroe's Blue Grass Boys in 1945, he brought with him a sensational technique that rejuvenated the five-string banjo, made his own name preeminent among country and folk musicians, and established bluegrass music as a national phenomenon.

The Scruggs banjo technique, known as the three-finger, rolling, or Scruggs' style, is the modification or perfection of traditional banjo

[26] Examples of the early Bill Monroe style can be heard on *Father of Bluegrass Music*, Camden 719.
[27] George D. Hay, *A Story of the Grand Ole Opry*, pp. 61–62.

styles.[28] Scruggs had learned and perfected the technique in his native western North Carolina, where he drew upon the playing styles of local talent who played at county fairs, fiddlers' contests, and similar festivities. Western North Carolina, where the piedmont merges into the blue haze of the Appalachian Mountains, was a fertile ground for country music and a repository of traditional styles and songs. It was one of the few areas in the nation where the five-string banjo continued to be popular with rural musicians, many of whom played a three-finger style not far distant from the one Scruggs perfected.[29]

Scruggs was born in 1924 on a farm near Flint Hill, North Carolina (outside Shelby),[30] and began playing the banjo when he was scarcely large enough to hold it. Scruggs' father and older brothers also played the banjo in a style peculiar to their own section of North Carolina. With Earl they learned from such recording groups as Fisher Hendley and His Aristocratic Pigs, the Carolina Tar Heels, Snuffy Jenkins (also a North Carolinian), and the North Carolina Ramblers. The Ramblers were led by Charlie Poole, who played the banjo in a three-finger style. Outside the ranks of professional country groups, Rex Brooks and Smith Hamett (both North Carolinians) stand high as five-string banjoists who influenced the development of the Scruggs style. Hamett, a distant relative of Scruggs', was probably the most influential. During the thirties Hamett became locally famous by playing in music contests and festivals throughout the Carolinas, where he inspired many young Carolinians to adopt his three-finger style.[31] Earl Scruggs was one of these.

As is true with most styles, it is difficult to point out one individual as the originator, since a style is the product of evolution and adaptation. Earl Scruggs did not invent the three-finger style, but he perfected it and carried it to greater technical proficiency than anyone else. When he joined Bill Monroe in 1945 as a twenty-year-old instru-

[28] A technical description of the Scruggs style can be heard on Pete Seeger's *The Five String Banjo Instructor* (with instruction brochure), Folkways F18303.
[29] For examples of these styles listen to *American Banjo Scruggs Style*, Folkways FA2314.
[30] Interview with Earl Scruggs, Nashville, Tennessee, August 23, 1961.
[31] *Ibid.*; Ralph Rinzler, notes, *American Banjo Scruggs Style*, Folkways FA2314.

mentalist, after having played earlier in Nashville with Lost John Miller,[32] he had already developed the style that was to make him the most famous banjoist in the country. He joined a group that included Lester Flatt on guitar, Chubby Wise on fiddle, Cedric Rainwater on bass and, of course, Bill Monroe on mandolin. This was the "original" group that to most bluegrass partisans will always rank as the foremost practitioners of the bluegrass instrumental style, and in the years from 1945 to 1948 the modern bluegrass sound came into being.[33] According to bluegrass authority Pete Kuykendall, the first recorded numbers that possessed all the elements of the bluegrass style were "Will You Be Loving Another Man," featuring the lead singing of Lester Flatt, and "Blue Yodel No. 4" (an old Jimmie Rodgers number), recorded for Columbia on September 16, 1946.[34] Since the group had been performing on road shows for several months before these recordings, young musicians had already had ample time to be exposed to the developing style.[35]

In this three-year period the banjo took on greater prominence in the Bill Monroe band than ever before, and an ensemble style of music, much like jazz in the improvised solo work of the individual instruments, came into existence. Throughout the country, completely unnoticed by the more commercial world of country music, a veritable "bluegrass revolution" got underway as both fans and musicans became attracted to the music. Young musicians began copying the sounds they heard on Bill Monroe records: the mandolin, banjo, and fiddle bursts of Monroe, Scruggs, and Wise, the guitar runs of Lester Flatt, and the high, hard harmony singing of Flatt and Monroe or the Blue Grass Quartet (the name used by the group when they sang gospel numbers). The emerging interest was not restricted to southerners. In New York, Chicago, and other large cities, young people

[32] Dixie Deen, "Goodness Gracious, It's Good!" *Music City News*, IV, No. 4 (October, 1966), 19.

[33] Mike Seeger, notes, *Mountain Music Bluegrass Style*, Folkways 2318.

[34] Kuykendall, "Bill Monroe and His Bluegrass Boys," *Disc Collector*, No. 13 (n.d.), 19.

[35] The important sounds and styles of the "original" bluegrass band can be heard on a series of Columbia reissues: *Bill Monroe and His Bluegrass Boys*, Harmony 7290; *Bill Monroe's Best*, Harmony 7315; and *Original Bluegrass Sound*, Harmony 7338.

who were interested in what they termed "folk music" became attracted to the Scruggs picking style as they had not been to other forms of country music.

The bluegrass "sound" did not become a "style" until other musical organizations began using the instrumental and vocal techniques first heard on Bill Monroe records. Neil Rosenberg believes that the Stanley Brothers' recording of "Molly and Tenbrooks," released in September, 1948, is "the first direct evidence" that musicians were copying the sound of the "original" bluegrass band. The Stanley Brothers learned their version from a Bill Monroe concert and actually recorded the song before Monroe's record of the exciting race-horse song was released. In their recording the Stanley Brothers featured the banjo played in the same style as that of Scruggs and entrusted the vocal duties to the mandolin-playing and tenor-singing Pee Wee Lambert, in an obvious copy of Monroe's vocal performance.[36]

Ralph and Carter Stanley, after leaving the army and forming a band called the Clinch Mountain Boys, got a job in 1946 singing on a radio station in Norton, Virginia[37] and, during the same period, made several recordings for Rich-R-Tone,[38] a small company in Johnson City, Tennessee. Also performing on the Norton station at this time was another group which would one day be recognized as major bluegrass performers. The group was headed by Jim and Jesse McReynolds, who came from the coal mining region of Carfax, Virginia.[39] In this period from 1946 to 1948 both the Stanley and the McReynolds Brothers featured string-band styles that, though similar to bluegrass, were more evocative of such pre-World War II styles as that of Mainer's Mountaineers, who have influenced virtually all of the major bluegrass bands. The McReynolds band had no banjo and featured instead the expert mandolin playing of Jesse McReynolds. While the Stanley Brothers included the five basic bluegrass instruments, their instrumentation was "old-time" rather than "bluegrass," and Ralph Stanley played the five-string banjo in the claw-hammer, or two-

---

[36] Rosenberg, p. 146.

[37] Smith, p. 252.

[38] The Stanley Brothers' Rich-R-Tone recordings have been reissued on *The Stanley Brothers: Their Original Recordings*, Melodeon MLP 7322.

[39] Dixie Deen, " 'Diesel on My Tail'—Jim and Jesse," *Music City News*, IV, No. 11 (May, 1967), 6.

finger, style taught to him by his mother in Dickenson County, Virginia.[40]

In 1948 the Stanley Brothers moved to Station WCYB in Bristol, Virginia, and by September of that year, when "Molly and Tenbrooks" was recorded, Ralph Stanley had abandoned the clawhammer for the three-finger style and the Clinch Mountain Boys had made the transition from old-time to bluegrass music.[41] The derivation of Ralph Stanley's three-finger technique cannot be conclusively pinpointed; Stanley insists that he learned the style from Snuffy Jenkins, a popular North Carolina banjoist.[42] Regardless of the influence exerted by Jenkins, Ralph Stanley did not use the style until about three years after Earl Scruggs had introduced the form on Bill Monroe's Columbia records. Whether Stanley already knew the style and merely ignored it until Scruggs demonstrated its popularity or whether he is merely reluctant to admit the influence of a competitor may never be known. Stanley certainly had ample opportunity to witness Earl Scruggs in action, because Flatt and Scruggs, who had recently left Bill Monroe, also performed over WCYB in 1948.[43]

After Flatt and Scruggs left the Blue Grass Boys in 1948, they formed the Foggy Mountain Boys, which included Mac Wiseman, Jimmy Shoemate, and another alumnus from the Monroe band, bassplayer Cedric Rainwater. After working for about three weeks in Hickory, North Carolina, they moved in the spring of 1948 to WCYB where they remained for about a year.[44] The next two decades were to see Flatt and Scruggs become the best-known bluegrass group in the nation and the most widely traveled organization in the entire country-music field. When their first Mercury recordings were released in early 1949, they became the third recorded group to feature a sound closely approximating that of the Bill Monroe band of the 1945–1948 period. The bluegrass sound was now becoming a style.

While new bluegrass bands were appearing, Bill Monroe's own organization was undergoing extensive personnel changes, as it has con-

[40] Interview with Ralph Stanley, San Marcos, Texas, February 6, 1964.
[41] Rosenberg, pp. 145–146.
[42] Interview with Ralph Stanley, February 6, 1964.
[43] Rosenberg, p. 145.
[44] Deen, "Goodness Gracious, It's Good!", *Music City News*, IV, No. 4 (October, 1966), 19.

tinued to do down to the present time. Monroe's band has continued to be a training ground for bluegrass musicians, and the three-finger banjo style has remained a consistent feature of the Monroe instrumentation. When Earl Scruggs left the Blue Grass Boys, he was replaced for a short period by Don Reno, from South Carolina, who quickly adopted the Scruggs style—as banjoists everywhere were doing. By 1949 Reno had followed the earlier path of Scruggs and had formed, along with guitarist Red Smiley, a popular group known as Don Reno and Red Smiley and the Tennessee Cutups. Reno, who alternated his three-finger style with jazzy techniques borrowed from electric-lead and steel-guitar players, attracted almost as many adherents as Earl Scruggs.[45]

By 1953 the bluegrass style was well established, with at least ten groups on commercial record labels performing under that designation.[46] Bluegrass music was building up its own loyal and devoted following who would purchase its records and attend its concerts. Although a bluegrass record rarely reached the hit proportions of the more conventional country numbers,[47] it sold on a steady and consistent basis, and some bluegrass groups did fairly well in the jukebox market. For example, in the mid-fifties guitarist Mac Wiseman, performing with a group called the Country Boys, gained national attention recording both pop and country songs, many of which he had learned in his native Shenandoah Valley.[48] With a voice similar to that of Bill Monroe and a propensity for old-time songs such as "I Wonder How the Old Folks Are at Home" (a Carter Family tune) and "When the Roses Bloom Again" (from the Delmore Brothers' repertory), Wiseman's songs were played regularly on country shows along with those of the more commercial performers like Faron Young and Jim Reeves. Wiseman delved deeply into old-time country and gospel music for his repertory, and sometimes into vintage popular music, as in his recording of "Love Letters in the Sand." Regard-

[45] Pete Kuykendall, "Don Reno and Red Smiley and the Tennessee Cutups," *Disc Collector*, No. 17 (n.d.), 18–20; Smith, pp. 252–253.

[46] Mike Seeger, notes, *Mountain Music Bluegrass Style*, Folkways FA2318.

[47] In a tabulation of songs that attained a position on *Billboard's* Country Chart for the period May 15, 1948, through August 31, 1963, only nine bluegrass performances appeared (*The World of Country Music*, pp. 187–199).

[48] Linnell Gentry, *A History and Encyclopedia of Country, Western, and Gospel Music*, p. 346.

less of the source, Wiseman's recordings were always characterized
by the intense, hard-driving bluegrass style and distinguished by his
own dramatic guitar playing.[49] Wiseman at one time had played
guitar for Bill Monroe, and his career was similar to that of Jimmie
Martin, whose records also attracted considerable juke-box popularity
in the mid-fifties. Martin, who had been lead singer and guitarist for
Monroe in 1949, came out of a Sneedville, Tennessee, farm background to form a group called the Sunny Mountain Boys, which recorded a string of relatively successful numbers, many of them in the
novelty vein. His singing of "Sophronie," "Hit Parade of Love," and
"I Like to Hear Them Preach It," augmented by the high harmony of
mandolinist Paul Williams, stand as examples of authentic bluegrass
music with expert instrumentation (particularly the five-string banjo
work of J. D. Crowe).[50]

During the mid-fifties, while country music as a whole became more
commercialized and akin to pop music, bluegrass music proliferated
and moved strongly toward the performance of authentic and old-
time country music. Although many bluegrass bands vied for recognition by the American audience, none equaled the success of Flatt and
Scruggs. Flatt and Scruggs, with the Foggy Mountain Boys, took their
brand of music into areas long alien to country music and, more than
any one group, implanted bluegrass music in the national music consciousness. Recording first for Mercury and later for Columbia,[51] Earl
Scruggs, the one-time farm boy from Flint Hill, North Carolina, and
Lester Flatt, a former textile worker from Overton County, Tennessee,[52] popularized bluegrass music in small southern hamlets and in
metropolitan New York and from the stages of village schoolhouses
and Carnegie Hall alike.[53] They joined the Grand Ole Opry in 1955

---

[49] Representative albums demonstrating the Wiseman style are *Tis Sweet to
be Remembered* (Dot DLP3084) and *Great Folk Ballads* (Dot DLP25213).

[50] Jimmy Martin, "My Childhood," *Country Song Roundup*, XVII, No. 91
(December, 1965), 30. A representative Martin album is *Good and Country*,
Decca DL4016.

[51] A Lester Flatt and Earl Scruggs discography, which is naturally not complete, has been compiled by Pete Kuykendall (*Disc Collector*, No. 14 [n. d.],
37–44).

[52] Deen, "Goodness Gracious, It's Good!" *Music City News*, IV, No. 4 (October, 1966), 8.

[53] One of their most successful albums includes a series of songs recorded live

and, using that institution as their Saturday-night base of operations, they toured all over the southeastern United States and appeared in towns and villages—some of them too small for a post office—sponsored by the Martha White Mills of Nashville.[54] And as their popularity increased in the late fifties, their schedule of concert tours expanded to take in the entire United States from Boston's Jordan Hall to Los Angeles' Ash Grove.[55] The success gained by the Flatt and Scruggs organization was paralleled by the rise in prosperity experienced by the Martha White Flour Mills. Cohen T. Williams, president of the firm that advertised Hot Rize (a self-rising ingredient found in the flour and meal), stated unequivocally that "Flatt and Scruggs and the Grand Ole Opry built the Martha White Mills."[56]

Although it is doubtful whether Flatt and Scruggs, who feel that their repertory has broadened into the sphere of musical eclecticism,[57] now consider themselves to be part of the bluegrass movement, bluegrass devotees definitely believe that the songs recorded by the Foggy Mountain Boys during the late forties and early fifties were among the most exciting in the entire bluegrass genre. These early Flatt and Scruggs recordings were characterized by verve and originality,[58] with much of the instrumentation performed at breakneck speed and the vocals rendered in an old-fashioned, high, hard harmony by such singers as Everett Lilly and Curly Sechler. The group first gave notice of its distinctiveness with the recording of such instrumental numbers as "Foggy Mountain Breakdown" (currently known as "The Theme from Bonnie and Clyde") and "Pike County Break-

---

before a Carnegie Hall audience (*Flatt and Scruggs at Carnegie Hall*, Columbia CL2045).

[54] Their rural audience is deeply devoted, and exhibits its loyalty by inviting Flatt and Scruggs back again and again. For example, they have appeared in Sandy Ridge, North Carolina, on at least twenty occasions (Nat Hentoff, "Ballads, Banjos, and Bluegrass," *Hi Fi/Stereo Review* [May, 1963], 49).

[55] *Billboard Music Week* (December 18, 1961), 42.

[56] Don Walker, "Music Built Mills: Martha White Head," *CMA Close-Up* (February, 1963), 3.

[57] See the comments made by Mrs. Earl Scruggs in Dixie Deen, "The Woman Behind the Man," *Music City News*, III, No. 5 (November, 1965), 22–23.

[58] Representative albums showing the early Flatt and Scruggs fire and enthusiasm are *Lester Flatt and Earl Scruggs* (Mercury MG20542) and *Country Music* (Mercury MG20358).

down" and a few Earl Scruggs originals like "Earl's Breakdown,"
"Flint Hill Special," and "Randy Lynn Rag" (named after one of his
sons). Songs of this type were often used as themes or fill-in numbers
on country disc-jockey shows; in fact, they were quite often the only
bluegrass songs included on the country radio shows.

By the middle of the sixties the Flatt and Scruggs group had won
success and affluence and their band had evolved into a well-
coordinated, precision-like unit which, though almost flawless in its
musical execution, lacked the fire and enthusiasm exhibited on the
early Mercury recordings. Lester Flatt now characteristically pitches
his vocals much lower than on such early recordings as "Jimmie
Brown the Newsboy" and "Roll In My Sweet Baby's Arms," and, possibly as a reaction against the Bill Monroe sound, the mandolin has
been dropped from the Foggy Mountain Boys' instrumentation. In
place of the mandolin a dobro steel guitar, played by Buck Graves,
was added in 1955. Graves, known in his comedian's role as "Uncle
Josh," plays the dobro with a rapid picking technique similar to that
of Scruggs on the banjo and did much to widen the basis of Flatt and
Scruggs' popular appeal.[59] Buck Graves, fiddler Paul Warren (who
had earlier played with Johnny and Jack), bassist Jake Tulloch
("Cousin Jake"), and Flatt and Scruggs exhibit an effortless stage
presence and collective musical interaction that is a delight to watch.

Perhaps the outstanding feature of Flatt and Scruggs' popularity
(and of bluegrass music as a whole) is the interest and enthusiasm
shown by people outside the usual country-music audience. People
who had never evinced the slightest interest in commercial country
music before, and who in fact would have dismissed it as a crass and
pseudo form of rural music, were now attracted to the bluegrass style
and described it in superlatives. Greenwich Village and Washington
Square habituees, college students in institutions like Fordham, New
York University, Vanderbilt, and the University of Illinois,[60] and
people who considered themselves "folk-music" partisans delighted

[59] Paul Charon, "Know the Nashville Musicians," *Country Music Review*, I,
No. 6 (February, 1964), 33.

[60] At least one of Flatt and Scruggs' college concerts has been recorded
(*Flatt and Scruggs Recorded Live at Vanderbilt University*, Columbia CL2134).
For a listing of their northern and college-based concerts, see *Billboard Music
Week* (November 10, 1962), 40.

in the bluegrass sound and tried eagerly to copy the Scruggs banjo technique. As the Flatt and Scruggs band roamed far and wide, everywhere Earl Scruggs' pre-eminence as a five-string banjoist was readily admitted. In 1959, Scruggs participated in the Newport (Rhode Island) Folk Festival and was the only country musician to be included.[61] Scruggs' performance at this and other functions evoked such interest that articles about his style and bluegrass music in general began to appear in the popular folk-music journals. In an article on the history of the five-string banjo *Compton's Encyclopedia* referred to Scruggs as a modern master of the instrument.[62] Scruggs' virtuosity is so impressive that some have compared his skill on the banjo to that of Paganini's on the violin.[63] By the early sixties, articles on Scruggs or the bluegrass style had appeared in such widely divergent magazines as *Time, Saturday Review,* entertainment periodicals like *Show* and *Show Business Illustrated, HiFi,* and even in sophisticated men's magazines such as *Playboy* and *Esquire.*[64]

The most significant of the above articles and one of the briefest was Alan Lomax's *Esquire* article, which possibly signaled the intellectual acceptance of bluegrass music. Lomax, who was one of the first American folklorists to recognize bluegrass as a vital form of our folk expression, gave country music the kind of breakthrough into intellectual respectability that it had always deserved. Many folk scholars and enthusiasts who otherwise would not have paid the slightest attention to bluegrass music were now compelled at least to tolerate it, since the well-known folklorist had given the musical-form his blessings. Referring to the music as "folk music with overdrive,"

---

[61] Scruggs' performances at the Newport Folk Festival can be heard on *Folk Festival at Newport,* Vol. 3, Vanguard VRS–9064.

[62] *Compton's Pictured Encyclopedia and Fact-Index,* II, 56.

[63] Robert Shelton, *The Country Music Story,* p. 140.

[64] "Pickin' Scruggs," *Time,* LXXVII, No. 27 (June 30, 1961), 53; Peter Welding, "Music From the Bluegrass Roots," *Saturday Review,* XLIV (June 10, 1961), 48; Bernard Asbell, "Simple Songs of Sex, Sin, and Salvation," *Show: The Magazine of the Performing Arts,* II, No. 2 (February, 1962), 88–91; Richard Warren Lewis, "Thar's Gold in Them Thar Hillibillies," *Show Business Illustrated,* II, No. 2 (February, 1962), 32–38; Hentoff, "Ballads, Banjos, and Bluegrass," *HiFi/Stereo Review,* (May, 1963), 48–52; Hentoff, "Folk, Folkum and the New Citybilly," *Playboy,* X, No. 6 (June, 1963), 95–98, 168–170; and Alan Lomax, "Bluegrass Background: Folk Music With Overdrive," *Esquire* (October, 1959), 103–109.

Lomax called bluegrass the "freshest sound" in American folk music. He was one of the first to recognize and call attention to bluegrass music's similarity to Dixieland jazz in its improvisation and lack of written arrangements. Either through lack of familiarity or in neglect of other country instrumental styles, such as honky-tonk and western swing, Lomax called bluegrass music "the first clear-cut orchestral form in five hundred years of Anglo-American music."[65]

Lomax's ground-breaking assertions about the bluegrass style were only a part of the growing body of academic discussion concerning the music. A review by D. K. Wilgus in a 1957 issue of the *Kentucky Folklore Record* was, perhaps, the beginning.[66] The remarks of Lomax and Wilgus were echoed and amplified in a variety of folk-music publications such as *Folkways, Caravan, Hootenanny,* and the *Little Sandy Review.*[67] Even the scholarly pages of the *Journal of American Folklore* and *Western Folklore,* in their record-review sections, regularly discussed albums released by such groups as Lester Flatt and Earl Scruggs, and the Stanley Brothers.[68] A further indication of bluegrass music's growing acceptance by the "folk music" coterie was the attention paid to it by the Folkways Recording Company. This company had always catered to a limited audience and for a long time had specialized in ethnic field recordings and performances by recognized city singers like Pete Seeger. In 1959, however, Folkways released an album entitled *Mountain Music: Bluegrass Style,*[69] which featured competent, but little-known, commercial bands from the southeastern United States. The notes to this album were written by Michael (Mike) Seeger, a member of the famous Seeger folk-music

[65] Lomax, "Bluegrass Background: Folk Music With Overdrive," *Esquire* (October, 1959), 108; see also Lomax's notes to Earl Taylor and His Stoney Mountain Boys, *Folk Songs from the Blue Grass,* United Artists UAL 3049.

[66] Cited in Rosenberg, p. 149.

[67] "Bluegrass: a Skeletal History and Survey," *Folkways,* No. 2 (n.d.), 22–24; Roger Lass, "Bluegrass," *Caravan: The Magazine of Folk Music,* No. 12 (August–September, 1958), 20–23; Ralph Rinzler, "The Roots of Bluegrass," *Hootenanny,* I, No. 2 (March, 1964), 54–55; *The Little Sandy Review,* No. 1 (n.d.), 31.

[68] For example, see the reviews written by D. K. Wilgus in *Journal of American Folklore,* LXXV, No. 295 (January–March, 1962), 88; and LXXV, No. 297 (July–September, 1962), 278–282; and those written by Ed Kahn in *Western Folklore,* XXII, No. 1 (January, 1963), 73–76; and XXII, No. 2 (April, 1963), 149–151.

[69] Folkways FA2318.

family and one of the most accomplished musicians among the urban folk fanciers. Seeger's interest in bluegrass music was another example of the appeal that the country style exerted upon the urban folk enthusiast. His research was similar to that of another young northern urbanite, Ralph Rinzler, who came out of a well-to-do New York family and college background to devote most of his life to the study and performance of old-time country and bluegrass music. An expert mandolinist who played for a time with a city bluegrass group called the Greenbriar Boys, Rinzler devoted considerable study to the work and career of his long-time idol, Bill Monroe.[70] Rinzler's study of Monroe described that individual's formative role in the development of bluegrass and provided an important corrective to those who, overcome with Earl Scruggs' instrumental proficiency, had exaggerated his role and unwittingly neglected Bill Monroe.

The number of bluegrass bands in both cities and hamlets has increased to uncountable proportions, and the word "bluegrass," originally applied to a specific style of music, has come increasingly and falsely to be applied to any kind of old-time country music that suggests the pre-electric instrumental style.[71] For example, Grandpa Jones, Stringbean (David Akeman), and the Louvin Brothers are sometimes labeled "bluegrass," although they regularly use electric guitars and play the banjo in the pre-Scruggs style.

Bluegrass music appeals to a diverse group of American listeners. Not only does it attract the basic rural audience, but as has been seen, it also appeals to many members of the "college set" and to urban intellectuals because of its expert instrumentation and use of traditional material. Bluegrass music even appears to be making some inroads into that broad middleground between the hillbilly audience and the cultural sophisticates, a middleground occupied by the middle-class listener whose only acquaintance with any kind of music is what he sees and hears on television. In 1962 CBS Television inaugurated a highly successful comedy series called "The Beverly Hillbillies" with the theme music provided by Lester Flatt and Earl Scruggs. The theme number, entitled "The Ballad of Jed Clampett,"

[70] See Rinzler's notes to *The Greenbriar Boys,* Vanguard VRS-9104.

[71] In his notes to *Mountain Music: Bluegrass Style"* (Folkways FA2318), Mike Seeger included a list of performers that contained some names, such as Don Gibson and the Blue Sky Boys, that have only the remotest relationship to bluegrass music.

recorded on a Columbia label, proved to be one of Flatt and Scruggs' most successful numbers.[72] The popular series, if not overly advantageous to bluegrass music, at least placed the name of Flatt and Scruggs before the public.

The "college set" may very well be the most enthusiastic audience that bluegrass music has had. Profiting from an over-all interest in folk music exhibited on college campuses, the bluegrass style is attractive as much for its use of traditional songs as for the use of the three-finger banjo technique. The bluegrass bands in the formative years of the style had moved without any outside pressures toward the inclusion of old-time songs in their repertories. Fiddle and banjo breakdowns—"Shady Grove," "Old Joe Clark," "Pig in a Pen," "Cumberland Gap"—were standard numbers in the bluegrass repertory. Bluegrass singers also placed great reliance upon sentimental melodies of an earlier era, such as "Maple on the Hill" and "I'll Be All Smiles Tonight." Occasionally a recorded version of an old ballad or event song like "White House Blues" (about McKinley's assassination) or "Story of the Lawson Family" (the tragic account of the murder of a North Carolina family in 1929) would appear. New event songs also appeared with regularity: for example, "The Springhill Disaster" (the Nova Scotia mine disaster of 1958), "Kentucky School Bus" (the crash that took the lives of several school children in 1957), and "The Flood" (the disaster that raged through Kentucky, Virginia, and Tennessee in 1957).[73]

Gospel songs from the evangelical and fundamentalist tradition also figured prominently in the bluegrass upsurge. Some of them, like "Angel Band," dated back to the shape-note tradition of the nineteenth century. Many of them, such as "I'll Fly Away" and "Where the Soul of Man Never Dies," came from the singing schools of the twentieth century. And a considerable portion came from the pens of modern songwriters, many of them the bluegrass musicians them-

---

[72] "The Ballad of Jed Clampett," Columbia 42606, is the only bluegrass tune ever to reach the number one position on the country popularity charts (*The World of Country Music*, p. 199).

[73] "The Springhill Disaster" was recorded by Bill Clifton in *The Bluegrass Sound of Bill Clifton*, Starday SLP159. "Kentucky School Bus" was recorded by Hobo Jack Adkins on Starday 363 and also by the Stanley Brothers with a different melody and under a different name, "No School Bus in Heaven," on Mercury MG71302. "The Flood" was also a Stanley Brothers' recording, found on *Country Pickin' and Singin'*, Mercury MG20349.

selves. Gospel songs had always been included in the material of every type of country singer, but more than any other group the bluegrass musicians seemed to be keeping the tradition alive. Two of the most important groups, the Stanley Brothers and Reno and Smiley, released almost as many sacred albums[74] as they did any other kind, and some bluegrass bands, such as Carl Story and the Rambling Mountaineers, Red Ellis and the Huron Valley Boys, and the Lewis Family, performed nothing but gospel music.[75] Evidently there still was an audience in the United States—small but loyal—that demanded the old-time gospel songs in the country style.

In reaching back into the past for songs—both gospel and secular —the bluegrass performers relied heavily upon early commercial hillbilly entertainers. The chief debt, perhaps, was owed to the Carter Family. One of Flatt and Scruggs' most successful early numbers was a Carter standard, "Jimmie Brown the Newsboy," and one of Mac Wiseman's best numbers was an old Carter favorite entitled "I Wonder How the Old Folks Are at Home" ("Homestead on the Farm"). At least two "memorial" albums by bluegrass entertainers (Flatt and Scruggs, and Bill Clifton) have been released in tribute to the Carter Family.[76] The Carter Family legacy, however, has been exerted primarily in the contribution of song material, not in the transmission of vocal or instrumental styles. Bluegrass performances, even when concerned with Carter Family songs, are radically different from those of the Carter Family. In contrast to the Carters' music, the guitar in bluegrass is seldom featured as a lead instrument;[77] the vocal harmony is higher pitched; and the tempos are considerably increased to accommodate the fiddle, mandolin, and banjo.

One of bluegrass music's chief contributions to country music has

[74] These include, for the Stanley Brothers, *Good Old Camp Meeting Songs* (King 805), *For the Good People* (King 698), *Old Time Camp Meeting* (King 750); and for Reno and Smiley, *Sacred Songs* (King 656) and *Sacred Songs*, (King 550).

[75] All of these groups record for Starday Records, and are among the most prolific of the bluegrass groups in their number of recorded albums. Record listings are available from Starday Records, Madison, Tennessee.

[76] Flatt and Scruggs, *Songs of the Famous Carter Family*, Columbia CL1664; Bill Clifton, *Carter Family Memorial Album*, Starday SLP146.

[77] Chief exception, however, is the stellar guitar instrumentation of Earl Scruggs heard most commonly on gospel recordings. For example, "God Loves His Children," on *Country Music*, Mercury MG20358.

been its maintenance or resurrection of old-time country styles, songs, and instruments. This contribution came in the period when country music as a whole seemed headed toward greater commercialization and amalgamation with popular music forms. Bluegrass resurrected the five-string banjo and dobro steel guitar and featured the fiddle when other country styles seemed to be abandoning it. The bluegrass bands have demonstrated that instrumental effectiveness is not limited by the absence of electric amplification, and they have revealed that the old rural high harmony is still very much a part of the southern musical style. The bluegrass groups have resurrected many of the old-time songs (either "antiques" or "evergreens"[78] depending on one's point of view) which the older people could recall with nostalgia and the young folks could view with novel interest as relics of a bygone era.

No one can prophesy with certitude the future course that bluegrass music will take, but at present it seems to have solidly insinuated itself into the nation's musical fabric and has won legions of followers abroad. Although the flurry of national excitement has died down from the high peak of the early sixties, scores of bluegrass bands, amateur and professional, still appear everywhere in the United States. The institutionalization of bluegrass music in American life has been evidenced in several ways: by the presence of four bluegrass bands on the Grand Ole Opry's permanent roster; by the appearance of journals, such as *Bluegrass Unlimited*,[79] which are specifically devoted to the genre; and by the establishment of several annual bluegrass festivals. The most important of these festivals is held each year near Berryville, Virginia. The Berryville festival, produced and directed by Carlton Haney and Ralph Rinzler, was created primarily to pay tribute to Bill Monroe.[80] The growing musical and academic recognition accorded to Monroe is, in fact, the most encouraging development of the bluegrass phase of the mid-sixties. Largely through the influence of Ralph Rinzler, who

[78] I first heard the terms used by Carter Stanley, of the Stanley Brothers, in San Marcos, Texas, February 6, 1964.

[79] *Bluegrass Unlimited* is a monthly publication (address: Box 1611, Wheaton, Maryland).

[80] Smith, "First Bluegrass Festival Honors Bill Monroe," *Sing Out*, XV, No. 6 (January, 1966), 65–69.

served for a time as his personal manager, Monroe has become a familiar participant at folk festivals and on college campuses.

Growing evidence suggests that bluegrass and other forms of country music are influencing each other. Bluegrass, after what seemed to be a brief flirtation with urban folk music, appears to be drifting back into the mainstream of country music as an increasing number of bluegrass entertainers, such as Jim and Jesse and the Osborne Brothers, record the same kind of songs as those associated with the honky-tonk singers. Some country singers long identified with other styles of music have recorded bluegrass albums: Joe and Rose Lee Maphis, Rose Maddox (a best-selling album with instrumentation provided by Bill Monroe and Don Reno and Red Smiley), George Jones and Melba Montgomery, and Porter Wagoner.[81] Within the bluegrass field itself a variety of styles prevail. The Barrier Brothers, Red Allen, the Lonesome Pine Fiddlers, the Lilly Brothers, and the master himself, Bill Monroe, continue to perform a style of bluegrass similar to that of the late forties. The Country Gentlemen (led by mandolinist John Duffy and guitarist Charlie Waller), perform in the Washington, D.C., area[82] and play in a supercharged style that surpasses in speed and intensity even the original bands of the Bill Monroe variety. The Country Gentlemen are characteristic of several very capable but little-known groups, such as Bill Harrell and the Virginians (Harrell now performs with Don Reno) and Earl Taylor and the Stoney Mountain Boys, who exaggerate the stereotyped features of the bluegrass style. Such groups might be termed "hyperbluegrass."[83] In other words, in their performances the tempos are just a little bit faster (often at breakneck speed), the guitar runs are more pronounced, the instrumentation is jazzier, and the harmony (such as that of John Duffy) is considerably higher. These groups often

[81] *Rose Lee and Joe Maphis,* Capitol T1778; *Rose Maddox Sings Bluegrass,* Capitol T1799; George Jones and Melba Montgomery, *Bluegrass Hootenanny,* United Artists UAL3352; and Porter Wagoner, *Bluegrass Story,* Victor LPM-2960.

[82] Biographical information on the Country Gentlemen can be found in the notes to their Folkways albums (Vol. 1, FA2409; and Vol. 2, FA2410). The Country Gentlemen can also be heard on *Bluegrass at Carnegie Hall,* Starday SLP174.

[83] For this term, and the idea behind it, the writer is indebted to Edward Mellon, mandolinist, bluegrass collector and authority, and chemist.

give a much more vital and enthusiastic sound to their performances than do the older, well-established organizations who have slowed down or mellowed with the passage of time and the increase in economic security.

Some of the bluegrass bands, including many of the hyperbluegrass organizations, play in a jazzy style that sometimes threatens to go beyond the bounds of country music. These include the Country Gentlemen and, before they formed competing units, Don Reno and Red Smiley and their Tennessee Cutups. Reno plays in a banjo style that is considerably more flexible and "progressive" than anyone else's. His repertory includes everything from gospel numbers and breakdowns like "Cotton Eyed Joe" to numbers like "The Bells of St. Marys" and "Washington and Lee Swing." Before parting company in 1964, Reno and Smiley recorded an extensive number of modern honky-tonk songs, original and otherwise.[84] Reno and Smiley were part of a growing company of bluegrass performers, including Jimmy Martin, Bobby and Sonny Osborne,[85] and Jim and Jesse McReynolds, who have performed recently composed songs of the tragic- and broken-love variety that are little different from their honky-tonk counterparts. Jim and Jesse McReynolds, whose fine duet harmonies resemble those of the Louvin Brothers and Blue Sky Boys, regularly carry musicians in their band who can play the electric guitar and drums as well as the conventional bluegrass instruments. When Jim and Jesse recorded an album of rock-and-roll songs written by Chuck Berry, they demonstrated what many observers often seem to forget, that no musical style remains pure very long.[86]

At the opposite pole from those who stress modern lyrics are the groups that rely heavily upon old-time music for their recorded repertory. In doing this, some of the groups reach far back into

---

[84] Reno and Smiley albums that include much honky-tonk and noncountry material are *Country Ballads* (King 621) and *Wanted* (King 718).

[85] Bob and Sonny Osborne, mandolinist and banjoist respectively, are known for their instrumental virtuosity and high-harmony singing. Representative albums are *Country Pickin' and Hillside Singin'* (MGM 3734) and *Cuttin' Grass* (MGM 4149).

[86] Deen, " 'Diesel on My Tail'—Jim and Jesse," *Music City News*, IV, No. 11 (May, 1967), 10. The album of Chuck Berry songs is called *Berry Pickin'*, Epic LN-24176.

antiquity to record songs such as "Barbara Allen,"[87] that have long been part of the Anglo-American heritage. And, more often, the tradition-minded bluegrass bands have delved into the American songbag to record tunes from the pioneer period or from the early days of commercial hillbilly music. This is done not so much as a conscious historical effort (such as poring over the pages of folk-music compilations) to find interesting songs that people have seldom heard, but merely as a presentation of songs that had long been familiar in the performers' musical heritage. The songs are performed not as archaic novelties, but as living documents that express prevalent and deeply ingrained ideas and mores. Many of the older performers, like Bill Monroe, Flatt and Scruggs, Hylo Brown, the Lilly Brothers, and the Stanley Brothers, perform songs learned during their childhood from relatives or neighbors at church services or at various social functions. Or they garner their songs from commercial and noncommercial sources, often forgotten, as they grew to manhood.

Of the tradition-minded bluegrass groups none had a wider-ranging, more old-time-based repertory than Virginia's Stanley Brothers. Born in Dickenson County near the Clinch Mountain area that also spawned the Carter Family,[88] Ralph and Carter Stanley achieved a reputation for having the most "old-timey" sound of any bluegrass organization. Carter Stanley was probably the finest lead singer in the bluegrass field and a collector of merit who revised and introduced some of the classic songs in the bluegrass genre, such as "Man of Constant Sorrow" and "Little Glass of Wine," that have become widely known among urban folk fanciers. Carter Stanley's death on December 1, 1966, saddened both those who knew him as an intelligent and humane gentleman and those who cherished and wished to perpetuate traditional country music.[89]

[87] Fine recordings of "Barbara Allen" have been made by the Lilly Brothers on *Folk Songs from the Southern Monutains*, Folkways FA2433; by Mac Wiseman on *Great Folk Ballads*, Dot DLP25213; and by Hylo Brown on *Bluegrass Goes to College*, Starday SLP204.

[88] Interview with the Stanley Brothers, San Marcos, Texas, February 6, 1964. The Stanley Brothers have one of the most active and professional fan clubs in the country-music field (details are available from Fay McGinnis, 1156 21st St., Wyandotte, Michigan).

[89] See John Cohen, "Tribute to Carter Stanley," *Sing Out*, XVII, No. 1 (February–March, 1967), 1.

The exceptional five-string banjo technique of Ralph Stanley placed the group firmly in the modern category, but their high, mountain harmony (also performed by Ralph) and their employment of old-time songs evoked a strong pre-bluegrass image. The lonesome sound of Ralph Stanley's harmony, rendered in one of the most unmistakably rural voices in country music, created mental images of winding mountain streams, hidden Appalachian coves, and village churchyards.

The Stanley Brothers recorded, on occasion, everything from honky-tonk songs like "The Wild Side of Life," and George Jones' "Window Up Above"[90] to at least one rock-and-roll number, "Finger Popping Time."[91] Their forte, however, were songs like "Little Birdie" (performed by Ralph in the pre-Scruggs banjo style), "Pretty Polly," "Little Maggie," gospel tunes like "Gathering Flowers for the Master's Bouquet," "No Letter in the Mail" (an old Monroe Brothers' favorite), and original arrangements that had the old-fashioned sound, such as "Little Glass of Wine."[92] The Stanley Brothers were an unusual group in that they were rarely heard on country disc-jockey shows or juke boxes; they were, however, quite popular and well known on college campuses, where they preferred to play.

Some of the younger performers depend on earlier commercial recordings for their repertory and quite consciously collect and listen to the vintage recordings of the twenties and thirties in their quest for material. Bill Clifton,[93] who sings in a relaxed and much lower-pitched style than most bluegrassers, leans heavily upon the Carter Family for his material. He has also relied, as have the Country Gentlemen, upon the recorded repertory of such groups as the Monroe Brothers, the Blue Sky Boys, Mainer's Mountaineers, and Charlie Poole and the North Carolina Ramblers. An even more striking example of the borrowing and conscious imitation of earlier commercial

---

[90] On *The Stanley Brothers Sing the Songs They Like Best*, King 772.

[91] On *The Stanleys in Person*, King 719.

[92] Two of the most valuable Stanley albums, in the traditional vein, are *Folk Concert* (King 834) and *Stanley Brothers* (Harmony HL7291).

[93] Clifton, who now resides in England, is also a successful businessman and entrepreneur of bluegrass music. His *Mountain Folk Songs*, Starday SLP111, is one of the finest bluegrass albums ever produced. Clifton also engineered the country-music segment of the Newport Folk Festival in 1963. See *Country Music and Bluegrass at Newport*, Vanguard VRS-9146.

groups is the case of the Greenbriar Boys. The Greenbriar Boys, originally composed of Ralph Rinzler, John Herald, and Bob Yellin, are a New York-based group who record for Vanguard and are among the very few northern urban groups to have gained any commercial success in performing in the bluegrass idiom.[94] Born and reared outside the southern rural environment, the Greenbriar Boys necessarily depend upon phonograph records for much of their musical guidance. As a result of their investigations of the old 78 rpm discs, they are authorities on early hillbilly music. Ralph Rinzler is the most notable of the group in this respect.

The recognition given to bluegrass music by college groups and folk enthusiasts has forced many organizations to perform the old-time songs when they might otherwise not have done so. The Flatt and Scruggs group is a case in point. Flatt and Scruggs, it is true, had recorded several old-time songs in their early career, but, after the college and folk interest set in, their recorded repertory took a dramatic shift toward the inclusion of old-fashioned material. They responded to the tastes of their new-found audience. They have recorded old-time country songs, but also some stereotyped songs long familiar to the urban folk enthusiast, such as "I Never Will Marry" and certain Woody Guthrie tunes like "This Land Is Your Land" and the mildly class-conscious "Hard Travelin'" and "Pastures of Plenty."[95] The Flatt and Scruggs group is now in the position of directing its country approach toward a basically city audience. However, the performances that Flatt and Scruggs have given at institutions like the University of Illinois are not necessarily the same that they would give at the Grand Ole Opry or in a small southern town like Sneedville, Tennessee. Ironically, in big city areas like New York Flatt and Scruggs, as well as other bluegrass organizations, may very well perform the more old-time rural numbers that the big city dwellers expect, and in the rural southern areas perform the slightly "citified" modern country songs emanating from Nashville.

The inclusion of old-time songs as a result of urban pressure is, of

[94] See Ralph Rinzler's notes to *The Greenbriar Boys*, Vanguard VRS-9104. For other examples of northern-based and collegiate bluegrass groups, see Shelton, *The Country Music Story*, p. 135.

[95] "Hard Travelin'" and "Pastures of Plenty" are heard on the Flatt and Scruggs' album *Hard Travelin'*, Columbia CL1951.

course, a healthy development for bluegrass music, but it is also evidence of a trend that might ultimately weaken the music's quasi-pure rural status. In an effort to satisfy the sophisticated urban audience the bluegrass bands might, as Flatt and Scruggs have done, record songs that were never native to the southern rural culture.[96] This would be an artificial process, and would be just as commercialized as anything the country-pop performers have done. It is true, however, that in recording "urban folksongs" the bluegrass groups might be dispensing songs that the country audience would accept if presented in a rural manner. But in recording the stereotyped urban folksongs as a result of urban pressure, the bluegrass groups thereby become less "folk" and move dangerously close to the "pop-folk" position occupied by such nonrural "folk" singing groups as the Tarriers and the Kingston Trio.

The enthusiastic reception given to bluegrass music by non-southern urban dwellers is only part of a general upsurge of interest in folk music throughout the United States. This enthusiasm, which approached the attention granted to rock-and-roll in the late fifties, has been termed the "urban folk revival."[97] The word "revival" is actually somewhat of a misnomer since the entire history of folk-music interest in the cities is a short one. Urban folk music dates back to the thirties when Library of Congress field-recording units and the Works Progress Administration stimulated an interest in America's grassroots music. At first the province of a dedicated and intelligent minority, mostly intellectuals and social workers who saw in the music an expression of social conscience,[98] folksinging gradually increased its audience as more and more capable performers joined its ranks. Burl Ives (who in many respects was the best of the group), Woody Guthrie, Huddie (Leadbelly) Ledbetter, Aunt Molly Jackson, Sarah Ogan Gunning, Josh White, Big Bill Broonzy, and others popularized the music on college campuses, in night clubs, and before union rallies. The depression-spawned interest was intensified during World War II when folksingings were used as anti-fascist

[96] Such as "New York Town," Columbia 42840 (also a Woody Guthrie creation).

[97] The writer does not know the origin of this phrase, but it is in common usage; for example, see Sandy Paton, "Folk and the Folk Arrival," *Folk Music*, I, No. 1 (1964), 14, 54–56.

[98] Bruno Nettl, *An Introduction to Folk Music in the United States*, p. 71.

rallies and in behalf of labor's organizational drives. The Almanac Singers were the prototypes of the groups who used folk music as a vehicle for social expression.[99] At the end of the war, "folk" music was still primarily a northern-based music with a limited following composed primarily of college students and intellectuals. And its overwhelming political bias, as is still true today, was to the left of the political spectrum.[100]

Urban folk music began to move out of its minority status in the late forties when groups like the Tarriers and Weavers placed songs like "Goodnight Irene" on the popular-music hit charts. Harry Belafonte continued the popularizing trend in the fifties by making the nation calypso-conscious.[101] Urban folk music was now becoming respectable and just another facet of America's popular music. Comfortable middle-class Americans without the slightest trace of social conscience could listen to the earthy ballads and feel that they were conforming to a national, and respectable, norm.

The tremors of interest in folk music in the late forties became a groundswell in the late fifties and early sixties. The intensification of interest, which saw the music assume the proportions of a national fad liked by young and old, was signaled by the success of a young singing group called the Kingston Trio. In 1958 the Kingston Trio (Dave Guard, Bob Shane, and Nick Reynolds) recorded a song called "Tom Dooley," an old North Carolina murder ballad,[102] which vaulted to the top position in the nation's popular hit charts. Following up this ballad with other very popular folksong offerings, the Trio became one of the biggest concert attractions in the United States. More than any other single recording, "Tom Dooley" set off the urban folk-music boom. In no time at all, a spate of Kingston Trio imitators bearing such names as the Brothers Four, the Cumberland Trio, the

[99] Woody Guthrie, *American Folksong*, pp. 5–6. A popular history of the urban folksinging movement is Oscar Brand, *The Ballad Mongers: Rise of the Modern Folk Song*.

[100] As one observer noted, "find a campus that breeds Freedom Riders, anti-Birch demonstrators, and anti-bomb societies, and you'll find a folk group" ("Hoots and Hollers on the Campus," *Newsweek*, LVIII, No. 22 [November 27, 1961], 84).

[101] Particularly through his best-selling album *Calypso*, RCA Victor LPM-1248.

[102] Capitol 4049. For the origin of the ballad see "The Legend of Tom Dula," *Caravan*, No. 15 (February–March, 1959), 44–47.

Chad Mitchell Trio, and the Wanderers Three appeared on record labels. The new groups, all quite young, directed their approach toward the college and high-school sets. The college folk interest at the beginning of the sixties differed from that generated during the depression and World War II years in that the modern folk movement was more inclusive and attracted a broad spectrum, including the fraternity and sorority groups, while the earlier movement had been identified with the more radical and intellectual segments of campus life. Although folksinging by the middle of the sixties had become deeply intertwined with the movements for peace and civil rights and had spawned an important body of protest material, such as that written by Malvina Reynolds, Phil Ochs, and Bob Dylan (in his early period),[103] the average folksong session (usually called a "hootenanny") attracted a wide assortment of Americans: the young and the old, the intellectual and the uneducated, the conservative and the liberal, and the poor and the prosperous. In short, nothing could be more "respectable" in the modern period than to be caught up in the folksong craze.

This folksong enthusiasm has been reflected in the appearance of a myriad of commercial folksinging groups, by the enormous increase in the sale of banjos and guitars, and by the appearance of a multitude of articles in popular magazines and ephemeral folksong publications explaining and extolling the folksong movement. The folksinging deluge came right on the heels of the rock-and-roll craze and can be explained partly as a fad which an amusement-hungry nation eagerly accepted. The urban folk phenomenon can also be interpreted, however, as a reaction against the noise and inanities of rock-and-roll and Tin Pan Alley popular music, and as a corresponding effort to find a simpler and more digestible musical expression. A highly complex and industrialized urban society, restless and ever changing, and beset by anxieties and nuclear fears, yearned to attach itself to something substantial and concrete. The folk movement, therefore, is partially an effort to find "roots" and regain the lost values of an earlier rural age.[104] The folksong, too, can be an escape mechanism much

[103] For examples of modern protest material see any issue of *Sing Out* or *Broadside*, the latter edited by Sis Cunningham in New York.

[104] Jacques Barzun noted that "we listen with more pleasure to the hillbilly in proportion as our urban life turns more and more into ferro-concrete" (*Music in American Life*, p. 91).

as the Western movie and television show are for the modern urban dweller. For displaced ruralites, folk music offers a halfway, or "respectable," means of regaining the old ways of life or tastes that they left behind when they moved to the city. They can accept "folk music" as a valid form of "culture," whereas hillbilly music, with which they had once been associated, connotes a "hayseed" background that they wish to forget. Most modern Americans long to be a part of the comfortable, status-seeking middle class, and an interest in folk music, as presently defined, has presented no obstacle. One can be interested in the rural past and yet not be a part of it. Whatever the source for the folkish enthusiasm, it has been a far-reaching one, and the appearance of folksinging groups, both amateur and professional, has shown few signs of diminishing. It seems that all one has to do to be a folksinger is to pick up a guitar or banjo, listen to a few Kingston Trio records, and begin singing.[105] Apparently one need not be a member of the folk.

As is true with country music, a variety of stylists exist within urban folk music. These range from such practitioners as John Jacob Niles and Richard Dyer-Bennett, who try to interpret the folksong as an art form, through popularizers like the Kingston Trio, Theodore Bikel, the Limeliters, and Peter, Paul and Mary to the "ethnic" group, including people like Jack Elliott (Elliott Adnopoz), Bob Dylan (Robert Zimmerman), and the New Lost City Ramblers, who try to "recreate" the sounds of the authentic folk. For the most part, the urban folksters have made little pretense to authenticity and merely attempt to present the songs as well as their talents will allow. The popularizers,[106] who have made up the bulk of the urban folksinging coterie,

[105] For an interesting view of the urban folk fad, and a criticism of its shallowness, see Robert Reisner, "Why I Detest Folk Music," *Folk Music*, I, No. 1 (1964), 6–7, 34.

[106] The popularization of urban folk music has inspired a prodigious number of articles, few of them scholarly. Among the best are Nat Hentoff, "Folk Finds a Voice," *The Reporter*, XXVI, No. 1 (January 4, 1962), 39–42; Hentoff, "The Rise of Folkum Music," *The Commonweal*, LXXV, No. 4 (October 20, 1961), 99–100; John McPhee, "Folk Singing," *Time*, LXXX, No. 21 (November 23, 1962), 54–60; "Hoots and Hollers on the Campus," *Newsweek*, LVIII, No. 22 (November 27, 1961), 84–85; and Alfred G. Aronowitz and Marshall Blonsky, "Peter, Paul and Mary," *The Saturday Evening Post* (May 30, 1964), 30–35. Among the several magazines devoted exclusively to folk music the best was *Hootenanny* (published bi-monthly in New York and edited by Robert Shelton).

devote little attention to folk scholarship and even less to folk styles. They are definitely popular singers using folk (or folk-sounding) material, and their styles of delivery, harmony, and stage patter are no different from those of their contemporary pop performers.[107] Their song material was learned, not from the folk, but from the urban folk-singers—the Weavers, Woody Guthrie, Pete Seeger, et al.—who had come before them.

A sizeable and increasingly important group, however, maintained that a performer should be true to his sources. The ethnic performers have endeavored to present a song without altering its melody or lyrics, and some of them have tried to re-create, exactly as they had heard them, the vocal and instrumental styles of the folk. This effort toward stylistic authenticity, the most insistent in urban folk music's brief history, brought country music the most recognition and scholarly acceptance it had ever received from the folk music world. Before the 1950's folklorists had scarcely given country music a second glance, except to dismiss it as something no better than commercial rubbish. Urban folksingers, too, seldom delved into the area of commercial country music to augment their repertory, and, when they did, the source was rarely acknowledged. Folksingers of an earlier period often relied on Library of Congress field recordings, the material disseminated among them by people like Woody Guthrie or Leadbelly, or the topical songs composed by themselves and their associates. Only occasionally—as in the case of Pete Seeger, whose banjo style was influenced by Uncle Dave Macon[108]—was the influence of a commercial hillbilly star admitted.

The modern ethnic performers, however, have readily identified their informants, and as a result, the pre-eminent position of commercial country music in American folk music has come to be recognized. In gathering their song material, the ethnic performers have done extensive research, both biographical and discographical, that the more reputable folk academicians had long neglected. There are

---

[107] This type of music has been termed "folkum" instead of folk by music critic Nat Hentoff, who claims that the term was first coined by the *Little Sandy Review* (Hentoff, "The Rise of Folkum Music," *The Commonweal*, LXXV, No. 4 [October 20, 1961], 99).

[108] Pete Seeger, notes to *Uncle Dave Macon*, RBF Records RF51.

many performers in the ethnic camp, but a few names predominate. Although Bob Dylan has moved through several stylistic worlds since the inception of his career and can now best be described as a poet rather than as a folksinger, he originally drew upon a diverse sampling of traditional sources. Jack Elliott has also relied on traditional material, and both he and Dylan leaned heavily upon Woody Guthrie as their mentor, as their styles will readily indicate; however, they also have drawn extensively upon various commercial country sources, including Jimmie Rodgers, Merle Travis, and a variety of Negro country-blues stylings.[109] The Greenbriar Boys learned their songs from early hillbilly recordings and presented them in the modern bluegrass style.[110]

Another group which has relied upon hillbilly records for their repertory, and in many ways the most distinctive of the urban folk performers, is the New Lost City Ramblers.[111] Composed of Mike Seeger, John Cohen, and Tom Paley (later replaced by Tracy Schwarz), the Ramblers have modeled their style and material after the hillbilly string bands of the twenties and thirties. They differ from almost all other urban groups, contemporary or early, in their use of the fiddle (played usually by Schwarz). In their performances they have achieved something that no other urban folk performers had ever attained or even tried before: they have come amazingly close to recreating the styles of a culture completely different from their own.[112] Their instrumentation sounds almost like a carbon-copy of the early hillbilly string-band styles. Their vocal styles, also intended to be as accurate as possible, do not fare quite as well; in many cases,

[109] Robert Shelton, "Bob Dylan," *Young Folk Song Book*, pp. 36–37; "Jack Elliott," *ibid.*, pp. 50–51. See also Shelton, "Joan Baez and Bob Dylan; the Voice Meets the Poet," *Hootenanny*, I, No. 2 (March, 1964), 10–11, 69–70; and the notes to *Bob Dylan*, Columbia CL1779.

[110] Alan Lomax, "The Greenbriar Boys," *Young Folk Song Book*, edited by Robert Shelton, et al., pp. 64–66. See also Ralph Rinzler's notes to *Greenbriar Boys*, Vanguard VRS-9104.

[111] Although Robert Shelton has written a short discussion of the Ramblers in the *Young Folk Song Book* (pp. 84–85), the best insights into the group's backgrounds and styles are in the notes to their various Folkways albums, particularly their first one, *The New Lost City Ramblers*, FA2396.

[112] See Billy Faier's review in *Caravan*, No. 15 (February–March, 1959), 32.

the New Lost City Ramblers give the impression of *trying* to sound country.[113]

Each member of the Ramblers' organization is capable of playing most of the hillbilly string instruments, but the most talented member of the group, and one of the more talented representatives of the entire urban folk-music world, is Mike Seeger.[114] Like the majority of urban performers, Seeger came from a nonfolk background (he is the son of a Harvard-trained musicologist, Charles Seeger), and is far removed indeed from the hillbilly culture of which he sings. Nevertheless, in his musical education Mike Seeger received a thorough indoctrination in the hillbilly style. Not only did his parents collect the Library of Congress field recordings (they were associated with the musical education phase of the New Deal's rural resettlement program), but unlike most scholars interested in folk music they collected also the early commercial hillbilly recordings. Almost from infancy, therefore, the young Seeger received a steady dosage of hillbilly music, which he supplemented through his own purchases and extensive research as he grew older.

During his military service in Baltimore, Seeger encountered bluegrass music for the first time and began playing in bluegrass bands throughout the Baltimore and Washington area.[115] As a result of this and his earlier training, he became interested in the older hillbilly styles and made them the all-consuming passion of his life. He mastered all of the hillbilly string instruments and, in fact, became one of the few individuals capable of picking melodies on the autoharp, an instrument usually reserved for rhythmic effect.[116] His absorption with early country music has made him one of the nation's leading authorities in that field and, because of his field-collecting forays in

[113] The Ramblers, however, never give the impression of singing down to the music or ridiculing it in any way. Their vocal styles are the reflections of deeply ingrained urban influences.

[114] In addition to the New Lost City Ramblers albums, Seeger has been featured on at least three albums of his own: *Mike Seeger*, Vanguard VRS-9150; *Old Time Country Music*, Folkways FA2325; and *Tipple, Loom, and Rail*, Folkways 5273.

[115] Jon Pankake, "Mike Seeger: The Style of Tradition," *Sing Out*, XIV, No. 3 (July, 1964), 9–10.

[116] For a discussion of the autoharp used as a melodic lead instrument see Pete Seeger, "The Autoharp Played Stoneman Style," *"Reprints From Sing Out*, IV, 58–59.

the southern region, led to the rediscovery of such important, but long forgotten, musicians as Eck Robertson and Dock Boggs.

Although Seeger's reputation as a singer, musician, collector, and historian is well recognized and deserved, some of his interpretive approaches toward country music can be questioned. He has recently given evidence of broadening his vision, but his devotion to the older styles has caused him to ignore most of the modern brands of country music, with the exception of bluegrass, and has therefore unwittingly created a false impression about the breadth, variety, and continuum of the country-music tradition. For example, his deep absorption with southeastern styles, and an almost romantic fixation on the southern mountains, has led to a virtual dismissal of the role played by southwestern musicians. Also, his glorification of bluegrass music to the exclusion of all other modern brands of country music (he has said some kind words about Buck Owens and Roger Miller)[117] downgrades the importance of such rural-oriented performers as Bob Wills and Hank Williams.

Aside from minor problems of interpretation, the historian can conclude only that Mike Seeger and such groups as the New Lost City Ramblers and the Greenbriar Boys have provided an immense service by broadening the concept of folk music and pointing out to interested urbanites the relatively untouched and neglected areas. It is clear that not only have these groups borrowed heavily from the country-music tradition, they have given back almost as much as they have borrowed. They have contributed to the increased national recognition and scholarly respectability accorded to country music and have actually influenced the song selections and stylings of some country musicians. Both the Stanley Brothers and Flatt and Scruggs have recorded songs which they learned from New Lost City Ramblers' albums.[118]

This kind of musical borrowing can be witnessed in the relations existing between other varieties of urban folk musicians and non-

[117] Mike Seeger, "A Contemporary Folk Esthetic," *Sing Out,* XVI, No. 1 (February–March, 1966), 59, 61.

[118] The Stanley Brothers' "Pretty Little Miss Out in The Garden," (on *Country Folk Music Concert,* King 864), was recorded earlier by the New Lost City Ramblers on *New Lost City Ramblers,* Folkways FA2491. Flatt and Scruggs' "Johnson Boys," (on *Folk Songs of Our Land,* Columbia CL-1830), was recorded earlier by the Ramblers on *New Lost City Ramblers,* Folkways FA2398.

bluegrass country performers. As urban folk music declined in popularity in the mid-sixties, it left its mark on country music just as rock-and-roll had done. The urban folk legacy, on the whole, was a beneficial one. It inspired many country performers to take a healthy look at their own folk heritage; it stimulated a cultural interchange between urban and country performers (as in Johnny Cash's recordings of Bob Dylan and Peter LaFarge tunes);[119] and it encouraged the creation of country songs which told stories and were folkish in theme. The creation of these songs is one of the strongest and most beneficial influences working to keep country music tied to its grand tradition of ballad-making and the event song.

Several country singers have shown evidence of an urban folk influence. Jimmy C. Newman, whose song selections had earlier run the gamut from honky-tonk tunes like "Cry, Cry Darling" to country-pop songs such as "A Fallen Star," delved into his Big Mamou, Louisiana, background and recorded several numbers, both singles and an album, from his Cajun heritage.[120] George Hamilton IV moved away from his earlier flirtations with rock-and-roll and country-pop to the performance of a number of folkish tunes like "Steel Rail Blues" and Johnny Hartford's "Gentle on My Mind" and in so doing found a style that was both commercial and well suited to his kind of delivery.[121] Another singer who like Hamilton often recorded urban-folk songs of the Bob Dylan and Gordon Lightfoot variety was Waylon Jennings. Jennings' eclectic approach has carried him into virtually every type of country music (he had once been the bass player for Buddy Holley's rock-and-roll unit), but in writing and recording such songs as "Julie" and "Anita, You're Dreaming," he presented the kind of story song, abounding in minor chords, which the urban folk audience delighted to hear.[122] Of all the country performers who have recorded this kind of material, Bobby Bare has been one of the most consistent

[119] Johnny Cash, *Bitter Tears*, Columbia CL-2248.

[120] Jimmy Newman, *Folk Songs of the Bayou*, Decca 4398, features the dobro and a Cajun-style fiddle.

[121] George Hamilton's folk-style songs can be heard on *Abilene* (Victor LPM-2778) and *Steel Rail Blues* (Victor LPM-3601).

[122] The Waylon Jennings' style can be heard on *Leavin' Town*, Victor LPM-3620.

and successful in the presentation of the story song.[123] He recorded many songs which earlier had been recorded by other country musicians, such as Hank Snow's "Miller's Cave," and Billy Grammer's "Detroit City," but in recording tunes like "Four Strong Winds," a song about Canadian migratory workers, he delved into the body of songs normally associated with urban folksingers. "Four Strong Winds," had been written and recorded by the Canadian team of Ian and Sylvia, and the song's popularity among country singers demonstrates the kind of mutual exchange that has occurred among country and urban artists. Ian Tyson and Sylvia Fricker (a husband and wife team) perform almost exclusively for sophisticated urban audiences, but many of their selections (for example, "Katie Dear," "Satisfied Mind")[124] reveal a knowledge of and a taste for country music. Both urban and country folk performers, therefore, seem to be giving increased indication of breaking down their mutual suspicions. With Johnny Cash becoming a common participant at prestigious folk festivals like the one at Newport,[125] and with singers like Buck Owens and Dave Dudley occasionally appearing at folk gatherings, at least some slight movement toward a merger of the two musical forms seems to be underway.

Despite the influence exerted by the New Lost City Ramblers and similar groups, the main catalyst that has worked to stimulate an interest in hillbilly music among urban folk fans was the issuance in 1952 of an important Folkways recording, *Anthology of American Folk Music*.[126] The *Anthology* is one of the most significant recordings ever issued in the field of folk music and, more than any one item, it introduced early country music to modern urban dwellers. Issued as six long-playing 33 1/3 rpm discs, the *Anthology* includes both white and Negro country selections recorded between 1927 and 1933, or from the advent of electrical recordings until the curtailment of field recordings during the depression. Taken from commercial re-

[123] Among the more folk-oriented albums by Bobby Bare are *Constant Sorrow* (Victor LPM-3395) and *500 Miles* (Victor LPM-2835).

[124] "Katie Dear" is on *Four Strong Winds*, Vanguard VRS-9133. "Satisfied Mind," is on *Play One More*, Vanguard VR5-9215.

[125] *Sing Out*, XV, No. 4 (September, 1965), 91.

[126] Folkways FA-2951, FA-2952, FA-2953 (hereinafter referred to as *Anthology*).

cordings drawn from the gigantic collection owned by Harry Smith, the *Anthology* was intended as an introduction to authentic country music of the days before the radio and phonograph had blurred regional distinctions.[127]

The *Anthology* introduced to urban folk enthusiasts such names as the Carter Family, Uncle Dave Macon, Buell Kazee, Dock Boggs, and Clarence Ashley. Marketed under the title of "folk music" and disseminated by the select Folkways Company, the *Anthology* has reached the ears of countless individuals who would have completely ignored it had it been dispensed under the title of "country" or "hillbilly" music. Songs from the *Anthology* have made their way into the repertories of urban performers,[128] who, with their appetites whetted by this initial introduction, resolved to learn more about songs and performers from the early hillbilly era.

Indicative of the new-found interest in hillbilly music is the case of Joan Baez,[129] the most respected of the modern singers of folksongs. Miss Baez is like the ethnics in her loyalty to her song sources, but she makes no effort to duplicate styles (except in her guitar work), and her vocal delivery, distinguished by her beautiful, clear soprano voice, is distinctively her own. She does not sound like a hillbilly or a member of the folk, but her clear and uncommercialized style has made her the biggest drawing card in urban "folk" music. Her uncommercialized style has, in fact, made her the most "commercial" of all folksingers. She draws upon a variety of both Negro and white sources for her song material, and her reliance upon recorded hillbilly music has been extensive. Her recordings of "Wagoner Lad," "Engine 143," and "Little Moses"[130] indicate that she either learned the songs from the *Anthology* or from someone who had access to the

---

[127] Notes (p. 2) to the *Anthology*, 2.

[128] The influence exerted by the *Anthology* upon urban folksingers has been discussed by Ed Kahn in "Folk Song Discography," *Western Folklore*, XXII, No. 1 (January, 1963), 74; and by Richard Rinzler in "The Friends of Old-Time Music," *The Little Sandy Review*, No. 28 (January–February, 1964), 38.

[129] Nat Hentoff, "Joan Baez," in *Young Folk Song Book*, edited by Robert Shelton, et al., pp. 18–19; Robert Shelton, "Joan Baez and Bob Dylan: The Voice Meets the Poet," *Hootenanny*, I, No. 2 (March, 1964), 10–11.

[130] "Wagoner Lad" (from the singing of Buell Kazee) and "Engine 143" (from the Carter Family) are heard on *Joan Baez*, Vol. II, Vanguard VRS-9094; "Little Moses" (from the Carter Family), on *Joan Baez*, Vol. I, Vanguard VRS-9078.

collection. Her recordings of "Wildwood Flower," "Gospel Ship," and "Little Darling, Pal of Mine,"[131] three Carter Family items, suggest that her interest in this early hillbilly group did not end with the *Anthology* selections; these songs were released by Columbia in a Carter Family album[132] well after the *Anthology's* issuance.

The awakened interest in early country music inspired by the *Anthology* generated a movement to reissue as many of the old recordings as possible. Although this movement has been largely stymied by the commercial recording companies who control the original masters, a number of important reissues have been placed on the market. Confronted with the conservatism of commercial recording companies, interested hillbilly fans and collectors have proceeded to issue long-play albums composed of old 78 rpm recordings originally released during the twenties and thirties. These recordings were taken from the private collections of hillbilly fans who had been painstakingly gathering them through the years. Among the more significant early reissues was an album containing selections by Gid Tanner and his Skillet Lickers, released by the Folk Song Society of Minnesota; and a Folkways album containing rare selections made by Uncle Dave Macon in the twenties.[133] Other than the individual items that sporadically reach the market, the two independent labels that have done most to reintroduce the old-time recordings to modern listeners are Old-Timey and County. Old-Timey, headed by Dave Strachwitz in California, and County, a company owned by David Freeman in New York,[134] have produced albums that include everything from string-band music to ballads and mountain gospel singing. These albums are important not only because of the recorded styles and songs conveyed but also because of the biographical and discographical notes that they contain. Historical

[131] These selections are heard respectively in *Joan Baez*, Vol. I, Vanguard VRS-9078; *Joan Baez in Concert*, Vanguard VRS-9112; and *Joan Baez*, Vol. II, Vanguard VRS-9094.

[132] *The Famous Carter Family*, Harmony HL7280.

[133] *Gid Tanner and His Skillet Lickers*, FSSMLP 15001-D (now out of print); *Uncle Dave Macon*, RBF Records album RF51.

[134] Information on records bearing the Old-Timey or County labels, and other hard-to-get items as well, is available from Disc Collector Publications, Box 169, Cheswold, Delaware 19936, and from County Sales, 311 East 37th St., New York, New York 10016.

scholarship on early country music has been significantly advanced by these recordings.

The movement of the commercial phonograph companies toward the reissuance of early recordings has been extremely cautious, but a slight but encouraging step has been taken in that direction. RCA Victor has been issuing albums by Jimmie Rodgers since 1949; but then, the Blue Yodeler's commercial appeal had never been doubted.[135] When RCA Victor introduced its Vintage Series, reissues of early country, race, and jazz recordings, it performed a valuable historical function. Among the more important of these collector's items is *Smoky Mountain Ballads* (LPV-507), which include songs by such people as Uncle Dave Macon, the Carter Family, and the Dixon Brothers; *Authentic Cowboys and their Western Folksongs* (LPV-522), which features such people as Carl Sprague, Jules Verne Allen, and Harry McClintock; and *The Railroad in Folksong* (LPV-532), a fascinating assemblage of talent which includes everybody from the well-known Vernon Dalhart and Jimmie Davis to the more obscure Rouse Brothers (whose classic "Orange Blossom Special" is far from obscure to country-music fans).

Before the introduction of the Vintage Series, Victor and Columbia had established cheaper subsidiary lines, called Camden and Harmony respectively, devoted to the reissuance of older recordings. For the most part these recordings were merely the more successful older songs of the big modern singers like Hank Snow and seldom went back more than ten years. In issuing an album of songs originally recorded in 1935 by the Carter Family,[136] the Harmony label definitely moved into the field of historical recording. In addition to the country fan, the urban folk devotee, whose appetite had been whetted by Folkways' *Anthology,* clamored for more recordings by the early country-music family. The Harmony album was soon followed by one from Camden (which had actually been released in Canada earlier than the Harmony album), then one from Decca, and still another from Harmony. Now that the demand was apparent, RCA Victor saw fit to release Carter Family tunes on the parent

[135] One source estimated that each of the Jimmie Rodgers LP's, in its first year of release, sold about 30,000 copies (Ren Grevatt, "Country Disk Acts Just Keep Selling," *Billboard Music Week* [October, 1961], 18).

[136] *The Famous Carter Family,* Harmony HL7280.

label.[137] Decca also gave some indications that it might be overcoming its reluctance to release the old material when it issued in 1966 an album of original Dave Macon recordings.[138] No one can as yet say whether the major commercial phonograph companies have been convinced of the financial feasibility of releasing the old-time recordings. The bluegrass craze has been responsible for the issuance of at least one set of old-time recordings by the Monroe Brothers, released in 1963 on the Camden label. One suspects that the desire for financial gain generated by the bluegrass boom rather than any regard for historical scholarship or folkloristic intentions inspired the issuance. The album was significantly titled *Early Bluegrass Music.*[139]

Among the smaller companies that have issued old recordings, King and Starday, both primarily country concerns, predominate. King, for example, has issued recordings by the Delmore Brothers, Carlisle Brothers, and Mainer's Mountaineers.[140] These recordings, however, date back no earlier than 1942 and do not include the real pioneer recordings of these groups (although the songs are the same as the originals). On the other hand, Starday, the company most instrumental in the dispensation of bluegrass music nationally,[141] moved in the early sixties, not toward the reissuance of old material, but toward the re-recording of old-time performers. Albums bearing the Starday label and featuring early, but still living, hillbilly entertainers like Ernest Stoneman, Arthur Smith, Lulu Belle and Scotty, Lew Childre, Sam and Kirk McGee, and the Crook Brothers have appeared from time to time.[142] Probably the most significant Starday

[137] *The Original and Great Carter Family,* Camden CAL586; *A Collection of Favorites by the Carter Family,* Decca DL4404; *Great Original Recordings by the Carter Family,* Harmony HL7300; *Mid the Green Fields of Virginia,* RCA Victor LPM-2772.

[138] *Uncle Dave Macon,* Decca 4760.

[139] Camden 774.

[140] These include the Delmore Brothers, *16 All-Time Favorites,* King KLP-589; Carlisle Brothers, *Fresh from the Country,* King 643; and Mainer's Mountaineers, *A Variety Album,* King 765, and *Good Ole Mountain Music,* King 666.

[141] Pete Welding, "Starday: The Bluegrass Label," *Sing Out,* XII, No. 3 (Summer, 1962), 63–65.

[142] *Ernest V. Stoneman and the Stoneman Family,* SLP200; *Fiddlin' Arthur Smith and the Dixie Liners,* SLP202; *Lulu Belle and Scotty—the Sweethearts of Country Music,* SLP206; *Old Time Get-Together with Lew Childre,* SLP153; *Opry Old Timers—Sam and Kirk McGee and the Crook Brothers,* SLP182.

old-time recording, and one of the most important released by any company, is an album composed of selections by the Blue Sky Boys. These songs, taken from radio transcriptions made in 1949, include old-time material performed in the same plaintive style that characterized the Blue Sky Boys recordings of the thirties.[143]

The biographical attention devoted to early hillbilly performers by the recording companies and by the independent groups who produced the reissues is part of at least a slight awakening by the general field of folk-music scholarship as to the importance of hillbilly music. Investigations by independently motivated hillbilly enthusiasts and by researchers working for Folkways have disclosed the existence of certain old-time performers long forgotten or presumed dead. Best of all, the old-timers are now being introduced to modern audiences via long-play albums and occasionally on the folk-concert circuit. Independent companies that have been instrumental in both finding and releasing songs by rediscovered entertainers include Bluebonnet, which has released albums by Bradley Kincaid and the Girls of the Golden West; Testament, which has released albums by Dorsey Dixon and Jimmie Tarlton; Kanawha, which has issued albums by Billy Cox and Clark Kessinger (a West Virginia fiddler); and Folk-Legacy, which distributed an important set of recordings by the Carolina Tar Heels.[144]

The major commercial labels were again rather slow in the rerecording of pioneer performers unless those entertainers had demonstrated an obvious and continuing commercial appeal. Two recordings, however, do merit special mention: The Blue Sky Boys'

---

[143] *The Blue Sky Boys—A Treasury of Rare Old Song Gems From the Past,* SLP205. RCA Victor has since released an even more important album of Blue Sky Boys' songs recorded in the thirties (*The Blue Sky Boys,* Camden 797).

[144] Bluebonnet, a company located in Fort Worth, Texas, has issued at least eight albums by Bradley Kincaid (BL 105, BL 107, BL 109, BL 112) and the Girls of the Golden West (BL 106, BL 108, BL 110, BL 113). Testament, a Chicago company, issued Dorsey Dixon songs on *Babies in the Mill,* (T-3301) and Jimmie Tarlton songs on *Steel Guitar Rag,* (T-3302). Kanawha, headed by Ken Davidson in Charleston, West Virginia, has issued one Billy Cox album (*The Dixie Songbird,* Kanawha 305), and two by Clark Kessinger (*The Legend of Clark Kessinger,* Kanawha 304; and *Sweet Bunch of Daisies,* Kanawha 306). Folk-Legacy, directed by Sandy Paton in Huntington, Vermont, isued the Carolina Tar Heels' recordings on *The Carolina Tar Heels* (FSA-24).

Capitol release, and the reunion of Sara and Maybelle Carter recorded on Columbia.[145] Both albums contained material previously unrecorded by those entertainers, but in both cases the vocal and instrumental approaches were identical to those used by the performers in their earlier recordings. Both Capitol and Columbia deserve commendation for producing two albums of tasteful simplicity, unencumbered by choruses, orchestras, and electric instruments.

Folkways continued to perform the valuable service for scholars and music lovers that it had rendered since the forties when it moved toward the re-recording of old-time country performers. Buell Kazee, the banjoist and balladeer who recorded for Brunswick in the twenties, was discovered in his native Kentucky, where he lived a quiet existence as a Baptist minister. His voice, as a soon-released Folkways album revealed,[146] was as rich and melodious as it had been in the twenties. Another very important discovery came when the indefatigable researcher, Mike Seeger, located five-string banjoist Dock Boggs in Virginia. Seeger subsequently engineered the recording of Boggs' Folkways albums.[147] Field investigations conducted by Ralph Rinzler and Eugene Earle revealed also that Clarence Ashley, another early five-string banjo player of note, still regularly performed the old songs along with his neighbors in East Tennessee. After recording two albums for Folkways[148] Ashley became a regular participant at folk festivals and, until his death in 1967, he enjoyed the resumption of a career that he had long thought was permanently ended. Ashley's two Folkways' albums had one very significant, and unexpected, side-effect: folk enthusiasts were introduced to another highly competent hillbilly performer, until then almost unknown. He is Arthel L. "Doc" Watson, one of Ashley's neighbors, and a blind guitarist, banjoist, and singer of distinction. Watson, who is a better instrumentalist than most of the well-known country-music performers, has become (along with his son Merle) one of the stellar attrac-

[145] *Presenting the Blue Sky Boys*, Capitol T-2483; *Historic Reunion*, Columbia CL-2561.

[146] *Buell Kazee Sings and Plays*, Folkways FS3810.

[147] *Dock Boggs*, Folkways FA2351 and Folkways FA5458.

[148] *Old Time Music at Clarence Ashley's*, Folkways FA 2355 and FA 2359. A tribute to Ashley and an announcement of his death was written by John Cohen for *Sing Out*, XVII, No. 4 (August–September, 1967), 30.

tions along the urban folk-concert circuit.[149] Folkways released also
an album by Ernest Stoneman,[150] an early hillbilly professional who
had ceased recording at the outset of the depression. His new recordings demonstrated that his style had changed little, although his
children, who played with him, have been strongly affected by the
bluegrass instrumental style. Stoneman's long career in country music
ended with his death in 1968.

In the decades before the fifties the folklorist's rejection of hillbilly music was as strong as the urban folksinger's refusal to perform the music (or at least his reluctance to admit that he might have
obtained a song from such a source). Folklorists combed the back-
country regions of the South collecting material from individuals who
had obviously learned their ballads and folksongs from hillbilly
records, but seldom was a remark made (except in a disparaging
sense) about the commercial hillbilly source. Scholars who sometimes wondered about the origin of a particularly quaint or interesting song they had "discovered" could have solved the riddle by
merely consulting the recorded repertories of people like Jimmie
Rodgers and the Carter Family. One suspects that the folklorists may
have rejected numerous hillbilly songs because those songs did not
conform to the scholars' esthetic standards or to the esthetic standards that the folk were "supposed" to have.

Although much more work needs to be done on this important
subject, Ed Kahn, in an excellent exploratory article in the *Journal
of American Folklore,* has pointed to the limited, but pioneering,
scholarship done by such folklorists and scholars as Herbert Halpert,
Guy B. Johnson, and Howard Odum on the relationship between traditional song and commercial recordings.[151] Alan Lomax has done
similar work. Although he has done little of a substantial scholarly
nature on commercial country music, as early as 1934 he and his
father had begun transcribing and publishing texts and tunes from
commercial records, many of which were included in *American*

[149] Watson has been recorded on several albums. These include *Doc Watson
and His Family* (FA 2366), *Jean and Doc at Folk City* (FA 2426), and, with
Flatt and Scruggs, *Strictly Instrumental* (CL-2643).

[150] *Stoneman Family,* Folkways FA2315.

[151] Kahn, "Hillbilly Music: Source and Resource," *Journal of American Folklore,* LXXVIII, No. 309 (July–September, 1965), 257–266.

Ballads and Folk Songs.[152] Not until 1947, however, did a discographic appendix appear in a standard folksong collection, *Folk Song, U.S.A.,*[153] edited by by Alan Lomax. Lomax had earlier recognized the importance of commercial recordings and in 1940 had issued what was intended to be merely an introductory guide to the subject. This was his *List of American Folk Songs on Commercial Records,*[154] which, of course, only skimmed the subject. In 1948, Charles Seeger reviewed in the *Journal of American Folklore*[155] a number of hillbilly and race recordings that had been released in previous years, marking the first time that the country's major scholarly folk publication had admitted the existence, or relevance, of commercial country music.

To intimate that the nation's folklore scholars have unanimously or enthusiastically accepted hillbilly music as a valid facet of folk culture would be, of course, a gross exaggeration. In fact, those who do recognize it, although a dedicated group, probably constitute a rather small (but growing) minority. Folklorists are divided, much as they always have been, between those who study the folksong as a form of art or as a piece of literature and those who view it in the anthropological sense as a living document that reflects the social and historical climate from which it emerged. The value of hillbilly music lies primarily in the latter category.[156]

No one has made a full-fledged attempt to ascertain the number of traditional songs found on commercial country records. Indeed, the

[152] John A. and Alan Lomax, *American Ballads and Folk Songs.* Archie Green has included a discussion of pioneer studies of folksong records in "A Discographic Appraisal of *American Balladry From British Broadsides: A Guide For Students and Collectors of Traditional Song,* by G. Malcolm Laws, Jr. (Philadelphia, American Folklore Society, 1957)" in *Caravan,* No. 15 (February–March, 1959), 7–13.

[153] John A. and Alan Lomax, *Folk Song: U.S.A.,* pp. 397–401.

[154] *List of American Folk Songs on Commercial Records* in Report of the Committee of the Conference on Inter-American Relations in the Field of Music, William Barrien, Chairman (Washington, D.C., Department of State, September, 1940).

[155] Charles Seeger, "Reviews," *Journal of American Folklore,* LXI, No. 240 (April–June, 1948), 215–218.

[156] See John Greenway, "Folk Songs as Socio-Historical Documents," *Western Folklore,* XIX (January, 1960), 1–9.

immensity of the task, if it were accomplished, almost staggers the imagination. Very limited approaches, however, have been made, as in the cases of Lomax and Ben Gray Lumpkin.[157] The most extensive attempt to date has been made by D. K. Wilgus, who wrote a master's thesis[158] on the subject in 1947, using his own extensive record collection for data. Wilgus in subsequent years has become perhaps the leading hillbilly-oriented folk scholar in America.[159] His *Anglo-American Folksong Scholarship Since 1898*, originally written as a doctoral dissertation, has been recognized as one of the most recent significant contributions to the field. Working first at Western Kentucky State College, where he edited the *Kentucky Folklore Record*,[160] and later as director of the Center for the Study of Comparative Folklore and Mythology at the University of California in Los Angeles, Wilgus gained a renown that, because of his interest, could work only to the advantage of hillbilly music.[161] *Anglo-American Folksong Scholarship* contained only a few references to hillbilly music, but its scholarly acceptance placed Wilgus in a position to promote the music through articles, record reviews, and scholarly papers. John Greenway, anthropologist and folklorist at the University of Colorado, made brief comments about a few hillbillies like Jimmie Rodgers, Merle Travis, and the Carter Family in his *American Folk Songs of Protest* (1953).[162] Greenway's *Journal of American Folklore* article on Jimmie Rodgers was the first article on hillbilly music to appear in a scholarly journal.[163] Wilgus and Greenway were

[157] Ben Gray Lumpkin, *Folksongs on Records*.

[158] Donald Knight Wilgus, "A Catalogue of American Folksongs on Commercial Records," unpublished master's thesis (Ohio State University, 1947).

[159] Wilgus is Record Review Editor of the *Journal of American Folklore*.

[160] For this journal, published by the Kentucky Folklore Society, Wilgus also compiled the discographical section, "On the Record," one of the first record-review sections to appear in a scholarly folk journal.

[161] In fact, in conjunction with the UCLA Committee on Fine Arts Production, Wilgus quickly created a Folk Music Festival that could vie with any in the United States. The Festival was prominent in its featuring of hillbilly talent. For example, in May, 1963, 12,000 people saw such performers as Clarence Ashley, Doc Watson, Maybelle Carter, and Bill Monroe (*Western Folklore*, XXII, No. 3 [July, 1963], 211).

[162] Greenway, *American Folksongs of Protest*, 7, 84, 100, 171–172, 205, 285.

[163] Greenway, "Jimmie Rodgers—A Folksong Catalyst," *Journal of American Folklore*, LXX, No. 277 (July–September, 1957), 231–235.

part of a small but growing fraternity that recognized country music's distinctive position within American folk music. The most impressive result of their intellectual labors thus far, and for the student the most important introduction to the scholarly study of country music, is the "Hillbilly Issue" of the *Journal of American Folklore* (LXXVIII, No. 309 (July–September, 1965). This landmark issue, specially edited by John Greenway and D. K. Wilgus, was devoted exclusively to country music. Norman Cohen contributed an article on the Skillet Lickers, and L. Mayne Smith presented what was probably the first scholarly introduction to bluegrass music. Ed Kahn, anthropologist and Executive Secretary of the John Edwards Memorial Foundation, wrote an instructive essay on the sources dealing with country music. The most significant article, however, and probably the most penetrating yet written on country music is Archie Green's "Hillbilly Music: Source and Symbol." Green, who is now Associate Professor of Labor and Industrial Relations at the University of Illinois, began as a student of labor and protest songs and his researches led him into an investigation of commercial hillbilly recordings. His studies have made him probably the most astute and knowledgeable critic of country music in the United States.

Many others, both within and on the periphery of academic scholarship, have contributed to a broader understanding of country music. Thurston Moore of Heather Publications in Denver, Colorado, has published four editions (1960, 1964, 1965, and 1966) of *The Country Music Who's Who*, a work designed as a tradebook but much more valuable because of its inclusion of historical data and rare photographs. In addition to the valuable contributions made by Moore, other work of both a scholarly and semischolarly nature has been done by the editors and contributors to the folksong magazines *Sing Out* and *The Little Sandy Review*;[164] by Robert Shelton, the folk-music editor of the *New York Times*; by Mike Seeger and John Cohen of the New Lost City Ramblers; by Ralph Rinzler, formerly of the Greenbriar Boys; by Judy McCulloh, of Urbana, Illinois; and by Neil Rosenberg and Richard Reuss, students at Indiana University. Regardless of his special area of interest, whether early string-

[164] *The Little Sandy Review*, circulated sporadically and sometimes not at all, is a high-quality little magazine of review, edited and published by Barry Hansen in Venice, California.

band styles or modern honky-tonk music, each of these scholars recognized that the music sprang from the folk, and in turn influenced the musical styles and repertory of the folk.

When scholars first made their hesitant entries into the field of country music, they found themselves seriously hampered by the lack of readily available source material. Many of the old-time performers had died, and few, if any, had left any kind of papers or memoirs. The recording companies had maintained few files on their performing personnel, and would disclose little information on the amount of record sales through the years. No reputable scholarly publication had considered country music worthy of attention. That the task of chronicling country music's significance and development has not been completely insurmountable is owed to a band of devoted hill-billy-music enthusiasts, unnoticed and unsung, who have been painstakingly gathering materials for decades. With little or no scholarly training, and with no motive other than a love for the music and a feeling that the older traditions should be preserved, these individuals labored indefatigably to compile both discographical and biographical data on country performers. A veritable network of hill-billy-record collectors,[165] not only in the United States but in countries such as England, Australia, Canada, and Japan, gathered the old records and songbooks and exchanged tapes and information with each other. People like Dave Wylie, Doug Jydstrup, Harlan Daniel, Gus Meade, Joe Hickerson, Peter Kuykendall, Joe Nicholas, Lou Deneumoustier, Eugene Earle, John Edwards, Bob Pinson, and Fred Hoeptner, who were in no sense trained folklorists, used their private funds and all the available time at their disposal to search through radio stations, record shops, and old junk stores for the out-of-print records of earlier years. They conducted the same kind of diligent, and often fruitless, search for information about the lives and careers of the old-time performers. Most of these collectors accumulated the early records indiscriminately, although some of them,

---

[165] Two of the most important outlets for record collectors were two mimeographed publications devoted to traditional country music, *Disc Collector* and *Country Directory*. Although they are no longer circulated, back issues can be obtained from their publisher, Lou Deneumoustier (Box 169, Cheswold, Delaware), who now publishes the *Disc Collector Newsletter*. Probably the best magazine currently devoted to hillbilly collecting is *Blue Yodeler*, published by Doug Jydstrup (P.O. Box 772, Minneapolis, Minnesota 55440).

like western-swing collectors Bob Pinson[166] and Fred Hoeptner, specialized in a particular area.

The most prolific hillbilly-record collector, and possibly the most informed, was John Edwards.[167] His collection, which numbered in the thousands (both disc and tapes), is all the more amazing because Edwards resided in Australia and never visited the United States. His collection, which initially included Australian issues of American hillbilly records, was expanded through the long-distance purchasing of discs and tapes from American collectors and other sources. His extensive information on the American performers was gained also through correspondence. Edwards' experience in collecting and disseminating information on American hillbilly performers was similar to that of his fellow collectors. With no recognized scholarly journals open to him, he relied upon magazines and periodicals devoted to country music[168]—usually obscure and ephemeral —for publication of his work. The independent research carried on by men like Edwards, oblivious of whether their work was academically respectable or not, laid the groundwork for full-scale scholarly treatment that might be made in the future. Edwards' own research was cut short on Christmas Eve in 1960 when he was killed at the age of twenty-eight in an automobile crash near Sydney, Australia. Death brought to an end a life-long labor to gain scholarly acceptance for hillbilly music. Along with American collector Eugene Earle, he had been planning a history of early American hillbilly music. The task will be completed by Earle, who was made the guardian of the entire Edwards hillbilly collection.[169]

---

[166] Bob Pinson, as one example of the country collectors, is a resident of Santa Clara, California. He has an enormous record collection, an almost exhaustive knowledge of country music, and a flair for research that would rival that of a professional historian.

[167] For John Edwards' biography and bibliography, see John Greenway, "John Edwards, 1932–1960," *Western Folklore*, XX, No. 2 (April, 1961), 109–111.

[168] A New Zealand publication, *Country and Western Spotlight*, edited by Garth Gibson, has issued a special edition which contains all of John Edwards' articles written for that magazine: Special John Edwards Memorial Edition, *Country and Western Spotlight* (September, 1962). Available only on special order from Garth Gibson, Kelso, No. 1 R. D. Heriot, Otago, South Island, New Zealand.

[169] Eugene W. Earle, "Tribute to John Edwards," *Disc Collector*, No. 19 (n. d.), 4–7.

An unexpected but positive result of the Edwards tragedy was the creation of an organization which will in time prove to be the greatest boon yet to the serious, scholarly study of country music: the John Edwards Memorial Foundation, conceived in 1960 and formally incorporated on July 19, 1962. The Foundation is directed by Eugene Earle, president; Archie Green, first vice president; Fred Hoeptner, second vice president; D. K. Wilgus, secretary; and Ed Kahn, treasurer and executive secretary. Its panel of advisers includes scholars, collectors, performers, and businessmen.

The purpose of the Foundation is to collect and catalogue every conceivable kind of material dealing with country music in order that students and scholars might effectively make use of it.[170] Beginning with John Edwards' own immense personal collection as a nucleus the John Edwards Memorial Foundation has gradually increased its holdings since 1960, largely through individual gifts. The Foundation, however, has always operated under the barest of budgets, and only through the tireless work, selfless devotion, and money of such people as Eugene Earle and Ed Kahn has the organization managed to survive and expand. Located at a very prestigious address, the Folklore and Mythology Center at the University of California in Los Angeles, the Foundation has at its command the best in academic personnel and resources. It needs only one thing to perform the kind of constructive research which country music has always needed: money. This all-important need has been partly met by grants from the Newport Folk Foundation, Wesley Rose of the Acuff-Rose publishing house and, most significantly, the Country Music Association.[171] If the affluent Country Music Association can be made to realize the pressing importance of this attempt to collect and preserve the historical record of early country music, then the John Edwards Memorial Foundation's greatest worry probably will be solved. As Robert Shelton has noted,[172] the CMA and JEMF should both realize that they complement each other, that their pro-

---

[170] *JEMF Newsletter,* I, Part 1 (October, 1965), 1. The *Newsletter* is edited by Norman Cohen and Ed Kahn and is published several times a year at irregular intervals.

[171] *JEMF Newsletter,* II, Part 2 (February, 1967), 20; Shelton, *The Country Music Story,* p. 228.

[172] Shelton, *The Country Music Story,* p. 229.

grams are not mutually exclusive, and that their actions can lead only to greater respect and recognition for country music.

The founding of two organizations, one devoted to commercial expansion and the other to scholarly research, symbolizes just how far country music has traveled from its early and simple beginnings. Emerging as the commercial offspring of a folk heritage, it has affected the development of that heritage, and has in turn produced songs and styles that have contributed to the growth of other folk traditions. In its earlier and less commercial days, it was given many designations: "old-time," "old-familiar," "mountain," and "hillbilly." As it increased in age and became more professional and lucrative, it acquired the more "respectable" term "country"; and, with the growing influence of southwestern-spawned rhythms and styles, the word "western" became a companion designation of synonymous meaning.

Country music has changed radically since the days of its commercial birth in the twenties, and the change, although partly directed by the musical entrepreneurs, has also been a product of the performers' improvisations and experimentations. And as the music's listening audience expanded into areas and generations unacquainted with the rural heritage, the performers changed, sometimes very slightly, to accommodate the tastes of the new audience. Country music has always been the reflector of the social milieu in which it was found. If it has taken on urban overtones, it is because the nation is rapidly becoming urbanized. The village hamlet or little mountain farm is only a short drive from the big city, or no farther away than a quick twist of the television or radio dial. Excessive commercialization, or the diminution of traditional styles in the interest of greater prestige or pecuniary gain, has of course been instrumental in altering country music. Let those who resent the influence of commercialization reflect on the fact that if it had not been for the work of radio stations and phonograph companies country music would never have been heard by most Americans. The effect that commercialization has had upon the purity of country music is one of the to-be-expected results of a system that stresses the distribution and sale of products at the highest possible profit.

For better or worse, a form of music divided into several styles and known by the general classification of "country" is very much a part of the nation's entertainment sector. Its growth and popularity give no signs of diminishing. Country music and its cultural cousin, urban folk music, are evidently bringing pleasure to millions of people all over the world. Aside from questions of folklore and the maintenance of traditional forms, the stimulation of happiness is the chief value that a music can possess. In a world beset with fears and anxieties, country music can play no greater role.

Summary and Epilogue

AS THE DECADE of the sixties ends, country music demonstrates no discernible evidence of disappearing from American life. In fact, despite the growing complexity and urbanization of modern America, the music almost daily increases in popularity. What then, in way of summation, can be said of such a viable phenomenon? What has been the true significance of its prior development, and what will be its future? An astute historian avoids predictions, but sometimes he can hazard an intelligent guess.

Country music—a musical form which can trace its lineage virtually to the beginning of American civilization—has had little more than forty years of commercial existence. Although some commercial outlets beckoned the individual performer before 1923, no recognized "industry" existed until performers like Fiddlin' John Carson, Vernon Dalhart, and Jimmie Rodgers demonstrated the economic potentialities of the music. In the decades since, this potential again and again has been realized. But if it were to be judged solely by its propensity for creating wealth, the music would have little value for the historian outside the province of business history. Country music is, or has been, much more than a business. It is a manner of viewing or reflecting life. To many people it has been a way of life itself. Regardless of how it may appear today, or of the gaudiness, pseudo sophistication, and commercialism of many of its performers, country music developed out of a folk tradition. And in each successive movement away from the folk culture toward the homogenizing, bland world of mass culture, country music has reflected the social and economic patterns of the people who created, disseminated, and digested it.

Any phenomenon that has experienced the longevity, the profitability, and the popularity of country music, and one that is so deeply involved with the social mores of a people, should require no defense of its historical and sociological importance. But as any of its devotees know, country music has not, until recently, been taken seriously either by historians or folklorists. There is scarcely any other musical form about which this can be said. Country music, like the jazz of an earlier era, is perhaps the only American musical style which is looked down upon because of the class connotations which it supposedly carries. In effect, it has been derided and dismissed because it is deemed to be "unrespectable," the province of musical illiterates whose natural habitat is the tavern. In a society such as ours, where one of the dominant trends of the last one hundred years has been the movement from the farm to the city, people have either romanticized the departed rural culture or have reacted against everything associated with it. Many people whose aspirations point them toward the chrome-plated, status-minded, suburban-dwelling middle class would like to forget (or have others forget) that they or their fathers ever walked behind a plow or pulled a cotton sack.

A scholarly investigation of opera, classical music, or jazz would provoke neither haughty contempt nor derision, because those musical forms are accepted as proper and respectable aspects of American culture. But none of them has attracted more adherents, nor gained more intense devotion, than country music, a musical form until recently considered unworthy of notice. Other musical styles are studied because they supposedly occupy higher positions in the American hierarchy of art or because they represent more accomplished musical disciplines. But the quality, or alleged nonquality, of country music has absolutely no relevance to its possible worth to a study of American culture or society. The mere fact that it touches the lives of so many millions and both reflects and shapes popular thought should be reason enough for its study. Let anyone who doubts the widespread appeal of country music venture into the South, or into those places where rural southerners have migrated. Everywhere he will encounter the omnipresent phenomenon. In thousands of homes, churches, cafes, taverns, auditoriums, dance halls, and radio stations, the music in its myriad forms still gives evidence of being the chief cultural staple of a large group of people who can neither understand nor accept any other form.

As the preceding chapters have attempted to show, country music sprang from diverse folk origins in the rural South. In the decades since 1923 it has changed as the South and the nation have changed. Successive changes have served to erase the old folk patterns and move country music toward a closer, and sometimes indistinguishable, amalgamation with popular music. Future investigations may reveal, however, that new folk traditions are being created within the commercial form.

The performers who made the initial recordings in the twenties were as authentic as any of those who performed for the Library of Congress field units in the thirties. In fact, in a few cases they were the same musicians. The earliest recorded repertory included a tremendous percentage of traditional songs, both American and British; perhaps of most importance, the songs were still performed in old-time styles relatively unaffected by commercial forces. The early performers not only recorded traditional songs, they also composed new ones which have found their way into folk tradition. The case of "Floyd Collins" can be multiplied many times. These early folk performers, who were yet commercial in that they hoped to make a few dollars, created songs and styles that have contributed heavily to both modern country music and the urban folk revival.

The history of country music since 1923 has been one of steady evolution toward commercialism and professionalism. But then, this evolution is equally apparent in sports, other art forms, and various facets of a once-informal American approach to entertainment. At first the commercial trend was imperceptible, but the phonograph, radio, sound motion pictures, television, and road shows all played their parts in obliterating regional distinctions, creating a relatively uniform brand of music, and moulding self-conscious commercial performers. The quest for profit, status, and prestige, which served to destroy the folk aura, was engineered not only by the entrepreneurs, but also, in large part, through the conscious efforts of the performers themselves. It is true that recording entrepreneurs emphasized the "star" system after 1940, but it is equally true that most country entertainers easily and enthusiastically succumbed to the lures of the "hit parade" and big-time show business. Thousands of young Americans have made the decision to become professional entertainers in the hope of emulating the success gained by such performers as Jimmie Rodgers, Eddy Arnold, and Hank Williams. Country music has been, for many people, a liberating force, an avenue that has taken them to the world of affluence and away from the culture of poverty and deadening labor that held their parents in bondage.

One factor contributing to the persistence of tradition within country music until World War II was the music's regional distinctiveness. It was confined largely to the South, and, as long as this was true, little pressure was exerted upon the performers to modify their styles. The performer and his audience had been subjected to similar cultural, social, economic, and religious influences. The performer, therefore, had little reason or incentive to change. And important for the maintenance of country music's purity was the fact that the musical entrepreneurs had little faith in the ability of the music to appeal to urban, middle-class listeners. Therefore, as long as they could see little profit to be gained, the promoters made no full-scale attempt to market the music on a national basis.

During the thirties, however, and despite the general neglect by the commercial world, country music became more widely distributed as it came under the influence of multiple factors. Professional techniques were introduced that have since become standard. Business concerns, such as Crazy Water Crystals, began using the music as an advertising medium on a national basis, and independent promoters became aware of the music's commercial possibilities. With the advent of the singing cowboy—exemplified by Gene Autry and Roy Rogers—the Hollywood movie industry exerted an influence that not only presented country music to a national audience but also helped to create a popular image that has remained with country music. Since the thirties the term "western" has become commonly associated with country music, and is evidenced today in the ostentatious, dude cowboy uniforms which most of the performers wear.

America's entry into World War II was the catalytic agent that made country music a national, and, later, an international phenomenon. Defense-work migrations and the Selective Service partially uprooted a static southern society and hammered at the southern shell of isolation. When the war ended, country music had infiltrated into every section of the nation, and trade publications such as *Billboard* had begun to take grudging notice. With the ending of wartime controls and the beginning of postwar prosperity, country music was ready for its greatest period of material advancement. It now had become a big business and was to experience its greatest commercial flowering in the fifties and sixties with the founding of the Country Music Association and the emergence of Nashville as a major recording center.

But what of the future of country music? Will the music survive, and if so, what forms will it take? At present, the country-music industry exhibits nothing but vigor and profitability. One need not worry about the industry; it is the music which is in danger of disappearing. It is altogether probable that for many years the term "country" will be affixed to a particular form of American music, but the designation itself will become meaningless. The meaning will vanish primarily because the "country" itself is disappearing. The statistics which tell of the vanishing family farm, the urbanization of the United States, and the amalgamation of American life also chronicle the disappearance of country music. In order to accommodate itself to an urbanized society and remain true to the interests of its listeners, country music must drastically change its forms. Country music will probably become known, as Ernest Tubb and publisher Wesley Rose have suggested,[1] by some name such as "Americana" or "American music." This change, though, will involve more than a switch in terminology.

The country music of the future will sound greatly unlike the "hillbilly" music of the twenties and thirties or the "country-western" music of recent decades. It is decidedly unrealistic to think otherwise. The elements that produced the rural sound are vanishing. No one will ever again sound like the performers of the early period. The factors that contributed to the vocal styles of performers such as the Carter Family or Blue Sky Boys were not synthetic commercial creations; these styles were the result of complex and deeply ingrained mores and behavior patterns bred by the southern rural environment. If one would preserve the rural musical styles, he must also preserve the culture that gave rise to them, a society characterized by cul-

---

[1] Interview with Ernest Tubb, Austin, Texas, March 24, 1962; interview with Wesley Rose, Nashville, Tennessee, August 28, 1961.

tural isolation, racism, poverty, ignorance, and religious fundamentalism. It is doubtful whether anyone would seriously suggest a return to such a society, despite the simplicity and sentimental attraction which such a society might hold.

If the older rural styles endure, it will be only because certain dedicated individuals make a conscious effort to preserve them. Instrumental styles can and will be imitated. Vocal styles can be imitated with less success, but there will doubtless be some individuals—like Mike Seeger and the New Lost City Ramblers—who will remain loyal to the older forms. But country music as a whole will develop in its own independent fashion, increasingly oblivious to any idea of tradition. As country music becomes a mammoth industry, it will act increasingly as big businesses invariably do: it will attempt to obtain larger profits by marketing a product that a host of consumers will buy. The product will become shinier and glossier; it may even completely alter its shape. The salesmen who market it—the entrepreneurs, the entertainers, and the disc jockeys—will continue to stress those techniques guaranteed to earn the most money. The performers, still for the most part southerners not far removed from rural backgrounds, will remain immersed in the characteristic American drive for respectability and success. In this urbanized middle-class quest there will be little room for a pure rural heritage. Every change, every modification, every surrender to the "popular" audience, and even the destruction of country music itself, will be rationalized under the general heading of "progress."

Whatever becomes of country music, one can hope that in our restless and complicated society some musical form will endure that will describe, in a simple and unaffected manner, the true, including even the unpleasant, aspects of American existence. Country music has played this role in the past, and should it abandon this responsibility there seems to be little else on the musical horizon to take its place (with the possible exception of urban folk music which has yet to prove that it is more than a transient phenomenon). Regardless of the shapes it may ultimately assume, country music can play a valuable function in American society if it maintains some kind of distinctiveness and remains close to the facts of life. If it fulfills this function, country music will remain as one of the naturalistic voices of American music.

BIBLIOGRAPHY

PRIMARY SOURCES

Unpublished Materials

INTERVIEWS

Roy Acuff, Nashville, Tennessee, August 26, 1961.
Mrs. Shelly Lee Alley, Houston, Texas, September 10, 1966.
Bill Anderson, Nashville, Tennessee, August 22, 1961.
Merle Shelton Attlesey, Dallas, Texas, September 7, 1963.
Bill Bolick, Greensboro, North Carolina, August 24, 1965.
Jim Boyd, Dallas, Texas, April 20, 1962.
Roy Lee Brown, Fort Worth, Texas, May 24, 1963.
Bill Bruner, Meridian, Mississippi, August 24, 1966.
Homer (Bill) Callahan, Dallas, Texas, August 23, 1963.
Maybelle Carter, Nashville, Tennessee, August 26, 1961.
Paul Cohen, Nashville, Tennessee, August 29, 1961.
Carr P. Collins, Dallas, Texas, April 20, 1962.
Ted Daffan, Nashville, Tennessee, August 21, 1961.
James Denny, Nashville, Tennessee, August 25, 1961.
Bob Dunn, Houston, Texas, July 17, 1966.
Lester Flatt, Nashville, Tennessee, August 23, 1961.
Herald Goodman, Carrollton, Texas, December 29, 1967.
Martin Haerle, Nashville, Tennessee, August 23, 1961.
Tommy Hill, Nashville, Tennessee, August 23, 1961.
Harlan Howard, Nashville, Tennessee, August 23, 1961.
George Jones, Austin, Texas, August 16, 1962.
Ed Kahn, Austin, Texas, July 26, 1963.
Ed Kahn and Don Howard, Del Rio, Texas, July 18, 1963. Made available
    to the author by Kahn.
Charles Lamb, Nashville, Tennessee, August 28, 1961.
James McConnell, Nashville, Tennessee, August 28, 1961.
Elsie McWilliams, Meridian, Mississippi, August 24, 1966.
Lottie Mixon, York, Alabama, August 25, 1966.

Bill Monroe, Nashville, Tennessee, August 23, 1961.
Tom Perryman, Henderson, Texas, September 7, 1966.
Don Pierce, Nashville, Tennessee, August 23, 1961.
Bob Pinson, Dallas, Texas, August 23, 1963.
William Ernest Porter, Dallas, Texas, September 13, 1966.
Ray Price, Austin, Texas, March 2, 1962.
Mary Adams Reeves, De Berry, Texas, September 7, 1966.
Ralph Rinzler, Austin, Texas, October 7, 1962.
Pearl Rodgers, Meridian, Mississippi, August 23, 1966.
Wesley Rose, Nashville, Tennessee, August 28, 1961.
Earl Scruggs, Nashville, Tennessee, August 23, 1961.
Jake Smith, Meridian, Mississippi, August 23, 1966.
Carl Sprague, Bryan, Texas, August 4, 1963.
Carter and Ralph Stanley, San Marcos, Texas, February 6, 1964.
Harry Stone, Nashville, Tennessee, August 28, 1961.
Ernest Tubb, Austin, Texas, March 24, 1962.
Claudia Rigby Vick, Meridian, Mississippi, August 23, 1966.
Audrey (Mrs. Hank) Williams, Austin, Texas, July 2, 1962.
Nate Williamson, Meridian, Mississippi, August 23, 1966.

LETTERS

George C. Biggar, Laguna Hills, California, March 18, 1967.
Bill Bolick, Greensboro, North Carolina, July 31, 1963.
Joe D. Boyd, Willow Grove, Pennsylvania, April 24, 1967.
Milton Brown, letters and business transactions in the possession of Roy Lee Brown, Fort Worth, Texas.
Norm Cohen, Los Angeles, California, February 25, 1967.
Ronald C. Foreman, Jr., Champaign, Illinois, February 9, 1967.
Archie Green, Champaign, Illinois, February 6, 1967.
Ed Kahn, Los Angeles, California, February 1, 1967.
Brad McCuen to Norm Cohen, New York, March 2, 1967. Made Available to me by Cohen.
Elsie McWilliams, Meridian, Mississippi, April 4, 1962.
Guthrie T. Meade, College Park, Maryland, February 21, 1967.
Bob Pinson, Santa Clara, California, October 21, 1963; and September 4, 1966.
Dave Wylie, Wilmette, Illinois, March 24, 1967; and April 3, 1967.

MANUSCRIPTS

Archie Green, "Hear These Beautiful Sacred Selections," unpublished paper on gospel songs found on early commercial recordings.

Judith McCulloh, "Hillbilly Records and Tune Transcriptions," read at the April 10, 1965 meeting of the California Folklore Society at UCLA.

Richard Ruess, "Woody Guthrie as Folk Informant and Folk Composer," read at the 1966 Annual Meeting of The American Folklore Society.

Neil V. Rosenberg, "From Sound to Style: The Emergence of Bluegrass," read at the 1966 Annual Meeting of The American Folklore Society.

Published Material

RECORD CATALOGUES

Brunswick Record Catalog. Chicago: The Brunswick, Balke, Collendor Co., 1926 through 1928.

Catalog of Victor Records. Camden, New Jersey: Victor Talking Machine Co., 1925 through 1934.

Columbia Record Catalogue. New York: Columbia Phonograph Co., 1923 through 1941.

MAIL-ORDER CATALOGUES

Montgomery Ward. 1927 through 1943.

Sears Roebuck and Co., 1928 through 1946.

NEWSPAPERS AND NEWSWEEKLIES

Billboard: The International Music-Record Newsweekly. Published weekly by the Billboard Publishing Co., Cincinnati, Ohio. 1928 through 1964.

Austin *Statesman,* August 5, 1964.

Dallas *Times Herald,* April 22, 1962.

Fort Worth *Star Telegram,* November, 1922, to May, 1923; and April 18, 1936.

Houston *Post-Dispatch,* December 20, 1931, December 24, 1931, and January 1, 1932.

Memphis *Commercial Appeal,* February 7, 1953.

Memphis *Press-Scimitar,* May 5, 1939.

RECORD ALBUMS CITED

Folk Origins

Banjo Songs of the Southern Mountains, Riverside RLP12-610. Notes by John Greenway.

Folksongs of the Louisiana Acadians, Folk-Lyric LFS-A-4. Collected and edited by Harry Oster, 1956–1959, under the auspices of the Louisiana Folklore Society.

The Five String Banjo Instructor, Folkways F18303. Performed and edited by Pete Seeger.

Blue Ridge Mountain Music, Atlantic LP1347. Recorded in the field and edited by Alan Lomax.

Texas Folksongs, Tradition Records TLP 1029. Notes by Alan Lomax.

The Blues Roll On, Southern Folk Heritage Series, Atlantic 1352. Recorded by Alan Lomax.

Early Commercial Country Music: The 1920's

MISCELLANEOUS ANTHOLOGIES

Anthology of American Folk Music, Folkways FA2951-53. Notes by Harry Smith.

A Day in the Mountains, County 512. An album stressing country humor; performed by various string bands of the 1920's.

Authentic Cowboys and their Western Folksongs, RCA Victor Vintage, LPV-522. Notes by Fred Hoeptner.

The Country Blues, RBF Records RF1. Early Negro blues recordings; edited by Samuel Charters.

Mountain Blues, County 511. White country blues recorded in the 1920's by various string bands.

Mountain Sacred Songs, County 508. Various string bands.

Mountain Songs, County 504. Secular songs and ballads recorded by an assortment of old-time performers.

Old-Time Fiddle Classics, County 507. Various old-time string bands.

Old Time Southern Dance Music: String Bands, Vol. 1, Old Timey X-100; Vol. II, Old Timey X-101.

The Railroad in Folksong, RCA Victor Vintage LPV 532. An assortment of early artists with notes provided by Archie Green.

Really! The Country Blues, Origin Jazz 1. Early recording by Negro performers.

Rural Blues, RF-202. A collection of Negro blues recordings.

ARTISTS

Clarence Ashley
  Old-Time Music at Clarence Ashley's, Folkways FA2355. Notes by Ralph and Richard Rinzler.
Dock Boggs
  Dock Boggs, Folkways FA2351. Notes by Mike Seeger.
  Dock Boggs, Folkways FH5458. Notes by Mike Seeger.
Carter Family
  A Collection of Favorites by the Carter Family, Decca DL4404.
  Country Sounds of the Original Carter Family, Harmony HL7422.
  The Famous Carter Family, Harmony HL7280.

Great Original Recordings by the Carter Family, Harmony HL7300.

Historic Reunion, Columbia CL-2561. New recordings made by Sara and Maybelle Carter in 1966.

Mid the Green Fields of Virginia, RCA Victor LPM-2772.

The Original and Great Carter Family, Camden CAL586.

Carolina Tar Heels

The Carolina Tar Heels, Folk-Legacy FSA-24. Notes by Archie Green.

Lew Childre

Old Time Get-Together With Lew Childre, Starday SLP153.

Buell Kazee

Buell Kazee Sings and Plays, Folkways FS3810.

Clark Kessinger

The Legend of Clark Kessinger, Vol. 1, Kanawha K304; Vol. II, Kanawha K306.

Bradley Kincaid

Bradley Kincaid, Bluebonnet 105, 107, 109, and 112.

Sam and Kirk McGee

The McGee Brothers and Arthur Smith, Folkways FA2379.

Opry Old Timers, Starday SLP182.

Uncle Dave Macon

Uncle Dave Macon, Decca DL4760. Notes by Ralph Rinzler.

Uncle Dave Macon, RBF Records RF51.

New Lost City Ramblers

New Lost City Ramblers, Folkways FA2396. Modern performers who play and sing in the styles of the 20's.

Songs From the Depression, Folkways FH5264.

Charlie Poole and the North Carolina Ramblers

Charlie Poole and the North Carolina Ramblers, Vol. 1, County 505; Vol. 2, County 509.

Jimmie Rodgers

Country Music Hall of Fame, RCA Victor LPM-2531.

Jimmie the Kid, RCA Victor LPM-2213.

My Time Ain't Long, RCA Victor LPM-2865.

Never No Mo' Blues, RCA Victor LPM-1232.

Train Whistle Blues; the Legendary Jimmie Rodgers, RCA Victor LPM-1640. Notes by Jim Evans.

Mike Seeger

Mike Seeger, Vanguard VRS-9150. A sensitive modern interpreter of the styles of the twenties.

Old Time Country Music, Folkways FA2325.

Tipple, Loom, and Rail, Folkways 5273. Notes by Archie Green.

The Skillet Lickers
  Gid Tanner and His Skillet Lickers, produced by the Folksong Society
  of Minnesota, Minneapolis, Minnesota.
  The Skillet Lickers, County 506. Notes by Norm Cohen.
Arthur Smith
  Fiddlin' Arthur Smith and the Dixie Liners, Starday SLP202.
  The McGee Brothers and Arthur Smith, Folkways FA2379.
Ernest Stoneman
  Ernest V. Stoneman and the Stoneman Family, Starday SLP200.
Jimmie Tarlton
  Steel Guitar Rag, Testament-3302.

The 1930's

OLD-TIME

The Blue Sky Boys (Bill and Earl Bolick)
  The Blue Sky Boys—A Treasury of Rare Old Song Gems From the Past,
  Starday SLP205.
  The Blue Sky Boys, Camden CAL797. Notes by Archie Green.
  The Blue Sky Boys, Capitol T2483. Notes by Ed Kahn.
Cliff Carlisle
  Cliff Carlisle, Vol. I, Old-Timey OT-103; Vol. II, Old-Timey OT-104.
Carlisle Brothers
  Fresh From the Country, King 643.
Billy Cox
  The Dixie Songbird, Kanawha 305.
Dorsey Dixon
  Babies in the Mill, Testament T-3301.
Delmore Brothers
  16 All-Time Favorites, King KLP-589.
Girls of the Golden West (Dolly and Millie Good)
  Girls of the Golden West, Bluebonnet 106, 108, 110, 113.
Sarah Ogan Gunning
  Girl of Constant Sorrow, Folk-Legacy FSA-26. Notes by Archie Green.
Woody Guthrie
  Dust Bowl Ballads, Vol. 1, Victor P-27; Vol. 2, Victor P-28. Reissued by
  Folkways as *Talking Dust Bowl,* FA2011 (FP11).
  Talking Union, Folkways FA5285.
Mainer's Mountaineers
  Good Ole Mountain Music, King 666.
  J. E. Mainer and His Mountaineers, King 765.
  J. E. Mainer's Mountaineers, Old-Timey 106.

Monroe Brothers
  Early Bluegrass Music, Camden 774.
Montana Slim (Wilf Carter)
  By Request, Camden CAL 701.
  Reminiscin', Camden CAL 668.
  32 Wonderful Years, Camden CAL 787.
  Wilf Carter, Starday SLP300.
  Wilf Sings, Camden CAL 527.
New Lost City Ramblers
  Songs from the Depression, Folkways FA5264.
Myrtle Eleanor and Scott Wiseman (Lulu Belle and Scotty)
  Lulu Belle and Scotty—the Sweethearts of Country Music, Starday
  SLP206.

WESTERN SWING

Western Swing, Old-Timey OT-105. Includes a variety of groups such as
those of Bob Wills and Bill Boyd.
Leon McAuliffe
  Mister Western Swing, Starday SLP171.
Bob Wills and Tommy Duncan
  A Living Legend, Liberty LRP3182.
  Best of Bob Wills, Harmony 7304.
  Mr. Words and Mr. Music, Liberty LRP3194.
  Together Again, Liberty LRP3173.

1941–1953

Roy Acuff
  King of Country Music, Hickory LPM 109.
  Roy Acuff and His Smoky Mountain Boys, Capitol T1870.
  Songs of the Smoky Mountains, Columbia HL9004.
  That Glory Bound Train, Harmony 7294.
Eddy Arnold
  All-Time Favorites, RCA Victor LPM-1223.
Bailes Brothers
  Avenue of Prayer, Audio Lab AL-1511.
Wilma Lee and Stony Cooper
  Family Favorites, Hickory LPM H106.
  Sacred Songs, Harmony HL7233.
Lloyd "Cowboy" Copas
  Mr. Country Music, Starday 175.
Little Jimmy Dickens
  The Best of Little Jimmy Dickens, Harmony 7311.

Red Foley
  Golden Favorites, Decca 4107.
  I'm Bound for the Kingdom, Vocalion 3745.
Jack Guthrie
  Jack Guthrie and His Greatest Songs, Capitol T-2456.
Grandpa Jones
  Real Folk Songs, Monument 8021.
Pee Wee King and Redd Stewart
  Country Barn Dance, Camden 876.
  Pee Wee King and Redd Stewart, Starday 284.
Louvin Brothers
  The Family Who Prays, Capitol T1061.
  Tragic Songs of Life, Capitol T769.
  Tribute to the Delmore Brothers, Capitol T1449.
Rose Maddox
  Rose Maddox Sings Bluegrass, Capitol T1799.
  The One Rose, Capitol T132.
Molly O'Day
  The Unforgettable Molly O'Day, Harmony HL7299.
Jimmie Osborne
  Jimmie Osborne, Audio Lab AL-1527.
Webb Pierce
  Wondering Boy, Decca 8295.
Carl Smith
  Best of Carl Smith, Harmony 7310.
  Sunday Down South, Columbia CL-959.
Hank Snow
  Last Ride, Camden 782.
  Old and Great Songs, Camden 836.
  Singing Ranger, Camden 514.
Hank Thompson
  Brazos Valley Songs, Capitol T-418.
Floyd Tillman
  The Best of Floyd Tillman, Harmony 7316.
Merle Travis
  Back Home, Capitol T-891.
  Folk Songs from the Hills, Capitol AD 50. An earlier issue of *Back Home.*
Ernest Tubb
  The Ernest Tubb Story, Decca DX-159.

Kitty Wells
  Dust on the Bible, Decca 8858.
  The Kitty Wells Story, Decca DX-174.
Slim Whitman
  Love Song of the Waterfall, Imperial 9277.
Hank Williams
  I Saw the Light, MGM 3331.
  The Lonesome Sound of Hank Williams, MGM 23803.
  On Stage, MGM 3999.

Modern Country and Western Music—1953–1960's

MISCELLANEOUS ANTHOLOGIES

  Bright Lights and Honky Tonks, Starday SLP239.
  Diesel Smoke, Dangerous Curves, Starday SLP250.
  Steel Guitar Hall of Fame, Starday SLP233.

ARTISTS

Bobby Bare
  Constant Sorrow, Victor LPM-3385.
  500 Miles, Victor LPM-2835.
Carl and Pearl Butler
  Avenue of Prayer, Columbia CL 2640.
Johnny Cash
  Bitter Tears, Columbia CL-2248.
  Fabulous Johnny Cash, Columbia 1253.
  Ride This Train, Columbia 1464.
  Songs of Our Soil, Columbia 1339.
Patsy Cline
  The Patsy Cline Story, Decca DX-176.
Dick Curless
  Tombstone Every Mile, Tower T-5005.
Skeeter Davis (Mary Frances Penick)
  The Best of Skeeter Davis, Victor LPM-3374.
  I Forgot More, Camden 818.
Jimmy Day
  Golden Steel Guitar Hits, Phillips PHM-200-016.
Roy Drusky
  All Time Hits, Mercury 12283.
  Songs of the Cities, Mercury 20883.

Dave Dudley
Truck Drivin' Son-of-a-Gun, Mercury 21028.
Songs About the Working Man, Mercury 20899.
There's A Star Spangled Banner Waving Somewhere, Mercury 21057.
Buddy Emmons
Steel Guitar Jazz, Mercury 20843.
Don Gibson
The Best of Don Gibson, Victor LPM-3376.
Merle Haggard
Swinging Doors/Bottle Let Me Down, Capitol T-2585.
George Hamilton IV
Abilene, Victor LPM-2778.
Steel Rail Blues, Victor LPM-3601.
Hawkshaw Hawkins
Country Gentleman, Camden 931.
Johnny Horton
Johnny Horton Makes History, Columbia 1478.
David Houston
Almost Persuaded, Epic LN-24213.
Jan Howard
Evil on Your Mind, Decca 4793.
Stonewall Jackson
All's Fair in Love 'n' War, Columbia 2509.
Sadness in a Song, Columbia 1770.
Waylon Jennings
Leavin' Town, Victor LPM-3620.
Waylon Jennings, Victor LPM-3523.
George Jones
George Jones' Greatest Hits, Mercury 20621.
George Jones Sings the Hits of His Country Cousins, United Artists 3218.
My Favorites of Hank Williams, United Artists 3220.
—— and Melba Montgomery
Bluegrass Hootenanny, United Artists 3352.
What's In Our Heart, United Artists 3301.
Loretta Lynn
Before I'm Over You, Decca 4541.
Blue Kentucky Girl, Decca 4665.
Roger Miller
Golden Hits, Smash 27073.
Melba Montgomery and George Jones
Bluegrass Hootenanny, United Artists 3352.
What's In Our Heart, United Artists 3301.

Jimmy C. Newman
  Folk Songs of the Bayou, Decca 4398.
Willie Nelson
  Willie Nelson Sings His Own Songs, Victor LPM-3418.
Buck Owens
  Buck Owens, Capitol T-1489.
  Buck Owens on the Bandstand, Capitol T-1879.
  Carnegie Hall Concert, Capitol T-2556.
  Dust on Mother's Bible, Capitol T-2497.
  The Fabulous Country Music Sound of Buck Owens, Starday SLP172.
Ray Price
  Night Life, Columbia 1971.
  Ray Price's Greatest Hits, Columbia 1566.
  Ray Price Sings Heart Songs, Columbia 1015.
  Ray Price Sings San Antonio Rose, Columbia 1756.
  Talk to Your Heart, Columbia 1148.
Charley Pride
  Pride of Country Music, Victor LPM-3775.
Jim Reeves
  A Touch of Velvet, Victor LPM-2487.
  He'll Have To Go, Victor LPM-2223.
Marty Robbins
  Gunfighter Ballads, Columbia 1349.
  More Gunfighter Ballads and Trail Songs, Columbia 1481.
Connie Smith
  Connie Smith, Victor LPM-3341.
Wynn Stewart
  It's Such a Pretty World Today, Capitol T-2737.
Porter Wagoner
  Blue Grass Story, Victor LPM-2960.
  The Cold Hard Facts of Life, Victor LPM-3797.
  Confessions of a Broken Man, Victor LPM-3593.
  Satisfied Mind, Camden 769.
Dottie West
  Here Comes My Baby, Victor LPM-3368.
Speedy West
  Guitar Spectacular, Capitol T-1835.
Roy Wiggins
  Mister Steel Guitar, Starday SLP188.
Wilburn Brothers
  Folk Songs, Decca 4225.
  Take Up Thy Cross, Decca 4464.

Bluegrass and the Folk Revival

ANTHOLOGIES

American Banjo Scruggs Style, Folkways FA2314.
Country Music and Bluegrass at Newport, Vanguard VRS-9146.
Folk Festival at Newport, Vol. 3, Vanguard VRS-9064.
Mountain Music Bluegrass Style, Folkways FA2318.

FOLK-ORIENTED

Joan Baez
    Joan Baez, Vol. I, Vanguard VRS-9078; Vol. II, Vanguard VRS-9094.
    Joan Baez in Concert, Vanguard VRS-9112.
Harry Belafonte
    Calypso, Victor LPM-1248.
Jimmie Driftwood (James Morris)
    Jimmie Driftwood Sings Newly Discovered Early American Folk Songs,
    Victor LPM-1635.
Bob Dylan
    Bob Dylan, Columbia 1779.
Everly Brothers
    Songs Our Daddy Taught Us, Cadence 3016.
New Lost City Ramblers
    New Lost City Ramblers, Folkways FA2396.
    Songs From the Depression, Folkways FH5264.
Mike Seeger
    Mike Seeger, Vanguard VRS-9150.
    Old Time Country Music, Folkways FA2325.
    Tipple, Loom, and Rail, Folkways FA5273.
Doc Watson
    Doc Watson and His Family, Folkways FA2366.
    Jean and Doc at Folk City, Folkways FA2426. An album recorded with
    Jean Ritchie.
    Strictly Instrumental, Columbia 2643. Recorded with Flatt and Scruggs.

BLUEGRASS

Hylo Brown
    Bluegrass Goes to College, Starday SLP204.
    Hylo Brown, Capitol T-1168.
Bill Clifton
    The Bluegrass Sound of Bill Clifton, Starday SLP159.
    Carter Family Memorial Album, Starday SLP146.
    Mountain Folk Songs, Starday SLP111.

Country Gentlemen
  Bluegrass at Carnegie Hall, Starday SLP174.
  The Country Gentlemen, Vol. I, Folkways FA2409; Vol. II, Folkways
  FA2410.
  On the Road, Folkways FA2411.
Flatt and Scruggs
  Country Music, Mercury 20358.
  Flatt and Scruggs at Carnegie Hall, Columbia 2045.
  Flatt and Scruggs Recorded Live at Vanderbilt University, Columbia
  2134.
  Great Original Recordings, Harmony 7340.
  Hard Travelin', Columbia 1951.
  Lester Flatt and Earl Scruggs, Mercury 20542.
  Songs of the Famous Carter Family, Columbia 1664.
Greenbriar Boys
  The Greenbriar Boys, Vanguard VRS-9104.
Jim and Jesse (McReynolds)
  Bluegrass Special, Epic 24031.
George Jones and Melba Montgomery
  Bluegrass Hootenanny, United Artists 3352.
Lilly Brothers
  Folk Songs from the Southern Mountains, Folkways FA2433.
Lonesome Pine Fiddlers
  Bluegrass, Starday SLP194.
Rose Maddox
  Rose Maddox Sings Bluegrass, Capitol T-1799.
Rose Lee and Joe Maphis
  Rose Lee and Joe Maphis, Capitol T-1778.
Jimmy Martin
  Good and Country, Decca 4016.
Monroe Brothers
  Early Bluegrass Music, Camden 774.
Bill Monroe
  Bill Monroe and His Bluegrass Boys, Harmony 7290.
  Father of Bluegrass Music, Camden 719.
  Original Bluegrass Sound, Harmony 7338.
Osborne Brothers
  Country Pickin' and Hillside Singin', MGM 3734.
  Cuttin' Grass, MGM 4149.
Reno and Smiley
  Country Ballads, King 621.
  Sacred Songs, King 656.

Sacred Songs, King 550.
Wanted, King 718.
Stanley Brothers
Country Folk Music Concert, King 864.
Country Pickin' and Singin', Mercury MG20349.
Folk Concert, King 834.
For the Good People, King 698.
Good Old Camp Meeting Songs, King 805.
Old Time Camp Meeting, King 750.
The Stanley Brothers: Their Original Recordings, Melodeon MLP7322.
The Stanley Brothers Sing the Songs They Like Best, King 772.
The Stanleys in Person, King 719.
Earl Taylor
Folk Songs from the Blue Grass, United Artists 3049.
Mac Wiseman
Great Folk Ballads, Dot 25213.
Tis Sweet to be Remembered, Dot 3084.

SECONDARY MATERIAL

Books and Pamphlets

A Check List of Recorded Songs in the English Language in the Archive of American Folk Song to July, 1940. Washington, D.C., 1940.

Alicoate, Jack (ed.). *The 1945 Radio Annual.* New York: Barnes Printing Co., 1945.

Allen, Frederick Lewis. *Only Yesterday.* New York: Harper and Brothers, 1931.

Allen, Jules Verne. *Cowboy Lore.* San Antonio: The Naylor Company, 1933.

American Society of Composers, Authors and Publishers. *Nothing Can Replace Music.* New York, 1933.

Atherton, Lewis. *Main Street on the Middle Border.* Bloomington: Indiana University Press, 1954.

Barzun, Jacques. *Music in American Life.* New York: Doubleday and Company, 1956.

Behind the Record of the Country Music Association. SEE Country Music Association.

Belden, Henry M., and Arthur Palmer Hudson (eds.). *The Frank C. Brown Collection of North Carolina Folklore,* Vol. II. Durham: Duke University Press, 1952.

Berendt, Joachim E. *The New Jazz Book; a History and Guide.* New York: Hill and Wang, 1962.

Billboard Music Week. *1962–1963 International Music Industry Buyer's Guide and Market Data Report*. New York, 1962.

Billboard. *The World of Country Music*. New York, 1963.

Boatright, Mody, et al. (eds.). *A Good Tale and a Bonnie Tune*. (Publications of the Texas Folklore Society, XXXII.) Dallas: Southern Methodist University, 1964.

Brand, Oscar. *The Ballad Mongers: Rise of the Modern Folk Song*. New York: Funk and Wagnalls, 1962.

Brockway, Howard, and Loraine Wyman. *Twenty Kentucky Mountain Songs*. Boston: Oliver Ditson Co., 1920.

Brunner, Edmund de S. *Radio and the Farmer*. New York: The Radio Institute of the Audible Arts, n.d.

Callahan, North. *Smoky Mountain Country*. New York: Duell, Sloan and Pearce, 1952.

Campbell, John C. *The Southern Highlander and His Homeland*. New York: Russell Sage Foundation, 1921.

Carpenter, Paul S. *Music, an Art and a Business*. Norman: University of Oklahoma Press, 1950.

Carson, Gerald. *The Roguish World of Dr. Brinkley*. New York: Rinehart and Company, 1960.

Cash, Wilbur J. *The Mind of the South*. New York: Alfred A. Knopf, 1941.

Charters, Samuel. *The Country Blues*. New York: Rinehart and Company, 1959.

Child, Francis James. *The English and Scottish Popular Ballads*. 5 volumes. Boston: Houghton Mifflin, 1882–1898.

Clark, Thomas D. *Pills, Petticoats and Plows: The Southern Country Store*. Norman: University of Oklahoma Press, 1944.

Coffin, Tristam P. *The British Traditional Ballad in North America*. (Vol. II of the Bibliographical and Special Series of the American Folklore Society.) Philadelphia: American Folklore Society, 1950.

Cohen, John, and Mike Seeger (eds.). *The New Lost City Ramblers Song Book*. New York: Oak Publications, 1964.

Compton's Pictured Encyclopedia and Fact-Index, Vol. II. Chicago: F. E. Compton and Company, 1960.

Couch, William T. (ed.). *Culture in the South*. Chapel Hill: The University of North Carolina Press, 1934.

Country Music Association. *Behind the Record of the Country Music Association*. Nashville, n.d.

Davis, Elise Miller. *The Answer is God*. New York: McGraw-Hill, 1955.

Dunson, Josh. *Freedom in the Air*. New York: International Publishers, 1965.

Eaton, Clement. *A History of the Old South*. New York: The MacMillan Company, 1949. Revised Edition, 1966.

Emmet, Boris, and John E. Jeuck. *Catalogues and Counters: A History of Sears, Roebuck and Company*. Chicago: The University of Chicago Press, 1950.

Ewen, David. *Panorama of American Popular Music*. Englewood Cliffs, New Jersey: Prentice-Hall, 1957.

Favorite Hymns and Folksongs (as sung by the Blue Sky Boys). n.p., n.d.

Feather, Leonard. *The Book of Jazz*. New York: Meridian Books, 1960.

Fox, John, Jr. *The Little Shepherd of Kingdom Come*. New York: Charles Scribner's Sons, 1903.

——. *The Trail of the Lonesome Pine*. New York: Grosset and Dunlap, 1920.

Frantz, Joe B., and Julian Ernest Choate, Jr. *The American Cowboy: The Myth and the Reality*. Norman: University of Oklahoma Press, 1955.

Freedman, Ronald. *Recent Migration to Chicago*. Chicago: The University of Chicago Press, 1950.

Gelatt, Roland. *The Fabulous Phonograph*. New York: J. B. Lippincott Company, 1955.

Gentry, Linnell (ed.). *A History and Encyclopedia of Country, Western, and Gospel Music*. Nashville: McQuiddy Press, 1961.

Gerould, Gordon Hall. *The Ballad of Tradition*. New York: Oxford University Press, 1957.

Grand Ole Opry History-Picture Book. Vol. I, No. 3. Nashville: WSM, 1957.

Greenway, John. *American Folksongs of Protest*. Philadelphia: University of Pennsylvania Press, 1953.

Guthrie, Woody. *American Folksong*. New York: Oak Publications, 1961.

——. *Bound for Glory*. New York: E. P. Dutton and Company, 1943.

Hank Snow Twenty-Fifth Anniversary Album, The. Nashville, 1961.

Hay, George D. *A Story of the Grand Ole Opry*. Copyright by George D. Hay, 1953.

Hays, Lee, et al. (eds.), *The Weavers' Song Book*. New York: Harper and Brothers, 1960.

Hentoff, Nat, and Albert J. McCarthy (eds.). *Jazz*. New York: Rinehart and Company, 1959.

Hillbilly Hit Parade of 1942. New York: Peer International Corporation, 1942.

Hillbilly Hit Parade of 1943. New York: Peer International Corporation, 1943.

Holbrook, Stewart H. *The Story of American Railroads*. New York: Crown Publishers, 1947.

Hudson, Arthur Palmer. *Folksongs of Mississippi and their Background.* Chapel Hill: University of North Carolina Press, 1936.

Hughbanks, Leroy. *Talking Wax: or the Story of the Phonograph.* New York: The Hobson Book Press, 1945.

Hughes, Robert, and Edith B. Sturges. *Songs from the Hills of Vermont.* New York: G. Schirmer, 1919.

Jackson, George Pullen. *White Spirituals in the Southern Uplands.* Chapel Hill: University of North Carolina Press, 1933.

Johnson, Charles A. *The Frontier Camp Meeting.* Dallas: Southern Methodist University Press, 1955.

Kephart, Horace. *Our Southern Highlanders.* New York: Outing Publishing Company, 1913.

KWKH's Louisiana Hayride. Shreveport, Louisiana: Radio Station KWKH, n.d.

Lomax, Alan. *List of American Folk Songs on Commercial Records.* (In Report of the Committee of the Conference on Inter-American Relations in the Field of Music, William Berrien, Chairman.) Washington, D.C.: Department of State, 1940.

———. *Mister Jelly Roll.* New York: Duell, Sloan and Pearce, 1950.

———. *The Folk Songs of North America.* New York: Doubleday and Company, 1960.

Lomax, John A. *Cowboy Songs and Other Frontier Ballads.* New York: Sturgis and Walton, 1910.

———, and Alan Lomax. *American Ballads and Folk Songs.* New York: The MacMillan Company, 1934.

———, and Alan Lomax. *Folk Song: U.S.A.* New York: Duell, Sloan and Pearce, 1947.

Lumpkin, Ben Gray. *Folksongs on Records.* Boulder, Colorado: Folksongs on Records, and Denver, Colorado: Alan Swallow, 1960.

Maclachlan, John, and Joe S. Floyd, Jr. *This Changing South.* Gainesville: University of Florida Press, 1956.

Meyer, Hazel. *The Gold in Tin Pan Alley.* New York: J. B. Lippincott Company, 1958.

Milburn, George. *Hobo's Hornbook.* New York: Ives and Washburn, 1930.

Moore, Thurston (ed.). *The Country Music Who's Who.* First annual edition. Cincinnati: Cardinal Enterprises, 1960.

———. *The Country Music Who's Who.* 1965 edition. Denver, Colorado: Heather Publications, Inc., 1964.

———. *The Country Music Who's Who.* 1966 edition. Denver, Colorado: Heather Publications, Inc., 1965.

McDaniel, William R., and Harold Seligman. *Grand Ole Opry.* New York: Greenberg, 1952.

McGill, Josephine. *Folk Songs of the Kentucky Mountains.* New York: Bosey & Co., 1917.

McNamara, Daniel I. (ed.). *The ASCAP Biographical Dictionary of Composers, Authors and Publishers.* New York: Thomas Y. Crowell Company, 1952.

Nettl, Bruno. *An Introduction to Folk Music in the United States.* Detroit: Wayne State University Press, 1960.

Odum, Howard. *Southern Regions of the United States.* Chapel Hill: University of North Carolina Press, 1936.

———. *The Way of the South.* New York: The Macmillan Company, 1947.

Oliver, Paul. *Blues Fell This Morning.* London: Cassell and Company, 1960.

Owens, William A. *Texas Folk Songs.* Dallas: The Texas Folklore Society, 1950.

Pope, Liston. *Millhands and Preachers.* New Haven: Yale University Press, 1942.

President's Research Committee on Social Trends. *Recent Social Trends in the United States.* New York: McGraw-Hill Book Company, 1933.

Radio Corporation of America. *The 50-Year Story of RCA Victor Records.* New York: Department of Information, 1953.

Randolph, Vance. *Ozark Folksongs.* 4 vols. Columbia, Missouri: The State Historical Society of Missouri, 1950.

Red Song Book. New York: Workers' Library Publishers, 1932.

Rodgers, Mrs. Jimmie [Carrie]. *My Husband, Jimmie Rodgers.* Nashville: Ernest Tubb Publications, n. d.

Schlappi, Elizabeth (compiler). *Roy Acuff and His Smoky Mountain Boys Discography.* (Country Research, Disc Collector No. 23.) Cheswold, Delaware: Disc Collector Publications, 1966.

Seeger, Mike, and John Cohen (eds.). *The New Lost City Ramblers Song Book.* New York: Oak Publications, 1964.

Sharp, Cecil. *Folk Songs From the Southern Appalachians.* London: Oxford University Press, 1917.

Shelton, Robert. *The Country Music Story.* New York: The Bobbs-Merrill Company, Inc., 1966.

———, et al. *Young Folk Song Book.* New York: Simon and Schuster, 1963.

Sherwin, Sterling, and Harry K. McClintock. *Railroad Songs of Yesterday.* New York: Shapiro, Bernstein & Co., 1943.

Silverman, Jerry. *Folk Blues: One Hundred and Ten American Folk Blues.* New York: The MacMillan Company, 1958.

Spaeth, Sigmund. *A History of Popular Music in America.* New York: Random House, 1948.

———. *Read 'Em and Weep.* New York: Doubleday, Page and Company, 1926.

———. *Weep Some More My Lady.* New York: Doubleday, Page and Company, 1927.

Sterling, William W. *Trails and Trials of a Texas Ranger.* Copyrighted by William W. Sterling, 1959.

Stuart Hamblen and His Lucky Stars Picture-Song Book. Chicago: M. M. Cole Publishing Company, 1942.

Tex Ritter, Mountain Ballads and Cowboy Songs. Deluxe edition. Chicago: M. M. Cole Publishing Company, 1941.

Texas Jim Robertson's Collection of Favorite Recorded Songs. New York: Bob Miller, Inc., 1943.

Thomas, Jean, and Joseph A. Leeder. *The Singin' Gatherin'.* New York: Silver Burdett Company, 1939.

Thompson, Warren S. *Growth and Changes in California's Population.* Los Angeles: The Haynes Foundation, 1955.

Thorp, Nathan Howard. *Songs of the Cowboy.* Estancia, New Mexico: New Print Shop, 1908.

Vance, Rubert B. *All These People.* Chapel Hill: The University of North Carolina Press, 1945.

———, and Nicholas J. Demerath (eds.). *The Urban South.* Chapel Hill: University of North Carolina Press, 1954.

Ware, Caroline F. (ed.). *The Cultural Approach to History.* New York: Columbia University Press, 1940.

Weisberger, Bernard. *They Gathered at the River: The Story of the Great Revivalists and their Impact Upon Religion in America.* Boston: Little, Brown and Company, 1958.

Wells, Evelyn Kendrick. *The Ballad Tree.* New York: The Ronald Press Company, 1950.

Wentworth, Harold, and Stuart Flexner. *Dictionary of American Slang.* New York: Thomas Y. Crowell Company, 1960.

Wheeler, Mary. *Steamboatin' Days: Folk Songs of the River Packet Era.* Baton Rouge, Louisiana State University Press, 1944.

Whitfield, Irene Therese. *Louisiana French Folk Songs.* Baton Rouge: Louisiana State University Press, 1939.

Wickham, Graham. *Darby and Tarlton.* (Special Edition of Doug Jydstrup's *Blue Yodeler.* Denver, Colorado: 1967.

Wilgus, Donald Knight. *Anglo-American Folksong Scholarship Since 1898.* New Brunswick, New Jersey: Rutgers University Press, 1959.

C. Vann Woodward, *Origins of the New South, 1877–1913.* (Vol. IX of *A History of the South.*) Baton Rouge: Louisiana State University Press, 1951.

World of Country Music, The. SEE Billboard.

Wright, Richardson. *Hawkers and Walkers in Early America.* Philadelphia: J. B. Lippincott Company, 1927.

Theses and Dissertations

McNeil, Norman L. "The British Ballad West of the Appalachian Mountains." Unpublished Ph.D. dissertation, The University of Texas, 1956.
Norris, Renfro Cole. "The Ballad on the Air." Unpublished M.A. thesis, The University of Texas, 1951.
Wilgus, Donald Knight. "A Catalogue of American Folksongs on Commercial Records." Unpublished M.A. thesis, Ohio State University, 1947.

Articles

"Albert Brumley," *Music City News,* III, No. 1 (July, 1965), 18.
"All States Broadcast Except Wyoming," *The Literary Digest,* LXXV, No. 6 (November 11, 1922), 29.
Anderson, Omer. "Fifty Million Europeans Can't Be Wrong," *Billboard,* LXXII, No. 28 (July 11, 1960), 1.
———. "Grass Roots Sprout," *ibid.,* No. 31 (August 1, 1960), 4.
Antrim, Doron K. "Whoop-and-Holler Opera," *Colliers,* CXVII (January 26, 1946), 18 ff.
Aronowitz, Alfred G., and Marshall Blonsky. "Peter, Paul and Mary," *The Saturday Evening Post* (May 30, 1964), 30–35.
Asbell, Bernard. "Simple Songs of Sex, Sin and Salvation," *Show: The Magazine of the Performing Arts,* II, No. 2 (February, 1962), 88–91.
Badeaux, Ed. "The Carters of Rye Cove," *Sing Out: The Folk Song Magazine,* II, No. 2 (April–May, 1961), 13–16.
Barter, Frieda. "Ferlin Huskey—What's in a Name," *Country and Western Jamboree,* I, No. 12 (February, 1956), 8–9.
Barthel, Norma. "Ernest Tubb," *Country and Western Spotlight,* No. 20 (October–December, 1957), 8–9.
Belz, Carl I. "Popular Music and the Folk Tradition," *Journal of American Folklore,* LXXX, No. 316 (April–June, 1967), 130–143.
Billington, Ray Allen. "Government and the Arts: The WPA Experience," *American Quarterly,* XIII (Winter, 1961), 466–479.
"Bluegrass: A Skeletal History and Survey," *Folkways,* No. 2 (n. d.), 22–24.
Bluestone, George. "The Changing Cowboy: From Dime Novel to Dollar Film," *Western Humanities Review,* XIV, No. 3 (Summer, 1960), 331–337.
Boggs, Dock. "I Always Loved the Lonesome Songs," *Sing Out: The Folk Song Magazine,* XIV, No. 3 (July, 1964), 32–37.

Bolick, William A. "Bill Bolick's Own Story of the Blue Sky Boys" (Introduction and commentary by William A. Farr), *Sing Out: The Folk Song Magazine*, XVII, No. 2 (April–May, 1967), 18–21.

Bradley, F. W. "Little Mary Fagan," *Southern Folklore Quarterly*, XXIV, No. 2 (June, 1960), 144–146.

Bryan, Charles F. "The Folk Music Enigma," *Tennessee Folklore Society Bulletin*, XV, No. 2 (June, 1949), 29–31.

Burdo, Eleanor M. "Montana Slim Story," *Disc Collector*, No. 12 (n. d.), 3–4.

Cameron, Stella. "Wilf Carter," *Country and Western Spotlight*, No. 19 (July–September, 1957), 8–10.

Carter, June. "I Remember the Carter Family," *Country Song Roundup*, XVII, No. 90 (October, 1965), 16–17, 30–32; and *ibid.*, XVII, No. 91 (December, 1965), 16–20.

Charon, Paul. "Know the Nashville Musicians," *Country Music Review*, I, No. 6 (February, 1964), 33.

CMA, Close-Up, January, 1967.

CMA Close-Up, February, 1967.

Cohen, John. "Clarence Ashley," *Sing Out: The Folk Song Magazine*, XVII, No. 4 (August–September, 1967), 30.

———. "Country Music Outside Nashville," *ibid.*, XVI, No. 1 (February–March, 1966), 40–42.

———. "Fiddlin' Eck Robertson," *ibid.*, XIV, No. 2 (April–May, 1964), 55–59.

———. "The Folk Music Interchange: Negro and White," *ibid.*, XIV, No. 6 (January, 1964), 42–49.

———. "Tribute to Carter Stanley," *ibid.*, XVII, No. 1 (February–March, 1967), 1.

Cohen, Norman. "The Skillet Lickers: A Study of a Hillbilly String Band and its Repertoire," *Journal of American Folklore*, LXXVIII, No. 309 (July–September, 1965), 229–244.

———, and Anne Cohen. "The Legendary Jimmie Tarleton," *Sing Out: The Folk Song Magazine*, XVI, No. 4 (September, 1966), 16–19.

Cohn, Lawrence. "Mississippi John Hurt," *Sing Out: The Folk Song Magazine*, XIV, No. 5 (November, 1964), 16–21.

Cooper, Texas Jim. "Cousin Herald Goodman," *Country Song Roundup Annual*, No. 5 (Winter, 1967), 76–77.

Country and Western Jamboree, II, No. 4 (July, 1956), 34.

Country and Western Jamboree, III, No. 5 (August, 1957), 26–28.

Country Song Roundup (Special Hank Williams Memorial Issue), I, No. 24 (June, 1953), 5–14.

Crichton, Kyle. "Thar's Gold in Them Thar Hillbillies," *Collier's*, CI (April 30, 1938), 24 ff.

Davis, David B. "Ten Gallon Hero," *American Quarterly*, VI, No. 2 (Summer, 1954), 111–126.

"Death of Three Recording Artists," *Hobbies*, LIII, No. 10 (December, 1948), 32.

Deen, Dixie, "Conway Rocks Right into Country Success," *Music City News*, IV, No. 8 (February, 1967), 3–4, 30.

———. "Country Music Hall of Fame Opens," *ibid.*, IV, No. 10 (April, 1967), 4, 8, 15–16.

———. "Diesel on My Tail—Jim and Jesse," *ibid.*, IV, No. 11 (May, 1967), 6, 8, 10.

———. "Goodness, Gracious, They're Good," *ibid.*, IV, No. 4 (October, 1966), 1, 8, 15, 19, 23.

———. "Merle Haggard: 'Someone Told My Story in a Song,'" *Music City News*, IV, No. 11 (May, 1967), 9–10.

———. "Purely Porter Wagoner," *ibid.*, IV, No. 9 (March, 1967), 3–4.

———. "'Six Days on the Road' Puts Ravin' Dave Dudley on Country Music Map," *ibid.*, IV, No. 1 (July, 1966), 11, 20.

———. "Skeeter Davis: Born to Sing," *ibid.*, No. 7 (January, 1967), 3–4; No. 8 (February, 1967), 6, 8, 9; No. 9 (March, 1967), 6, 9; No. 10 (April, 1967), 30.

———. "The Crown Prince of C-W Music," *ibid.*, No. 2 (August, 1966), 1, 31.

———. "The Woman Behind the Man," *ibid.*, III, No. 5 (November, 1965), 17, 22.

———. "The Woman Behind the Man," *ibid.*, No. 10 (April, 1966), 5, 14, 19.

———. "Tom T. Hall's Touch of Greatness," *ibid.*, V, No. 2 (August, 1967), 3–4.

Dolin, Eva. "Does Roger Miller Know What He Wants?" *Country Song Roundup*, XVII, No. 87 (February, 1965), 28–29.

Earle, Eugene W. "Bill Cox Discography," *Disc Collector*, No. 13 (n. d.), 2–5; No. 14 (n. d.), 9–13; No. 15 (n. d.), 2–7.

———. "Tribute to John Edwards," *ibid.*, No. 19 (n. d.), 4–7.

Eddy, Don. "Hillbilly Heaven," *The American Magazine*. CLIII (March, 1952), 29 ff.

Edwards, John. "A Tribute to Riley Puckett," *Disc Collector*, No. 12 (n. d.), 8–10.

———. "Bradley Kincaid, The Story of the Kentucky Mountain Boy," *ibid.*, No. 11 (n. d.), 4–5.

———. "Buell Kazee: A Biographical Note," *Caravan: The Magazine of Folk Music* (June–July, 1959), 42–43.

————. "The Delmore Brothers," *Country and Western Spotlight* (Special John Edwards Memorial Edition, September, 1962), 16.

————. "Memories of Jimmie Rodgers," *Disc Collector*, No. 15 (n. d.), 16–18.

————. "The Mystery of the 'Texas Drifter,'" *Country and Western Spotlight* (Special John Edwards Memorial Edition, September, 1962), 31.

————. "McFarland and Gardner," *ibid.*, 15.

————. "The Old Labels—No. 2," *ibid.*, 14–15.

————. "Old Time Singers—Tex Ritter," *ibid.*, 40–41.

————. "The Sons of the Pioneers," *ibid.*, 34.

————. "The Story of a Great Folk Artist—Cliff Carlisle," *ibid.*, 9.

————. "Wade Mainer," *ibid.*, 24.

"Ernest Tubb Discography," *Disc Collector*, No. 10 (n. d.), 2–3.

Everly, Ike. "Father Calls Mother Secret of Amazing Success," *Country and Western Jamboree*, IV, No. 1 (Summer, 1958), 10–16, 33, 38.

Faier, Billy. "Review," *Caravan: The Folk Music Magazine*, No. 15 (February–March, 1959), 32.

Fortune, Phillip. "Who the Old Time Western Bands Consisted Of," *Disc Collector*, No. 12 (n. d.), 11.

Fox, Daniel M. "The Achievement of the Federal Writers Project," *American Quarterly*, XIII, No. 1 (Spring, 1961), 3–20.

Furnas, J. C. "Country Doctor Goes to Town," *Saturday Evening Post*, CCXII, No. 43 (April 20, 1943), 12–13, 44 ff.

Gillis, Frieda Barter. "In the Spotlight—Sonny James," *Rustic Rhythm*, I, No. 4 (July, 1957), 19–24.

————. "Johnny Cash," *ibid.*, No. 2 (May, 1957), 7–13.

Glover, Tony. "R & B," *Sing Out: The Folk Song Magazine*, XV, No. 2 (May, 1965), 7–13.

Green, Archie. "A Discographic Appraisal of *American Balladry from British Broadsides: A Guide for Students and Collectors of Traditional Song*, by G. Malcolm Laws, Jr. (Philadelphia, American Folklore Society, 1957)," *Caravan: The Magazine of Folk Music*, No. 15 (February–March, 1959), 7–13.

————. "An Aunt Molly Jackson Discography," *Kentucky Folklore Record*, VII, No. 4 (October–December, 1961), 159–169.

————. "Born on Picketlines, Textile Workers' Songs are Woven into History," *Textile Labor*, XXI, No. 4 (April, 1961), 3–5.

————. "Dorsey Dixon: Minstrel of the Mills," *Sing Out: The Folk Song Magazine*, XVI, No. 3 (July, 1966), 10–13.

————. "Hillbilly Music: Source and Symbol," *Journal of American Folklore*, LXXVIII, No. 309 (July–September, 1965), 204–228.

————. "The Carter Family's 'Coal Miner's Blues,'" *Southern Folklore Quarterly*, XXV, No. 4 (December, 1961), 226–237.

———. "The Death of Mother Jones," Reprint Series No. 82, University of Illinois Bulletin, Institute of Labor and Industrial Relations, Vol. LVII, No. 70 (May, 1960). Reprinted from *Labor History*, I, No. 1 (Winter, 1960).

Green, Ben A. "Dunbar Cave Always Reflects Roy Acuff's Love for People," *Country and Western Jamboree*, III, No. 5 (August, 1957), 8, 34.

Greenway, John. "Folk Song Discography," *Western Folklore*, XXI, No. 1 (January, 1962), 71–76.

———. "Folk Songs as Socio-Historical Documents," *ibid.*, XIX (January, 1960), 1–9.

———. "Jimmie Rodgers—a Folksong Catalyst," *Journal of American Folklore*, LXX, No. 277 (July–September, 1957), 231–235.

———. "John Edwards, 1932–1960," *Western Folklore*, XX, No. (April, 1961), 109–111.

Grevatt, Ren. "Country Disk Acts Just Keep Selling," *Billboard Music Week*, LXXIII, No. 42 (October, 1961), 18.

Hartwell, Dickson. "Caruso of Mountain Music," *Colliers*, CXXIII, No. 10 (March 5, 1949), 26, 39, 42.

Healy, Bob. "The Beverly Hillbillies," *Country Directory*, No. 3 (1962), 30–31.

———. "The Light Crust Doughboys," *ibid.*, 21–29.

———. "Ocie Stockard and the Wanderers," *Disc Collector*, No. 18 (n. d.), 19–20.

———. "The Prairie Ramblers," *Country Directory*, No. 3 (1962), 4–14.

———. "Roy Newman and His Boys," *ibid.*, No. 4 (n. d.), 24–26.

———. "The Ted Daffan Story," *ibid.*, 27–32.

———. "W. Lee O'Daniel and His Hillbilly Boys," *ibid.*, 6–11.

Hentoff, Nat. "Ballads, Banjos and Bluegrass," *Hi Fi/Stero Review* (May, 1963), 48–52.

———. "Folk, Folkum and the New Citybilly," *Playboy*, X, No. 6 (June, 1963), 95–98, 168–170.

———. "Folk Finds a Voice," *The Reporter*, XXVI, No. 1 (January 4, 1962), 39–42.

———. "The Rise of Folkum Music," *The Commonweal*, LXXV, No. 4 (October 20, 1961), 99–100.

"Here's Willie Nelson," *Music City News*, II, No. 7 (January, 1965), 10.

"Hit Maker—Ray Price," *Rustic Rhythm*, I, No. 2 (May, 1957), 11–15.

Hoeptner, Fred G. "Country or Western—It's a Choice of Words," *Country and Western Jamboree*, IV, No. 1 (Summer, 1958), 36–38.

———. "Folk and Hillbilly Music: The Background of their Relation, Part II," *Caravan: The Magazine of Folk Music* (June–July, 1959), 20–21.

——. "The Story of an Early Fiddle Band: East Texas Serenaders," *Disc Collector*, No. 17 (May, 1961), 8–11.

"Hoots and Hollers on the Campus," *Newsweek*, LVIII, No. 22 (November 27, 1961), 84.

Hooper, Russ, and Randy Slacum. "The Dobro Guitar and Bluegrass," *Bluegrass Unlimited*, I, No. 11 (May, 1967), 2–4.

Hurst, Jack. "Hound Dog Wails of Fires and Corn Whiskey," Nashville *Tennesseean* (January 15, 1967).

Jarman, Rufus. "Country Music Goes to Town," *Nation's Business*, XLI (February, 1963), 44–51.

JEMF Newsletter, I, Part 1 (October, 1965), 1.

JEMF Newsletter, II, Part 2 (February, 1967), 20.

Kahn, Ed. "Folk Song Discography," *Western Folklore*, XXII, No. 1 (January 1963), 74.

——. "Hillbilly Music: Source and Resource," *Journal of American Folklore*, LXXVIII, No. 309 (July–September, 1965), 257–266.

Killian, Lewis M. "The Adjustment of Southern White Migrants to Northern Urban Norms," *Social Forces*, XXXII, No. 1 (October 1953), 66–70.

Kuykendall, Pete. "Bill Monroe and His Bluegrass Boys," *Disc Collector*, No. 13 (n. d.), 19.

——. "Don Reno and Red Smiley and the Tennessee Cutups," *ibid.*, No. 17 (May, 1961), 18–20.

——. "Lester Flatt and Earl Scruggs Discography," *ibid.*, No. 14 (n. d.), 37–44.

Lass, Roger. "Bluegrass," *Caravan: The Magazine of Folk Music*, No. 12 (August–September, 1958), 20–23.

"The Legend of Tom Dula," *Caravan: The Magazine of Folk Music*, No. 15 (February–March, 1959), 44–47.

Legere, Bill. "Carter Family Discography," *Country and Western Spotlight*, No. 34 (June, 1961), 6–14.

Leverett, Wilbur. "The Kelly Harrell Story," *Disc Collector*, No. 11 (n. d.), 5–6.

Lewis, Richard Warren. "Thar's Gold in Them Thar Hillbillies," *Show Business Illustrated*, II, No. 2 (February, 1962), 32–38.

Lieberson, Goddard. "Country Sweeps the Country," *The New York Times Magazine* (July 28, 1957), 13 ff.

Life, XV, No. 11 (October 11, 1943), 55.

Lomax, Alan. "Bluegrass Background: Folk Music With Overdrive," *Esquire*, L11, No. 4 (October, 1959), 103–109.

——. "Folk Song Style," *American Anthropologist*, LXI, No. 6 (December, 1959), 927–955.

Long, Hubert. "Faron Young," *Rustic Rhythm*, I, No. 2 (May, 1957), 16–20.

"The Louvin Brothers," *Country and Western Spotlight*, No. 21 (January–March, 1958), 6–7.

McCuen, Brad. "Bill Boyd and His Cowboy Ramblers Discography," ―*Country Directory*, No. 3 (1962), 15–21.

―――. "Blue Sky Boys Discography," *ibid.*, No. 1 (November, 1960), 20–25.

―――. "Monroe Brothers Discography," *ibid.*, No. 2 (n. d.), 14–16.

McPhee, John. "Folk Singing," *Time*, LXX, No. 21 (November 23, 1962), 54–60.

Martin, Harris. "Buck Owens Riding All Time Height of Popularity," *Music City News*, II, No. 12 (June, 1965), 1, 4.

"Marty Robbins," *Rustic Rhythm*, I, No. 1 (April, 1957), 21.

"Meet Charlie Bowman," *Disc Collector*, No. 16 (n. d.), 3.

Movie-Radio Guide, XI, No. 3 (October 23–31, 1941), 6.

Movie-Radio Guide, XI, No. 28 (April 18–24, 1942), 33.

Munden, Kenneth. "A Contribution to the Psychological Understanding of the Cowboy and His Myth," *American Image*, XV, No. 2 (Summer, 1958), 103–147.

Music City News, V, No. 4 (November, 1967), 32.

Newman, Clarence B. "Homespun Harmony," *The Wall Street Journal*, XXXVII, No. 141 (May 3, 1957), 1, 6.

Newsweek, XLI, No. 3 (January 19, 1953), 55.

Nichols, Lewis. "The Ubiquitous Juke Box," *The New York Times Magazine* (October 5, 1941), 22.

"Noted Country Collectors," *Country Directory*, No. 1 (November, 1960), 4–5.

Pankake, Jon. "Mike Seeger: The Style of Tradition," *Sing Out: The Folk Song Magazine*, XIV, No. 3 (July, 1964), 9–10.

―――. "Sam and Kirk McGee from Sunny Tennessee," *ibid.*, No. 5 (November, 1964), 46–50.

Parkman, Mrs. Henry. "Now Come All You Good People," *Colliers*, LXXXIV, (November 2, 1929), 20–24, 58–59.

Pass, Fred. "Singin' Man," *Texas Parade*, XXIII, No. 1 (June, 1962), 31–33.

Paton, Sandy. "Folk and the Folk Arrival," *Folk Music*, I, No. 1 (1964), 14, 54–56.

Peer, Ralph. "Discovery of the First Hillbilly Great," *Billboard*, LXV, No. 20 (May 16, 1953), 20–21.

―――. "Rodgers' Heritage," *ibid.*, LXVI, No. 21 (May 22, 1954), 17.

"Pickin' Scruggs," *Time*, LXXVII, No. 27 (June 30, 1961), 53.

Pinson, Bob. "The Callahan Brothers," *Country Directory*, No. 2 (n. d.), 5–13.

———. "The Musical Brownies," *ibid.*, No. 4 (n. d.), 11–17.

"Platter War," *Business Week* (November 10, 1934), 14.

Record Research, No. 23 (June–July, 1959), 13–16.

Reisman, David. "Listening to Popular Music," *American Quarterly*, II, No. 4 (Winter, 1950), 359–372.

Reisner, Robert. "Why I Detest Folk Music," *Folk Music*, I, No. 1 (1964), 6–7, 34.

"Removing the Last Objection to Living in the Country," *Country Life*, XLI, No. 4 (February, 1922), 63.

Rinzler, Ralph. "The Nashville Scene: The Roots of Bluegrass," *Hootenanny*, I, No. 2 (March, 1964), 54–55.

Rinzler, Richard. "The Friends of Old-Time Music," *The Little Sandy Review*, No. 28 (January–February, 1964), 38–40.

Rosenberg, Neil V. "From Sound to Style: The Emergence of Bluegrass," *Journal of American Folklore*, LXXX, No. 316 (April–June, 1967), 143–150.

Seeger, Charles. "Music and Class Structure in the United States," *American Quarterly*, IX, No. 3 (Fall, 1957), 281–295.

———. "Reviews," *Journal of American Folklore*, LXI, No. 240 (April–June, 1948), 215–218.

Seeger, Mike. "A Contemporary Folk Esthetic," *Sing Out: The Folk Song Magazine*, XVI, No. 1 (February–March, 1966), 59–61.

Seeger, Peter. "The Autoharp Played Stoneman Style," *Reprint From Sing Out*, IV (New York, Oak Publications, 1962), 58–59.

Shelton, Robert. "Country from Another Country," *Cavalier*, XVII, No. 11 (September, 1967), 18–19.

———. "Joan Baez and Bob Dylan: The Voice Meets the Poet," *Hootenanny*, I, No. 2 (March, 1964), 10–11, 69–70.

Smith, L. Mayne. "A Reply to John Cohen," *Sing Out: The Folk Song Magazine*, XVI, No. 3 (July, 1966), 31, 33.

———. "An Introduction to Bluegrass," *Journal of American Folklore*, LXXVIII, No. 309 (July–September, 1965), 245–256.

———. "First Bluegrass Festival Honors Bill Monroe," *Sing Out: The Folk Song Magazine*, XV, No. 6 (January, 1966), 65–69.

"Songs From Texas," *Time*, XXXVII, No. 12 (March 24, 1941), 36.,

Spivacke, Harold. "The Archive of American Folk-Song in the Library of Congress," *Southern Folklore Quarterly*, II, No. 1 (March, 1938), 31–36.

Stand By (November 2, 1935), 9.

Tamony, Peter. "Hootenanny: the Word, its Content and Continuum," *Western Folklore*, XXII, No. 3 (July, 1963), 165–166.

Time, XXXVI, No. 10 (September 2, 1940), 45.

Time, LXXVII, No. 17 (April 21, 1961), 69.

Todd, Charles, and Robert Sonkin. "Ballads of the Okies," *The New York Times Magazine* (November 17, 1940), 6–7, 18.

Variety, CCVI, No. 3 (March 20, 1957), 35.

Waldron, Eli. "Country Music: The Death of Hank Williams," *The Reporter*, XII, No. 10 (May 19, 1955), 35–37.

———. "Country Music: The Squaya Dansu from Nashville," *ibid.*, No. 11 (June 2, 1955), 39–41.

Walker, Don. "Music Built Mills; Martha White Head," *Close-Up* (February, 1963), 3.

Walsh, Jim. "Favorite Pioneer Recording Artists: Vernon Dalhart" (Part I), *Hobbies: The Magazine for Collectors*, LXV, No. 3 (May, 1960), 33–35, 45; (Part II), No. 5 (July, 1960), 34, 36–37, 55; (Part III), No. 6 (August, 1960), 33–35; (Part IV), No. 8 (October, 1960), 34–36, 44.

———. "Death of Three Recording Artists," *Hobbies*, LIII, No. 10 (December, 1948), 32.

Welding, Pete. "Music from the Bluegrass Roots," *Saturday Review*, XLIV (June 10, 1961), 48.

———. "Starday: The Bluegrass Label," *Sing Out: The Folk Song Magazine*, XII, No. 3 (Summer, 1962), 63–65.

Wilgus, D. K. "Aunt Molly's 'Big Record,'" *Kentucky Folklore Record*, VII, No. 4 (October–December, 1961), 171–175.

———. "An Introduction to the Study of Hillbilly Music," *Journal of American Folklore*, LXXVIII, No. 309 (July–September, 1965), 195–204.

———. "On the Record," *Kentucky Folklore Record*, VII, No. 3 (July–September, 1961), 125–127.

———. "Record Reviews," *Journal of American Folklore*, LXXV, No. 295 (January–March, 1962), 87.

"Willie Nelson the Songwriter, 'One in a Row,'" *Music City News*, IV, No. 6 (December, 1966), 24–25.

Zolotow, Maurice. "Hillbilly Boom," *The Saturday Evening Post*, CCXVI (February 12, 1944), 22 ff.

INDEX

INDEX OF SONG TITLES